# TRADE, AID, AND ARBITRATE

*In remembrance of Maggie's parents, Minnie and Harry Fein, and their home on Windermere Road, Auburndale, Massachusetts.*

# Trade, Aid, and Arbitrate

## The Globalization of Western Law

RONALD CHARLES WOLF
*Member of the Bars of New York and Vermont, USA*

ASHGATE

Published by
Ashgate Publishing Limited
Gower House
Croft Road
Aldershot
Hants GU11 3HR
England

Ashgate Publishing Company
Suite 420
101 Cherry Street
Burlington, VT 05401-4405
USA

Ashgate website: http://www.ashgate.com

**British Library Cataloguing in Publication Data**
Wolf, Ronald Charles
Trade, aid, and arbitrate : the globalization of Western law
1.Arbitration, International 2.International law
I.Title
341

**Library of Congress Cataloging-in-Publication Data**
Wolf, Ronald Charles.
Trade, aid, and arbitrate : the globalization of western law / Ronald Charles Wolf.
p. cm.
Includes bibliographical references and index.
ISBN 0-7546-2285-1
1. Foreign trade regulation. 2. Arbitration and award. 3. Debts, Public. 4. International trade. 5. Globalization. I. Title.

K3943.W65 2003
343'.087--dc22

2003052366

ISBN 0 7546 2285 1

Printed and bound in Great Britain by MPG Books Ltd, Bodmin, Cornwall

# Contents

## PART 3: INTERNATIONAL ARBITRATION AND THE GLOBALIZATION OF WESTERN LAW

# Preface

*Let us pretend*

The practice of law is an empirical adventure with an emphasis on social conflict and daily evaluation of community norms. From this milieu, the counselor-at-law naturally begins to form ideas about the nature of the law and society. Cast forth from the halls of study, the attorney daily confronts the dramas of human life. Quickly, the practicing lawyer discovers that behind the contractual conflicts, the strident judicial contests, the anguished claims, the dialectical court sentences, are, for the most part, economic questions. The headline court cases affecting the heart are the exception. Pass by a court house and any tribunal clerk will inform you the litigation calendar is replete, more likely inundated, with contractual claims and inheritance disputes.

Mercantile needs germinate legal principles much as the earth sprouts forth its plant life. The broad scheme of the present investigation has been succinctly described by an eminent scholar, '... the social practice comes first and the law comes tumbling after'.[1] Or even more pithily from the same author, 'Society calls and the law responds'.[2] Clearly economic principles cannot be separated from social consequences. Envisioning the law, with its pillar of commercial principles, as an independent compartment of human society alongside other cultural institutions, is a mistake. Society is substantially an economic social pattern stabilized by legal principles. Economics weaves its wants into all facets of society, dragging along with it the relevant legal concepts.

Law, then, is a fertile field for the exploration of sociological phenomena. Accordingly, the material presented in this book is almost exclusively a factual exploration into the many less familiar aspects of international economic life which are determining the course of social history. Various conclusions are extricated throughout this treatise; but in general it can be affirmed that private international commercial law is subject to the hegemony of Western law which is itself substantially influenced by US law. Western commercial law is going global with its neoliberalism and market economy policies and principles. The description of the globalization of Western law is '... the story of the law merchant all over again',[3] where the words 'law merchant' have been expanded to now include international commercial practices.[4] The methodology[5] adopted to reach this conclusion is one familiar to all investigators: the examination of data, a synthesis of the facts, and finally a general deduction as to principles. Anyone who finds the facts convincing but not the conclusions deduced or inferred at least has the advantage of the reported data.

But before we begin our journey certain further assumptions need to be explicitly stated. This permits the reader to evaluate the material offered within a general theory of the sociology of the law. It would be unfair to plunge the reader into a wide array of disjointed data without an initial theoretical framework which will serve to coordinate the ensuing chapters. There are new, important sources of norms governing the social communities of most nations streaming forth from autonomous institutions. It has aptly been denominated by an prominent scholar of globalization 'global governance without global government'.[6] They range from the unobtrusive international arbitration panels to the sovereign credit-rating agencies to the recondite Bank for International Settlements in Basle. The standards emanating from all these founts, and many others to be portrayed, eventually regulate the lives of citizens everywhere. The international institutions are dictating the rules which are generating global legal principles. Their functioning and effects commands our understanding just as we want to comprehend better how our national assemblies operate.

But these extra-judicial creeds are not just a mélange of assorted values. They bear substantial similarities in their content. They are significantly under the influence of Western social and economic mores and in particular those of the US. They are derived from Western principles of what is a just society and a sensible economic system. In short, democracy and free markets are considered the correct postures for social life and this message is forcibly conveyed to other nations through the various multilateral institutions dominated by the industrialized nations.

Moreover, as these values emerge from sources not chosen by the electorate, the result is the prevailing beliefs diffused are denationalized. They have little to do with the identity of nations and everything to do with the political and economic tenets of organizations and their functionaries. The values in question, then, have not evolved from the particular history of a nation but are rather superimposed on sovereigns by authority figures. Citizens everywhere are disenfranchised and violently display this sentiment on the streets for there is no one elected institution which can respond to their cries of alienation.

Buttressing this trend is the composition of the many multilateral and supranational associations now a constant feature, some would argue threat, of human organization. They are constituted by technocrats, gifted and trained professionals, who dominate thoroughly the issues and problems brought to their establishments. Thus, one of the significant movements of the twenty-first century is the denationalization of intellectual capital and its indispensability. Heretofore, nations and entrepreneurs have had recourse to material capital to secure their power positions. The twenty-first century is witnessing the emergence of intellectual capital able to be furnished by a variety of people without regard to family fortunes, race, creed, sex, or any of the traditional false divisions erected by societies. Technical prowess cannot tolerate artificial barriers and world trade requires the trained specialist.

Furthermore, the integration of financial markets and the ease of international communications — one of the hallmarks of economic globalization[7] — spurred by the advent of the information society, now makes it possible for new forms of business organizations to coordinate the production, marketing, and sale of goods and services through the virtual network. No longer is it necessary to rely on the capital-intense, brick and mortar, stodgy multinational headquarters to command worldwide commercial affairs. Contracts implemented by digital information transfer means the virtual corporation, invisible to governments, difficult to locate, immune to national laws, subject only to international arbitration through legal covenants, escapes the application of national legal doctrine. Through arbitration, the new law merchant, or *lex mercatoria*, as it is denominated — and christened 'new' because its origins in the medieval English law merchant are now transplanted onto the global scene — is becoming the standard for international commercial transactions. But of course, the legal principles of the *lex mercatoria* are a consensus of Western mercantile law as developed through centuries of trading. National precepts enunciated by municipal courts are becoming irrelevant to the development of international commercial law. With the emergence of the *lex mercatoria* as a corpus of international commercial law, the dominance of Western legal principles is further solidified on a global scale as the Western nations are the principal international traders.

Hence the publication in your hand is both a sociological and legal review of the consequences of international trade and the laws generated from this activity. Of course, the attentive reader is pleased to be informed as to the nature of our inquiry, a description as to the attributes of 'law', so that we all may agree as to our subject matter. Unfortunately, the nature of the law defies a consensus of opinion as to its characteristics. The amount of tomes seeking to define the law exceed the yearly avalanche of culinary publications. And while at least the results of the latter may be accompanied by a fine glass of wine, and disappointment assuaged with mellow reminiscences, the former often drives us to despair and the need for a more elevated degree of alcohol. Without doubt, the social scientist requires patience.

Nevertheless, one premise is certain. What we recognize as law is pluralistic and hardly dependent on local courts for its proliferation. Summarizing one scholar,[8] it is not possible to distinguish in practice between legislative laws and community norms. By community, we of course include the various international associations and multilateral institutions. This is what is meant by pluralism: society is governed by laws from a variety of origins, and whether we call them norms, mores, legislative acts, judicial decisions, group and peer pressures, their function is the same. A plurality of sources governs social conduct and is recognized as such by the members of the community. We may describe this as the daily encounter with the prescribed rules of social conduct and they are learned early. The law profession does not have a monopoly on the understanding of laws.

But this book is not another venture into the intellectual problems of legal pluralism.[9] It proceeds from the fact of its existence. On the one hand, for many writers legal pluralism is marginalized. To these scholars, the law is monist, wherein the state has a monopoly, and positivist — what is not created by the state is not law. Such a view has been clearly shown to be erroneous by a distinguished philosopher of the law.[10] To your author, also, legal pluralism is uncontestable. One further step is taken. This treatise departs from the premise that if we are governed by a pluralism of laws it is because the law is a grammatical construction which serves to prevent the dissolution of any society which is itself imagined.[11]

Being in great part fables woven by power alliances, the idea of law can be advocated by any group for any reason provided it seeks to consolidate beliefs. The laws of a country club are no more sacred than the edicts of a national assembly. We might even stride further in our theoretical implications and classify the law as a 'triumph of image over substance'.[12]

Any stable community is a truce where the lines of power and protection of rights are drawn.[13] Some societies do it well; others fail. All is in flux. Law and society have no existence other than in the mind of the beholder. Drawing on material from anthropological, sociological, economic, and legal texts, there is here presented evidence of the mutable, fluid, adaptable nature of the law which permits members of a community to more or less function with a minimum amount of recourse to violence. We may envision society as a constellation of varied bodies, ruled from without and within, by principles and policies from diverse sources, the whole held together by the grandiose scheme of law but no one can find, at least easily, the unifying dogma. If the search for a unifying principle has eluded physicists, so has it the social scientist. But, for the most part, community life functions, almost, for social order is always prone to disintegrate into chaos when norms are seriously challenged.

Such a scheme is not meant to be utopian; far from it. Nor does it presume 'this is the best of all possible worlds'; surely this can hardly be true. In fact, stumbling towards cohesion and trying to hold hands describes better how most societies are organized. The seesaw between cooperation and aggression characterizes communal life in the majority of nations, particularly the industrialized populations where the right to dissent is emphasized. From this proposition, it is natural that the law commands respect from social forces by offering incentives to its members. Relative social harmony is one, as is an ambient for conducting business. If law has no sacred origins, then clearly the law must offer practical rewards for the underlying norms to be accepted. This proposition permits an explanation of many of the phenomena of our present international community of nations.

With such a professed vision of society, there is also collated in this book the varied and, at times, unusual sources of material and social forces which are mounting an assault upon the cultural diversity of sovereign nations. The result is a tidal wave of influences prodding community life in the trading nations towards a globalization of commercial law. Many of the vital issues affecting community life in countries wishing to join the integrated commercial markets will be determined by the basic principles of Western law with its underlying economic and political beliefs. One may be tempted to characterize this book as a portrait of legal imperialism. Such is not the intention. Indeed, conquest by any means, cultural or military, hardly explains the origins of the occupation. The democratic process in the West, even if erected on a disinterested citizenry, is still subject to social pressures. The annals of human activity recorded in this book point to the merchant class as a prime cause of norms. The political sector has spawned an entire industry of lobbying. To assume the polity of a nation is composed of idealistic representatives defies the information available in any media source. Commerce enables the citizen. Commerce creates power and the average person dons with energy the role of the power broker.

There are no value judgments in these assertions. And the conclusion is confined to those sovereigns and their nationals who are desirous of being part of the international commercial route for such is the material gathered in this text. Yet, the assertion is probably true for any organized society, as all communities exercise trade. This is the price to be paid. International trade, and then international aid, usually accompanied by the agreement to arbitrate, constructs norms of behavior. It is a circle dominated by the industrialized nations. Law is an expression of a community's mores without which there would be no society. Presently, the dominant mores emanate from the West for reasons of capital and trade.

To understand better this process, the ensuing chapters describe many of the fountainheads which are forging the legal globalization of commercial norms. The chapters are broad brush strokes. Each chapter warrants a separate book. It would be presumptuous, therefore, to attribute any philosophical analysis to the myriad topics analyzed. Rather, by identifying the functioning of entities such as the International Monetary Fund (IMF), the World Bank, the Organization for Economic Co-operation and Development (OECD), combined with a description of various other sources of legal norms, there is revealed to the reader how unending is the process of legal globalization. The presentation which follows is an empirical reflection. This should permit further investigation.

Of course, commercial life is not sensibly separated from other spheres of civil life. Because of this, the legal globalization of commercial life on a global scale will have its repercussions in other aspects of social life. The exploration of patent rights must inevitably collide with the social weal. Property rights are invariably linked to civil duties. Commentators often link globalization with the loss of personal liberties. This is determining the winners and losers without offering either alternatives to the process of globalization or failing to explain what 'win and lose' means. Such a determination requires the construction of an entire body of community norms. Such a laudable mission is not considered in this study.

Ultimately, the present volume must be considered more as an investigation into the wide-ranging, highly-influential commercial activities of our present era rather than as the elaboration of a theoretical model. Our point of departure is the international commercial aspects dominating our present epoch and with these words of explanation, and also leaving behind any pretense to constructing a sociology of the law, we will commence our chronicles.

## Notes

[1] Shapiro, Martin, *Globalization of Freedom of Contract*, pages 269-298, footnotes pp. 361-363, in Chapter Nine of *The State and Freedom of Contract*, ed. Harry N. Scheiber, Stanford University Press (1998) at p. 270.
[2] Ibid at p. 297.
[3] Ibid at p. 271.
[4] Ibid. This equation is not to be attributed to Prof. Shapiro. It is my own interpretation.

[5] I am grateful to Dr. Rachel Sieder, Senior Lecturer in Politics, at the Institute of Latin American Studies, University of London, for her analytical review of one of the drafts of this book and her insightful observations which led me to address certain questions in this introduction.
[6] Stiglitz, Joseph, *Globalization and its discontents*, Penguin Books (2002) at p. 21.
[7] Ibid, at page 9, but this strict interpretation of globalization emphasizes market economics without considering other social consequences. As will be divulged throughout the chapters in this text, our definition of globalization is more broad for we are describing a general set of rules generated by world markets and institutions. Rules, not markets, are the attributes of legal globalization, a definition advocated by Martin Shapiro, *The Globalization of the Law*, Indiana Journal of Global Studies, 1(1) (Fall 1993) and adopted by your present author.
[8] Woodman, Gordon R., *Customary Law in Common Law Systems*, <www.ids.ac.uk/ids/govern/acc/ust/pdfs/idswoodman.pdf>, accessed 9 April 2003, and see references in this article replete with insightful observations and scholastic critiques.
[9] For a comprehensive definition of legal pluralism and further references see Griffiths, John, under entry 'Legal Pluralism' in the International Encyclopedia of the Social Sciences (2001).
[10] Twining, William, *Globalisation and Legal Theory*, Northwestern University Press (2000).
[11] Unger, Roberto Mangabeira, *The Critical Legal Studies Movement*, Harvard University Press (1986), '... society is understood to be made and imagined rather than merely given' at p 18.
[12] Tomkins, Richard, *No logo can sell the true horrors of battle,* The Financial Times, 20 March 2003, at p. 15, where, in another context, the author summarizes the view that present-day warfare has become a marketing campaign for public support and the true battlefield is consumer loyalty to the cause, normally described in appealing terms such as 'Operation Blus Spoon' (US invasion of Panama) or 'Operation Desert Storm' (US invasion of Iraq). In fact, the same logic applies to legal precepts. Their initial emergence is essentially a marketing exercise in the sale of a product.
[13] Ibid.

# Acknowledgements

In 1999, I undertook studies in the Department of Social Studies at the University of Manchester, UK to obtain an M. Phil. in the social sciences. I was privileged to be accompanied by two outstanding scholars and teachers: Professor John Gledhill, Department of Social Sciences, and Professor David Milman, Faculty of Law. I am indeed indebted to them for their encouragement and academic guidance which eventually led to receiving my degree in 2001.

After receiving my degree, I decided to expand my thesis into a book by incorporating more material and furthering my analysis. When I submitted an outline of my intended text to John Irwin, Consultant Publisher, Ashgate Publishing Ltd., I received a positive reply and immediate support. Through the subsequent years of gathering material and writing, John Irwin made many valuable suggestions as to my intended presentation.

After many revisions, I sent the text to numerous scholars. I received many pertinent and critical observations which tempered my thoughts. Without in any way implying endorsement of the present book, I would like to thank, in alphabetical order, the following scholars: John Griffiths, Faculty of Law, University of Groninger, Groningen, The Netherlands; Anita Kon, Pontifica Universidade Catolica de São Paulo, São Paulo, Brasil; Rachel Seider, Institute of Latin American Studies, University of London, London, UK; Martin Shapiro, School of Law, University of California at Berkeley, Berkeley, CA; Francis Snyder, Co-Director, Academy of International Trade Law, Macão, China; William Twining, School of Law, University of Miami, Coral Gables, FL; Gordon R. Woodman, School of Law, University of Birmingham, Birmingham, UK.

The editing of my manuscript was done under the aegis of Sarah Horsley, Desk Editor, Ashgate.

Finally, to my wife, Marilyn, my gratitude for her loving support during the many years I was sequestered in my study. It was indispensable to know she was always present.

# PART 1
# INTERNATIONAL TRADE AND THE GLOBALIZATION OF WESTERN LAW

## Chapter 1

# The Globalization of Western Law

*The general idea is ... trade, aid, and arbitrate*

Without deliberate design, economics fashion laws and dictate social principles. Dependent on commerce and the recognition of property rights for survival, the isolated, culturally homogenous community bows to regulation, whether informal or enforced. From this description, law can be explained in a variety of ways: a cultural phenomenon of which law is one component; a relationship of class domination where property rights are protected to reinforce dominant social positions; or even a method for problem-solving so as to restrain social conflict.[1]

Yet there are further explanations. Law is also a grammatical construction to venerate a reality which does not exist and permits the realization of income. A parcel of land is leased. The expression 'lease' requires a definition. You do not find leases in nature. The definition of a lease is a social and economic statement. The law is thus an artifice permitting a dominant economic process to expand its reach through analytic and juridical reasoning. Patent rights for computer-chip manufacturing are licensed to a third party. The 'right' conceded contains a lengthy history of economic philosophy.

Law, then, not being a reality, admits and requires various explanations and social insights to understand its functioning at any particular moment of history. In our present century, the social organizing function of hamlet economics has given way to international commerce and institutional lending. The ensuing consequences are varied but global in their repercussions. These forces of international trade and aid are greater than the cultural anchors of a particular society; the need for survival is greater than the habit of individuality conferred by an indigent culture. Trade and aid insist upon legal convergence in the name of commerce. As business goes frenetically international and markets become more integrated each day, the results are predictable: we are swept up in a trend towards legal globalization generated by the explosion in world trade.[2]

The formulations of laws are no longer confined to national frontiers and sanctified by the enforcement powers of the sovereign nation. Transnational institutions, international arbitration boards, global regulatory agencies, standard documents, generalized commercial customs, and ad hoc tribunals are founded on the assumed general laws of justice. From a concern with dried fodder to genetically modified foods, the wand of regulators sees a sensible, moral international uniformity.[3] The alleged existence of the general principles of law of civilized nations is seldom questioned.[4]

Accountability before the bar of humanity is the desired end not compliance with the edicts of local courts. International commerce must not be restrained by local customs or public mores. Recognizing cultural variety confuses and debilitates the global merchant. As if to humiliate further the touted arrogance of local jurisprudence and national courts, the hoary doctrine of 'the King can do no wrong' has been assaulted by international conventions.[5] Under present doctrine, the acts of a nation are no longer immune to liability for being the acts of a state if commercial interests are involved.

The new legal order is, however, under the dominion of Western law, particularly US jurisprudence. Due to unrivalled economic expansion, the US has extended its legal hegemony under the *Pax Regis* of its mercantile scepter. As this has been done through trade, it is natural that we look to the trading actors and their activities for the economic and social results. The existing, convincing statistics suggest the profound effect of international commerce on our global community. In the year 2000, global trade achieved 26 per cent per cent of world gross domestic production.[6] Propelling international commerce are the widespread bilateral investment treaties between nations whose declared purpose is to stimulate more trade.

As bilateral investment treaties foster international arbitration, national, (often called municipal), court jurisdiction is avoided; such circumvention contributes to the globalization of the law. The ensuing arbitration awards are not founded on a prior, stable, legal repository of precedents. Rather arbitrators predicate their awards on general principles of law whose existence, if true, rests more on a moral vision than any legislative support. Consequences from international mercantile activity are further augmented by the social behavior of various public and private institutions, which prompts trade and aid, but at the same time imposes neoliberal legislation in diverse, dissimilar nation states.

It is common and public knowledge public international institutional loans are conditioned on the borrower enacting Western economic and social principles. With the major international public lenders under the firm tutelage of the US, it is natural that US social culture impregnates and influences the philosophies of these organizations. Additionally, the multi-sovereign bodies such as the Organization for Economic Co-operation and Development (OECD) or the World Trade Organization (WTO) as well as the multilateral trade agreements, often designated regional trade blocs, encourage international arbitration. As a result international arbitration law supplants local court jurisprudence; but international arbitration law is stateless, anational, and disconnected from any particular cultural tradition. International arbitration boards, therefore, permit the emergence of a transnational legal order without any parliamentary support.

Furthermore, there is a widespread range of independent international activity such as, for example, international conventions, uniform laws, model laws, academic publications, standard form of contracts, and commodity agreements, all of which affect various aspects of international trade. The cumulative effect is to contribute to the formation of a transnational legal order which, while sufficiently diffused and varied, is homogenous. Successful commercial ventures are launched on anticipated uniformity of legal principles with their subjacent concepts.

Consequently, legal standardization is the result of the commercial acts of trade, aid, and arbitrate. The historical sovereignty of the nation state is presently confronted with the ubiquitous realities of international commerce. Integrated markets and international commerce have brought their own rules and principles to local communities. Today, the idea of sovereignty is pluralistic, composed of competing social influences, and international commerce is a powerful contender for primacy. Yet sovereign pluralism must not cloak a disturbing reality. Economics is not a humanitarian ally to social welfare. Economics requires the social peace but makes no judgment on its contents. Thus, the trend towards legal uniformity is intimately linked to the economic and social forces dominating world trade and their adjacent philosophies.

### *A definition of globalization as distinct from internationalization*

The *globalization*[7] of the law may be defined as the transposition of laws from one culture to another. The social structure of the host society is affected in such a way that its thoughts about how objects and people are regulated are altered; the legal imagination of the host society changes. The globalization of the law is not about volume, speed, or compression of distance; these are descriptions of the *internationalization* of products or ideas. As modest examples of international commerce, we have the export of popular culture, integrated capital markets, omnipresent multinationals, and manufacture through virtual factories: standardization in its most varied and often distasteful form. Nor can we forget the fast-food franchises, internet cafes, and androgynous fashion shops found in all cities and villages. All these, and more, are evidence of how the world is contracting into a compact unit so that cultural information interchange is instantaneous.

Nevertheless, legal globalization is a different attribute. Legal globalization is the construction of a transnational jurisprudence; the forces are dispersed, not confined to a legislative source, nor sponsored by a particular community. Autonomy reigns, but scattered motives are similar to rivers — eventually concurrence is reached as ideas flow into the main stream of commercial activity. The globalization of an idea is different from its internationalization. The food franchise syndrome may change the eating or drinking habits of a country, but it hardly affects the ideas people have about one another and how they are related, obligated, adopted, disinherited — all the thoughts which express social ties (or their dissolution) between human beings. Fashion and fads are internationalized, laws are globalized — they are not given a boisterous reception as performers at a rock concert. The globalization of the law is a silent, but invasive process; the globalization of an idea requires it to cause people to reformulate the stories about their culture. Internationalization of an idea may precede, assist, or facilitate globalization, but they are different processes.

Thus globalization is more than a process of degree[8] although it certainly contains aspects of integration and cooperation across national borders.

Nevertheless the globalization of the law is a mental attitude or receptivity, depending on your viewpoint. Hence, lawyers study the content of our laws — what some might call fables; sociologists describe their consequences; historians explain their origin; legislators engineer new myths; social anthropologists reveal their universality. The entire human race lives within a mental reference of fancies and fictions, what we baptize as laws, against which are played out the birth and death of the family according to consensual, or at least passively accepted for a while, folk ballads. As frequently happens with songs, they become popular and even attain a worldwide audience. The chants of the successful commercial nation become acclaimed hits and even achieve world patrimonial status.

### *The common law of global law*

There are those who will argue that legal globalization requires an intentional, legislative effort. There flourishes among many people the conviction that democratic societies are distinguished by deliberative, positive law and any progress towards the establishment of a global law will require a similar framework. It is natural to think that what has been the legal history of the nation state is a valid reference for the future global community.

Parliaments discuss; legislators give due respect to all opinions; the minority voice through representation is heard; a consensus is reached; the law is published. Public notice wisely counsels all citizens with regard to reasonable and permitted conduct through legislation, the essence of positive law. The nation state has a complex apparatus to compel enforcement; judges contribute by adapting the law to society's realistic expectations. This constellation of legal activity may be characterized as discussion, participation, consensus, notice, enforcement, and judicial relevancy. They are the perceived and esteemed values of democracy and therefore, it is argued, must be repeated on an international level in order to have a world, legal community. In other words, the emergence of a global law is dependent on the extension of the legislative process to the world community. Wise heads will draft laws which impede mutual destruction and after global peace is established the cauldron of social tranquility will permit our ultimate, genetically manipulated destiny. World justice, it is thought, must follow the same process as law in the nation state.

But, as students of history well know, and common sense dictates, humanity was not born into a world of written, codified standards of conduct. It is convenient to emphasize at the outset of our analysis that the description of the normal legislative and judicial processes in current industrialized nations is just one possible method for regulating social conduct; therefore it is perfectly possible for laws to appear without the process just described. Unwritten law, normally custom, was the process of the English common law which led to the varied, complex legal regimes which governed and still regulate the social lives of the English, the Americans, and other nationalities of English influence. True, much of the common law has been superseded by legislation and codes; but for centuries custom, which is consensual social order, maintained moral cohesion.

With a clear vision of the non-parliamentary formation of the law, we will understand how the law is maintained and articulated without any elaborate legislative and judicial machinery. This will facilitate comprehension and concurrence as to the probable, silent sources of the fountain heads of justice on a global scale. Without any international parliamentary structure, it is possible for a global legal order to emerge. The necessities of international commerce have led to the construction of a common law applicable on a world scale. It is being assembled from myriad sources, some written, others assumed to exist, but in reality reflecting the cultural thought of diverse participants.

*The myths of the law*

Human life is organized around economics, even when the reigning, dominant social values appear to have a religious aspect;[9] human society is currently dominated by trade and organized according to prescribed social behavior.[10] Laws summarize beliefs and customs, particular to a social group; they are imagery, and have no independent existence, but articulate ideas about objects and people. Laws are not discovered — they are either written or spoken and thus entirely dependent for their logic, or lack of it, on the mental process of the human being.

Once, in many parts of the world, marriage was the sale of a female human being to a male human being. Many jurisdictions now recognize that the legal content of marriage has no specific meaning and unions are permitted between members of the same sex. Marriage and unions as legal concepts converge with many similar results, such as the possibility of inheritance or the right to social security benefits received by one of the partners to the union. Legally, the parable of what a marriage is has changed. The frontiers of legal ideas are fluid: there are no logical boundaries, only functional consequences.

The laws regulating the more important aspects of social organization are ideas, fables, allegories, stories, venerated legends, whatever you want to call them — ephemeral, subjective concepts which may originate because of society's economic structure. They may be a response to the moral choices posed by variegated human activity or based on historical incidents or philosophical thoughts about the nature of mankind, including divine origin. They are often theories so that one social faction can snatch control from another.

With the appearance of the industrial nation, legislation, in the form of social engineering, has always been a headwater for laws. Increasingly it is becoming the major source for social consensus which is presently difficult without a centralized assembly hall characteristic of smaller communities. Finally, of course, law comes from judicial interpretation which adapts legal thought to contemporary reality. It is a further fact of social life that humanity is contentious by nature, prone to quarrel and armed conflict. Avoidance of violence is one of the primary functions of the law(s) and whatever is considered a handy icon will be certainly appropriated. Laws, surging by necessity from the collective psyche, strive to contain violence by enumerating what is acceptable conduct at a given historical moment.

Thus, the origins of laws are myths, various, not subject to any logical delineation, but they all have one thing in common: useful creeds which permit society to be organized around values and allows us to proceed with our biological destiny — feeding and raising a family in the best manner permitted, and, of course living the longest, possible. Characterizing them in this fashion does not in any way demean or detract from their universal importance; rather it deflects our academic inquiries into their function. With the knowledge of the cultural relevancy of the law, it is comprehensible that trade and its components assume a cardinal role in creating law.

*The nature of the law is, ... , well, yes, ... , human nature*

There is no lack of theories as to either the nature or origins of the law. A sensible method would be to have a general consensus reached as to what the law is, but a definition of the law will prove to be as elusive as its remote origins. The effects of the law are so integral a part of human society everywhere, that many authors have attributed it to a divine manifestation in the human spirit. From this view point, *homo sapiens*, a flawed reflection of a perfect deity, instinctively seeks to recreate a world of eternal truth and justice. The intellectual foundations of Western law or other legal systems, such as Islamic or Roman, are a pale image of a more profound, universal energy; yet all preach a universal justice.

But, so vast and complex is the law that we must realistically put aside questions of a highly theoretical nature and instead study that which can be observed: how societies normally establish social order. Surely one of the aspects of the real existence of the law is social stability, rules people accept in the majority, moral guideposts for human conduct, the cultural definition of what is right and wrong. If a dog knows the difference between a caress and a kick, obviously people can determine if they are surrounded by order or chaos.

Utilizing this methodology, multiple social anthropologists[11] have described the existence of basic legal procedures in various non-technical societies which do not have elaborate judicial machinery or formal parliamentary structures. Such authors have produced convincing studies of the natural propensity of human society to self-regulate itself without parliaments, published decrees, judges, and lawyers. What is present is consensus and, certainly as much as in industrialized societies, the minority dissenter is also heard.

Revealed through extensive field studies in the most diverse parts of the globe, from herders of cattle to traders in crops, from forest scavengers to stock brokers on an exchange, is a pattern of social units organized around an economic means of subsistence. Such investigations demonstrate that the tendencies of people to engage in power struggles, mercantile strife, and local violence, are restrained by the necessity for mutual defense, family succor, parental love, and accumulation of assets for generation survival. As has been suggested by some biologists, the evolutionary history of humanity may not be the elimination or suppression of instincts but the addition of more. This is illustrated in the existing inclination of most people to avoid violence and seek compromise.[12] Therefore, societies produce mechanisms for dispute resolution and impregnate social customs with venerable, ancestral attributes, so as to standardize behavior patterns and diminish armed conflict. The American constitution is no more hallowed in origin than the American Indian totems.

Consensus and discussion, adherence to prescribed moral conduct, conflict-solving techniques, are the sensible contours of social aggregations, otherwise the recalcitrant faces ostracism. Human societies everywhere must naturally develop pacific solutions to conflict or face internecine extinction. The nature of humanity lies in its genome and not in its locale; hence, the tendency towards social order, buried among the helix of human genetics, relies on the same psychological traits to avoid chaos and annihilation. The law manifests itself through social order, and ergo, where there is social equilibrium there is law.

Of course, this exposition hints at being tautological. Law is social order; social order is law. Circular reasoning may indeed be present, but he who has lived in a social environment where the expected rules of conduct are put into question on a daily basis hungers for such a definition![13] In any event, equating law with social order is not to contest other possible sources of the law but rather to emphasize its functional factors. The relevancy of this brief delineation should now be apparent. Societies with only oral skills and tools are able to maintain order through the tradition of their customs, without deliberate, complex, legislative procedures. Naturally, then, the same necessity for economic stability should permit the debut of a global legal order under propitious circumstances without the advent of a world parliament.

Law follows the economy, and if the market is international, the law will strive to achieve a global unison. International trade cannot prosper in a milieu of radically different legal cultures; there always lurks behind every agreement, oral or written, the unspoken fear of conflict. The construction of a world legal community, even if composed of highly technological units, is in the same situation as the mountain hamlet. No formal international social mechanisms have yet been made mandatory; an obligatory, international constitution is lacking.

Naturally, public international enforcement is halting. The forums where voices can be heard are dispersed and uncoordinated. Rather, there is a growing international congregation where various and variegated factors are at work to deflect conflict into dispute settlement mechanisms. The participants know litigation comes from commerce as do raisins from grapes. Consequently, one of the most powerful and pertinent conditions fostering the foundations of a world legal order are the activities associated with international trade.

### *Trade winds bearing their legal cargo*

The present globalization of the law owes its impetus to the gigantesque proportions that international trade has assumed. This is, naturally, a further development of the importance of commercial activity and its consequences upon the social structure of a society emphasized by many social anthropologists.[14] Without doubt, economics, in the industrialized societies, is a major element in shaping social organization; it is arguably the primary social force whose reigning values and commercial activity dominates our global civilization. The devouring, pervasive forces of commerce seem uncontestable — although some have argued, with great scholarship and probably in desperation, that this is only a temporary historical fact.[15] Moreover, the mercantile invasion of Europe and parts of Asia by US industry and its advisers has seen the principles of the common law and US legal concepts in the area of commercial law substantially influence jurists and legislators in those countries.[16] To do business with US, Inc. you must execute documents prepared by their counsel.

The velocity, volume, and impact of globalization by international trade has put it leagues ahead of the admirable, modest efforts at harmonization by international jurists. The galleons of trade carry common freight and their captains' legal cargo. However, you cannot buy Western goods without their being agreement as to what is legally, a 'purchase'; it is a bundle of complex rights and duties. There exist a multitude of international conventions concerning the sale and purchase of goods.[17] If you want to do business with the West, then it will inevitably be framed within legal concepts emanating from this source. Global trade is thus not a mere commercial occurrence — not only a change in ethos from an earlier epoch,[18] but one with profound cultural consequences. The laws of the caravan arrive and stay long after the merchants depart; behind are left the tangible evidences of Western law: invoices and receipts.

The invisible but real cargo of galleons is the laws of the exporters.

*Trade, aid, and arbitrate in the global economy*

It should be apparent that the more standardized the mercantile rules across the globe are the more international trade will be stimulated and, since everyone wants commerce, the incentive for legal constancy is irresistible. However, the normal drift towards international trade rules is often interrupted and distorted by the litigious character of human society. Trade generates profits and also a lot of disputes.

As might be expected, the prudent tradesman does not enter into a commercial venture if there is a possibility of the transaction being subject to the strange laws and precepts of a country not in the mainstream of international commerce. When faced with the fact of an unfamiliar system of law being applied to any transaction, there arises a law-shy reaction. Dispute settlement mechanisms are sought which avoid the application of strange or funny laws. Most merchants either want their national laws applied or the dispute must be referred to an entity which will apply laws couched in familiar cultural references. This is the point of view of the Western entrepreneur who is also the main world trader. Of course, generally, there are no funny laws, only perplexed onlookers. A legal system which has been constructed by any society could hardly be funny; it simply is not understood by others. But such comprehensive approaches to legal diversity will not convince your chairman of the board of directors of a US or UK corporation. Other solutions have to be found.

The answer has been the rush, or perhaps, more accurately, gallop to international arbitration which is seen as an avoidance of municipal laws. International arbitration may be described as an out-of-court dispute settlement procedure, an ad hoc board, subject to its own rules, involving citizens, and including sovereign states, of diverse origin. Of course, the resolution of the dispute depends on the law to be applied and unless the arbitration agreement provides for a selection of the relevant law, the arbitrators will have to decide this for themselves.

Thus, the distinguishing characteristic of international arbitration is not its alleged informality — in truth this rarely exists — nor even the diverse citizenship of the parties which can easily be the situation in an usual international commercial venture . Rather the lack of certainty as to the law to be applied, an aspect not often emphasized, is the watermark of international arbitration. In a municipal court case, the applicable law is usually a question of local law. In international arbitration, the applicable law may or may not have been selected by the parties to the arbitration agreement. It is this uncertainty as to the substantive law which has made international arbitration a significant fountain-head for global law. The importance of international arbitration takes on added primacy for global law when we consider the actions of public entities who are stimulating the procurement of international arbitration in international trade.

International trade is not an activity only confined to individual volition. By intervention of international groups in the trade process, ranging from public entities composed of national governments to the publicly sponsored institutions, the repercussions from trade are hardly restricted to the mere exchange of goods. As a simple illustration, international commerce is often encouraged by the already mentioned bilateral investment treaties between nations or international conventions which encourage international arbitration. With a significant number of treaties[19] in existence supporting arbitration, it is easy to understand the global activity of international arbitration.

The public lending institutions such as the World Bank or IMF fulfill a significant role in the funds they make available for infrastructures to promote foreign investment. However, the extension of aid carries with it the obligation on the part of the recipients to adapt neoliberal social and economic legislation. This frequently includes foreign investment laws which recognize the relevancy of international arbitration.

The broad multilateral trade agreements such as the WTO or the more restricted regional associations such as the North American Free Trade Agreement (NAFTA) create the economic conditions for augmenting trade but also encourage and provide for international arbitration. In fact, NAFTA allows a private investor to compel a government, or any of its subdivisions, to submit to arbitration — a significant innovation in international law.

Then there are the multi-sovereign organizations, such as the UN or the OECD, who are responsible for a great deal of policy recommendations to their members and the drafting of various model laws. Many of them contain guidelines for international arbitration. Such associations are composed of most of the nations of the world and are in effect a consensus-building forum for a wide variety of commercial matters including foreign direct investment. These groups promulgate suggested laws and principles to guide commercial practices. Their importance lies in the convergence of opinion on a variety of topics, legal and economic, which range from model clauses in contracts to approved rules of conduct for multinational companies. We can summarily refer to all of these international groups as supranational organizations.

In addition to the supranational organizations, the preference for international arbitration finds support in various legal instruments such as international conventions, or professional work groups proposing uniform and model laws. There are also the standard form of contracts suggested by trade associations and the multiple arbitration institutes[20] in the major capitals of the world who market their services to the commercial public. Nor can we overlook the commodity associations with their uniform rules adopted for the most varied forms of business imaginable, such as transport documents and telecommunications.

Finally, but of considerable importance, is the sprawling cadre of international lawyers trained in Western laws that have shown a decided preference for arbitration over litigation in court.[21] For attorneys with international clients, international arbitration has become a necessity when counseling them.[22]

Unfortunately for the clients, while national laws are avoided, there is no agreement as to its substitute. The student of international arbitration law will not find a developed body of arbitration law from which to formulate a system of jurisprudence. International arbitration law is still in its growth phase and as such is highly dependent on the individual arbitrators and their cultural preferences.

### *International arbitration and the globalization of Western law*

The emergence of a global legal order, whose presence is now sufficiently articulated not to be ignored, naturally raises questions as to its origins, causes, nature, and future course. Unfolding on a significant scale is an uncoordinated movement towards the globalization of the law under the hegemony of the commercial laws of the industrialized nations. Often such jurisprudence is described as Western law, a convenient but imprecise label which needs further clarification to be useful.

By Western law, we mean precepts emanating from those countries dominating world trade, substantially under the influence of either the common or civil law of the US and Europe: nations possessed of a parliamentary democracy; social units whose political economy acknowledges the consensual basis of society and the primacy of individual liberties.

Furthermore, such republics are themselves substantially under the commercial sway of this century's major economic power — the US — so that the principles of Western law which emerge as a global order cannot be in contradiction to the basic tenets of American law. The more important international, commercial jurisprudence may complement US laws, or even amplify them, but the world's largest international trader establishes the paradigms.

The globalization of American law is not the result of deliberate actions by the US government or US multinationals in their quest for economic dominance; the forces at work are varied, subtle, scattered, disorganized. In fact, many of the elements contributing to the diffusion of Western global law are not even American in source or identity, although obviously under its influence.

Consequently excluded, although not because of any logical defect or cultural impropriety, are all the ideologies of those nations and their laws who are recipients of Western trade and services. Precisely because world trade is between or from industrialized societies to others, the flow of social ideas, in particular legal concepts, is heavily unilateral. We import from China but we know little of its laws. We sell to Tunisia but we are indifferent to its local legislation. We ship to Ecuador but the bill of lading with binding legal terms emanates from Spain. International trade, dominated by the West, conducts trade on its terms, its legal documents, and its jurisprudence.

Moreover, the business of the US and other Western nations is not only business. It is also corporate lawyering, bringing juridical notions everywhere there is trade, stockpiles of legal documents transferred digitally all around the world to legal correspondents who modify, without substance, the US legal concepts to sound as if they were home spun out of distant native soil. Dominated by Western technology and commerce, the global society being constructed by many factors is apt for the reception of a global legal order based on its jurisprudence.

Certainly, the diffuse implantation of US neoliberal economics in most parts of the world has made common law principles familiar to European and Asian jurists. The industrialized countries account for 81 per cent of world output of which 31 per cent comes from the US, 26 per cent from the European Union, and 15 per cent from Japan.[23] Contrary to popular imagination, 81 per cent of US direct investment overseas goes to high-income countries.[24] With US investments totaling billions in such countries, it is a survival necessity to understand its laws and commercial principles. The understanding of the influence of American law becomes even more acute when it is realized that countries such as China, India, Brazil, and Mexico only account for 5 per cent of total global exports.[25]

Moreover, as it is the entrepreneurs of capitalism who are circulating the legal documents for signature we would not expect the contracts in question to contain references to legal systems foreign to one of the major participants. It is difficult to imagine a major US electronic manufacturer doing business in Iran to submit to arbitration according to the principles of Islamic law, although the latter may be eminently suited to the dispute.

Rather, the penetration of US, or if you prefer, industrialized nation economics into the far corners of the world has brought with it the complement of arbitration and with that, either a reference to the general principles of law and justice, or instead, to one of the major arbitration institutes in the Western world, which is the same thing. Selecting an arbitration institute is not choosing a system of law.

Understandably, the arbitrators cannot be expected to have an allegiance to any particular nation state but rather to their mandate, to judge according to justice. And for the most part, the arbitrators' legal system has been the application of principles familiar to them. Invariably, this means Western legal principles, plus a generous portion of private opinions as to what is equitable. In this way, the foundations are laid for the emergence of a global law, without any municipal law allegiance and founded on Western legal principles. The results vary in accordance with the subjective interpretations given by the various arbitrators. Without clear standards, it is to be supposed that international arbitrators will seek tutelage in the various policy statements of international organizations, conventions, treaties, and many other diverse legal instruments.

Trade and aid eventually cause many of its participants to arbitrate. The avalanche of international commerce is bound to generate disputes. Combined with the favorable orientation of public international institutions, the role of international arbitration is seen to be of primordial interest in fomenting the arrival of a global system of law. In addition to being heavily influenced by Western legal principles, international arbitration admits of much individual determinism.

While the results appear difficult to harmonize due to their scattered origins, a pattern is emerging. Sovereign courts are unable to retain their historic privileges over international commerce. With no specific body of law upon which to draw, international arbitration is fostering a transnational world order under the aegis of the various, national economic powers and their contentious merchants.

The economic alliance of trade and aid are conducive to arbitration. The social aspects of international commerce are mirrored in the cultural traditions of the arbitrators. Without the restraints of a national assembly nor subject to review by municipal courts,[26] international arbitration contributes significantly to the trend towards legal globalization under the aegis of Western economic and legal thought.

## Notes

[1] Moore, Sally Falk, *Certainties undone: fifty turbulent years of legal anthropology, 1949-1999*, The Journal of the Royal Anthropological Institute, vol. 7, 95-116 (2001).

[2] Wolf, Martin, *Economic Globalization, An Unfinished Revolution*, Special Report, The World: 2003, The Financial Times, 23 January 2003, at page III, reporting that world trade as a percentage of world gross domestic product, has risen from 7 per cent in 1950 to 24 per cent per cent in 2001.

[3] Dombey, Daniel et al., *The power that sits over Europe*, The Financial Times, 22 August 2002, at page 7.

[4] International Criminal Court (ICC) established by the Rome Treaty entered into existence on 1 July 2002. For details see the official website at <www.un.org/law/icc>, accessed 17 March 2003. While the existence of the ICC is without doubt an indispensable step towards the globalization of human rights, its creation is founded on the assumption that universal moral values are an obligatory part of any civilized nation. More implicit in the existence of the ICC is the statement that *homo sapiens* is not a mechanical composition but contains other intangible and sacred elements.

[5] See the North American Free Trade Agreement (NAFTA) available on <www.lanic.utexas.edu>, accessed 9 January 2002 whose provisions permit an individual or corporate investor to sue the host state.

[6] Roach, Stephen, *Back to borders*, The Financial Times, 28 September 2001, extracting these statistics from a report by Morgan Stanley.

[7] See Shapiro, Martin, *The Globalization of the Law*, Indiana Journal of Global Studies, 1 (1), Fall 1993. I am indebted to Prof. Shapiro for his succinct definition of globalization 'By globalization of law, we might refer to the degree to which the world lives under a single set of rules', and which led me to slightly alter this definition for the purposes of my analysis.

[8] Braithwaite, John and Drahos, Peter, *Global Business Regulation,* Cambridge University Press (2001)where the authors cite with approval a description of globalization as being 'the intensification of ...' all aspects of social life across borders.

[9] A clear conclusion from Tawney, Richard Henry, *Religion and The Rise of Capitalism*, Pelican Books, 1938 ed., London.

[10] On law and anthropology, see extensive bibliographies of the social anthropologists Gluckman, Max, *Politics, Law and Ritual in Tribal Society*, Basil Blackwell, 2nd ed., Oxford (1967); Merry, Sally Engle, *Anthropology, Law, and Transnational Processes*, Annual Review of Anthropology, 1992.21, pp. 357-379; Moore, Sally Falk, *Social Facts & Fabrications 'Customary' Law on Kilimanjaro*, Cambridge University Press, Cambridge (1980). For an exhaustive review of the literature in footnote form by a lawyer with a profound knowledge of social anthropology and the law, see Snyder, Francis, *Law and Anthropology: A Review*, EUI Working Papers Law No. 93/4, European University Institute, Florence (1993).

[11] Gluckman, Max, *Politics*, supra, n. 4; Moore, Sally Falk, supra, n. 4; also Moore, Sally Falk, *Law As Process*, Routledge & Kegan Paul, London (1978).

[12] Ridley, Matt, *Genome: The Autobiography Of A Species In 23 Chapters*, HarperCollins, New York (1999), has a good summary of current literature on the topic of evolutionary history in chapter seven, accompanied by a suggested reading list and notes.

[13] In Portugal during the 1974-75 Revolution, new laws were like news: they changed almost daily. Revolutions destroy quickly the thought of the hallowed traditions which come to us from our ancestors. In circumstances of agitated social change, laws become a vehicle for implementing power through myth creation.

[14] Moore, Sally Falk, supra, n. 7; for a multi-analysis of economics on state sovereignty and its consequences see Gledhill, John, *Power & Its Disguises*, Pluto Press, London and Boulder, Colorado (1994).

[15] Tawney, Richard Henry, *The Acquisitive Society*, Harcourt, Brace and Howe, Inc., New York (1948), arguing that the ethos of economics has presently superceded the ethos of morals but this can and should be reversed.

[16] See report in The Financial Times, 28 September 2001 concerning DaimlerChrysler which apparently has become the first German-based company to adopt Anglo-Saxon corporation governance rules by selecting non-executive directors to sit on the 'chairman's council'.

[17] The interested reader is counseled to see the web sites of the United Nations, UNIDROIT, or UNCITRAL for typical, legal texts at, respectively, <www.un.org>, <www.unidroit.org>, <www.unicitral.org>.

[18] Veblen, Thorsten, *The Nature of the Business Enterprise*, Augustus M. Kelley ed., New York (1975).

[19] As of 16 September 2002, 153 nations have signed the Convention of the International Settlement of Investment Disputes, <www.worldbank.org/icsid>, accessed 6 October 2002.

[20] Random examples are the London Court of International Arbitration, the China International Economic and Trade Arbitration Commission, the Japan Commercial Arbitration Association, the American Arbitration Association, the Stockholm Chamber of Commerce, the Chamber of Commerce and Industry of the Russian Federation, and the Belgian Centre for Arbitration and Mediation, all being a modest listing of arbitration centers existing in the various nations of the world.

[21] Asken, Gerald, *Arbitration and Other Means of Dispute Settlement*, pp. 287-291, at p. 287, in *International Joint Ventures: A Practical Approach to Working with Investors in the U.S. and Abroad*, American Bar Association, Section of Law Practice (1990).

[22] See extensive article by Craig, W. Laurence of the international law firm of Coudert Brothers, *Trends and Developments in the Laws and Practices of International Commercial Arbitration*, published on the website <www.coudert.com/practice>, accessed 5 October 2002. This article contains various footnotes to substantiate the conclusions set forth.

[23] Wolf, Martin *The markets are too eager to discount the cost of war*, The Financial Times, 26 March 2003, at p. 15.

[24] The Economist, survey *The Case for Globalisation*, 29 September-5 October 2001, at p. 6, table 1.

[25] Ibid, p. 11.

[26] In legal theory, appeals from arbitration awards are possible. However, various international conventions, such as the Convention On The Recognition And Enforcement Of Foreign Arbitral Awards restrict the reasons upon which an appeal can be predicated. Recourse to reasons such as, for example, the parties were not given due notice, or the subject matter of the award was not submitted to arbitration, requires protracted litigation in a municipal court. The average participant in an arbitration procedure is not prepared to thereafter undergo lengthy and expensive court litigation.

## Chapter 2

# The Social Logic of Dispute Settlement

*The importance of being argumentative*

The satirical view of legal dispute procedures with their scriveners or stooped lawyers murmuring Latin rituals to a drowsy judicial officer is reasonably correct. Yet we must not be lulled nor mistaken by routine cabalistic procedures; they are the stuff from which national dramas are wrought and which significantly affect social life. Often seen as a component of legal pluralism, dispute settlement procedures are additionally a source of legal norms in contradiction to judicial interpretations or legislative edicts. Dispute settlement procedures constitute a challenge to the authority of the judicial establishment which is most evident in commercial matters.

The invocation of a default clause in a sovereign debt can put an entire nation into jeopardy. Failure to meet bond maturity dates raises the specter of bankruptcy procedures, followed by creditor cost-effective demands and the loss of thousands of jobs. The cliché, as usual, is accurate. The pen — in this case the printed indenture of national debt or the terms of the bond — is mightier than the sword. Dispute settlement procedures, rarely transpiring beyond the court house or arbitration panels, have more social consequences than the daily reported lurid crimes.

This is because dispute settlement procedures are an integral part of the social life of communities everywhere — and we will want to know who hears the dispute, a court or an arbitration panel; it does make a difference. The procedural as well as the content of the dispute settlement procedures can vary considerably with profound social results. A court might apply a national law while an arbitration panel may seek a solution in broad, generalized concepts not identified with a particular, local system of law. Dispute settlement mechanisms, whether national or international, are a fertile source of sociology and jurisprudence.

Dispute settlement mechanisms conciliate divergent views and are crucial to a stable community. But beyond the function of maintaining a social equilibrium, how disputes are resolved will determine to what degree social standards of behavior become law and, more dramatically, the possible influences beyond a particular jurisdiction.

Thus, if a private club is able to expel a member for breach of its internal rules, we will not be concerned as to the nature of such rules. They are not expected to have repercussions beyond the club milieu. But if the club were the OECD, or the

WTO, or a sovereign nation, then the nature of the norms and how they are enforced is entirely different. Moreover, the nature of the dispute settlement mechanism will have a direct influence on the source of the legal norm invoked. Reverting to our private club, with the right of expulsion the club can maintain its internal rules unaltered without third-party interference. Were the club, by its own rules, required to refer an alleged violation to arbitration, then we can imagine different results. The reasonableness of the infraction might be questioned, even if subjectively, by those empowered to hear and try. The how of dispute settlement is not a legal technicality but a significant social tool.

Yet dispute settlement mechanisms have even a further dimension. Whoever determines the issues of litigation must have a standard of social norms which are methods for separating right from wrong. Therefore, while a private club member may have a straightforward perception of right and wrong, since the club rules are presumably accessible, an arbitration panel member in a WTO hearing may have considerable trouble establishing the 'law of the case'. In our WTO hearing, defining where responsibility lies in a dispute between sovereigns is a Herculean task. The range of social norms applicable to a dispute becomes more spacious or restrictive dependent on the origin of the dispute and the entity entrusted with its determination.

Moreover, the nature of the entity charged with dispute resolution has innumerable consequences. When matters are heard before a municipal court, the dispute is cast within a cauldron of national myths and social concepts. National courts normally affirm a nation's mythology — who are the heroes, what were their moral inspirations; more important, who are the villains and why. Tribunals not anchored to a municipal court system must create their own ideology. One cannot compare a WTO arbitration panel hearing to an arbitration tribunal assessing claims by bond holders against a sovereign nation, or to a local civil court in a major metropolitan city.

Thus dispute settlement conditions a variety of social issues: how laws are formed, their sources, their influence beyond national frontiers, what social norms are selected to be decreed as a law, the importance of the composition of the tribunal, and the criteria the tribunal uses. All of these themes are inter-related by litigation mechanisms. Dispute settlement is an eminently social endeavor.

Among the different community spheres available for analysis, the sociology of dispute settlement is conveniently studied through the prism of international commerce. While it can also be analyzed through the varied aspects of private civil litigation, for the most part such conflicts are confined to national courts. International commerce divorces the development of the law from the history of a nation; national law is irrevocably associated with the origins of the realm. In fact, one of the reasons for the popularity of international arbitration is the fear by the parties that national law will favor one over the other in a dispute in a municipal court. The social logic of international arbitration is diametrically different from that of national arbitration. When disputes are heard before a municipal arbitration panel, appeals to the court are facilitated. Hovering above national arbitration panels are the municipal guards ready to enforce national law.

Opposed to this trend, is the merchant's desire for liberty of commercial rules not encumbered by a variety of jurisprudence whose development has been linked to national foundations. While the battle for this goal is still being fought, there are no doubts of the fundamentally distinct approach to international litigation by arbitrators. Arbitration, for the most part, strives to assist the expansion of international commerce, which is why it is so popular among the merchant class. Equally importantly, the theme of globalization lurks ceaselessly alongside the growth of international commerce. Through legal globalization, the degree to which the world lives under a single set of rules is augmenting.[1] What we cavalierly describe as rules are also custom, legislative fiat, judicial interpretation, and arbitration norms.

The study of international commerce and dispute settlement inevitably introduces us to the concept of globalization and to what extent dispute settlement influences its growth or contains it. But prior to a further consideration of the theory of dispute settlement, a panorama of international commerce and its complementary effects is relevant and useful.

*Brothers in law*

Transnational mercantilism has invaded the globe spawning international litigation. Significant multinational organizations such as the WTO are engaged in promoting and regulating international commerce; the UN played a significant part in the promulgation of the UN Convention for the International Sale of Goods. This treaty, regulating the international sale of goods, is adhered to by a multitude of nation states and is considered a repository of the common law of international sales. Being a treaty, its legal effects are not dependent on municipal courts although the interpretation of it by national tribunals is unavoidable. Nevertheless, it is a notable example of efforts by teams of jurists to craft international rules for international commerce. The World Bank and regional development banks are also assisting in the drafting and harmonization of laws. Multinational enterprises, the so-called MNEs, have become the dominant species of international commercial creatures.

Sparking difficult questions of law arising from international commerce, MNEs awaken jurists to the need for uniformity; otherwise, the result will be international chaos, and not commerce. Understanding commerce as a communal activity whose purport surpasses income and gain adds a necessary dimension to our understanding the process of legal globalization. Partially imperialistic, but also derived from consensual contributions, merchants and jurists converge on the practical, hands-on approach to dispute resolution.

Imperialistic or not, the surge of international commerce characteristic of our present epoch matters, is effecting our lives in all aspects. A decent income for all on our planet, prolonged life expectancy, reduced infant mortality, extinction of child labor, universal education for the humble as well as the privileged, environmental preservation, the protection of human rights, available medical care, cultural diversity, secure retirement funds, national sovereignty — there are no social limits to the consequences of global business.

It should come as no surprise that trade and laws are inseparable. Perhaps we do not need trade for law, but commerce without norms is a frenzied, twitching, decapitated corpus. While our attention is frequently drawn by the media to the trials of the ethically depraved before an international war crimes tribunal, such events are only a sporadic part of the less obvious but steady and silent process of legal globalization now in progress stimulated and shaped by the practices of the MNEs.

With the growth of global law operating outside of any specific parliamentary structure, the contents of this law will be the ideology of the dominant trading partner. If merchants seek sureness, their own jurisprudence appears the most sensible and therefore the chosen favorite. Changing a person's diet, usually an insuperable obstacle will appear a minor hurdle when compared to altering a merchant's view as to what is a sensible law or not. Once the dominant trading partner is able to establish a legal beachhead, it is only a matter of time before differences in legal theories among the trading groups begin to disappear.[2] There is a confluence of ideas which gravitates about the theories of the preeminent trading partner. However, this is only possible if a freedom is created from the dictates of local courts, since judicial decisions are bound to follow the precedents and juridical concepts of their nation. The international merchant class does not want to be frustrated in the expectation of its contractual obligations voluntarily assumed with other parties by the idiosyncrasies of the various municipal courts.

Science cannot proceed without standardization of quantities or measurements nor can international commerce flourish without an identifiable body of law: impartial, stable and predictable. Thus the merchants and the professional classes associated with them seek other forms of dispute settlement. To avoid local courts, arbitration becomes the desired forum, demanded by the merchants and insisted upon by their counselors. This is what has happened. Moreover, as soon as commercial law begins to assume a certain harmony, it is natural that concepts will be borrowed from the commercial world and applied to civil, or personal, rights.

The trend toward the globalization of the law is substantially in the area of international commercial law. Yet so strong is the need for the global village to have a common set of norms that there are now visible laudable efforts towards the globalization of criminal law and suggestions for other specialized areas of international law.[3]

Were these trends merely confined to a narrow segment of international trade, the movement towards the globalization of the law would hardly make substantial progress, if any. However, trade ordinarily is accompanied by financial aid. International institutions are formed dedicated to lending and promoting industrial development, but the lenders require changes to the laws of the borrower, which encourages international foreign investment. International commerce responds to the incentives created by the sovereign states in their need for capital: international alliances are established; trade and capital begin to circulate more freely. Yet the more integrated markets become, the more they need their laws harmonized with those of other nations.

Regional trade associations such as NAFTA, or the six-nation South American customs union, MERCOSUR, or the Andean Community are formed to facilitate commerce. Protectionism bends, eventually collapsing, before the lure of larger markets with the same results. Open markets require less nationalism in the law. Likewise, trade issues are raised in bodies such as the WTO in an effort to obtain even more barter within a consensual framework and rules are established to govern trade. Subscription to, and hearty acceptance of, the economic and political beliefs espoused by the dominant members are part of the adherence procedure. The result is increased international commerce. Furthermore, organizations, such as the OECD, exist to gather consensus on a wide variety of topics, certainly including recommended legal norms for multinational social behavior. From this effort, international commerce receives a further impetus in the guise of a dedicated pursuit by technocrats.

Complementary to such vast, diverse labor of technocrats and specialists in numerous organizations is the appearance, in unprecedented scale, of integrated capital markets, transnational corporations, regional trade associations, international conventions, model laws, uniform laws, international courts, trade associations, standard contracts, and non-governmental organizations. This list is by no means exhaustive, but all contribute to the law-making process provoked by international commerce.

The results produced from people associated with treaties, associations, organizations, private interest groups, professional committees, and scholastic teams are not usually coordinated in such a way as to produce a harmonious body of international private law. The effect is more of independent pockets of activity, generating through competent toil, a confluence of ideas concerning the basic legal norms affecting private international commerce. Such a confluence of activity is held together by various social bonds but dispute settlement, litigation, the contentious aspect of social life plays a positive, significant role in spite of its divisive appearance. The law of dispute settlement reveals the social fabric of a society, with regard to both the degree of its development and its secular beliefs. Reinforcing social norms and circulating them in the form of court sentences or arbitration awards adds to the pacification of international commerce.

### *Social comfort from commerce in conflict*

When we invoke dispute settlement and litigation, we enter the world of legal symbolism. The law, as an object, does not exist; it is entirely a mental concept. Litigation is about invasions by others which disrupt our mental images concerning our concepts of right and wrong. Yet our gauges of morality are usually orientated by reference to the real world. For a large part of the population everywhere this means commerce impregnated by income, profit, capital gain, and accumulation. Early land law is frequently seen by historians as a source of norms at a time when commerce was still marginal in contrast to our present economic phase. Feudal law is seen as a system of reciprocal rights and duties couched in family terms, an unhappy euphemism which conceals the abject serfdom involved. How curious, yet early land law was regulating the only major commodity which could then be utilized — realty and all the commerce derived from it.

Clearly, economics is the unrivaled motor of legal symbolism. Without the necessity of trade, the law would be confined to the social aspects of family, inheritance, and criminal law.[4] Commercial contract law is the patron of international commerce and ultimately international commercial relations; the development of contract law has permitted trade to grow with reduced uncertainty. And the more international trade expands and becomes the dominant ethos of dispersed societies, the more urgent is the need for the elimination of legal risk, the pressing requirement of removing legal uncertainty, the demand for a uniform legal framework, and the drive for laws corresponding essentially to commercial expectations and not political objectives. The consumers spur the markets and the merchants lobby the politicians. Western democracy is essentially an uninhibited game of commercial influence circumscribed by rules of supposed fair play.

In legal, economic parlance this is described as minimizing the transaction costs, reducing indirect, direct and anticipated expenses associated with any commercial contract to the minimum possible. But it also brings cultural threats, as the forces of commerce are deemed more immediate. Legal and cultural diversity must yield to harmonization. It is natural that the social dynamics conducive to legal globalization find their most powerful expression in multilateral organizations created to condition an orderly growth of international commerce.

From the significant contractual union of many sovereigns representing the major and minor nations of the world, bound together by the objectives of more trade, common codes and principles are easily asserted from above.[5] The mercantile spirit is at the same time adventurous for new markets, but hostile in its attitude towards foreign rules and standards. Supranational governance from the top permits legal harmonization which than translates into globalization. Dispute settlement, formerly the province of local courts, is shifted to international arbitration boards which are thus understood as a separate source of legal norms easily in conflict with municipal courts. A world global legal order is emerging from this source because it is conducive to more trade.

If the persistent invasion of our lives by international commerce is now an acceptable fact, the same institutions which reduce tension in a local community, the courts, or their equivalent, will have to emerge to the satisfaction of the international merchant community. Dispute settlement in the local society has not the same objectives as in the international community. While the material is vast and prompts many academic specialities, one aspect of national law is to protect minority views. This is not the objective of international commercial law. As a matter of principle, there is no reason why a bill of rights for international commerce should not exist. However, as merchants desire uniformity and not diversity, the effect on commerce of an international commercial bill of rights probably would be to stultify it. International trade is simply not going to take any risks in the face of uncertain legal conclusions nor favor idiosyncratic commercial rules. Through dispute settlement on an international level, eventually there will arise a body of harmonious law which will encourage even more commerce.

International commerce does not require the law of the jungle. It thrives on monotony.

*Closing statement by counsel*

Where once dispute settlement was exclusively the province of wise minds, gray heads, and the occasional tipsy advocate, it is now understood as a dynamic, social process involving multiple, diverse participants. Dispute settlement conditions what social norms become laws; the formalities, or lack of them, defines the source of the norms. The entity judging the dispute makes possible the range of norms invoked, whether narrow or ample. In the same fashion, the enabling act of the judging entity, whether local or international, will permit the results to have local or transnational scope.

Accompanying the growth of international commerce, are the multiple financial institutions, public and private, conceding aid and credit, which stimulates further commerce. Multilateral and multinational organizations are established to regulate various aspects of international trade while private associations are formed to emit standard rules and regulations for a variety of activities, ranging from food additives to bills of lading.

Dispute settlement and aid are an integral part of trade. As international commerce demands a relatively expeditious resolution of conflicts in order to progress, international arbitration has become a major source of dispute settlement, preferred by the traders and the financial markets. Resulting from these activities is the invisible hand of legal globalization, diffusing social norms, harmonizing cultural differences, suggesting model forms and clauses, insisting on legislation before aid is granted, inserting a firewall between the traditional sovereign state and the supra-national structure.

The social logic of international trade predicts international arbitration will produce social norms which will often be at variance with municipal court views. Hence, dispute settlement, whose perplexity anciently was confined to deciding between a writ in chancery or a plea at the common-law courts, is now seen as a fountainhead of innumerable social and legal precepts.

## Notes

1 See Beynon, John & Dunkerley, David, *Globalization: The Reader* (2000) for a compilation of multiple articles by various authors on the most varied aspects of globalization although not the law; see also Shapiro, Martin, *The Globalization of the Law*, Indiana Journal of Global Studies, 1 (1), (Fall 1993).

2 For the view that Asia will be more resistant to legal changes, see Katzenstein, Peter J., *A World of Regions: America, Europe, and East Asia* (1993), <www.ijgls.indiana.edu>, accessed 17 December 2001, stating '... because ... East Asia embody different norms and are endowed with different capacities, globalization will not lead to homogenization. The spread of legal norms will remain politically contested'.

3 Of course, the constitution of *ad hoc* tribunals to try war crimes and the use of military courts to replace, temporarily, the normal jurisdiction of a criminal court are examples of

this trend. Additionally the International Criminal Court established by the Rome Treaty entered into existence on 1 July 2002. For details see the official website at <www.un.org/law/icc>, (accessed 17 March 2003). Another academic discussion in vogue is the constitution of a world court to hear international antitrust issues and thus strive for a coherent, global doctrine on this crucial material, cf. Guzman, Andrew T., *International Antitrust and the WTO: The Lesson from Intellectual Property*, UC Berkeley Law & Economics Research Paper No. 2000-20, <www.law.berkeley.edu>, accessed 15 December 2001.

[4] In some societies, the prime function of law courts is confined to the enforcement of criminal law precepts, for example, see Shin-yi Peng, *The WTO Legalistic Approach and East Asia: From the Legal Culture Perspective*, 1 Asian-Pacific Law & Policy Journal 13 (2000), where he describes how civil disputes in China are handled informally, through kin networks, without the intervention of the judiciary system. Recourse to the law courts for resolution of, for example, contractual disputes, is considered a disgrace and brings dishonor to all the participants.

[5] Oloka-Onyango and Udagama, *The Realization of Economic, Social and Cultural Rights: Globalization and its impact on the full enjoyment of human rights*, UN Doc. E/CN. 4/Sub.2/2000/13-15 June 2000 available at <www.unsystem.org>, accessed 8 February 2002.

# Chapter 3

# Finally Giving Citizens Everywhere Their Lawful Investment Rights

*We, the people*

Simultaneously legal instruments and technical documents, they rarely provoke editorial comment in the media. Yet bilateral investment treaties ('bits'), with their arbitration provisions, have a profound influence on the globalization of the law. Bits breach the legal insularity of the nation's courts regarding foreign investment. Whereas local courts look to their own legal principles for guidance, international arbitration relies on a supposed common denominator of imagined, universal legal principles.

As foreign investment issues range over a multitude of commercial law principles, bits irremediably constrict national sovereign jurisdiction over international commercial issues. Bits allow commercial international law to develop without national law restrictions. The result is a continuing expanding sphere of international commercial law principles though there is no international civil court or international legislative assembly.

Equally noteworthy, the historical subjugation of the individual to the interests of the nation state has changed with the advent of investment treaties.[1] The importance of public international law in defining and regulating the commercial rights of individuals, if ever they had any, has been altered significantly.[2] The appearance and the proliferation of bits is a convincing testament that international law is no longer confined to relationships between states but also includes and protects the individual.[3]

Such a fortuitous development has resulted from bits granting to individual investors the right to arbitrate disputes with the host country before an international arbitration board. Individual justice, when it is decreed, is dependent on the dispute settlement process. International arbitration fostered by bits has commuted justice to the private investor.

This recognition of the individual in international law is the inevitable outcome of increased world trade. Through bits, rights have been granted to individuals to sue governments who consent to have the claims heard in arbitration. Channeled through bits, the foreign investor can expect to have considered and defined legal concepts in arbitration such as equal national treatment, expropriation, and exchange controls, among the more frequent causes of litigation. The reasons for such contemporary sovereign flexibility are not a matter of principle; it is economic necessity. The imperatives of commerce write the contents of the law.

Because nations require trade and capital investment, they must accept the demands of the capital exporters and offer inducements. And the source of this new commercial power and exercise of rights by individuals is made possible through dispute settlement resolved in arbitration. Trade expands; merchants clamor for international arbitration as a safe haven from undesirable local politics; international arbitration is consecrated in a plethora of investment treaties; the jurisdiction of local courts retracts. One cannot say that any nation or private group set about to denationalize international trade; but that has been the result. This process has elevated individual commercial rights to the level of international law protection. Private international commercial law has earned an honorable status as a de facto commercial bill of rights.

A brief, historical review will assist in understanding this dramatic legal changes in which individual rights are achieving international law status and, more importantly, why.

Formerly, and with specific reference to foreign investment in other lands, international law, public or private, did not generally recognize the right of an individual to have a claim against a sovereign nation.[4] The spokesman for the citizen was the government. Nations dealt with one another, not nations with individuals.[5] Prompted by the Mexican expropriation of American assets which started in 1915,[6] the US government, in opposition to this juristic lacuna, announced what is now known as the *Hull* doctrine.[7] Nations had to compensate foreign investors when their assets were expropriated by 'prompt, adequate, and effective' indemnities.[8]

Although from the remote past, one still hears clearly the imperial words of the US Secretary of State Cordell Hull:[9]

> The Government of the United States merely adverts to a self evident fact when it notes that the applicable precedents and recognized authorities on international law support its declaration that, under every rule of law and equity, no government is entitled to expropriate private property, for whatever purpose, without provision for prompt, adequate, and effective payment therefore.

Invoking the image of gunboat readiness, such bombastic language appealed to other industrialized nations who were emotionally in sympathy with the patriotic Hull. If the doctrine was not heeded, a nation would invoke its commercial and possibly military prowess in defense of its citizens' investment and property rights. Perhaps the individual had no standing in court, but its country had, hopefully, a stationary army ready for action. Understandably, the industrialized nations applauded the appearance of the *Hull* doctrine.

In opposition to the *Hull* doctrine, the Latin American states, when expropriating or taking other action against foreign-owned assets, invoked the *Calvo* thesis.[10] The *Calvo* doctrine followed upon the armed intervention in Mexico by France in 1838 and 1861 and, in contrast to the *Hull* doctrine, advocated that countries, without interference from other nations, are free to act as they wish within their jurisdiction. Sovereign pride will not admit of instructions from another realm as to rights over assets within its territory. All disputes must be resolved in the local courts, where, it must be presumed, US or other national insistence on adequate compensation would be tempered considerably.[11]

Perhaps looking over his shoulder to see if any gunboats were arriving, the Mexican Minister of Foreign Affairs in 1938, proffered the classical definition of the *Calvo* doctrine:[12]

> My Government maintains ... there is in international law no rule universally accepted in theory nor carried out in practice, which makes obligatory the payment of immediate compensation nor even of deferred compensation, for expropriations of a general and impersonal character ...

With time, and with the United Nations as a forum, the emerging economies and underdeveloped nations also did not want to accept the *Hull* doctrine as a standard for their emerging economies. The results were multiple resolutions upholding the rights of sovereign nations to protect their resources.

Thus we have various UN Resolutions, such as the 1962 Resolution on Permanent Sovereignty over Natural Resources,[13] endorsing 'appropriate' compensation for expropriation; another Resolution on Permanent Sovereignty over Natural Resources in 1973[14] clarifying that 'appropriate' was a rejection of the *Hull* requirement of 'adequate'; the 1974 Resolution Declaring a New International Economic Order[15] which considers unacceptable any sanctions against a country because of expropriation; and finally the Charter of Economic Rights and Duties[16] which gives nations the right to exercise authority over foreign investment in accordance with their national objectives.

All these resolutions were destined to give supremacy to nations over assets in their various forms within their jurisdiction. National interests were deemed superior to individual economic rights. Yet it is not hard to understand the dismay of international merchants, encouraged to invest abroad, but faced with national attitudes hostile to excessive foreign investment protection. It is probably fair to say that until the proliferation of investment treaties, the *Hull* doctrine was being supplanted by a consensus that lesser developed countries should and would pay less than adequate compensation when properties were expropriated.[17]

Even then, national interests had to be tempered. Foreign investment might dwindle and central bank reserves would evaporate. Sovereignty could stand firm in the face of commercial rancor but then the shipments of needed goods would slow to a trickle. Bills of lading require payment in a hard currency which is an attribute that merchants and their Central Banks have.

Law being a fickle icon, the results the individual under international law depended on the nation state involved, the court, and the political balance of power which is always silently present. Inevitably, the justice of national reason had to give way to the realities of international commerce. Which philosophy was adopted, that of *Hull* or that of *Calvo*, was dependent on power politics.

With trade as the dominant leitmotif and ally of industrialization, the need for emerging nations to attract resources and skills, and the circulation of capital dependent on freedom from local legal biases, a pattern emerged. A solution was encountered which appears satisfactory to all parties, merchants and nations. Nations interested in trading with one another execute investment treaties. The nations' signatory to the treaties agrees to have disputes affecting individuals referred to international arbitration.[18]

The sovereign consent to arbitration withdraws jurisdiction over the subject matter, usually a commercial question of investment or its consequences, from the local courts. The doctrines applied by international arbitrators thus constitute a source of international law for the individual not anchored to a national system of law. With the appearance of bits is the demise of the doctrine of international law that individuals have no standing in court, only nations. Executing investment treaties for economic reasons also brings the obligation by nations to arbitrate. Local courts are avoided. Theories of law are developed by arbitrators and not judges.

The columns of a global law are thus in construction, supplanting effectively any scholastic international law principle allegedly regulating the rights between individuals and nations. Academic arguments on behalf of the individual, when they were proclaimed, have now been transposed to treaty language. Emerging from legal uncertainties as how to breach the traditional immunity of the nation, two significant events command our attention: the individual is recognized as having rights under international law; in parallel, there are emerging doctrines of law as developed by the arbitrators.

Both of these conclusions emanate from the investment treaties. Such agreements have forged a network amongst nations for how disputes will be resolved and for the adoption of arbitration as the preferred method over local court litigation. The bits concede the right of arbitration to the foreign investor but the mechanics need regulating. Arbitration without an agreed upon mechanism would probably be counter-productive, raising vexing questions as to arbitration procedure instead of law issues.

The motor of efficiency and perceived need for arbitration has resulted in the Convention on the Settlement of Investment Disputes between States and Nationals of Other States ('Convention') opened for signature on 18 March 1945.[19] This Convention, *inter alia*, establishes the International Center for the Settlement of Investment Disputes (ICSID), which operates under the aegis of the World Bank, and contains dispute settlement rules regulating arbitration procedure.

In an attempt to satisfy different legal viewpoints, and as a concession to the diversity of legal cultures, the laws to be applied are couched in generalizations. The unintended result is to afford to arbitrators the ability to create law. Investment treaties are an avenue for the development of private international commercial law through the ICSID.

We are not dealing with an obscure convention. The significance and influence of this model treaty becomes apparent when we are advised[20] that in 2002 there were in existence over 2000 bits and that approximately 150 nations[21] have adhered to the Convention.

Bits and adhesion to the ICSID Convention create a closed system encompassing the trading world and fomenting its own commercial rules while clearly disseminating the globalization of the law under Western legal principles.

*Investment treaties, the corner stones of a global law*

Describing a treaty as an 'investment' treaty is susceptible to inducing two errors. The first is that the treaty deals with investment commonly associated with stock exchanges and the second, a more serious oversight, that there is a pure, typical investment treaty.

As used in bits, the subject matter is intended to be what we more commonly think of as the varied forms of foreign direct investment, including the establishment of companies, acquisitions, joint ventures, real property rights, intellectual property rights, loans, mortgages, shares, all as simple illustrations. That there is only one model of investment treaty is inaccurate. There are also multilateral trade agreements, regional trade associations, investment provisions in various treaties[22] that are not bits, so that we can more accurately speak of bilateral, regional, multilateral or plurilateral, legal relationships which protect investment rights.

Nor can we exclude the possibility of arbitration clauses appearing in the enormous schedule of international conventions regulating commerce from the transport of dangerous chemicals to the hunting of whales. Nevertheless, the bits rank as a primary source for promoting international arbitration by conceding to individuals private international commercial law rights. It has been a slow development.

The World Bank has given a succinct history of bits:[23]

> Modern BITs have retained broad uniformity in their provisions ... [V]irtually all bilateral investment treaties cover four substantive areas: admission, treatment, expropriation and the settlement of disputes. Almost all modern BITs include provisions dealing with disputes between one of the parties and investors having the nationality of the other party. In this respect most provide for arbitration under the Convention on the Settlement of Investment Disputes between States and Nationals of Other States.

In the typical bit, each nation state who is a signatory obligates itself with another nation state that each will permit and protect investments by each other's citizens. With subsequent amendments, designated by the terms 'Additional Facility', the ISCID is now prepared to hear cases from individuals even if one party is not a citizen of a signatory or the 'investment' does not fall within the terms of the Convention provided the necessary consents are obtained. The ICSID is thus able to act as an international arbitration forum provided there is compliance with its jurisdiction rules.[24]

But, of course, the fact that an arbitration center is being extensively used does not mean its stated object is to foment its own law. Indeed, any arbitration center publicly stating this function and further printing it would hardly receive the approval of national governments. Still, the evidence is inescapable that the use of facilities such as the ICSID permits the displacement of the usual function of the interpretation of the law by courts to an arbitration center. This happens because the standards of interpretation consecrated in such investment treaties are substantially indefinite. Thus, we are informed on good authority,[25] that almost all of the bits in existence contain provisions that guarantee 'fair and equitable' treatment.

Once a treaty introduces such laudable concepts, whoever is called upon to interpret these words faces a complex cultural question: a definition of fairness and equity. Such standards can only be interpreted within a framework of cultural relevancy. The importance of bits and their contribution to global law increases to critical proportions when we learn that in the vast majority of bits[26] the signatories are encouraged to submit their differences to international arbitration procedures, more specifically to the ICSID.

However, the ICSID is active not solely by virtue of references through bits. From claimants all over the world, claims have been presented to the ISCID, among others, concerning hotels, mutual funds, radio stations, and toll bridges,[27] disputes clearly within the commercial experience of most people. Bits and other investment treaties foster recourse to international arbitration.

Yet we must not lose sight that what appears to be protecting a private investment becomes a method for subtracting municipal court jurisdiction from the signatories.

### *The ICSID, almost a world law tribunal*

The ICSID has performed a critical role in promoting international arbitration and stimulating awards not beholden to any one sovereign jurisdiction; what is colloquially described as 'stateless' awards.

Pursuant to the Convention, the ICSID provides facilities for the conciliation and arbitration of disputes between member countries and investors who qualify as nationals of other member countries as well as those who are not if one of the parties to the dispute is a signatory. Recourse to ICSID conciliation and arbitration is entirely voluntary. All ICSID Contracting States, whether or not parties to the dispute, are required by the Convention to recognize and enforce ICSID arbitral awards.

Arbitration under the auspices of ICSID is similarly one of the main mechanisms for the settlement of investment disputes under four recent multilateral trade and investment treaties, NAFTA, the Energy Charter Treaty, the Cartagena Free Trade Agreement and the Colonia Investment Protocol of Mercosur.

The ICSID has maintained a low public profile. Nevertheless, its mechanism for international arbitration represents a significant step towards creating 'stateless' awards and initiating a new order of legal principles not having allegiance to any municipal law system. The bits obligate the signatories to refer any dispute to the ICSID but this remission does not state what will be the rules of law to be applied.

As to the law to be applied, the ICSID has appropriate language. If the parties do not reach agreement on the matter, which they seldom do, then Article 42(1) of the Convention specifies, in part, that the Tribunal will apply:

> … the law of the Contracting State party to the dispute (including its rules on the conflict of laws) and such rules of international law as may be applicable.

The reference to the rule on the conflict of laws is a reference to what law the contracting state believes has application over the subject matter. In practical terms this often becomes impossible to define because, *a priori*, we are presuming a fact which may not be true: that all nations have a conflict of laws rule.

Even if a nation does have a conflict of laws rule, it has to be interpreted, and this may present innumerable legal problems of proof. It can be expected that the rules of international law as understood by the arbitrators designated by the ICSID will be frequently utilized as it is a simpler course of action. Arbitrators without a specialized training in the law will not easily immerse themselves in a crash course on the conflict of laws, an area of the law which purports to assist a court in determining what national law is applicable to a particular dispute. An understanding of the theory of the conflict of laws requires a substantial training in legal theory. For the average arbitrator, commonsense solutions are preferable, particularly since arbitration is intended to avoid the lengthy, complex ideational content typical of law cases.

Moreover, we are not given any guidance as to what is the source of this 'international law'. International law can be obtained from treaties, conventions, uniform laws, model laws, customary law, law merchant and a host of international cooperative agreements between various governments.

The content of international law is thus fluid, imprecise, and permits international arbitrators to decide what is and what is not 'international law'.

### *The boundaries of trade are as the frontiers of the human mind, limitless*

The recourse to ISCID arbitration rules obeys no particular geographical logic other than a signatory or party has to be interested in international trade, which is to say, investment treaties are like water, they cover pretty well the surface of our commercial globe.

The UK has many bilateral investment treaties.[28] Executed since 1975, they now number more than 75 and all contain similar provisions,[29] ranging from Albania, Sri Lanka, to Turkmenistan, and Zimbabwe. The US Department of State makes various typical bits available on its web site. They are numerous. With the US, we have bits with such diverse countries as Croatia, Jordan, Trinidad and Tobago, and the Ukraine. The list is extensive.[30]

The US is only one of many nations which has executed bits and an examination of the countries executing bits includes all modern nations of today, such as the UK, Germany, France, to name but a few in Europe.[31] In South America, a vast majority of the countries have signed at least one bilateral investment treaty.[32] Such is the power of trade that the cherished *Calvo* doctrine has been decidedly overturned by the countries of the hemisphere in which it originated. But the planetary presence of bits is not confined to a particular hemisphere or stage of economic development. Without any order or significance, a random review of bits already signed includes Madagascar/Sweden (1966), Netherlands/Tanzania (1970), Egypt/Switzerland (1973), Nepal/UK (1993) Czech Republic/Tajkistan (1994), Denmark/Hong Kong (1994), Italy/Mongolia (1993), and finally Hungary/Malaysia (1993).

*The justice in bilateral investment treaties*

Bits generally permit the parties to the treaty to have arbitration according to the terms of the Convention with the ICSID. At first glance, this might seem a sensible direction towards the search for an international conception of justice and impartiality. International trade must be liberated from the concepts peculiar to any national jurisdiction. Yet such a method has its harmonization consequences.

By withdrawing law issues resulting from foreign direct investment from the tribunals of the host country and compelling the parties to seek arbitration of their dispute before the ICSID, the contours, its contents, and the particulars of the local legal culture of the host country are being declared not relevant for purposes of foreign direct investment.

What is being created is a special court, in this case, an international arbitration tribunal, for foreign direct investment. This permits arbitrators to disregard rules of law promulgated by courts and instead seek a different standard, one predicated upon 'justice', or 'equity', or 'the principles of international law'. Standards are difficult to define. Thus, international trade, freed from the shackles of municipal court determinations, develops according to the doctrines emanating from the international arbitration tribunals. As the standards for justice contained in arbitration treaties are idealistic, but without specific content, the realities of international commerce will finally reverse the *Calvo* doctrine and its subsequent national adherents.

Historical irony is emphasized when we realize the Mexican doctrine born south of the border has been blatantly revoked by its own national legislators with the adhesion to NAFTA which entered into force on 1 January 1994.[33] By virtue of this treaty, foreign investors are given the right to sue directly the Mexican government and have their investment claims decided in arbitration by the ISCID. In order others should not think this was a neighborly oversight, the Mexican government executed a bit containing arbitration mechanisms with Spain on 22 June 1995 and Switzerland on 10 July 1995.[34]

Modern commerce has brought to an end the vaudeville act of *Hull* and *Calvo*.

## Notes

[1] See review of this development in Andrew T. Guzman, *Explaining The Popularity of Bilateral Investment Treaties: Why LDCs Sign Treaties That Hurt Them,*

<www.jeanmonnetprogram.org/papers/97/97-12>, accessed 14 December 2001. The same article also contains an extensive bibliography on issues affecting customary law and the emergence of bits.

[2] See the historic summary by Elihu Lauterpacht, *International Law and Private Foreign Investment* <www.ijpls.indiana.edu/Vol4/no.2/laugp>, accessed 14 December 2001.

[3] Ibid.

[4] The International Court of Justice at The Hague is considered the primary source of international law. Set up in 1945 by the UN, Article 34(1) of the Statute of the ICJ reads: '1. Only states may be parties in cases before the Court'. Sources of international law include conventions, treaties, scholarly essays, and customary practices between nations.

[5] Supra, n. 1.

[6] Supra, n. 1.

[7] The former US Secretary of State, Cordell Hull, expressed his views in 1938 involving the expropriation of American assets by Mexico, see, for an exchange of notes on this dispute, 3 Green H. Hackworth, Digest of International Law Sec. 228 at pgs. 655-65 (1942).

[8] For a clear, succinct explanation of this doctrine see above, fn. 2.

[9] Reproduced in 3 G. Hackworth, Digest of International Law 658-59 (1942).

[10] Carlos Calvo, (1824-1906) an Argentine jurist who argued that legal questions involving the acts of national sovereignty must be resolved exclusively in the local courts. Foreign investments should not be afforded more favorable treatment than national investments. This is in stark contrast to the US Monroe Doctrine whereby the US would enforce foreign debts, by force if necessary.

[11] R. Doak Bishop & Jame E. Etri, *International Arbitration in South America*, <www.kslaw.co/library>, accessed 14 December 2001.

[12] Supra, n. 1.

[13] Resolution 1803, 15 UN Doc. A/5217 (1962).

[14] Resolution 3171, 52 UN Doc. A/9030 (1974).

[15] Resolution 3201, UN Doc. A/9559 (1974).

[16] Resolution 3281, UN Doc. A/9631(1974).

[17] See discussion as to history of UN resolutions ostensibly granting sovereign nations more rights than prevalent under the *Hull* doctrine, supra, fn. 1.

[18] See article by Margrete Stevens, Senior Counsel, ICSID, Washington, DC in the International Business Lawyer, entitled *Experience in Arbitrations under ICSID Rules Pursuant to Bilateral Investment Treaties*, 29(8), pgs. 377-380 inclusive, September 2001.

[19] Supra, n. 18.

[20] See report on international arbitration <www.freshfields.com.practice.corporate.publicationspdfs.2431>, accessed 20 May 2002.

[21] This is the quantity stated by the ICSID on their home page <www.worldbank.org/icsid>, accessed 14 December 2001.

[22] See NAFTA and various links on portal <www.lanic.utexas.edu>, accessed 9 January 2002.

[23] Edited by this writer. See home page of World Bank and links to bilateral investment treaties at <www.worldbank.org>.

[24] Supra, n. 23, for details concerning basic documents of the Convention, additional facilities, the signatories, and details as to each treaty.

[25] Supra, n. 18.

[26] Ibid.

[27] Ibid.

[28] Ibid.

[29] Ibid.
[30] The web site of the US Dept of State is <www.state.gov>, with relevant links, accessed 22 February 2002,
[31] Supra, n. 18.
[32] See *Investment Treaties in the Western Hemisphere: A Compendium*, in <www.alca-ftaa.oas.org. > accessed 14 December 2001.
[33] A regional trade agreement composed of the US, Canada, and Mexico. See various links on portal <www.lanic.utexas.edu>, accessed 9 January 2002.
[34] See <www.worldbank.org>, and links to bilateral investment treaties, accessed 8 October 2002.

# Chapter 4

# Some Regional Trade Agreements are a Sorry Lot

*A place in the sun*

Without dispute settlement procedures, the declarations of political and commercial convenience canonized in RTAs (RTAs), sometimes confusingly referred to as preferential trading agreements, cannot go beyond the consequences of political rallies and trade exchange. Originally conceived as a form of one nation granting trade preferences to another, it is true the more recent RTAs now extend their provisions into domestic issues.[1] For this reason, the term 'preferential trading agreement' is misleading as it conceals other agreement objectives such as harmonization of trade policies.

However, while some RTAs are more arresting than others, or afford more extensive coverage as to the underlying rights protected, time will dissipate their din. Without clear rules for the protection of individual rights and a formal dispute settlement procedure, RTAs will always be captive to volatile governmental opinion.

Nevertheless, the foundations for global commercial law are being erected by at least one notable example of a regional trade agreement. NAFTA, with its arbitration provisions, between Mexico, Canada, and the US, is a fertile source of law principles being developed independently of national courts. For the time being, the majority of RTAs are still in their embryonic stage.

But in spite of their being imperfect entities, containing amorphous legal structures, it is through the creation of regional, supranational courts, or arbitration boards, that RTAs will contribute towards the convergence of globalized commercial law concepts. It is only a matter of time. The South-east Asian countries and China have signed an agreement to establish a broad free trade area by 2010.[2] The US is negotiating a long list of bilateral agreements to promote trade liberalization with multiple countries such as Morocco, Central American countries, the five members of the Southern African Customs Union, and various nations in South East Asia.[3] In some cases, the bilateral agreements will not evolve beyond a tariff schedule; in others cases, the bilateral agreements are adjacent and complementary to the general trend towards a Free Trade Area of the Americas which will eventually unite into one zone from Canada to Argentina.

For these reasons, while an analysis of a particular RTA confers historical and social insights, the irregular pattern requires a methodology and the panorama presently offered is an attempt to establish such an academic framework for the study of RTAs. The importance of RTAs towards the globalization of the law justifies the task.

Any doubt as to the prevalence of RTAs and their potential for globalizing law is quickly dispelled by the published academic literature. The WTO reports[4] that as of December 2002 250 RTAs have been notified to GATT/WTO. Over 170 are currently in force and it is expected that by the year 2005, the number of RTAs should approach 300.[5] Some of the notified RTAs have been discontinued but the original signatories involved are parties to redesigned agreements.

Nor are RTAs eccentric solutions chosen by marginal economies. International trade conceals its neighborly origins. Although world commerce is seen as largely responsible for globalization, in fact, within the RTAs is where most of the merchandise exchange takes place. Heralding a new era and economy, the trade liberalization movements and privatization processes are inevitably pressuring regions all over the world to unite, legislate, harmonize, and adjudicate. Unfortunately, the politically aware social forces in the various territories comprising regional agreements are not often in agreement. The progress of RTAs is hesitant and fragmented.

Additionally, about 50 per cent of world trade is conducted under RTAs.[6] Trade pursuant to these agreements is augmenting more rapidly than global trade.[7] Over ninety (90) per cent of the members of the WTO belong to RTAs.[8] Furthermore, many of the RTAs are inter-related with countries participating in more than one RTA.[9] More important than the number of RTAs is the population affected by such agreements. Thus, the agreements linking the various nations of the Americas and the European Union's regional agreements with Central, Eastern Europe, and the Mediterranean each comprise more than 500 million people. Nor are the RTAs isolated, self-contained trading blocs.[10] Multiple are the RTAs between countries not geographically adjacent.[11]

Yet, in spite of their omnipresence, RTAs are the *enfants terribles* of the trend towards consecrating the rights of the individual in confrontation with the nation, being, for the most part, promissory starts followed by a languid existence. They are potential constellations of individual rights which will ultimately detach private commercial international law from local, national courts; but for the moment political forces interact with commercial objectives while clear legal principles are yet to be formalized and clearly established within the relevant RTA.

For this reason, to some, RTAs are simply geographical and trade alliances,[12] legitimate and necessary economic defenses against major, mercantile blocs and not intended to disrupt local court jurisdiction over its citizens. When they are poorly structured, it is doubtful if they constitute little more than provincial voices, calls, and appeals for the strengthening of common interests.[13] To others, RTAs are cast as part of a resurrected globalization process, attempts by sovereign nations to accompany the trade liberalization in course, and remembrances of nasty past-memories of slave traders, and other unpleasant, historical comparisons surface.[14]

Moreover when discussing RTAs, conclusions can not be precipitated. The subject matter is ambiguous, academic contours difficult to establish. The terminology is imprecise, definitions seem elusive,[15] their characteristics not yet systemized, the reasons for their existence controversial,[16] their consequences the focus of much theoretical study[17]. Still, one aspect is certain. Regional trading agreements are augmenting[18] and with their increased presence come a powerful mechanism to avoid local laws through the establishment of regional, or supranational courts, and even more incisively, at times permitting, or even obligating, international arbitration.[19]

Dependent on the regional trading agreement, the judicial aspects of some RTAs thus become imbued with expansive consequences. Regional frontiers are illusory. While in theory affecting only a few nations, a whole hemisphere may easily be involved.[20] Thus we see efforts throughout South America where through a variety of institutions RTAs have spurred attempts at the harmonization of both public and private law.[21]

Once a regional court or international arbitration is mandated by a regional trade agreement, judicial standards become suffused with vague references to 'international law',[22] or 'in equity',[23] or 'fair and equitable treatment',[24] since anything more definite is likely to impede the adoption of the RTA by fearful political forces. But the phrase international law, similar to the word fair or equity, is a non-objective reference which means what the declarant wishes it to mean.[25] By such allusions, lawyers, judges, or arbitrators are able to invoke contemporary common sense or changed mores as a substitute for legal precedent. A regional trading agreement, whether through a court of justice or arbitration permits local investors and the international entrepreneurs to escape the confines of their own local courts. Efficient trade, and not local politics, becomes the hub of the wheel. *Stare decisis*[26] is replaced by 'is this a workable commercial rule?'.

However, even in these circumstances, the contribution of RTAs to the development of a global legal order is unsteady because many RTAs are defective in treaty language as regards the private citizen. For the most part, they are political aspirations.[27] The RTAs are far from maturity, whether as administrative organisms or legal entities. Truly, they are the orphans of public and private international law, with no tutelage.

Yet there are notable, important exceptions which affect a large, significant population.[28] And because of the existence and dynamics of this restricted, but highly significant group, it is fair to say that RTAs are an augmenting influence in the establishment of a world legal order. This is particularly evident in the Western hemisphere, under the influence of The North America Free Trade Area (NAFTA)[29] and in the Southern hemisphere under the dominion of MERCOSUR.[30]

A coherent academic organization of RTAs, which will facilitate a prediction as to their influence, an understanding of their potential, a realistic appraisal of their potential contributions, will require a systemic classification.

### *Name calling*

Presently, current nomenclature concerning RTAs refers to unilateral, bilateral, and multilateral trade agreements.[31] However, RTAs can also be grouped by the categories of preferential trading agreements applicable to a portion of goods or services; a free trade agreement whereby trade barriers amongst the signatories are abolished; and a customs union where the parties adopt a common external trade barrier but which may graduate to a harmonization of national policies.[32] The final step is of course a federation of sovereign nations or states, as is the US, where law, economics, fiscal policy, foreign affairs, and national security, come together in unison under a centralized government.

Such objectives are within the horizon of the European Union and when achieved, the European Union, as the US, will achieve a federation structure. When this happens, it makes no sense to think in terms of regional trading agreements for the prior sovereign parts now have a unity and judicial existence. A new nation is born and the regional trade agreement implodes. But for every classification contrived or definition given, exceptions can be found, doubts arise, and there appears to be no academic concurrence as to the categories. Without a logical graduation, an analysis of RTAs can only result in political or economic insights, which does not contribute towards a social science methodology. This is a clear indication that a taxonomy of RTAs needs to be constructed in accordance with less subjective aspects, such as proximity, and more objective criteria. They exist.

Buried within the preambles and articles of the RTAs lie the absence or presence of legal norms. Without the articulation of juridical concepts a RTA is a political tract, the vision of statesmen or prophecies which may or may not materialize. It has been suggested[33] that the legal criteria of the direct effect of laws in the region concerned, the standing of citizens, the supremacy of the law over domestic law, the transparency of laws, and their enforcement, offer an analytic tool. This is unquestionably true, although the elements concerned require a substantial legal background for use as a working tool.

Nevertheless, proceeding from this basis, a broad, interdisciplinary classification is possible. In conformity with this suggestion, an organization of RTAs can be made which focuses on the degree of apperception, or not, of private international law rights by the sovereign(s) and its enforceability. The following is a suggested methodology for RTAs. The resulting classification separates RTAs from those only recognizing rights between nations and those which also grant this important protection to private individuals even though a sovereign is a party. Public international law, private international law, conciliation, arbitration, enforcement of decision, these are the minimum variables upon which a methodology should be constructed.

### *Public Law RTAs*

RTAs where there is recognized the rights and duties of the signatories so that public international law is the significant legal norm. However, there is no mechanism to resolve differences between the signatories. Such an RTA is dependent on power politics.

### *Public Law Conciliation RTAs*

RTAs where there is incorporated into the relevant treaty a conciliatory dispute settlement mechanism for public parties but enforcement aspects are voluntary.

Conciliation requires a voluntary meeting of the minds of the interested parties with their being absent any obligatory mechanism.

*Public Law Judicial Constituent RTAs*

RTAs where there is incorporated into the relevant treaty a judicial or arbitration settlement mechanism for public parties. Naturally, unless the losing sovereign accepts the verdict or award, enforceability is always possible by recourse to war.

*Public and Private Law Conciliation RTAs*

RTAs where there is incorporated into the relevant treaty a conciliatory dispute settlement mechanism but enforcement procedures are voluntary. Public and private rights are recognized but private parties have to seek permission to have their claims heard or all parties must agree to the arbitration procedure. It is expected the parties will attempt to conciliate their differences by private negotiation before initiating formal procedures.

*Public and Private Law Judicial Constituent RTAs*

RTAs where there is incorporated into the relevant treaty a judicial or arbitration settlement mechanism for public and private parties. Here, the individual, possessed with a favorable decision or award, can seek enforcement, at least for damages, in a judicial forum.

The comparisons here sought are the formal structures of the regional trade agreement, if any exist. Within each classification, we will want to know the powers of each organ of the community, the areas of competence, what areas of the law are contemplated, the beneficiaries of the particular treaty, the remedies made available to public and private entities. Further, the existence or not of tribunals created by RTAs, and their scope as well as source of jurisprudence, is all useful when examining RTAs. This will permit investigators to identify various standards against which to measure other RTAs.

Furthermore, there are topics such as proper parties, interpretation, harmonization, complexity of legal redress, sources of laws, efficacy of judicial sentences, appeal rights, courts vs. arbitration, methods of selecting judges or arbitrators, judicial independence, and enforcement. All of these factors and more itemization is possible, will influence the social and legal consequences of the RTA in question.

With such a methodology, the focus of scholastic interest will shift from public international law, the principles which regulate the rights between sovereign nations, and where often occult compromises occur, to private international law which is the domain of the citizen and where transparency naturally reigns. Private international law is directed towards the protection of the aureole of rights inherent in the individual. We think of international investments, international contracts, establishment of companies, freedom of labor movement, constitutional privileges, and the right to be heard in an impartial international tribunal. This shorted list, for no attempt has been made to be exhaustive, are the issues of private international law and which investment treaties have significantly enhanced on an international level. It now remains for RTAs to achieve this same stage of development.

In summary, at the simplest level, are the public law RTAs which are essentially political organizations whose implementation is dependent on individual will and persuasion. The various RTAs which have no developed legal structure can hardly be viewed as anything more than political documents, subject to the vagaries of national assemblies and the sorry politics of power.

Far more complex are the public and private law judicial RTAs where compliance can be enforced and further where there is an opportunity for the principles of international private law, our primary interest, to be announced. Of concern to the investigator of the globalization of the law are those RTAs which have created a judicial or arbitration dispute settlement mechanism to determine to what degree such RTAs contribute to the formation of a transnational legal system.

Additionally, as the organizational structure of an RTA will vary with the classification suggested, there should be a correlation between the category in which falls an RTA and its degree of permanency and sphere of influence. Examples of the utility of this method which makes apparent the deficiencies and attributes of a selected group of RTAs are included here as an annex.

## Annex

## Selected Regional Trade Agreements and Methodology

*NAFTA*

With this regional trade agreement, the US, Canada, and Mexico[34] inaugurate a new era which may serve as a model for a future Free Trade Area of the Americas. NAFTA confers rights upon an individual investor to sue a sovereign and obligate the issues be tried before the international arbitration board, ICSID, under the auspices of the World Bank. NAFTA represents a public and private law constituent RTA and, in deference to its importance, is discussed separately in the next chapter.

In alphabetic order, other RTAs of interest are as follows:

*The Andean Community*

Signed in 1969, The Agreement of Cartagena established the Andean Community[35] with the objectives of creating a free trade area. The Andean Community juridical system has a supranational nature. It is distinguished from municipal Andean law and from public international law.

Andean provisions are binding throughout the territory. This also means that the citizen acquires rights and obligations whose fulfillment must be recognized by both national courts and the Andean Community at all levels.

Thus the Andean Group Court of Justice is in a position to formulate rules of law independently of municipal law. Most importantly, and fundamental for the development of a regional law, the Court is empowered to hear cases from third parties, individuals or companies, who believe their rights have been violated by any provision of the Andean Community.[36]

The Andean Court of Justice is also empowered to hear matters agreed to be arbitrated upon by private parties and is specifically given the authority to apply principles 'in equity' in accordance with the Andean legal system.[37]

We are thus confronted with an all-encompassing regional agreement which grants private parties standing in court, a basic and first element in the construction of a regional legal system whose influence will be beyond local, municipal courts.

In as much as all private parties must consent to an arbitration before the Andean Court of Justice our methodology suggests the Andean Community is a public and private law conciliation RTA.

*APEC and ASEAN*

Contrasting with the RTAs evolving towards a legalistic form of governance are the RTAs based on the opposite concept. Dispute is to be resolved through consensus. The Asia-Pacific Economic Cooperation Forum (APEC)[38] was formed but it is a 'loose, consultative forum, … characterized by a spirit of pragmatism'.[39]

Moreover, 'The paradigm of APEC is essentially a mechanism based on voluntary consensus and peer pressure. This kind of "soft law" ... is the preferred Asian way'.[40]

In similar fashion are the constituent members of the Association of South East Asian Nations (ASEAN).[41] As with APEC, consultation and conciliation are the indicated methods of dispute settlement. So much so, that the applicable agreement expresses this clearly:

> 2. However, neither compensation nor the suspension of concessions or other obligations is preferred to full implementation of a recommendation to bring a measure into conformity with the Agreement or any covered agreements.[42]

Referring to our methodology, APEC and ASEAN are public law RTAs.

*CARICOM*

The Caribbean Community and Common Market (CARICOM) was founded in 1973.[43] Its general purpose is to construct a common market.[44] A proposed Caribbean Court of Justice (CCJ) will be the regional judicial tribunal.[45] With CARICOM, we find that the proposed provisions establishing the CCJ direct the court to judge according to '... such rules of international law as may be applicable'.[46]

However, there is a division among political circles and the legal profession in CARICOM as to whether or not restrictions will be put upon the court's powers. For some, the reference to 'international law' implies 'public law' issues and that means only sovereign states will be allowed to appear before the court. To others, the court must be given independent powers and the right to interpret the CARICOM treaty, drawing parallels to the European Court of Justice,[47] even when the rights of individuals are affected.[48]

The controversy over the full scope of the CARICOM Court of Justice indicates typical areas of investigation provoked by RTAs. Our legal norm analysis permits us to identify potential areas of conflict and different stages of development.

Juridical identity confronts a loose association: whether public or also private international law issues are admitted; restricted powers or full autonomy for the court; these are the tags of whether we are dealing with RTAs or legislative aspirations; regional members of an international community, or sovereign nations which merely seek help to compete internationally.

Our legal norm analysis permits us to conclude that CARICOM is in a transitional state from exclusively public law issues to also contemplating international private law rights and, dependent on the outcome of the political debate, CARICOM may fall within the category of a public and private law RTA. Were this to happen, then we can expect contributions to global law forthcoming. When private international law becomes a reference, there is immediately created a distance from the confines of municipal law.

*ECOWAS*

The fifteen (15) West African States that constitute The Economic Community of West African States, (ECOWAS),[49] is intended to be an economic community and its treaty and protocols[50] establish a Community Court of Justice and an arbitration tribunal. Unfortunately, the reference to these institutions is dependent on a protocol as yet not executed.

Moreover, the reference in the relevant protocol to the Community Court of Justice intends the decisions to be binding on individuals but we are not given any indication if individuals can seek recourse directly to the court or arbitration tribunal. Consequently, public and private law matters appear to be contemplated but the treaty and protocols are not sufficiently implemented for any clear understanding.

In these circumstances a legal norm analysis leads us to conclude that ECOWAS as a regional trading agreement is very much in its infancy and we are dealing with an incipient public law RTA.

*MERCOSUR*

MERCOSUR,[51] also known has the Southern Common Market, is regulated by a Treaty and various protocols. Private rights are recognized but it is the nation member which raises the issue before the competent authorities. Arbitration as a method of dispute settlement is recognized but only if all parties agree, both public and private. Each of the signatories will ' ... ensure fair and equitable treatment to investments of investors of another Contracting Party ...'.[52]

Additionally, the Protocol of Brasilia,[53] applicable to the MERCOSUR group, specifically dictates that the arbitration tribunal will have recourse to, *inter alia*, '... the principles and dispositions of international law ... '.[54]

Finally, if the parties agree, the arbitrators may decide the controversy '... ex aequo et bono ...'[55] which may be translated as 'in justice and fairness' or according to what 'is just and good' or even 'according to equity and conscience'.

Albeit under restricted circumstances, the MERCOSUR legal structure grants some protection to the citizen if the respective nation is responsive, establishes arbitration as a valid alternative to court action, and expressly permits the use of equitable principles. Municipal law is no longer the exclusive source of law. Nevertheless, MERCOSUR falls within the methodology of a public and private law conciliation constituent RTA since the individual is not automatically given rights.

The above classifications permit us to determine with reasonable accuracy if a particular regional trade agreement is a mere political declaration or has procedures which will lead to judicial pronouncements. Our methodology establishes a graduated scale which culminates in the recognition of private rights under international law against a sovereign nation.

When a particular regional trade agreement falls within the category of a public and private law judicial constituent RTA, we can then anticipate and predict that concepts of private international law will be recognized and superimposed upon municipal law concepts. RTAs will eventually form a network of independent commercial law principles that constitutes an anational body of law and which will form part of a larger corpus of international commercial law designated by the technical term *lex mercatoria*.[56]

## Notes

[1] Jo-Ann Crawford et al., *RTAs and the WTO*, Credit Research Paper No. 00/3, paper prepared for a meeting of the North American Economic and Finance Association in Boston, 6-9 January 2000, <www.dti.gov.uk/worldtrade/regional>, accessed 17 December 2001.

[2] Amy Kazmin, *Asean and China sign deal for free trade area*, The Financial Times, 5 May 2002, at page 6.

[3] Edward Alden, *Countries line up to sign US trade deals*, The Financial Times, 1 April 2002, at page 10.

[4] See home page of the World Trade Organization, <www.wto.org>, accessed 25 March 2003, and links to 'regional trade agreements'.

[5] Ibid.

[6] Ibid.

[7] Ibid.

[8] See n. 1.

[9] Ibid.

[10] Ibid.

[11] Ibid.

[12] Guy de Jonquières, *Popular Trend is at odds with global free trade,* The Financial Times, 20 November 2001.

[13] See the web sites for Asian countries such as ASEAN at <www.asean.org> and SAARC at <www.saarc.com>, accessed 5 January 2002 .

[14] Norman Girvan, International Meeting on Globalization and Development Problem, Jan 18-22, 1999, Havana, Cuba, <www.genderandtrade.net> accessed 5 January 2002: 'Prior rounds of globalization involved slavery, indentureship[sic], the free movement of labor, and (European) inter-state rivalry in the Caribbean.'

[15] L. Alan Winters, *Regionalism versus Multilateralism*, The World Bank, International Economics Department, International Trade Division, November 1996, <www.sice.oas.org/geograph/westernh/regmulea.asp>, accessed 17 December 2001: 'I will define 'regionalism' loosely as any policy designed to reduce trade barriers between a subset of countries regardless of whether those countries are actually contiguous or even close to each other. I will not define 'multilateralism' precisely, however, because — to my surprise and regret — I find that I cannot easily do so.'

[16] Lloyd Gruber, *Rethinking the Rational Foundations of Supranational Governance: Lessons from the North American Free Trade Agreement*, Harris School Working Paper Series: 99.18, <www.harrisschool.uchicago.edu.>, accessed 24 December 2001.

[17] See n. 1

[18] Ibid.

[19] See <www.nafta-sec-alena.org/english/index> with links, accessed 9 January 2002. Under NAFTA, arbitration is obligatory.

[20] Geographically including the whole of North America and, with some minor exceptions, Central and South America, the various, intermittent attempts to establish a Free Trade Area of the Americas is an example.

[21] Jorge M. Guira, *MERCOSUR As An Instrument for Development*, 3-Sum NAFTA: L. & Bus. Rev. Am 53m (1997).
[22] See infra, n. 43, indicating web site of CARICOM and links. Thus Article XVII of the 'Agreement Establishing the Caribbean Court of Justice', exhorts its members to apply '... such rules of international law as may be applicable.'
[23] See <www.americasnet.net/Trade_Integration/ftaa_tutorial/155> accessed 2 January 2002.
[24] For details of agreement, see <www.MERCOSUR.org>, accessed 9 January 2002.
[25] 'When I use a word', Humpty Dumpty said, in a rather scornful tone, 'it means just what I choose it to mean, neither more nor less.' <www.sundials.org/about/humpty>, quoting excerpts from *Alice in Wonderland*, accessed 8 January 2002.
[26] To abide by decided cases.
[27] The Treaty establishing CEFTA (Poland, Czech Republic, Slovakia, Hungary, Slovenia, Romania, and Bulgaria) is a good example, see <www.cefta.org>, accessed 8 January 2002. CEFTA is a free trade area. It is a political tract committed to eliminating tariffs and encouraging trade. However, it contains no mechanism for resolving differences which are binding on the parties. Being basically a political document, we can assume that as the Central European nations seek membership to the European Union, CEFTA will become irrelevant.
[28] The Andean Community, MERCOSUR, and NAFTA are RTAs which have taken steps but in different degrees, towards creating regional courts or arbitration tribunals.
[29] For NAFTA treaty, see <www.sice.oas.org/trade/nafta/chap-111.asp#A1110>, accessed 30 January 2002.
[30] For general information on MERCOSUR, see <www.MERCOSUR.org>, accessed 9 January 2002. MERCOSUR is composed of Argentina, Brazil, Paraguay, and Uruguay, with Chile and Bolivia as associate members.
[31] Supra, n. 15 for an analysis of RTAs according to various criteria such as objective function, symmetrical or asymmetrical, interaction between countries, as examples among others.
[32] Tim Martyn, *A Complete Guide to the Regional Trade Agreements of the Asia-Pacific*, <www.arts.monash.edu.au/ausapec/RTA/entirereport/PDF >, accessed 26 December 2001.
[33] Prof. Andrea K. Schneider has made an incisive analysis on the various criteria in Andrea K. Schneider, *Democracy and Dispute Resolution: Individual Rights in International Trade Organizations*, 19 U. Pa. J. Intl Econ. Law, 587 (1998).
[34] For articles of agreement see links on portal <www.lanic.utexas.edu>, accessed 9 January 2002.
[35] See <www.americasnet.net/Trade_Integration/ftaa_tutorial/155>, accessed 2 January 2002. Initially, the Andean Community was made up of Colombia, Peru, Ecuador, Bolivia, and Chile. Later, Venezuela joined but Chile withdrew in 1974. In September 1995, Panama applied for admission and presently is an observer.
[36] See <www.comunidadandinha.org/ingles/trea/ande_trie2>, accessed 2 January 2002.
[37] Ibid, see Article 38 of the Treaty creating the Court: 'The Court will issue its arbitration award, either in law or in equity, …'.
[38] In 1989, Australia invited twelve nations to form an organization to be entitled APEC. The membership has grown and is diverse containing countries as different as Australia, Canada, Chile, People's Republic of China; Hong Kong, Indonesia, Japan, Republic of Korea, Mexico, Peru, Russia, Singapore, USA, Vietnam. For full details see <www.apecsec.org.sg>, accessed 28 January 2002.

[39] Shin-yi Peng, *The WTO Legalistic Approach and East Asia: From the Legal Culture Perspective*, 1 Asian-Pacific Law & Policy Journal 13 (2000), and footnotes 100 et seq. to his article.
[40] Ibid.
[41] The Governments of Brunei Darussalam, the Republic of Indonesia, Malaysia, the Republic of the Philippines, the Republic of Singapore, the Kingdom of Thailand and the Socialist Republic of Vietnam, Member States of the Association of South East Asian Nations (ASEAN), see <www.asean.org>, accessed 18 February 2002.
[42] Ibid, with links to dispute settlement agreement.
[43] For details on CARICOM see web site <www.caricom.org>, accessed 7 January 2002. The present members of CARICOM are Antigua, Bahamas, Barbados, Belize, Dominica, Grenada, Guyana, Haiti, Jamaica, Montserrat, St Kitts-Nevis, St Lucia, St Vincent and the Grenadines, Suriname, Trinidad, and Tobago.
[44] Ibid.
[45] Ibid, see links to questions and answers about the Caribbean Court of Justice.
[46] Article XVIII of the relevant protocol states, in part:

> 1. The Court, in exercising its original jurisdiction under Article XII (b) and (c), will apply such rules of international law as may be applicable.
> 2. The Court may not bring in a finding of non liquet (author's note: adjudication is not possible since the law is not clear) on the ground of silence or obscurity of the law.

[47] The Court responsible for the interpretation of the laws of the European Union.
[48] Duke Pollard, *The Caribbean Court of Justice(CCJ): Challenge and Response*, 3 May 1999, <www.CARICOM.org>, accessed 7 January 2002.
[49] Treaty signed 24 July, 1993, the signatories are Benin, Burkina Faso, Liberia, Mali, Cabo Verde, Niger, Cote D'Ivoire, Nigeria, Gambia, Ghana, Senegal, Guinea, Sierra Leone, Guinea Bissau, Togo, see <www.ecowas.int>, accessed 30 December 2001.
[50] Ibid, for reference to protocols.
[51] MERCOSUR is composed of Argentina, Brazil, Paraguay, and Uruguay, see <www.MERCOSUR.com/in/info/tratados_acuerdo_MERCOSUR_ue>, accessed 2 January 2001. Bolivia and Chile are associate members.
[52] Ibid.
[53] For details see <www.MERCOSUR.com/in/info/tratados_protocolo_brasilia>.
[54] Ibid, my translation from the Spanish, Article 19(1) of the Protocol.
[55] Ibid, Article 19(2).
[56] See the discussion in Chapter 20 entitled 'International Arbitration: The Global Customs of Merchants' for a review of the doctrine of *lex mercatoria* and its contribution to the globalization of the law.

## Chapter 5

# The NAFTA Investor and Legal Globalization

### *NAFTA*

None of the RTAs approximate the crown jewel: NAFTA,[1] nor its contribution to the globalization of the law. NAFTA stimulates foreign investment by affording direct remedies to the investor. Moreover, NAFTA mandates arbitration when disputes arise between the investor and the sovereign. Because of its importance as a major RTA, NAFTA merits a separate, brief, and independent survey within the material of RTAs.

For the moment, NAFTA provisions are confined to Mexico, Canada, and the US. However, there are constant US initiatives to establish a Free Trade Area of the Americas (FTAA) for all of Latin and South America. Should the political and economic ambitions of US neoliberal statesmen become a reality, it can be expected that NAFTA will serve as a legal model. In addition to being an important contributor to the globalization of Western law, NAFTA is a reliable harbinger of the legal future for the entire North and South American continents.

When NAFTA entered into force on 1 January 1994, it granted rights to private entities to have their disputes with a host investment NAFTA nation subject to obligatory arbitration. Surely one of the unexpected results was the dramatic change NAFTA arbitration panels exerted upon the development of private international commercial law. NAFTA arbitration panels have made substantial theoretical contributions to the emancipation of the foreign investor from the domain of the local national courts. While such an evolution should be considered laudatory, criticism has not been absent. On the one hand, many non-governmental bodies see NAFTA as permitting law suits which make it difficult for authorities to enact environmental, health, safety, or even labor regulations. Others are claiming the attempt by the Commission to restrict the ambit of NAFTA destroys the original intent to protect investors. If the American government thought its investors were sufficiently protected to generate capital flows to Mexico,[2] others have been quick to put the US into the dock. Thus it is claimed NAFTA is used by investors as a cover for demanding damages for indirect expropriation, an act of state prohibited without just compensation,[3] and not permitted under the provisions of NAFTA. Through NAFTA, it is alleged, foreign investors are able to thwart local authorities from protecting national interests, such as the environment.[4]

Although a mixed blessing dependent on the issue involved and your social convictions, deeply integrated RTAs such as NAFTA which are substantially more than tariff preference agreements are providing general, international legal standards which are aloof from municipal law against which to measure sovereign acts. Investors are entitled to the protection of 'international law' and 'fair and equitable treatment',[5] our nebulous treaty benchmark for universal justice. Once it is agreed by treaty that the laws of a sovereign nation must withstand scrutiny by international law standards, there naturally arise questions as to the source of these ideals and what are the content of such references. Such inquiries will result in, quite frankly, bewilderment. These are interrogations jurists have asked themselves for centuries without satisfactory responses. There are some modest, helpful guidelines, although as legal yardsticks they only point in the direction of an illusory, hazy state of society — desirable, but defying detailed description. One source is the International Court of Justice at The Hague.

The statutes of the International Court of Justice (statutes), which hears claims by one sovereign against another, is regarded by jurists as the prime source of public international law. The statutes recognize various categories by which to analyze disputes submitted to it and they offer guidance as to the contents of public international law. They are: international conventions, international custom, the general principles of civilized nations, and the teachings of eminent jurists.[6] These are also the possible parameters when arbitration boards are called upon to decide if a sovereign nation has fulfilled its obligations pursuant to a regional trade agreement and which establishes international law as a means for dispute settlement.

While the statutes are intended as a point of reference for public international law — the regulation of rights between sovereigns-their generality, both as to form and reference, make them equally usable for private international law dispute resolution. Obviously, such references lack specificity. If the principles are valid for public law issues they are appropriate for private law disputes when a sovereign is involved. With references in the generality and with wide scope for interpretation, application, and uncertain understanding, the statutes are ideal norms. Neither judges nor arbitrators normally state publicly or in writing that their laws are founded on the principles of uncivilized nations.

With sources indicated by the statutes as a convenient starting point for inquiries and theoretical considerations by arbitrators as to the just and equitable, most any conclusion is possible given the fertile perambulations which make the human mind notorious for its creativity. Not having obligatory references containing specific content, NAFTA arbitrators rely on their own cultural heritage to define what is 'just' or 'equitable' or the principles recognized by civilized nations. Nebulous standards are an irresistible invitation to personal ideology. The statutes reinforce private norms.[7]

In an attempt to broaden and harmonize the social aspects of foreign investment, NAFTA as a fully integrated RTA has embraced legislation which seeks to establish uniform labor and environmental rules for its signatories and thus provides a human dimension to a commercial treaty. This it accomplishes by virtue of the North American Agreement on Environmental Cooperation[8]and the North American Agreement on Labor Cooperation[9].

Clearly, then, NAFTA is concerned not exclusively with public international law, but also private international law, and not only with investment but also labor and the environment. NAFTA is a public and private law judicial constituent RTA.[10] Unlike the RTA of Mercosur where all parties must agree to arbitrate for this mechanism to be initiated,[11] NAFTA is the only RTA to specifically grant rights to the individual to have controversies with a sovereign decided by arbitration in accordance with the ICSID Convention[12] or the United Nations Commission on International Trade Law (UNCITRAL).[13] These references to ISCID and UNCITRAL are to organizations whose provisions also permit the application of general principles of law. The relevant articles of NAFTA establish clearly that the dispute will be heard without considering obligatory the municipal law[14] and this is reinforced by the articles of ICSID and UNCITRAL.

One of the principal uses of the NAFTA treaty by private investors seeking redress against a sovereign nation has been recourse to the now famous Chapter 11 of NAFTA which deals with protection to investors against measures of nationalization or expropriation.[15] But Chapter 11 is more than just a haven against confiscation in its varied forms. Chapter 11 of NAFTA is a leap forward into erecting minimum standards of justice which must be applied by NAFTA nations towards investors. NAFTA exhorts nations to 'accord to investments of investors of another Party treatment in accordance with standards of international law, including fair and equitable treatment and full protection and security'.[16]

With the sources of international law dependent, in part, on the relevant statutes of the International Court of Justice,[17] NAFTA directs standards of law not contingent on the domestic law of the host nation.[18] This being so, it will happen that the investor may receive better treatment than if he sought relief in a domestic court.[19] Beyond this freedom from the confines of municipal law lies another horizon which demonstrates how the globalization of the law impacts upon the multitude of treaty networks regulating international commerce.

If general international law treatment requires adherence to treaty obligations, which it apparently does, then it should be possible to formulate a claim against a NAFTA signatory based on WTO obligations which have been violated by a nation host state signatory to WTO.[20] Failing to comply with a WTO obligation is to violate the international law of good faith and therefore is in breach of Article 1105 of Chapter 11.[21] No doubt in response to this feared consequence, a Free Trade Commission (Commission) was constituted according to the provisions of NAFTA.[22] On 31 July 2001, the Commission issued a clarification, purportedly binding on an NAFTA arbitration tribunal[23] and it stated:

> B. 1. Article 1105 (1) prescribes the customary international law minimum standard of treatment of aliens as the minimum standard of treatment to be afforded to investments of investors of another Party.

The Ministers composing the Commission wished to make it quite clear that the reference in Article 1105 of NAFTA to 'fair and equitable treatment' is not intended to confer any rights superior to those indicated above.[24] The Commission's statement may be seen as an attempt to restrict the import of NAFTA articles so as to preclude arbitration panels from seeking principles of international customary law which go beyond generally understood rights of fairness and due process and thus avoid extrapolation to WTO provisions.

This restrictive attempt at restricting the provisions of Chapter 11 has been incited by the various cases brought against the US alleging illegal expropriation because of governmental regulations aimed at curtailing pollution or eliminating toxic materials from the subsoil and which directly affects a foreign investor who must accept such zoning requirements in order to do business.[25] The variety of possible claims is substantial but the keynote should be obvious. Whereas the US was concerned its investors would receive less than adequate standards of justice by Mexico, both US and Canadian citizens are now utilizing NAFTA against the US government. It is not surprising, therefore, that in bilateral treaty negotiations with Chile and Singapore, the US is striving to insert into the applicable treaties language which will restrict legal remedies available to US investors.[26] Contrasting with decades of insisting on stronger foreign investor protection through international arbitration, the US now faces lawsuits arising out NAFTA provisions. Canadian investors are claiming US regulatory provisions amount to expropriation under NAFTA.[27]

However, it is not only regional trade agreements such as NAFTA which are granting private international law rights to individuals against nations. There are also the ubiquitous bilateral investment treaties and the hopes for a unified trade block throughout the Southern Hemisphere, the much coveted FTAA.[28] For the moment, the alliance of RTAs such as NAFTA and bilateral investment treaties are prescribing standards of international justice devoid of specificity and sufficiently idealistic to incorporate the dominant moral and social ethos of a particular era. Private international law standards erected on Western jurisprudence are the contemporary holy grail for global investors and politicians. The future realization of the FTAA will bring to investors open markets for their goods, the disappearance of fixed exchange rates, the elimination of national frontiers and protectionism, the firm anchor of an agreement that links nations with the powerful US economy.[29] And its laws. With the US in active pursuit of bilateral investment treaties,[30] US economic policies, underpinned by its laws, will determine the future course of private international commercial law.

That the US will also be a frequent defendant in a law suit under NAFTA articles is an eloquent testimonial to the impartiality of Western law.[31]

## Notes

[1] A regional trade agreement composed of the US, Canada and Mexico. See various links on portal <www.lanic.utexas.edu>, accessed 9 January 2002 for articles of agreement.

[2] Patrick Dumberry, *Expropriation Under NAFTA Chapter 11 Investment Dispute Settlement Mechanism: Some Comments on the Latest Case Law*, Int. A.L.R. 2001, 4(3), 96-104 (2001), after reviewing some of the decided cases states in his Conclusion '... such an extensive interpretation of the concept of expropriation goes beyond what the NAFTA parties had in mind ... It [the arbitration decision] poses a fundamental challenge to the government ability to regulate any economical activity in the general interest of its citizens'.
[3] UAW, *NAFTA'S hidden impact*, Solidarity August 2002 at page 4.
[4] See *Metaclad Corporation v. The United Mexican State*, where Mexico was held liable to a foreign investor although the claimed expropriation was an attempt to enforce an environmental law, see case reported on the ISCID website, <www.worldbank.org/icsid>, Case no. ARB (AF)/97/1, accessed 22 January 2002. Date of award is 30 August 2000.
[5] Article 1105 of NAFTA requires NAFTA governments to 'accord to investments of investors of another party treatment in accordance with international law, including fair and equitable treatment and full protection and security'.
[6] Article 38 of the statutes of the International Court of Justice at the Hague. The full text of the statutes may be consulted at <www.icj-cij.org>, accessed 1 February 2002. Article 38 of the Statutes of the International Court of Justice refer to international treaty obligations, international custom, customary practices of nations, general principles of law, international law principles, opinions of highly qualified writers, and international law experts.
[7] See Chapter 17 on 'Investment Treaty Disputes Will Make You Wonder' for case illustrations.
[8] See <www.epa.gov/region5>, accessed 8 October 2002.
[9] See<www.naalc.org>, accessed 8 October 2002.
[10] A suggested methodology was set forth in Chapter 4, **Annex.**
[11] Mercosur is composed of Argentina, Brazil, Paraguay, and Uruguay, see <www.mercosur.com/in/info/tratados_acuerdo_mercosur_ue>, accessed 2 January 2001.
[12] Details of the ICSID Convention and references to all articles can be found on <www.worldbank.org/icsid/basicdoc/9>, accessed 7 January 2002. ISCID arbitration procedures can be found therein.
[13] United Nations Commission on International Trade Law, see home page <www.uncitral.org/en-index>, accessed 3 January 2002.
[14] Article 1105 of NAFTA, supra, fn. 1. To further support the abandonment of municipal law, we find the following language:

> Article 1121: Conditions Precedent to Submission of a Claim to Arbitration.
>
> 1. A disputing investor may submit a claim under Article 1116 to arbitration only if:
>
> (a) the investor consents to arbitration in accordance with the provisions of this Subchapter; and
>
> (b) both the investor and an enterprise of another Party that is a juridical person that the investor owns or controls directly or indirectly, waive their right to initiate or continue before any administrative tribunal or court under the domestic law of any Party any proceedings with respect to the measure of the disputing Party that is alleged to be a breach of Subchapter A of this Chapter...

In other words, arbitration is automatic unless the foreign investor waives this right.

[15] Article 1110 of Chapter 11 of the NAFTA treaty reads as follows:

> No Party may directly or indirectly nationalize or expropriate an investment of an investor of another Party in its territory or take a measure tantamount to nationalization or expropriation of such an investment except:
> (a) for a public purpose;
> (b) on a non-discriminatory basis;
> (c) in accordance with due process of law …; and
> (d) on payment of compensation …

[16] Excerpt from Article 1105 of Chapter 11 of NAFTA treaty, see <www.nafta-sec-alena.org.> accessed 28 January 2002.

[17] Supra, n. 6.

[18] Todd Weiler, *NAFTA Article 1105 and the Free Trade Commission: Just Sour Grapes, or Something More Serious?*, International Business Lawyer, December 2001, at page 5: 'It is generally accepted that the purpose of a provision such as NAFTA Article 1105 is "to provide a basic and general standard which is detached from the host State's domestic law", citing Rudolph Dolzer and Margrete Stevens, *Bilateral Investment Treaties*, Martinus Nuhoff, The Hague (1995).

[19] The United States of America on Behalf of George W. Hopkins v. United Mexican States (Docket No. 39, 1926) reported at 21 Am. J, Intl Law 160.

[20] Supra, n. 18.

[21] Ibid.

[22] Article 1132 of NAFTA, see web site supra, fn. 16.

[23] Supra, n. 17. Article 1132 reads:

> 2. An interpretation by the Commission of a provision of this Agreement will be binding on a Tribunal established under this Section.

[24] Supra, n. 18.

[25] See n. 4.

[26] Edward Alden, *Washington alters line on US investor protection*, The Financial Times, 2 October 2002, at page 8.

[27] Ibid.

[28] Richard Feinberg, *A vision for the Americas*, The Financial Times, 7 August 2002 at page 11.

[29] Ibid.

[30] Edward Alden, *Countries line up to sign US trade deals*, The Financial Times, 1 April 2002, at page 10.

[31] See Chapter 17 'Investment Treaty Disputes Will Make You Wonder' for case illustrations.

# Chapter 6

# The World Trade Organization Spawns Legal Globalization

*A view of the top by those at the bottom*

Inherently powerful in its capacity for supranational commercial governance as well as evoking hope for a rule of law, the WTO,[1] often referred to as the 'Marrakesh agreement',[2] has disappointed its supporters and aggravated the ire of many an organization. Composed of 146 members,[3] consisting of both the world's largest as well as the smallest economies, the WTO continues to be a world assembly of power politics unable to attain its inspirational origins. From strident essays lamenting its partiality towards the multinational world to the frenzied street battles in protest against its alleged protection of neoliberal capitalism, the WTO stirs controversy and cries of Western economic imperialism.

For investigators of international trade, the WTO represents the realization of multiple philosophies: the culmination of the irreversible trend towards international commerce, non-existent trade barriers, unimpeded capital transfers, and the protection of intangible personal rights, from patents to services — a modest recitation from a lengthy multilateral agreement with 21 annexes. All these objectives would naturally proceed in a more orderly fashion if regulated by the rule of law. Unfortunately, this vision has failed because the provisions creating the WTO are flawed and unenforceable. WTO dispute settlement panel awards — one of the innovations of the multilateral trade agreement — lack an execution mechanism. Once again, dispute settlement procedures reveal themselves to be the lynchpin of social order through which the impartial will of the community can be implemented. International trade history illustrates the dependency of the law on economic logic and dispute settlement procedures.

Following World War II, politicians envisioned three major international organizations to harmonize world trade. They were the IMF, the International Bank for Reconstruction and Development (World Bank) and the ill-fated International Trade Organization (ITO).[4] Due to the hostility of the US Congress, the ITO was never formed. Instead, in the Spring of 1947, at Geneva, Switzerland, the General Agreement on Tariffs and Trade (GATT 47) was signed. During its 47 years of existence, GATT 47 achieved many successes in the field of international trade, particularly in reducing tariffs. Yet it must be stressed that GATT 47, and its brief successor GATT 94, were compromise agreements founded on power politics essentially linked to economic influence. Alleged violations of its provisions could only be decreed by the unanimous consent of all the nations, which was infrequently achieved. Even assuming a uniform consensus was achieved, there were no enforcement procedures. GATT 47 and 94 were unable to decisively resolve trade conflicts. The reason is obvious. Nations reacted to sanctions from GATT 47 and 94 in inverse proportion to their world influence. The more powerful the nation, the less likely it was to accept encroachments upon its sovereignty. Drawing upon almost 50 years of frustrated and disobeyed GATT panel decisions, and the majority of nations' convictions that world order required world law, there emerged in 1995 a modern multilateral agreement, the WTO. Introduced were new, if not revolutionary, concepts into international trade agreements.

In addition to the general principles which characterized the prior GATTs,[5] trade in goods and services were given explicit treatment[6] as were investment[7] and intellectual property rights.[8] A deliberate effort was made to encompass all the major sectors possibly subject to international commerce, from tangible goods to intangible rights. The declared philosophy of the WTO is to foment open trade, stimulate international market access, and create a legal order for international trade.[9] In contrast to many of its detractors, the WTO does not lack commentators who believe the benefit from its provisions and philosophy will inure to consumers all over the world:

> ... [I]ncreased international competition leads to product and process innovation, further reducing costs and expanding consumer choices.[10]

Beyond expanding the concept of goods to include the traditional intangible rights now dominating our economies, a further major, critical novelty was introduced into the regulation of world trade. There was inaugurated a dispute settlement mechanism, independent of any national court system, whose decisions are binding unless unanimously rejected by all the members of the WTO. This is a significant departure from prior GATT agreements[11] which had required confirmation of any dispute decision to be confirmed by all members. Whereas the GATTs emphasized the conciliation process and political consensus was sought before a decision was reached, the WTO embarked on a familiar Western concept — the rule of law.[12] At the core of law, both substantive and procedural, lies the appeal process. The rule of law, so treasured by the law profession as it expands indefinitely the possible expenditure of time, requires recourse by appeal to reverse a ruling by a court, an arbitration board, or administrative agency; otherwise, the sentence from which the appeal was taken remains binding and enforceable. Law emerges as a formal institution when the decision-making process demanded by disputes is withdrawn from conferences based on persuasion and power politics.

The appeal process now forms part of the WTO. A WTO dispute panel award is valid unless reversed on appeal. This introduction of the rule of law is derived from the unhappy legal experience of both GATTs. The drafters of the WTO sought to avoid what were seen as many of the shortcomings of the prior systems. The GATT dispute settlement mechanism was awkward and unanimous consent usually meant inaction. No one wants to shake rudely a lumbering giant who, when provoked, might abruptly cease providing much needed foreign currency to a particular GATT member. The required unanimity of votes hardly ever occurred. No GATT member would be so foolish as to be identified by a 'yea' vote.

Rather then be faced with unpleasant alternatives — condemn your trading partner or be silent — the world's nations wisely selected a platform of the rule of law. Thus, WTO provides for a reversal of roles. What is decided by a WTO dispute panel board is binding unless the entire WTO membership votes to revoke it. As the decision would have to be contrary to the most elementary sense of justice, no one will raise their voice in protest unless convinced of a 100 per cent adherence. In this aspect, the Western internationalists have triumphed and so has the rule of law. At least this is *prima facie* the impression. But an enlightened comprehension of the WTO agreement and its annexes reveals that the rule of law established has no enforcement mechanism. The rulings emitted by the WTO adjudicative bodies must rely on voluntary compliance. There are no methods available in the WTO to compel obedience. Without impartial enforcement, we cannot speak of law but only a convergence of opinion or a generalized body of norms, customs, or mores — generally effective provided there is no defiance by a powerful WTO member.

We have returned to the inept days of the GATT. Only instead of nations remaining silent and tolerating abuses — after all, better to receive the occasional loan/grant than be a gadfly — a further unexpected result has surfaced. If WTO panel members know their rulings may be spurned by a recalcitrant member, every reason exists to strive to announce precepts which are likely to be acceptable to the largest, most powerful economic communities possible.

WTO rulings on technical aspects of tariffs can be politically assimilated by the offending WTO members. Nations will voluntarily abide by panel decisions which trace and define complex issues relating to tariffs, schedules, procedures, matters to which the general public does not usually direct its attention. And there are thousands of such rulings under the GATTs which were accepted by the members in question. Not so with sensitive national issues, such as health or environment, or the strong economic interests of a nation's rights over fishing. These are explosive issues which bring out onto the streets the enlightened public or refusal of the defendant nation to accept the ruling.

The US continues to defy the WTO, holding its foreign sales corporation tax was not an illegal export subsidy, and as a result faces sanctions from other members in the amount of $4 billion dollars. Nor has the US acknowledged that it intends to comply with the latest WTO dispute settlement panel ruling that it is illegally imposing steel tariffs.[13] The foreign sales corporation tax and steel tariff levies follow upon at least a half a dozen cases in which the WTO has ruled against the US.[14]

Fear of unleashing vociferous public opinion or economic retaliation by an irate nation naturally will cause the WTO when emitting panel decisions to choose principles which strengthen sovereignty and not weaken it. With no means of enforcing its decisions, the WTO is in the same position as its predecessors GATT 47 and 94, except there is a further, ironical variation. Now, decisions are valid and not dependent on member ratification, but since they cannot be enforced and voluntary compliance is still needed, a sensible WTO panel is going to pronounce principles of law which incorporate the legal principles with the largest common denominator so as to secure voluntary compliance from the contestants. The largest common denominators in the law are those principles of which all nations and individuals are naturally endowed: equity, justice, and good-faith. At least this is the self-proclaimed objective you would reach when reading the national constitutions.

Thus there arises on the international scene a fortuitous convergence for foreign investors and sovereigns among bits, regional trade agreements, and the WTO. All will seek an accommodative posture and consequently WTO economic sanctions will be forced into compromises. If the US Congress refuses to amend its foreign sales corporation tax, an alleged subsidy to US companies, it is difficult to see what other WTO members can do by way of compelling compliance.

Generalities and appeals to broad concepts, as are those used in other international arbitration panels, flow from the pens of the WTO panel members. When discussing the EU import ban on meat containing hormones, the WTO appellate body had to consider whether or not the EU's precautions on banning US import meat containing hormones formed part of 'a general customary rule of international law'.[15] The appellate body found the EU's precautionary principles were not valid as the EU had failed to undertake the required risk assessment. Nevertheless, the US, after four years of imposing sanctions on more than $100 million of EU exports, has failed to have the EU lift its hormone-beef treated ban.[16] The WTO finding appears to be in conformity with the role of a dispute settlement system which expressly incorporates the customary rules of interpretation of public international law.[17]

All participants, the panel members of the WTO, the arbitrators appointed by the RTAs or through the bits, rest their decisions on the universal principles of public and private law rights, for that is the path to acceptance. Whereas municipal courts can assume anti-establishment postures in the form of judicial sentences, because they can enforce them, the supranational organizations and arbitration panels rely on sovereign opinion. The rule of law announced by the WTO has eliminated the need for unanimous consent as to the contents of its panel decisions. Enforcement of its decisions are left to the conscience of defendant nations, as if such a mental reference makes sense. A nation is composed on social parts engaged in power struggles. Nations neither possess a collective will nor a collective conscious.

The laudatory objective of regulating international commerce by providing a judicatory mechanism has been severely compromised by a confusing constituent constitution which offers no enforcement mechanisms. This has permitted trade law to develop without any specific guidance. The direction of trade law is left to drift according to the will of the major economic players who know adverse decisions can still be ignored. Although not an item on the ballot boxes of the various candidates, the popular elected governments of the US, Europe, and Japan determine the trade politics of WTO.[18] This is a direct consequence of the lack of enforcement authority of the WTO which must rely on each member nation accepting voluntarily trade norms decreed as applicable.

*The world's laws at your fingertips*

But the WTO has taken further original steps with as yet untold consequences and which makes less probable the development of a coherent body of trade law on the substantive issues. The framers of the WTO understood that trade is multifaceted and includes goods, services, and ideas. Trade in one is an important as in the others. Adopting a generalist approach, the primary WTO agreement is relatively short and seeks to encompass all major areas of trade, whether goods, services, or ideas, through other annexed agreements.[19] While a respected technique when drafting commercial contracts, incorporation by reference as used in the WTO constitution, particularly when there are so many other texts involved, is to yield the document to interminable interpretation. The theory of incorporating many other ideas through annexed documents has probably brought irremediable problems to the WTO, for a reference to one document often justifies a reference to another document. The linkage of references becomes indeed stretched with unpredictable results. The result has been from fears the WTO requires privatization of public services, such as libraries or hospitals, to charges the WTO protects multinational pharmaceutical patents when they least make sense: in impoverished nations.

As a legal document, the WTO demonstrates many of the defects typical of multilateral agreements. The mercantile pressures to open markets and harmonize international trade overwhelmed and subjugated the normal prudence which accompanies the drafting of treaties. Our analysis of the agreement establishing the WTO reveals that its inherent structure is conducive to fomenting legal globalization due to its inept legal formulation. What emerges from an inclusive analysis of the WTO are some discordant observations. To begin with, the agreement creating the WTO is essentially the statement of the chairman of the board of a multinational anxious to convince others of the benefits to be derived from international commerce.

The preamble[20] of the agreement establishing the WTO exhorts us that the '... field of trade and economic endeavour should be conducted with a view to raising standards of living ensuring full employment ...'; and '... allowing for the optimal use of the world's resources ...'; but of course '... with the objective of sustainable development ...'; culminating in promises to the developing countries to '... secure a share in the growth in international trade commensurate with the needs of their development'.

Surely, no one can quarrel with such commendable aims nor does one doubt the sincerity of the author(s) of these words. But no sooner do we feel inebriated with such a public declaration of idealism, then despair enters when we search for details. In fact, there are none. For information as to how the enabling agreement creating the WTO is to be implemented, we are referred to a 'List of Annexes', twenty one agreements in all. Among this list, are the various covenants regulating matters as diverse as agreements on the application of sanitary and phytosanitary measures to trade-related aspects of intellectual property rights. A salutary reading of the WTO agreement causes us to pause over Article XVI, impishly denominated

'Miscellaneous Provisions'. Here, oddly, we find what is surely one of the basic obligations created by the WTO agreement:

> Each Member will ensure the conformity of its laws, regulations and administrative procedures with its obligations as provided in the annexed agreements.[21]

Thus, the WTO constitution has a bill of rights sprawled throughout 21 annexes. Derived from this construction, there can be articulated the principle which has sent shudders through the pen of many an academic writer. On matters affecting WTO issues, the domestic laws of the nations must conform to the standards of the Marrakesh agreement,[22] although the norms are absent. We are not advised whether the conformity is only on trade issues but also on domestic affairs which may contravene the precepts of the WTO.

Recently Canada decided to salvage its newspaper industry from the avid preference of Canadian readers for American journalism.[23] Canada sought to defend its culture from American business. In contravention of WTO/GATT principles, Canada imposed an excise tax on certain non-Canadian periodicals as well as granting subsidies to Canadian journals. The measures were declared invalid. Adepts of local culture may recoil from the implied principle that local culture cannot contravene supranational precepts. But such moral indignation is due to the legal nature of the WTO agreement which states norms without content, much as a national constitution.

When the WTO establishes norms prohibiting domestic measures which prevent access to local markets, or ban quotas, or permit measures necessary to protect human, animal or plant life or health, the standards announced must be interpreted by a dispute settlement panel. The WTO has been granted authority to interpret without the power to enforce.

### *Dispute mechanisms without enforcement is as health without food*

Unfortunately, nowhere in the enabling act of the WTO will we find any helpful reference to the source of the law to be applied when a dispute arises. Since the application of laws only arise in disputes, we are not surprised that one of the annexed agreements, annex 2, is entitled 'Understanding on Rules and Procedures Governing the Settlement of Disputes' (DSU).[24]

By the terms of the DSU there is instituted a mechanism for judicial settlement of disputes by the Dispute Settlement Body (DSB). Here, then, surely, is the source of WTO law. The WTO agreement, what fairly could be described as the most contemporary, significant, international commercial constitution, avoids any clear declaration of legal principles. Rather, confining itself to moral allusions, the WTO has delegated to another body, the DSB, the responsibility for interpretation of the world's most notable trading agreement. This will prove to be a fruitless delegation — abortive, but a respectable legal technique which is confounding the development of public international law with private law. The US Constitution is interpreted by the US Supreme Court. The unwritten constitution of the UK is interpreted by the courts of England. Only there is a significant difference. Domestic law cannot be confused with public international law.

The laws of the US and the UK are rooted in centuries of common law decisions and the laws of other nations similarly have their inspiration in countless, local judicial decisions so that domestic law constitutes for each society a repertoire of custom and culture transposed into legal language. The interpreters of national constitutions normally have centuries of judicial scholarship to assist them in the task of adapting fundamental rights to new social exigencies.

Understandably, the WTO, a multilateral agreement heretofore a political agglomeration, has not this legal history, other than humanity's past fostered on ancient trade routes. Regrettably, the main, indeed, the only apparent source of WTO law through delegation is to be found in Article 3 of the DSU which contains the sole explicit statement of applicable law:

> 2. The dispute settlement system of the WTO is a central element in providing security and predictability to the multilateral trading system. The Members recognize that it serves to preserve the rights and obligations of Members under the covered agreements, and to clarify the existing provisions of those agreements in accordance with **customary rules of interpretation of public international law** [emphasis added]. Recommendations and rulings of the DSB cannot add to or diminish the rights and obligations provided in the covered agreements.

We are thus advised that the WTO agreement will be construed according to the customary rules of public international law. To further compound any hope of detailed legal guidance, for the customary rules invoked are indeed evocative of aspirations, but little more, Article 11 of the same agreement extends this dictate to all of the annexes which of course means to the entire range of activities foreseen by the WTO.

Again, a brief quotation of the relevant part of Article 11 is elucidative.

> The function of [the dispute panels] is to assist the DSB [dispute settlement body] in discharging its responsibilities under the Understanding and the covered agreements.

Covered agreements means the annexes which include topics such as intellectual property rights, trade in goods, services, sanitary measures, tariffs, in short the world of commerce and the stuff of which profit is made. In order to understand what laws will be invoked when a WTO dispute concerning all possible sources of WTO dominion arises, we are thus faced with one, and only one, legal reference: customary rules of interpretation of public international law. Yet our search for the customary rules is fraught with ambiguity. Nor could it be otherwise. To alter what passes for popular wisdom,[25] 'the custom of one is the nightmare of another'.

The WTO has erected a legal system whereby custom reigns and enforcement is dependent on nations agreeing on a particular custom. The main source of customary interpretation under public international law is dictated by the Vienna Convention on the Law of Treaties and the Statutes of the International Court of Justice.

*Vienna Convention on the Law of Treaties*[26]

While denominated the 'Law of Treaties', the Vienna Convention clearly includes a document such as the WTO agreement.[27] Unfortunately, the Vienna Convention offers modest direct assistance for purposes of interpreting the WTO. Specifically, Article 31 (1) of the Convention states, among other provisions, that there will be applicable:

> (c) any relevant rules of international law applicable in the relations between the parties[28]

By international law must be understood 'public international law' since the Vienna Convention only applies to treaties between nations.[29] In as much as public international law is the referred standard, we must encounter a source which contains the 'relevant rules of international law'.

There is unanimous academic consensus[30] that one of the sources of public international law is the statutes of the International Court of Justice,[31] and specifically Article 38. Before demonstrating what was probably not the intention of the framers of the WTO, the far-reaching horizons of Article 38 merit reproduction:

> 1. The Court, whose function is to decide in accordance with international law such disputes as are submitted to it, will apply:
> a. international conventions ...;
> b. international custom ...;
> c. the general principles of law recognized by civilized nations;
> d.... judicial decisions and the teachings of the most highly qualified publicists of the various nations ... .

This is surely an extraordinary result. By virtue of the series of references commencing with the mandate of Article 3 of the DSU, there is transmitted through the WTO, the principles of public international law. Yet there is no agreement by nations as to the content of these principles.[32] The WTO arbitrators are cast adrift without any legal moorings and asked to find the relevant custom for a particular dispute.

Even more dramatic are the consequences of the covered agreements annexed to the WTO. Many of these agreements relate to interests of vital social concern such as health and the exploitation of natural resources via patent rights; the right to investment without fear of expropriation unless there is paid just compensation; the freedom of establishment of services in other countries; the protection against discrimination by a nation against private entities in fields also occupied by public entities. The list is indeed long as there are 21 agreements in question without seeking related texts by implication or even legal logic.

But there is no need for social alarm. In fact, the outcome, for some, is eminently satisfactory. The WTO and the private law arbitration boards are now operating on the same set of principles, custom, conventions, civilized principles of law, the teachings of qualified publicists, and all those familiar sources which have held word order together till the present. What we do not know is what are the customs and general principles which will be applied.

Fortunately, there already exists a substantial body of international arbitration decisions which has had to consider and apply these very same principles, those maxims of custom and civilization. International arbitration law will provide us with endless principles, basically private opinions, which will confirm the dominion of Western legal principles. As Western multinational corporations dominate international commerce, this is indeed a satisfactory outcome for adherents to world trade.

Such a conclusion contrasts with thoughtful observations by others who allege the WTO is not intended to be a forum for elements of civil society.[33] Perhaps it was not so intended. Yet, the dispute settlement provisions, in conjunction with the annexed agreements relating to trade in services, investment, and intellectual property rights have dramatically altered the prior, consensus rule of nations to one of laws and private property founded on international economics. And global commerce does require global laws. One without the other will eventually cause deflation, that dreaded virus which is no less devastating than any pestilence. But global laws also displace community customs and curtail the power of the nation state.

The WTO, a world organization, is also becoming a municipal law system[34] but still subject to power politics. Not intended to be so, the WTO continues to be a forum for the discussion of what are the customary rules of trade. Customary international law and customary trade rules are ill-defined and uncertain[35] and hence foment substantially the globalization of Western law. Trade is controlled by the West and the industrialized nations will dictate what the customs of the world are. Powerless to enforce its decisions, the WTO when considering private property rights will have to have recourse to the same sources of law as the international arbitration tribunals.

These fountainheads are the common customs of international commerce, defined and dominated by the Western economic powers.[36] Jurists refer to these customs as 'the law merchant', or, if you prefer Latin, the *lex mercatoria.*[37] The WTO, for all its elaborate dispute settlement procedures, is forced to rely upon the same content for law as other supra-national organizations and international arbitration boards. The more there are established or created supra-national organizations and administrative organs the more likely it is that there will emerge a stable body of international commercial principles which will be seized upon by these very same civil associations.

As we shall see in a subsequent chapter,[38] the lack of enforcement mechanisms has rendered the WTO more a forum for trade policy discussion than for implementing rights of one member against the other. As in all forums, there are voices given more weight than others.

## Notes

[1] The WTO assumed its legal existence on 1 January 1995. For a complete history of the WTO see the WTO web site at <www.wto.org > accessed 11 February 2002.
[2] The agreements constituting the WTO and its annexes were signed on 15 April 1994 at Marrakesh, Morocco, see Final Act Embodying the Result of the Uruguay Round of Multilateral Trade Negotiation, April 15, 1994, reprinted in 33 I.L.M. 1125 (1994). The WTO has succeeded to GATT (General Agreement on Tariffs and Trade). The history of GATT and the WTO can be simplified. Essentially there was first GATT 1947, which was then superceded by GATT 1994. The present WTO incorporates the provisions of GATT 1994 as well as prior judicial decisions rendered pursuant to that agreement. Of course there are differences between GATT 1947 and GATT 1994 and many questions unresolved with the incorporation of the latter in the WTO. However, these issues are not germane to the discussion in the present survey.
[3] This is the membership as of 4 April 2003. For details see home page of WTO at <www.wto.org> accessed 22 April 2002.
[4] For a comprehensive description of the history of the WTO, see Thomas J. Dillon, *The World Trade Organization: A New Legal Order for World Trade*, 16 Michigan Law Review 349 (1995).
[5] The basic postulates of the prior GATT and present WTO agreements are:

- The most favored nation principle. Privileges given to one nation must be given to all.
- National treatment. Foreign entities can not be discriminated against.
- Tariffs will be generally lowered. Free trade, with no tariffs, is the goal.
- Import quotas, also denominated quantitative restrictions, are to be eliminated.
- Ceilings will be fixed for goods and services already subject to duties, known as 'binding'.
- Competition is to be fomented.
- Subsidies are to be eliminated.

Both agreements further strive to remove non-tariff barriers, such as antidumping and countervailing duties, valuation of goods, voluntary restraint agreements, product, labor, and environmental standards, where all of these are used to create obstacles to the free flow of goods and services.
[6] General Agreement on Trade in Services (GATS), see web site of the WTO supra, n. 3.
[7] Agreement on Trade-Related Investment Measures (TRIMS), see web site of the WTO supra, n. 3.
[8] Agreement on Trade-Related Aspects of Intellectual Property Rights (TRIPS), see web site of the WTO supra, n. 3.
[9] See Kevin C. Kennedy, *The GATT-WTO System at Fifty*, 16 Wis. Int'l L. J. 421 (Summer 1998) for a detailed, clear history and concise summary of GATT-WTO.
[10] Ibid, at page 422.
[11] The two GATT agreements of 1947 and 1994 relied exclusively on political consensus.
[12] See Shin-yi Peng, *The WTO Legalistic Approach and East Asia: From the Legal Culture Perspective*, 1 Asian-Pacific Law & Policy Journal 13 (2000), summarizing Asian approach to dispute settlement and raising doubts whether the Western system of the 'rule of law' will be adopted in the short term by the region.
[13] On both issues, see lead editorial in The Financial Times, 28 March 2003, on page 18.

[14] Edward Alden, *US steel tariffs illegal, rules WTO*, The Financial Times, 27 March 2003, at page 8.
[15] WT/DS26?AB/R, EC-Measures Concerning Meat and Meat Products Panel Decision and Appellate Body Report.
[16] Guy de Jonquières, *Europe hopes to 'hit the White House where it hurts*, 26 March 2002, at page 8.
[17] J. Patrick Kelley, *The WTO and Global Governance: The Case for Contractual Treaty Regimes*, 7 SPG Widener L. Symposium. J. 109 (2001). However, Prof. Kelley has serious reservations about the WTO dispute panels relying on general customary international law. He explains the hormone-meat finding as one in which the WTO panel affirmed the duty of EU to undertake risk assessment as mandated by one of the annexes to the WTO agreement.
[18] Ibid.
[19] There are 21 in all, see <www.wto.org >accessed 18 February 2002.
[20] Supra, n. 3.
[21] Supra, n. 3.
[22] This principle has been stated more eloquently by Prof. Joel P. Trachtman, *The Domain of WTO Dispute Resolution*, 40 Harv. Int'l L. J. 333 (1999): 'With regard to domestic law, it is clear that applicable WTO law trumps conflicting domestic law, at least as a matter of WTO law'.
[23] Complaint filed in 1996 with results rendered 1997, WTO panel decision reported in Canada — *Certain Measures Concerning Periodicals*, WT/DS31/R modified by WT/DS31/AB/R available on the WTO web site under document downloads, accessed 18 February 2002.
[24] Article 3 of the 'Understanding on Rules and Procedures Governing the Settlement of Disputes' states that the dispute settlement system of the WTO 'is a central element in providing security and predictability to the multilateral trading system'. The full text of this 'Understanding' can be found on the WTO web site, supra, n. 3.
[25] 'What is meat for one, is poison for another'.
[26] The Convention was adopted on 22 May 1969 and opened for signature on 23 May 1969 by the United Nations Conference on the Law of Treaties. For full details of Convention see <www.un.org/law/ilc/texts/treaties> accessed 16 February 2002.
[27] Supra, fn. 26, Art. 2 of the Convention '... "Treaty" means an international agreement concluded between States ...'.
[28] Ibid.
[29] Ibid, Article 1.
[30] See David Palmeter et al., *The WTO Legal System: Sources of Law*, 92 American Journal of International Law 398 (1998).
[31] For the full text see <www.icj-cij.org> accessed 14 February 2002.
[32] Mark B. Baker, *Tightening the Toothless Vise: Codes of Conduct and the American Multinational Enterprise*, 20 Wis. Int'l L. Rev. 89 (2001) stating A.1., 'Customary international law is a nebulous and evolving concept, referring to basic international norms of civilized society'.
[33] Padideh Ala'i, *A Human Rights Critique of the WTO: Some Preliminary Observations*, 33 Geo. Wash. Int'l L. Rev. 537 (2001).
[34] David Palmeter, *The WTO as a Legal System*, 24 Fordham Int'l L. J. 444 (2000).
[35] Supra, n. 17.
[36] Francis Williams, *WTO arms Europeans with weighty weapon*, The Financial Times, 31 August-1 September 2002 at page 2, where it is reported the EU is not anxious to enforce $4 billions of sanctions against the US for fear of retaliation. 'Brussels says the system [ed:

WTO] puts too much emphasis on retaliation, harming trade without necessarily obliging countries to comply with WTO rulings'.

[37] For a discussion on the *lex mercatoria* see the chapter 'International Arbitration: The Global Customs of Merchants'.

[38] Chapter 18.

## Chapter 7

# The OECD Quietly Governs the World

### *Laws and oligarchies*

Independently, and we should not think in any sense coordinated, multilateral organizations, associations, and multinational enterprises are establishing a coherent, international, commercial legal order.[1] Institutions and organizations, such as the WTO, the IMF, the World Bank, and NAFTA,[2] along with international arbitration boards and a multitude of civil associations, are dispensing, dependent on the entity, global guidance on international trade,[3] inducing legislation which affects political structures, and permitting citizen investment rights to be raised against sovereigns before international arbitration boards. Common commercial legal principles form the intellectual corpus of these groups.

In the industrial nation, groups of citizens, usually utilizing the corporate model, dominate commercial sectors of the nation through mega-corporations. Beyond the statistics from multiples sources as to foreign trade and foreign investment, the pervasiveness of this social factor is attested to by the numerous anti-trust and competition laws which are a standard feature of the legal systems of the industrialized nations. Fearful of a parallel government, the legislatures enact competition laws designed to curb the activities of national oligarchies. Yet the power struggles continue unabated between the multiple oligarchies for control of commercial sectors in a community.

The volumes of books on competition law throughout the US and the EU confirm the uselessness of these legislative attempts. Competition laws would not be necessary if competition truly existed and legal tomes would have no readership if the competition laws produced lasting results. With national governments everywhere enacting similar competition laws, with the multinational corporations ostensibly playing the rules so as to comply, yet in reality hiring teams of lawyers to devise apparent obedience to the laws but not to its objectives, the result can only be the spread of similar legal principles affecting competition. The commercial oligarchies, dominating trade globally, find it convenient for the same legal principles to accompany their activities. The participants want the same rules so strategies can be formulated. In this way, their final objective will be achieved. Given that competition laws impact considerably commercial law when large companies and international trade are involved, globalization of competition law has to affect other legal areas.

In addition to discretely avoiding anti-trust laws, the commercial oligarchies are also able to formulate global policy through clubs, from the small chambers of commerce to the international institutions. An obvious and well-known conduit to the globalization of the law operating through commercial oligarchic practices is exemplified by the OECD,[4] an association of the world's industrialized nations. Unlike the WTO or NAFTA, the OECD has no procedures for the settlement of disputes, nor could it. The declared objective of the OECD is to provide an international commercial forum for the dissemination of ideas. With convincing clarity, the OECD throws into relief the vices and virtues of the lack of a dispute settlement mechanism in a multilateral organization, allowing us also an insight into the origins of legal norms. The WTO has a dispute settlement mechanism but no enforcement procedures. The OECD has neither one, nor the other, yet it obtains extraordinary results in the promulgation and harmonization of a wide variety of laws. The explanation may lie in the diverse composition of the WTO where the conflicts of interest are interminable while the OECD is a homogenous oligarchy. Still, there is another plausible explanation.

When dispute settlement mechanisms exist, there are the possibility minority rights and cultural diversity will develop and thrive as adjudication forces transparency and impartiality. Dispute settlement mechanisms, if conducted with neutrality, promote variances from the general norms. Such is the function of litigation. The supposed wisdom of the majority is prevented from culturally exterminating the minority. Dispute settlement mechanisms are an effective and necessary barrier against legal globalization provided such procedures offer concise references. Dispute settlement mechanisms deflect social tension into an acceptable forum. Without enormous public pressure, the general myths cementing the social group are unlikely to be altered. But the occasional concession to the spirit of the minority is articulated. The absence of dispute settlement produces a different result.

When specific standards are missing for purposes of adjudication, then the established dispute procedures, vague in construction and references,[5] are only window-dressing. The vacuum leaves substantial opportunity for dominant economic forces to impose and influence others to their will. Without any dispute settlement procedures, a significant amount of social stability and harmonization can be achieved through the process of consensus generated by the economic prowess of a group. The social lesson is that dispute settlement procedures without clear enforceable norms are less effective than a committee of those possessing economic authority.

For this reason, do not be lulled into thinking a commercial forum such as the OECD is merely a chatty reunion of technocrats with similar, committed commercial ideals. This would be a grave error of judgment and social analysis.

### *The social stability of oligarchies*

But before reviewing the highly efficient, non-litigious mechanisms of the OECD, it will be relevant to consider, in the abstract, a number of assumptions of social behavior. They are all derived from the observable fact that oligarchies, such as clubs, tribes, houses of worship, do not need formal dispute settlement procedures in order to achieve their goals. To understand this premise, it is necessary to return to the fundamentals of social organization.

Without procedures for resolving differences, the social norms of a society fall prey to the dominion of the traders. It is in the exchange of goods, or its possibility, that dominion of one group or individual over another is made possible. Economics fosters social norms which in turn give birth to legal customs. The hoe requires ownership of land and title to realty is contrived into a legal doctrine which logic can amplify. Unless there is an impartial arbiter, the inconvenient, burgeoning legal norms of the economic minority wither.

The lack of formal dispute procedures requires community stability to be based on consensus. With resources in their possession, the dominant mercantile interests form an oligarchy and establish agreement on commercial norms. This tends to foment uniformity with little legal space for divergent views. The only way contentious issues can be resolved without formal mechanisms is through persuasion and the dispossessed, short of a street revolution, are normally ineffective. Democracy without dispute mechanisms is at its best, a fragile fiction. Minority groups, without recourse to an impartial arbiter of social norms, have no power structure to support them.

Since there is no way legally to oppose the consensus, the basic legal tenets established by the economic plurality, usually in the mathematical minority, become the rule of reason. Those who have economic power wield it. It is the primary reason for wanting this social, economic weapon. It offers access to all services of a society. Although this appears to be materialistic determinism,[6] it is in fact only a description of the origin of legal norms which is not dependent on a particular economic system, but rather is the result of the dominant economic forces. No matter what the economic tenets of the oligarchy, nor their origin, legal norms are generated which accommodate the underlying economic premises. It is not legal norms which shape the economic premises but mercantile history which grants credence and authority to various legal beliefs.

Furthermore, when economic power is concentrated in an oligarchy which in turn has a global influence, as do the multinationals, the consensus has global implications. Unison in this situation leads to globalization of legal norms. All of this because without formalized dispute settlement procedures there is no effective way for the dissent to be heard, much less enforced. Logically, globalization incited by an oligarchy naturally chooses the topics of concern to its interests. While our age is more socially aware, and there are many multinationals who take seriously their social responsibilities,[7] yet it is natural that commercial issues of prime importance such as taxation, foreign investment, competition, and capital movement loom significantly in such groups. To say that multinationals are only interested in commercial profit is to criticize birds for flying.

Moreover, by definition, such groups are not democratic conventions. After all, economic oligarchies do not develop from a sense of civic obligations. Mutual interests are the unifying element and there is no necessity to attend to divergent views. Sporadically, the lean chief financial officer jogging through the city park laments the destruction of vast forest reserves and a note is made to address the local 'green is great' club on tree conservation, especially when our executive notes his city park trees are becoming moribund due to gasoline pollution. Still, one socially aware executive is not representative of the multitudinous anonymous boards of directors responsible for the commercial objectives of corporations with pension funds and individual shareholders clamoring for distribution of dividends and capital appreciation.

Besides uniformity, legal globalization produces a democratic deficit. With common objectives and an easily created network of contacts between technocrats from different nation members, legislation, often induced through personal networks, is primarily directed towards the economic sectors. Additionally, an oligarchy in one area, such as trade, will find its counterpart in other segments, for example in public international loan agencies, whose existence is to foment international trade which is dependent on multinational foreign investment. Convergence arises between such oligarchies and the globalization is even more effective. Finally, such groups are quite efficient in creating sanctions. Beyond its own membership, those nations or trading partners who do not conform to predetermined standards are easily excluded.[8] Recalcitrant third parties are not able to conduct business with the major economic participants and obedience is quickly compelled. It is highly effective legislation without the need for a parliamentary debate.[9] Either you comply or you commence the long-delayed financial diet.

These are some of the results a faulty, or absent, dispute settlement system generates. As for virtues, there is probably only one: something gets done although at times we may question if it is what we want to see accomplished. There are some who will see in such highly effective oligarchies a diplomatic manner of achieving a harmony of laws and a common commercial viewpoint without the need for prolonged, at times irrelevant, public debate. It is no surprise that the presence or absence of dispute settlement procedures produces contradictory results in their social impact. The reason is simple. Obligatory dispute settlement mechanisms insulate and protect minorities. Cultural, including legal, variations are allowed to flourish. When dispute settlement procedures are informal, or have no enforcement power, necessity and consensus converge on uniformity, a simple epithet for globalization.

### *An oligarchy called the OECD*

While the WTO often garners strident public attention, accompanied by prolonged and contentious street protests, it is the less conspicuous OECD who is far more efficient in having model laws and conventions, drafted by its elite staff, transmitted to, and adopted by, various sovereign nations. This it does without a parliament or tribunals, panel hearings, or even conciliation procedures. Composed of thirty (30) sovereign members,[10] this private club is simultaneously a management consultancy group, a think-tank, an 'unacademic [sic] university'[11] and a legislative body without elected deputies.[12] Two-thirds of the world's goods and services are produced by its members.[13] Twenty-nine of the world's 100 largest organizations are multinationals. The US company Exxon is larger than all but 44 national economies. These companies accounted for 4.3 per cent of the world gross domestic product in the year 2000. The gross domestic product of Exxon is equal to that of Pakistan and surpasses that of Peru. Ford and General Electric are comparable to the economies of Nigeria while Phillip Morris approximates that of Tunisia or Guatemala.[14] Economic growth and expansion of world trade are the leitmotif of the OECD charter.[15] Imports and exports between OECD members are dominated by firms from the USA and the UK.[16] Significantly, the largest country with foreign direct investment in Europe is the US.[17]

With a membership more diverse than the EU or NAFTA, a staff of 1,850 people, an annual budget of about US 200 million,[18] 25 per cent of which is provided by the USA,[19] yet more restrictive in charter than the WTO or the UN, the OECD is a closed forum with an open agenda. Nevertheless, OECD membership is not comparable to the UN or the WTO, both open to nations of various social currents or philosophies. To join the OECD requires a commitment to a 'market economy and a pluralistic democracy'.[20] Hence, while in theory the OECD is composed of sovereign nations, the representatives of the members and the staff employed should be committed to the charter obligations of their principals. Since the economic cudgels of the members are held by the multinationals when dealing with international trade, it is not a fancy nor flight to see in the OECD an oligarchy dominated by multinational interests.[21]

Being an oligarchy does not mean it is an anti-community coterie. In fairness, the 'themes'[22] occupying the OECD at times display a considerable social concern: ageing, society, health, international migration, insurance and pensions, sustainable development, are but a few from a lengthy list.[23] Fortunately, even the declared purpose of a market economy does not impede the OECD from its concern with public values. Moreover, contrary to the imperfectly conceived WTO, structured to hear disputes but with no means to enforce decisions, the OECD performs efficiently the function of a super-government encompassing all the necessary attributes.

Model laws or conventions are approved by the members and then adopted in the individual, national assemblies through a highly efficient network of technocrats and their counterparts in the various member nations. Indirectly, legislation is promulgated through the OECD. That there are no elected deputies presents no enactment difficulties nor moral scruples. Thus, among other model conventions, the OECD has drafted and had approved a convention on capital flows which once transmitted to a national jurisdiction directly regulates this indispensable natural resource: investment funds. The OECD has made a substantial contribution to the globalization of capital markets.[24]

Consequently, although the OECD has neither enforcement mechanisms, nor even dispute procedures as does the WTO, it is able through the tribal technique of exclusion, to bring non-members into conformity with policy attitudes approved by the members. The OECD directed its Committee on Fiscal Affairs to seek a global cooperative framework to counteract tax competition which was eventually endorsed by the OECD Council of Ministers. Countries which do not adhere to the general standards will face sanctions.[25]

Furthermore, as if it were an entrepreneur's university, the OECD engages in research, publishes statistics, writes reports, makes recommendations, and engages in policy discussions with technocrats from the governments of its members and non-members. Such activities are consecrated in its charter which expressly directs it to work with non-member States or organizations.[26] Possessing a staff of lawyers, economists as well as other professionals, the OECD maintains extensive consultations and conferences with its members and non-members. It maintains co-operative relations with over 70 non-members.[27] This it does through 'national contact points' which means each member designates entities with whom the OECD can dialogue. It functions pragmatically as a 'my buddy' network. The OECD publishes books, over 250 new titles a year.[28] It maintains consultations and dialogue with the business and labor sectors through the Business and Industry Advisory Committee and the Trade Union Advisory Committee.[29] Finally, the OECD has official relations with the International Labor Organization, the IMF, the World Bank, and various United Nations agencies.[30] If we accept the contours of its economic philosophies, the OECD is a professional, productive, organization of qualified technocrats orientated to promulgating neoliberal laws.

For the moment, the OECD is dedicated to a market economy. The OECD does not purport to issue decrees, or regulate commerce. It is, in charter, a permanent congress for international trade. Captive to governments dominated by industrial power and capital resources, the OECD is a continuation of insistent lobby interests contesting influence with the civil government. It does legislate and regulate, although with persuasion and consensus, no doubt often through the conduit of the national contact points. Global governance is achieved through the promulgation of model legislation which is adopted by the various nations.[31] The results coincide with our introductory assumptions. The OECD, an oligarchy of potent commercial forces, is a powerful mechanism towards the globalization of law because it does not encounter any dispute settlement obstacles. From an economic oligarchy defined by its multinational members there flows, as water into the estuary, a number of social and legal consequences.

Some examples are elucidative. They illustrate how legal globalization is occurring under the auspices of the OECD.

### *Corporate governance and the citizens of the world*

Corporate governance is how the rights and obligations between the various units of a corporation such as the board of directors, management, shareholders, and third parties are formulated. Increasingly, good corporate governance implies a concern for the welfare of the community. There are good reasons for concern with this topic. It is technical but also infused with humanistic goals.

Corporations are social units although with economic objectives. The social milieu today requires that corporations accept their community responsibilities.[32] It is apparent, then, that the more rights shareholders have in diverse areas of the world, and the more these rights bear a similarity, the more there will be substantial globalization as to shareholder activism. Shareholder rights have been selected because of the obvious rise of shareholder activism all over the world.[33]

Shareholder activism is also not an esoteric specialty. It concerns how corporations will socially perform in their community environment.

A number of organizations exist to monitor the social responsibility of corporations.[34] The Investor Responsibility Research Center in the US is an independent, not-for-profit corporation which conducts research and publishes reports on major corporations and international investors, social issues, and the reciprocal effect of each upon the other. Another American organization, the Council of Institutional Investors, represents government and union pension funds, and publishes an annual list of companies. Management teams of several companies included on the list have acknowledged and taken steps to explain poor financial performance and corporate strategies to improve their social responses.

Global Proxy Services Corporation in the US manages corporate governance activities and exercises voting rights for institutional investors with holdings of over $200 billion US dollars in corporate securities in over 50 markets.[35] American ownership of shares in foreign companies inevitably means shareholder activism will be exported all over the world.

California Public Employee's Retirement System (CalPERS) is the third largest pension fund in the world. It considers itself a permanent shareholder and not a trader. CalPERS has set guidelines for UK and French governance. Moreover, it will only invest in emerging equity markets that conform to its moral and financial standards.[36] CalPERS maintains a list of countries in which it can or cannot invest.[37] In order to be put on the permissible list for investment, high-ranking officials from emerging countries confer with CalPERS as to their markets.[38]

The same trend is occurring in Europe. A group of Europe's largest investors, mutual and pension funds, under the auspices of ISIS Asset Management and the Universities Superannuation Scheme, have written to the world's 20 top pharmaceutical companies with a list of good social practices. As an example, this statement calls for the industry not to prevent poor people obtaining drugs because of intellectual property laws,[39] laws which by virtue of the WTO are supposed to be recognized by its members. Such a statement is a mixture of shareholder activism and corporate governance. Implicit in the statement is the threat to withdraw investment in the targeted companies if they fail to comply with the objectives of the list.

Thus, besides the substantial shareholder interests represented by pension funds, there is a rising tide of corporate governance issues being looked at by religious groups.[40] Located in the US, the Interfaith Center on Corporate Responsibility (ICCR) groups 275 religious institutions who are using shareholder rights to review human rights, workers privileges, and global warming. The ICCR controls $110 billion in pensions which is invested in various ways, including share ownership. In 2002, ICCR members backed 144 shareholder resolutions affecting social and environmental topics at 99 companies. ABP, Europe's largest pension fund is considering establishing a $250 million fund for investment in socially responsible companies.[41] Social awareness by multinationals is now a significant concern for corporate managers and the OECD has responded to such interest by publishing its guidelines: 'OECD Principles of Corporate Governance'.[42]

## *Corporate governance on the high seas of globalization*

Legal globalization is a reflection of multinational power.[43] Of the world's first 100 economies half are corporations.[44] Further, the top 25 multinational enterprises are richer than approximately 170 nations. Manufacturing by foreign companies in the European Union in the 1990s increased significantly translating into the trend towards economic union.[45] Were the world exclusively determined by market economy and its associated laws, various companies might be able to purchase several nations.[46]

The OECD Principles of Corporate Governance, intended to be adhered to by the powerful multinationals, strive to protect shareholders' rights so that shareholders will be able to compel transparency, not be subjected to a captive management, avoid discrimination and promote equitable treatment of all shareholders, facilitate voting, ensure due notice of general assemblies, instill objectivity in the board of directors, and permit simple access to corporate information. The precise details of the OECD Principles of Corporate Governance pale before their commendable purpose. Only by stimulating shareholder activism within a transparent, informed corporate environment will the abuses of corporate dictatorships over shareholders be mitigated. When we refer to shareholder activism we invoke shareholder democracy. And as American ownership of foreign corporations is a well-recognized phenomenon,[47] shareholder activism is equivalent to exporting from America its economic and legal corporate concepts.

If we inquire of what interest is the consecration of shareholder activism in various parts of the world, our answer is that the multinational must ensure its capital interests are protected. Good corporate governance permits the multinational to raise its necessary capital, dispersed through millions of shareholders all over the world. Commercial logic thus reveals itself to produce unexpected social results.

With multinationals concerned that their capital investments may be prejudiced by perceived secretive boardroom transactions, shareholder activism requires them to recognize the rights of their own shareholders. The parameters of the 'OECD Principles of Corporate Governance' benefit both management and the shareholder. The cabalistic conferences and hushed exhortations to board members, management, and others interested in sharing the profits and, alas, at times plundering through insider trading, have produced their results. Thus we are agreeably informed by the OECD[48] that Australia, Canada, Czech Republic, Denmark, France, Germany, Greece, Italy, Japan, Korea, The Netherlands, New Zealand, Poland Portugal, UK, the US, and the EU are, in varying degrees, embracing the fundamentals of the OECD Principles of Corporate Governance. The multinational continues to have access to capital.

Nor is the OECD only concerned with the governance of corporations. The OECD has recently published its 'OECD Guidelines for Pension Fund Governance'.[49] Total assets of private pension funds within the OECD countries for 2001, preliminary data, are $8,985.6 billion.[50] Such assets constituted nearly 30 per cent of OECD financial assets in 2000.[51] Behind the publication of the guidelines is the clear intent by the OECD to set international standards for the management and safety of collective pension funds.[52] Contained within the guidelines are the 'appropriate legal and governance structures to ensure funds are managed in the best interest of plan members and beneficiaries'.[53] Although the OECD will monitor the implementation of the guidelines, the World Bank and the IMF will use such guidelines as part of 'their regular assessment of international standards'.[54] The guidelines assume global significance when it is realized that all over the world countries are having their public pension plans managed privately.[55]

Shareholder activism as developed and theorized in the industrial nations is obviously a hallmark for shareholders everywhere. Global business brings global shareholders. Pension plans and religious institutions will bring to bear social pressures.[56] The received commercial truths of the OECD will contribute, if not dramatically, at least effectively, to the spread of Western shareholder activism and corporate governance with its accompanying economic theories and legal myths. Acting as a supranational legislative assembly, the OECD is promoting the globalization of shareholder interests and corporate governance throughout the industrial world and its satellite trading partners.

Logically related to corporate governance are the OECD guidelines on multinationals.

*There are 11 lofty commandments more 4 investment obligations*

'The OECD Declaration and Decisions on International Investment and Multinational Enterprises: Basic Texts'[57] (Guidelines) is intended to make uniform the general rules of foreign investment and entrepreneur activity in another jurisdiction. The Guidelines contain various principles of good conduct for enterprises. They are 11. They encourage good corporate behavior. They range from contributing to the social progress of the community to abstaining from politics.[58] But there is a downside. The host nation, where the multinational is operating, also has obligations, four of consequence.

Countries acting as host to foreign investment are supposed to adhere to the OECD guidelines. They are: to protect foreign investors according to the principles of international law; to afford foreign investors equal treatment with domestic investors; that this impartial national treatment will be extended to all the territories of the host nation; and finally, the host country will avoid imposing conflicting requirements on foreign investment so that the investor is not caught between opposing legal principles, those of its origin, and those of the jurisdiction in which it is operating. These are the essential principle of the guidelines and they are of course a declaration of the globalization of the law. Nor is this a fortuitous coincidence. Because the OECD reflects the interests of a coterie of multinationals which are the economic motors of the member nations, this supranational assembly strives for equality of treatment wherever business is conducted, which is pretty much everywhere. Everywhere is a synonym for globalization.

The principles of international law can only mean the law of industrialized nations. The member nations are not expecting to be governed by the laws of rural or nomadic communities. In a clear effort to harmonize commercial laws, the host country is asked to minimize onerous obligations on the foreign investor so that it, the company investor, is not subject to conflicting legal norms. The Guidelines have attracted wide attention and generated substantial activity on the part of the member nations. The UK advised all British posts abroad to actively promote the Guidelines.[59] Sweden has sent copies of the Guidelines to all its embassies.[60] Canada provides information through seminars to its overseas staff.[61] When seeking permission for investment in Germany, the application form contains a reference to the Guidelines.[62] The Finnish Parliament wants its export credit insurance group to advise applicants of the existence of the Guidelines.[63]

The US is holding discussions with the Export-Import Bank, the Overseas Private Investment Corporation, and the Department of Commerce to have applicants for these services aware of the Guidelines.[64] The material just described is a modest part of a more complete report vividly conveying how the Guidelines are being marketed to various nation members and non-member observers.[65] The Guidelines are no more, nor less, than a decree law on foreign investment, drawn by an assembly of mercantile deputies, whose consequences are global.

Closely related to foreign investment is, unhappily, the specter of bribery.

*Bribery is not naughty unless you are caught*

The OECD Convention on 'Combating Bribery of Foreign Public Officials in International Business Transactions'[66] (Convention) is intended to deter subornation. The Convention makes clear its object of '... combating bribery of public officials in connection with international business transactions ...'[67] The Convention includes all 30 OECD Member countries and 4 non-member countries (Argentina, Brazil, Bulgaria and Chile). All signatories commit themselves to pass legislation necessary for its ratification and implementation into national laws.[68]

It is difficult to imagine how bribery would achieve legislative status other than through the OECD, being such polemic material. No doubt the impetus lies with the multinationals who want a level field of competition. Nevertheless, although clearly an acclamatory standard, the basis of this legislation is attributable to Western standards of law as envisioned by the industrialized countries and which will have direct application throughout the trading world. After all, there would be no need to prohibit bribery, a condemned practice under Western law concepts, unless it was an acceptable practice in some jurisdictions. Thus the tentacles of competition law are complemented by criminal sanctions.

*Paradise is a jug of wine, a loaf of bread, and the end of tax havens*

There is no international treaty of fiscal law obligatory in the various sovereigns. Consequently, globalization and internalization have spurred the emergence of tax havens and harmful tax regimes to escape the authority of the sovereign.[69] Without examining the details which separate one haven from the other, what occurs is that substantial tax revenue is diverted from jurisdictions, income which could be used to develop a country's infrastructure and promote social welfare. Originally, the international tax problems created by international commerce were resolved through the proliferation of double taxation treaties and the OECD made a significant contribution to a solution with its promulgation of its 'Model Double Tax Convention' of 1977.[70]

However the inherent right of sovereigns to enact their own tax legislation has resulted in various sovereigns attracting foreign capital with low, and at times, non-existent tax rates. Such tax havens naturally raise suspicions of money laundering in addition to practices of unfair competition in attracting foreign companies with their capital and technology. In response, the OECD has undertaken a number of initiatives, culminating in two reports[71] which provide member nations with a list of defensive measures which can be taken to bring international taxation into a global governance in accordance with an OECD international taxation model. Some of America's corporations[72] are operating from off-shore tax havens. For some, this is an united affront to sovereign taxation rights. To others, it will be a much needed response to an unjust situation: those who work, pay, and those who speculate, avoid. Two of the largest US public pension funds[73] have threatened to withdraw their investment in off-shore tax haven US companies on the grounds tax havens impede effective corporate governance by shareholders. Their combined potential investment is more than $1,000 billion. Any significant sale of shares in such companies would depress their quoted exchange value.

The stance of the OECD is a clear example of the globalization of international taxation law for surely the efforts of the OECD will prove fruitful. How surprising the results. Whereas the WTO has a dispute settlement mechanism, as an organization it is unable to enforce its own panel decisions. The OECD, not possessed of any judicial attributes, achieves considerable global consensus on a variety of social issues, through its informal oligarchy.[74] In the face of shareholder activism and corporate governance issues, the multinationals have to accept their fiscal duties. The fear of insolvency by a sovereign is greater than the lobbying power of the multinational. With tax havens, the OECD has favored the sovereign.

From corporate governance to bribery, our lessons from the OECD permit the formulation of a norm of the sociology of the law. Without enforcement powers, the law must depend on consensus. Consensus is formed from the dominant economic groups. Without judicial procedures to contest the majority will, the minority view on legal norms will eventually be eliminated or rendered ineffective. Oligarchies have their social function. As they establish legal norms, they are a substitute for more formal organizations which decree standards, such as a legislature or a judicial system. Imperfect by faulty representation, oligarchies such as the OECD continue to govern an imperfect world.

## Notes

[1] Stephen Thomsen, *Investment Patterns in a Longer-Term Perspective*, Working Papers on International Investment, Number 2000/2, available on the home page of the OECD, infra, n. 15.

[2] NAFTA is a regional trade agreement composed of the US, Canada, and Mexico.

[3] Danielle S. Petito, *Sovereignty and Gobalization: Fallacies, Truth, and Perception*, 17 N.Y.L. Sch. J. Hum. Rts. 1139 (2001).

[4] Organisation for Economic Co-operation and Development.
[5] Such as various regional trade agreements or the WTO.
[6] T. B. Bottomore and Maximilien Rubel, eds, Karl Marx, *Selected Writings in Sociology and Social Philosophy*, Penguin Books 2nd Ed. (1963).
[7] Alison Maitland, *Businesses are called to account*, The Financial Times, 28 March 2002, at page 1.
[8] Alexander Townsend, Jr, *The Global Schoolyard Bully: The Organization for Economic Co-operation and Development's Coercive Efforts to Control Tax Competition*, 25 Fordham Int'l L. J. 215 (2001).
[9] Andrew Parker et al., *OECD ponders action against tax havens*, The Financial Times, 19 April 2002, at p. 6.
[10] By accession dates, Australia: 7 June 1971, Austria: 29 September 1961, Belgium: 13 September 1961, Canada: 10 April 1961, Czech Republic: 21 December 1995, Denmark: 30 May 1961, Finland: 28 January 1969, France: 7 August 1961, Germany: 27 September 1961, Greece: 27 September 1961, Hungary: 7 May 1996, Iceland: 5 June 1961, Ireland: 17 August 1961, Italy: 29 March 1962, Japan: 28 April 1964, Korea: 12 December 1996, Luxembourg: 7 December 1961, Mexico: 18 May 1994, Netherlands: 13 November 1961, New Zealand: 29 May 1973, Norway: 4 July 1961, Poland: 22 November 1996, Portugal: 4 August 1961, Slovak Republic: 14 December 2000, Spain: 3 August 1961, Sweden: 28 September 1961, Switzerland: 28 September 1961, Turkey: 2 August 1961, United Kingdom: 2 May 1961, United States: 12 April 1961.
[11] Both the spelling and description are from the home page of the OECD, infra, n. 15.
[12] James Salzman, *Labor Rights, Globalization and Institutions: The Role and Influence of The Organization for Economic Cooperation and Development*, 21 Mich. J. Int'l L. 769 (2000).
[13] Ibid.
[14] All statistics in this paragraph are derived from *United Nations Conference on Trade and Development* quoted in Guy de Jonquières, The Financial Times, 13 August 2002, at page 3.
[15] Article 1 of the 'Convention on the Organisation for Economic Co-operation and Development' the text of which is available on the OECD home page <www.oecd.org> accessed 28 April 2002.
[16] Supra, n. 1, at p. 6.
[17] Supra, n. 1, at p. 8. See also Guy de Jonquières, *Foreign direct investment flows drop sharply after 2000 record*, The Financial Times, 4 July 2002, at p. 6.
[18] See home page of OECD, supra, n. 15.
[19] Ibid.
[20] Supra, n. 15.
[21] The OECD Guidelines for Multinational Enterprises: Text, Commentary and Clarifications, JTOO115758, 31 Oct 2001, home page of OECD, supra, n. 15, page 6: 'The activities of multinational enterprises, through international trade and investment, have strengthened and deepened the ties that join OECD economies to each other and to the rest of the world'.
[22] This is the designation given by the OECD on its home page to the various topics presently under its ken.
[23] OECD web site, supra, n. 15.
[24] Jost Delbruck, *Globalization of Law, Politics, and Markets — Implications for Domestic Law — A European Perspective*, 1 Ind. J. Global Stud. 9 (1993).
[25] Supra, n. 8.
[26] Article 12, supra, n. 15.

[27] Supra n. 15 and link to 'history'.
[28] Ibid.
[29] Ibid.
[30] Ibid.
[31] Supra, n. 8.
[32] Peter Nobel, *Social Responsibility of Corporations*, 84 Cornell L. Rev. 1255 (1997) stating that: 'In Europe, providing credit is considered to be a social obligation'. Under German and French law, a corporation acts within a social environment.
[33] OECD Steering Group on Corporate Governance, 26-27 April 2001, DRAFT, Room document 1, posted on the web site of the OECD, supra n. 15.
[34] The information in this paragraph et seq. was derived from the extremely informative article, Mary E. Kissane, *Global Gadflies: Applications and Implementations of US — Style Corporate Governance Abroad*, 17 NYL Sch. J. Int'l & Comp. 621 (1997).
[35] Ibid.
[36] Elizabeth Wine, *CalPERS sticks to ethical stance*, The Financial Times, 20 February 2003, at p. 17.
[37] Ibid.
[38] Ibid.
[39] Geoff Dyer, *Investors to increase pressure on drug groups*, FT*fm* (The Financial Times fund management supplement), 24 March 2003, at p. 1.
[40] Elizabeth Wine, *Ethical Crusaders resolve to redeem the corporate sinners*, The Financial Times, 30-31 March 2002 at page 24. The material which follows on this theme was extracted from the article by Ms. Wine.
[41] Simon Targett, *ABP to open $250m SRI fund to other investors*, FT*fm* (The Financial Times fund management supplement), 28 October 2002 at p. 1.
[42] SG/CG(99)5, Ad Hoc Task Force on Corporate Governance dated 16-19 April 1999.
[43] Mark B. Baker, *Tightening the Toothless Vise: Codes of Conduct and the American Multinational Enterprise*, 20 Wis. Int'l L. Rev. 89 (2001).
[44] Ibid.
[45] Peter Marsh, *Multinationals more efficient*, The Financial Times, 28 March 2002.
[46] Ibid.
[47] The North American investment fund One Equity Partner, affiliated with Bank One of Chicago, bought 75 per cent of the shares of the German naval constructor HDW, reported in the Portuguese Diario de Noticias, *Americanos controlam construtora naval alemã*, 03 May 02, at p. 5.
[48] Supra, n. 15.
[49] Supra, n. 15, links to pension fund governance, accessed 26 October 2002. The complete pension guidelines are published online.
[50] Ibid.
[51] Ibid.
[52] Ibid.
[53] Ibid.
[54] Ibid.
[55] Ibid
[56] Simon Targett et al., *Investors to fight tax barriers*, FT*fm* (The Financial Times fund management supplement), 22 April 2002, at p. 1, revealing a coalition of US and European fund managers are demanding that the EU Commission take action against countries with tax regimes of protectionism that discriminate against foreign investment houses.

[57] The OECD Declaration and Decisions on International Investment and Multinational Enterprises: Basic Texts, DAFFE/IME(2000)20, 8-9 November 2002, available on the home page of the OECD, supra, n. 15.
[58] Supra, n. 57, page 11, paragraph II. General Principles.
[59] The OECD Guidelines for Multinational Enterprises: First Annual Meeting of the National Contact Points, Summary Report, 21 September 2001, available on the OECD web site, supra, n. 15.
[60] Ibid.
[61] Ibid.
[62] Ibid.
[63] Ibid.
[64] Ibid.
[65] Ibid.
[66] The text of the Convention can be found on the homepage of the OECD, supra, n. 15.
[67] Supra, n. 15, Preamble to the Convention.
[68] The implementing nations to date are Australia, Austria, Belgium, Brazil, Canada, Denmark, Finland, France, Germany, Greece, Hungary, Iceland, Japan, Korea, Luxembourg, New Zealand, Norway, Spain, Sweden, Switzerland. Information posted on the OECD home page, supra, n. 15, as of 29 April 2002.
[69] Supra, n. 8, at page 7.
[70] Available on web site of OECD, supra, n. 15.
[71] Available on web site of OECD, supra, n. 15, 'Harmful Tax Competition: An Emerging Global Issue 9' (1998) indicating need to identify tax havens and other harmful tax regimes and provide guidelines to eliminate these practices; also 'Towards Global Tax Co-operation: Progress in Identifying and Eliminating Harmful Tax Practices' (2000) highlighting harmful tax practices and publishing defensive measures to be taken).
[72] As an example, Everest Reinsurance Group, Foster Wheeler, and Ingersoll-Rand, are some of the companies cited in Julie Earle, *US pension funds may cut links with 22 groups*, The Financial Times, 12 August 2002, at page 16, reporting on two of America's largest public pension funds threatening to withdraw their investment in corporations operating in off-shore tax havens.
[73] Supra, n. 72, California Public Employees' Retirement System (CalPERS) and California State Teachers' Retirement System (Calstrs).
[74] James Canute, *Bahamas will reconsider reforms*, The Financial Times, 27 August 2002, at page 4, where it is reported the government of the Bahamas is reviewing legislation implementing recommendations made by the OECD and the international Financial Task Force to persuade off-shore finance and banking centers to alter their way of doing business.

Chapter 8

# Sovereign Independence Depends on Your Credit Rating

*The opinion of others is what counts*

As observed in irony by one legal scholar,[1] the two major superpowers are the US and Moody's Investor Service. Whereas the US can destroy you with its military might, Moody's[2] of the US can decapitate a nation by merely downgrading its sovereign bonds.[3] To which thoughts we must add that Moody's has been given an undeserved sanguine prominence. Besides Moody's, the 'oligarchic trinity'[4] also includes Standard and Poor's (S&P's) of the US as well as Fitch Ratings from France.[5] Either of the three are formidable adversaries which sovereign independence must confront but before whom it can not prevail. Observations by any of the three can cause shudders to the executive branch of the sovereign in cause. Sovereign credit rating effectuates legislative reforms in the bond issuer as efficiently as legislative action.

These three agencies command such hegemony because US official entities and the international bond market have conferred the scepter of authorization by conceding to them the designation of national recognized statistical rating organizations (NRSROs), a concept at once honorific and horrific, for it is devoid of any specific content as we will shortly see. Nor is not without relevance that it is the US which has created the power structure of the credit agencies. American capital mechanisms are widely emulated, its standards of appraisal globally appreciated, and the Delphic pronouncements of our trinity are followed throughout the international bond investment world.

As to sovereign bonds, their credit rating affords a penetrating insight into the effects the world of finance exerts upon nations and their encirclement by the forces of legal globalization. Hence, the economics of sovereign bonds also contains a sociological factor. The ratings of sovereign bonds have a profound influence ultimately on the social lives of citizens and merits the scrutiny of all interested in the social consequences of apparently technical legal topics. Sovereign bonds are a social kaleidoscope. In the years 1999, 2000, 2001, and 2002, there were issued, respectively, by sovereign nations throughout the world bonds in the amount of $1,408, $1,270, $1,419, and $1,650, in US billions. In four years almost $US 6 trillion in sovereign bonds were issued.[6] By being able to influence the flow of investment funds through their opinion as to the safety of the sovereign bond, the rating agencies influence considerably the global economic order.

The economic logic behind the convenience of ratings is quite simple. Nations who wish to participate in the global economy must attract foreign capital. One common method is to issue a sovereign bond subscribed in a foreign currency, such as US dollars or Euros, as opposed to the issuer's. Such obligations are a popular financial instrument because of, in theory at least, the broad range of assets possessed by a sovereign. In the words of a well-known American banker, 'countries do not go bankrupt because they always own more than they owe'.[7] The premise of this observation may be suspect as a country's main resources are its fixed assets, such as land and hardly able to be levied upon and taken away. But, nevertheless, it indicates a truism hardly ever contested in the investment world: a good rated sovereign bond is a safe investment.

Not surprisingly, then, the rating given by one of the triumvirate is assiduously followed by the foreign sovereign bond international investment market which is a disbanded, substantial source of funds from the Americas to Asia. If a nation has a poor credit rating, the bond market will either ignore the sovereign bond issue or will demand a premium in the form of a high yield bond. Obviously, foreign potential bankrupt nations are not desirable candidates for international trade or foreign direct investment. Sovereigns therefore crave and require favorable credit ratings for their issues.

Fortunately for the bond industry, sovereign nations, similar to hotels, films, kitchen equipment, and restaurants,[8] now have at least these three guides to classify their performance and advise the international capital markets. Of course, the object of the inspection is neither comfortable lodging, entertainment, nor appetizing cuisine, but instead the expectation of receiving payment. Nevertheless this ostensible investment grade attribute also has repercussions regarding the economic and social policies of the issuing sovereigns. By rating well or ill, and stimulating or depressing the salability of a sovereign bond, it is within the grasp of rating agencies to dictate to governments all over the world what should be the principles of their political economies. Of the many world nations, three rating agencies are at the helm of governments without any electorate having chosen them. From economics to law is but a short step, as the economic aspects of law and the legal aspects of economics are improbably separated.

We are discretely confronted with an example of a 'growing trend towards private ordering of traditionally public functions'.[9] Particular entities, varied in accordance with the subjacent activity, perform the functions of governmental bodies but subject to market pressure and therefore considerations of cost and efficiency. Social values tumble before the laws of the market. In order to obtain favorable ratings for their sovereign bonds, governments all over the world are subject to the analysis, through economic and social prisms of the agencies, as to their political policies. The results can be advantageous or not, but the result is surely the globalization of legal principles. The correct mixture of political economy, which by its nature has to contain legal principles, is imposed upon the sovereign debtor under penalty of a lower credit rating. As two thirds of the agencies are US, and the other is French, our imagination as to the correct political economy for sovereign debtors has only one example upon which to draw: US neoliberal capitalism moderated modestly by French social concerns.

The reasons for this have to do with the authority gratuitously granted to these agencies by powerful public organizations. In 1975, the US Securities and Exchange Commission (SEC) adopted the 'Net Capital Rule' whereby credit ratings of 'nationally recognized statistical rating organizations' would be used to measure the liquidity of financial institutions under its jurisdiction. In other words, a high credit rating indicates a credible degree of liquidity in the secondary bond market and qualifies towards any obligatory cash reserves. As of 23 December 2002, the only credit rating agencies to have been recognized as NRSROs are our trinity.[10]

Although such an edict certainly has the protection of investors as an objective, yet there appears a glaring logical lapse in this attitude. The SEC protects and enshrines our American oligopoly 'because of the status they have been accorded by the regulatory agency of the largest economy in the world. They are [classified as] "nationally recognized statistical rating organizations" (NRSROs), but without the US Securities and Exchange Commission (SEC) ever having defined them!'[11] In other words, the authority of the SEC over American financial entities obligates a credit agency wishing to compete for global rating business to have secured the status of a nationally recognized statistical rating organization. Those credit rating agencies which have received this status are referred to as NRSROs and being such are able to comment upon the viability of sovereign bonds for purposes of regulation compliance.

However, the standards and criteria to achieve this status are nowhere clearly defined. The administrative criteria to concede this status is as illusory as the standards by which the NRSROs judge the sovereigns. This bewildering state of affairs can only be a cause of distress to the affairs of the nation under analysis. Other official references to the utility of credit ratings can be found in US regulations concerning the quality of the bond portfolios of US national banks; US Comptroller of the Currency prohibitions on banks purchasing securities not of investment quality; and covenants in bond which stipulate a default will be deemed to have occurred if there is a downgrading of the bond in question.[12] By extending a semi-official status to these credit rating agencies, the US government, and the bond market in general, subject both corporate and sovereign acts to private scrutiny and appraisal.

At this juncture of our analysis, we marvel at the unabashed cartel which no anti-trust authority seems to question.

### *Anti-trust laws in abundance but the cartels go on*

The three rating agencies dominating the sovereign bond market operate through an extensive network. Moody's has 16 offices around the world and rates at least 100 sovereign nations. Nearly every country which issues sovereign bonds is rated by Moody's.[13] From rating 11 countries in 1980, Moody's now rates 78 sovereign bonds, both in domestic and foreign currency.[14] S&P's employs over 5,000 people and maintains offices in 18 countries.[15] Fitch has a presence in 75 countries with 40 offices world wide. They maintain a staff of 1,200 personnel.[16]

The importance of the rating agencies is further exemplified by the rules of the Basle Committee on Banking Supervision which in its proposed capital adequacy requirements for banks all over the world is considering assessing the risk of banks in direct proportion to the ratings of the debts they hold for investment.[17] Nor is it only the SEC or the US Comptroller of Currency which looks to the trinity for guidance. Sovereign bond classifications are widely quoted in the financial media and are indispensable for proper investment guidance. Denial to the classifications conceded by the rating agencies may even justify a formal, legal complaint.[18] Nations can hardly engage in any activity without their activities being commented upon and then rated by various agencies. Such agencies assess the risk associated with the obligations of a central government. While this activity appears technical and of interest confined to the financial sector, such is not the case.

What is at issue is national independence and whether or not a sovereign will govern its citizenry according to local laws deemed to be in resonance with its culture or by those thrust upon it because this is the requirement for an investment grade credit rating. In theory, a national legislature is beholden to an electorate. Our three credit rating agencies owe a duty of corporate governance only to their shareholders. The sovereign credit bond market thus propels citizenry into confrontation with shareholders our citizens will hardly ever meet. Yet, although a complex sovereign performance schedule is in use, and various criteria are published on the relevant web sites, we are not sure what the intangible elements are being measured against. Prospects of a stable economy, the object of the credit investigation, implies we have an absolute standard of national stability, which is as absurd written as spoken. Were this just a marginal pastime to gainfully employ the occasional errant economist who finds evaluating sovereign achievement an intellectual challenge our interest would be equally sporadic. But, no, this is not the case.

The rating agencies wield such authority as to cause the concept of sovereignty to be cast in doubt. No nation escapes the scrutiny of the international credit rating agencies. They are the sovereign power brokers. Nor is there wrath confined to the struggling emerging economies or underdeveloped nations. Being a member of the club of industrialized nations does not offer any immunity. The Bank of Japan is advised by Moody's to take 'more vigorous measures' to stimulate the economy.[19] The failure to heed this advice will be a downgrade of its 'sovereign debt'. In patrician tones, a senior credit officer at Moody's counsels Japan to change its current policies otherwise their debt rating will be reduced.[20]

As Moody's already lowered Japan's rating to the level of a number of developing countries, such as Botswana,[21] any further degradation of Japan's credit position is catastrophic. Their sovereign debt represented in bonds will trade at a deep discount and further international capital sovereign financing will require an increased interest rate as premium for the assumed risk. In the event the Japanese government is not reading the admonitions from Moody's, Fitch downgraded Japan's largest banks, apparently in the belief their nationalization was probable due to their lack of financial strength.[22] Fitch is frustrated with the progress of economic and corporate reform in Japan.[23] Although Fitch does not occupy any honorary position on Japan's governmental councils, its frank warnings indicate its awareness of the power sovereign rating agencies possess. Without reform according to the economic and social principles of Fitch, foreign investment will be discouraged.

Apparently the credit agencies feel no need to confine their observations to economic issues. Moody's downgraded its projections for the South Korean economy during the month of February 2003 because of the crisis with North Korea over their nuclear weapons program. The comments by Moody's generated a wave of currency and share selling threatening to destabilize the South Korean economy.[24] If all roads lead to Rome, obviously the credit agencies have no trouble in arriving. S&P's determination to lower its outlook on Italy's sovereign debt affects basic premises about eurozone debt.[25] One of S&P's credit analysts warns Italy about its 'budgetary imbalances'.[26] Presumably, it is taken for granted that the economic ministers of all nations have their shadow counterparts dispersed throughout the credit rating agencies. Although not yet a member of the European Commission, Moody's feels it is necessary to warn France that its budget deficit 'may have reached three per cent of GDP in 2002'[27] which would mean the EU Stability Pact[28] is being violated. '[I]f the trend persists over the long term, it could put the rating [France] under pressure'.[29]

Good economic performance is rewarded with further foreign investment. However, a warning, if unheeded, will result in more costly bond issues if not provoke a downright flight of capital. No doubt the government of India was enthralled to learn that Moody's was going to upgrade its sovereign obligations.[30] We can wonder at the audacity of the credit rating agencies in their appraisals of sovereign nations. The credit agencies must evaluate not only issues of solvency, but also the soundness of political institutions, social harmony, and economic progress.[31] Obviously, such laudatory objectives from the viewpoint of the credit analyst cause great consternation to a national community.

The reason is simple enough. What is being judged is apparently sovereign solvency but this bait is a definite red herring. The economic and social policies of the sovereign are under review by Western analysts and truth is in the eyes of the beholder. Thus the international credit rating agencies, secure in their cartel, are just another force driving nations towards convergence in spite of the omnipresent anti-trust laws. As the buttresses of social and economic policies are the laws of the nation, sovereign credit agencies, as absurd as it may appear at first sight, in fact cajole and threaten nations into adopting recommended economic, legal, and social programs.

The private bond ratings of sovereigns continue and will do so for the indefinite future. Apparently, the major sovereign credit-rating agencies have no hesitation in advising other nations on what constitutes good government.

### *The branch is not permitted to fall far from the tree*

It is not without relevance that the trinity are private companies[32] obviously committed to the pursuit of profit, if not the public weal. S&P's is a division of The McGraw-Hill Companies, a major US publisher. Moody's is located in NY and a significant part of its shares are held by an American investor.[33] Fitch Ratings is owned by Fimalac of France whose principal business is hand tools and garage equipment. It is through Fitch Rating[34] that they have diversified into the international sovereign rating business.

So the destiny of sovereigns all over the world, or at least their access to global commerce, is justly in the hands of those equally committed to the free market. But the free market has its rules and policies. It is instructive for purposes of social consequences to understand more in singularity what are the details of these programs. Moody's approach to sovereign rating[35] is general and comprehensive. Besides the foreign debt of the sovereign in question, they analyze the qualitative factors and economic fundamentals. Groups, races, dispersion of income, cultural diversities, economic administration, fiscal and monetary policies, natural resources and their exploitation, to name only the obvious. In short, Moody's attempts to obtain an exhaustive understanding of the nation under review. From its understanding of the cultural content of a particular nation, comparisons surely are made with the social references of analysts employed by Moody's.

S&P's publishes on its web site[36] the elements which guide it in their classification of a sovereign bond. Although S&P's methodology claims to be directed towards an analysis of credit risk, this determination, by its own announcement, is both quantitative and qualitative. It is the qualitative aspect which interests us and which constitutes S&P's a self-elected member of all national assemblies whose bond issues it has decided to 'rate'. This becomes obvious when we examine the particulars. Thus S&P's is concerned with the stability and legitimacy of political institutions. It is influenced favorably with the popular participation in the political process and the orderliness of leadership succession. Transparency in the legislative process, quite rightly, is a positive element. More relevant to the topic of legal globalization is the view S&P's has of the sovereign's economic status. S&P's are frank in their interest in the prosperity, diversity, and degree to which the sovereign's economy is market orientated. In its opinion, a market economy is less prone to policy error. Naturally, many elements must be weighed to evaluate how disposed towards blunders is the sovereign.

Hence, the income of the sovereign should be equitably distributed. There should be a broad tax base and low rates. The sovereign should evidence signs of fiscal flexibility and the creation of public infrastructures. We are instructed the Republic of Singapore receives a high rating because of compliance with this program.[37] Certain contradictions appear in the S&P's published methodology which implies that the judges are not entirely independent. While an excessive government debt burden will ordinarily lower a sovereign's rating, Japan, Belgium, and Italy, although among the most indebted nations, receive a favorable rating. This is, in the opinion of S&P's, because they have wealth, a high level of development, and the revenue-raising ability.[38] In other words, at times the club members must be treated paternally. And if this seems unfair, well, so be it. Any signs of market favoritism are greeted with enthusiasm. Chile is complimented because it has mandatory, privately financed pension funds. This is a contributing factor to improving the sovereign's credit standing.[39]

Fitch Ratings, under the dominion of French entrepreneurs, presents a more statistical approach and is not so apparently biased towards the Western model of democracy. In its published web site 'Checklist of Sovereign Rating Criteria',[40] more emphasis is given to economic details but political aspects are not ignored. Yet the biases towards a market economy are evident. Consequently, without any pretension towards a schematic presentation, Fitch seeks information concerning trade union density and days lost through industrial action; self-employment and its trend; framework for ensuring competition; description of the method for privatization; independence of the central bank; policy towards trade liberalization and foreign investment; any negative legal regimes directed towards foreign investment.

From this summary, we see that sovereign credit rating organizations deem it appropriate, if not obligatory, to ensure the destiny of their sovereign ward adheres to the policies considered correct.

### *Credit the credit agencies for their contribution to legal globalization*

The credit rating of sovereign bonds is subject to the hegemony of Moody's, S&P's, and Fitch Ratings. In addition to the two of our trinity being American owned, all three are firmly within the camp of a free market economy. Given the fact that all three base their credit ratings on a number of factors which have no technical standards — culture, economic progress, social cohesion, political stability — it appears a forgone conclusion that approval, or the withdrawal of it, will be influenced by the rater's point of reference.

We are thus forced to conclude that the private capital market dictates the same terms to sovereign nations as do the public international financial organizations such as the IMF and the World Bank. For those sovereign nations who wish to engage in development plans, attract foreign capital, raise hard currency in the international bond market, these aspirations can only be satisfied by obedience to the value system of the creditors and the donors. As these values are a reflection of Western economic and social beliefs, we can only expect that as economic, social, and political demands are made upon sovereign nations in the guise of credit ratings, the laws which articulate such norms must also conform to the expected standards. Sovereign nations now find themselves subject to legal specifications conceived and designed by three credit rating agencies.

Surely this is one of the oddities of the legal globalization movement in course. Even more absurd is the fact that the issuers of sovereign bonds, not only depend on the credit agencies for their ability to attract funds, but they are obligated to pay a fee for the preceding investigation.[41] This medley of conflict of interest might be tolerated with resignation if there was significant utility in the sovereign ratings. However, according to a scholarly study of sovereign ratings, '... sovereign credit ratings fail to anticipate banking and currency crises'.[42] Yet, in spite of the probable futility of credit ratings, they are assiduously studied and compared and sovereigns are obligated to accede to the rater's imperatives. The course of legal globalization finds its support in the social beliefs of the credit-rating agencies and with the continued integration of capital markets this trend can only accelerate the process.

Credit rating agencies are the global regulators of solvency. They wield global power. As noted by one commentator, 'Yet all but one of the agencies is US-based

(Fitch is French owned) making the entire world's credit-worthiness assessed and regulated by the US'.[43] Still, Fitch feels no threat to its own capabilities as observed by its threat to downgrade Germany's sovereign bonds.[44] In Fitch's view, Germany's widening budget deficit and sluggish reforms will have to be corrected.

The oligarchy is under assault. On 23 February 2003, the US Securities & Exchange Commission granted Dominion Bond Rating Service (DBRS), a Canadian company, the status of a nationally recognized statistical rating organization (NRSROs).[45] DBRS has not formally announced its entry into the sovereign credit rating industry. Yet, even if DBRS were to foray into this field, the privileged position of the holy trinity is unlikely to be dislodged. A US Congressional subcommittee has publicly stated its fear that the US government '... has created an oligopoly, eliminating the checks and balances that would serve the public interest in a free market'.[46]

The same Congressional subcommittee has reminded the US SEC that the NRSROs failed to advise the public about the fraudulent accounts of several well-known, publicly listed US corporations while several credit rating agencies not having this exalted status did issue timely warnings.[47] But these are the failures in the credit assessment of the private sector. The public sector presents even more difficult credit determinations. Independent sovereignty today is a credit risk, particularly for national autonomy.

## Notes

[1] Frank Partnoy, *The Siskel and Ebert of Financial Markets?: Two Thumbs Down For The Credit Rating Agencies*, 77 Wash. U. L. Q. 619 (1999).

[2] Moody's Investors Service usually referred to as 'Moody's'.

[3] Supra, n. 1. A sovereign bond is an obligation to repay a debt issued by a nation.

[4] General information concerning these three credit rating agencies can be found at <www.moodys.com>, which is US owned, <www.standardandpoors.com>, which is US owned, and <www.fitchholdings.com>, which is French owned, all accessed 27 January 2003.

[5] The legal entity is now FitchIBCA because of various acquisitions. At times in the professional literature there are references to Fitch, Inc.

[6] Päivi Munter, *Flight to bonds sends yields sliding to new lows*, The Financial Times, 29 January 2003, at p. 15 and the graphs presented.

[7] Attributed to Walter Wriston when he was head of Citibank, and quoted in Fitch Sovereign Ratings, Rating Methodology, available on Fitch web site, supra, n. 4.

[8] Supra, fn. 1. We are grateful to Prof. Partnoy for his wry comparisons.

[9] Steven L. Schwarz, *Private Ordering of Public Markets: The Rating Agency Paradox*, 2002 U. Ill. Rev. 1 (2002).

[10] Daniel Gross, *Busting up the Ratings Cartel*, 23 December 2003, available at <www. slate.msn.com/id/2075959>, accessed 29 January 2003.

[11] Article (untitled) by Chakravarthi Raghavan dated 15-28 February 2002 available on <www.twnside.org.sg/title/twe275f.htm>, accessed 29 January 2003.

[12] Jonathan R. Macey, testimony before the US Committee on Governmental Affairs concerning Nationally Recognized Statistical Ratings Organizations, March 20, 1932, available on <www.senate.gov/~gov_affairs/032002macey>, accessed 31 January 2003.

[13] Statistics culled from Moody's Investors Service web site, supra, n. 4.
[14] Jenny Wiggins, *Sovereign ratings seen as stable*, The Financial Times, 10 February 2003, at page 19.
[15] Statistics culled from Standard & Poor's web site, supra, n. 4.
[16] Statistics culled from Fitch web site, supra, n. 4.
[17] Supra, n. 9. The central bank Governors of Belgium, Canada, France, Germany, Italy, Japan, Luxembourg, the Netherlands, Sweden, Switzerland, the UK and the US established the Basle Committee. Also participating in bank reunions are senior representatives of bank supervisory authorities and their respective central banks.
[18] Jane Croft, *Online group files S&P complaint*, The Financial Times, 27 January 2003, at page 16, where Ms. Croft reports that Absreports.com, a provider of online information concerning the European securitisation industry, filed a complaint with the Office of Fair Trading (UK), alleging S&P's was acting in an anti-competitive manner by restricting access to its classifications. In other words, so vital is the information, that Absreports.com considers it a public duty for S&P's to make their determinations freely accessible. It is to be noted that S&P's claims its ratings are available on its own web site free of charge.
[19] David Pilling, *Moody's calls on BoJ to reflate economy*, The Financial Times, 15 January 2003 at p. 6.
[20] Ibid.
[21] Ibid.
[22] David Ibison, *Fitch downgrades Japanese banks*, The Financial Times, 31 January 2003, at p. 13.
[23] Ibid.
[24] Andrew Ward, *Agency downgrades S Korea outlook as nuclear crisis grows*, The Financial Times, 12 February 2003, at p. 6.
[25] Päivi Munter and Aline van Duyn, *S&P warns Rome to put its finances in order*, The Financial Times, 17 January 2003, at page 13.
[26] Ibid.
[27] Aline van Duyn, *Moody's warns of French deficit*, The Financial Times, 29 January 2003, at p. 22.
[28] Under the Stability Pact of the European Union, all members agree budgets must not exceed 3 per cent of gross domestic product. Otherwise, sanctions may be applied.
[29] Supra, n. 27.
[30] Supra, n. 4, home page of Moody's, where there is presented in linear form various credit actions recently taken. The reference to India's upgrading is dated 3 February 2003.
[31] Richard Cantor and Frank Packer, *Current Issues in Economics and Finance*, Federal Reserve Bank of New York, 1 (3) (June 1995), available at <www.newyorkfed.org/rmaghome/curr_iss/ci1-3> accessed 21 January 2003.
[32] All information concerning Moody's, S&P's, and Fitch recited in this chapter is available on the respective company web sites.
[33] Warren Buffet, the paradigm of American capitalism, or through one of his family-controlled corporations such as Berkshire Hathaway.
[34] Fitch IBCA.
[35] All comments concerning Moody's methodology are derived from D. Johannes Jüttner and Justin McCarthy, *Modelling a Rating Crisis*, available on <www.econ.mq.edu.au./staff/djuttner/SOVEIG.2>, accessed 2 February 2003.
[36] Supra, n. 4. All facts discussed concerning the methodology of S&P's can be found published on their web site.
[37] Ibid.

[38] Ibid.
[39] Ibid.
[40] Supra, fn. 4.
[41] Supra, fn. 12.
[42] Carmen M. Reinhart, *Sovereign Credit Ratings Before and After Financial Crises,* 21 February 2001, available on <www.puaf.umd.edu/papers/reinhart>, accessed 5 February 2003.
[43] John Adams, *Crisis? What crisis?*, FT Expat, February 2003, at p. 45, quotation from an 'insight column: ratings agencies' signed by James Featherstone.
[44] Päivi Munter, *Fitch has bearish view of Germany*, The Financial Times, 19 February 2003, at page 21.
[45] Vicent Boland, *Congress to investigate SEC's role in policing credit ratings*, The Financial Times, 14 April 2003, at page 21.
[46] Ibid.
[47] Ibid.

# PART 2
# INTERNATIONAL AID AND THE GLOBALIZATION OF WESTERN LAW

## Chapter 9

# The Free Market Logic of International Aid

*Aid, like trade, may possibly contaminate*

Aid and trade are the ideal partners, a vaudeville team whose stage is the world. They complement each other in a harlequin duet, each assisting the other, trade needing aid, and aid fomenting trade. We can term this a cozy commercial partnership with accompanying acrobats. As for its audience, there is no lack of paying playgoers. But the price of the ticket is not always known beforehand. Nor could it be, since sometimes the price is stipulated on purchase; other times it is claimed later; and there are even instances when the price is variable, depending on unforeseen circumstances. All this is possible because aid is not a single transaction whereby sums are loaned. It is a complex, never-ending social transaction with the participants often having to modify their social structure. Some simple examples will suffice as to the social aspects of aid.

Trade functions on credit. Goods and services are sold with payment delayed for a period of time customary to the particular trade. Most commerce is not cash self-sufficient. Even the transnational corporations seek financing for their many needs. Corporate finance is largely devoted to the management of debt. When the credit is needed by nations, it is denominated international aid and often arranged by public institutions. When private banking institutions are involved, the extension of credit is denominated a loan. Between aid and loans are different philosophies for furnishing funds, but the end result, legally, is the same. The debtor is drawn into the web of Western legal principles.

Both public and private lending institutions prior to the concession of credit will examine carefully the reliability of the borrower. In the case of private lenders, the loan analysis may not be concerned with the borrower's distasteful social policies. If the borrower is not a political ally, this is not an insuperable obstacle. With the proper guarantees, often given by the lender's government who actually may be politically hostile to the borrower, a loan is forthcoming. These are the inconsistencies of international finance. The public institutional lender does not have the political luxuries available to the private lender. Using allegedly taxpayer funds, loans are granted to emerging economies in conformity with the lender's assessment of progress, a notably subjective activity.

Were need the only cause of international aid, it would be enough to extend the domain of Western culture over those sovereigns interested in commerce. Which probably means the entire repertoire of nations. However, simply wanting does not necessarily mean the aid will be forthcoming. Aid and credit carry with them a cultural component. Public lending institutions require assurances from their borrowers as to legislative enactment which will make the borrower viable, prosperous, and this is most easily accomplished by laws attractive to foreign investors. Welcoming laws are Western legal principles written in the language of the host country.

Moreover, countries are adept at emulating the competitors and even surpassing them in their own skills. Through the last decades, the Asian nations have built up substantial surpluses of US$ reserves, becoming arbitrators as to currency exchange values. Far from being material of mere academic interest, exchange rates affect the life of a nation as to its fiscal and monetary policies. Nations holding large surpluses of a currency can inundate the forex market and drive down the value of the currency in question. This causes the depreciated currency to seek refuge in higher interest rates to defend its value, a social consequence of grave proportions.

But the private lending sector also has its substantial influence in extending the domain of Western lending law over other national borrowers. The private lending institutions form part of a complex banking network which is overseen by professional and institutional consent, particularly the various worlds Central Banks, through the Bank for International Settlements[1] and the Basle Committee on Banking Supervision.[2] Both organizations are located in Basle, Switzerland. Both organizations receive strict adherence to their recommended banking standards for a simple reason. National banks who do not accept and adhere to the published voluntary recommended standards for reserves, determination of individual credit worthiness, transparency requirement from borrowers, public revelation of the financial condition by the national bank, prohibition against insider lending, and condemnation of credit given because of the 'ye ole buddy network' will surely find themselves blacklisted.

The breadth of the bankers from Basle is extensive and effective. It is also a further confirmation of the true reach of Western debtor law. The essence of banking law radiates from Switzerland. Its sound and conservative banking principles, intended to protect depositors and foment growth, rests upon Western ethics which have profound historical roots.[3] These morals, springing from the mores of thrift and labor, have given rise to a legal structure which is not founded on rewards for laxity and carelessness. Whatever our religious convictions, the triumph of commerce in displacing other forms of social life, is reflected in the morality imbuing present day commercial Western law, a bit tarnished from its origins, but the remnants are visible.

Once a loan is obtained, the obligation of repayment arises. But as trade is not always a peaceful pursuit so the public paths of international aid and loans also have hurdles. Aid and loans require payments but unfortunately maturity dates are not always met. The debt obligation becomes converted into a sovereign or private default. When defaults do occur, the consequences for public borrowers are more serious than for the private enterprises. The law of debt for private enterprises is normally a matter of municipal law and is highly developed. Protection against creditors is an entrenched legal mechanism. Time is given to the debtor, against the wishes of the creditor, to refinance and recuperate, or else declare bankruptcy.

Public defaults raise questions of law which to date have not been satisfactorily resolved. More seriously, the fate of debtor nations, normally emerging market economies, is in the hands of the Western industrialized nations who are debating what innovations should be made to the law of bankrupt sovereign nations.[4] At times the debate rages not over what laws should be applied, but the preservation of commissions to the investment bankers which market the public debt.[5] One of the options as to the treatment of sovereign debt includes 'collective action clauses'. This is a mechanism suggested by the US Treasury which requires a majority of creditors to unite for any legal action against the debtor. For the moment, the present situation generally allows creditors to take whatever individual action the law of the relevant jurisdiction permits.

The IMF favors the US Treasury suggestion while other investment groups prefer the opportunity to purchase default sovereign bonds and act independently. They can be bought at a deep discount. There are always hopes the debtor nation will be bailed out of difficulties and the bonds eventually repaid. If not, the first to the courtroom may cross the collection line ahead of the others. Whatever alternative appears sensible or correct, we are not informed of the opinion of the debtors. Lenders ponder and sovereign borrowers await the outcome. Capital operates in its own stratosphere, but without the presence of the one necessary party, the debtor.

Regardless of the law to be applied for bankrupt sovereigns,[6] sovereign default can mean a halt to further international financing. Once a line of credit for foreign currency is terminated, panic sets into the markets, both locally and internationally.[7] Sovereign debtors normally will accede to the demands of the public institutions who in their turn call for all manner of draconian remedies. That they may be justified does not detract from their social effects.[8] With international lenders mostly under the influence of the Western law of debt, sovereign defaults thrust the potential debtor upon the mercy of Western creditors and its bankruptcy laws. Sovereign aid invariably means that Western law concepts will be applied, whether through bond default clauses, international bankruptcy procedures, or judicial moratoriums conceded by laws which are anticipated to become standard procedures.

Sovereign aid is a conduit for the transmission of Western debt culture. Invariably, there will be defaults due to disagreements as to the interpretation of loan clauses, allegations of misuse of loan funds, vulture funds anxious to buy doubtful sovereign debt in the hopes of compelling payment in court, and defaults which need renegotiation but it is only forthcoming on conditions imposed by the lender. The panorama is, of course, more detailed. While international trade is an optimistic venture, with its participants expecting rewards for their labor, there is a dark side to international aid which needs revelation. Along with international trade, international aid unintentionally advances the increment of disputes as Western law is not founded on altruism in business. But the consequences of international aid lurch beyond fomenting, through trade, more litigation. The social consequences of international aid are more diffuse due to the people and operations involved.

*Legal documents are a precious aid*

International aid, whether private or public, is normally given for the purposes of assisting countries in developing various national infrastructures. Roads, dams, power lines, hospital, airports, harbors, these are some of the typical, major ventures it is hoped will be served by international aid. Yet, a moment's reflection should convince us that it is highly unlikely the citizens of the borrower will have a substantial part in the development other than by contributing labor. Otherwise the borrowers would be the local population and with the funds received they would be the contractors. In fact, the infrastructures will be realized but with the assistance and under the direction of foreign companies and their staff who bid for these public projects. Normally, the foreign contractor will establish a local subsidiary so as to be able to compete for the bid as a national company.

The presence of foreign contractors, or other skilled foreign investors, is why public aid is often given. It is, naturally, not the only reason. Frequently, humanistic principles guide the concession of public loans. But as these institutions are under the governance of Western economists, it does not escape the attention of the technocrats that aid will assist the lender's' economies. Moreover, the cadre of merchants is mostly corporate in the form of multinationals but of course collective societies are represented by individuals who include financial officers, marketing executives, engineers, lawyers, scientists, personnel counselors, technological advisers, the exact composition dependent on the nature of the corporate activity. Not unexpectedly, the possibilities unleashed by international aid transpose to the borrower and its community a broad range of skills such as accounting methods, corporate structure, personnel policies, communication equipment, marketing platforms, corporate strategy, so that the interplay between the borrower and the host contractor is indeed a complex encounter requiring an aptitude for learning by the recipient and the transference of new knowledge. The establishment of the simplest foreign subsidiary always implies a conduit for the traffic of know-how.

Furthermore, the arrival of the engineers and other professionals has been preceded by multiple legal documents. Business is not conducted through handshakes. Voluminous contracts identifying the work to be done, the promises undertaken, the payments expected, the technology transferred, the warranties and guarantees, the default clauses, the companies to be established, the capital of operating joint ventures, the share structure, the voting rights, all of this is just a glimpse of the material to be discussed and debated. From this partial recitation of human activity and required legal documents, it is surely apparent that the beneficiary of the aid, the borrower, must understand and accept the legal concepts addressed. Without a concurrence as to the operative legal norms nothing will be finalized. It is the stalwart borrower who will seek to alter significantly the controlling legal forms. Lawyering becomes commuted to adopting the legal norms of the lender and its counsel to the local jurisdiction. International aid thus transmits currency and contemporaneously the jurisprudence of the lender.

International aid, instructing how contemporary business is done and the legal concepts underlying it, becomes a vehicle of ideas accepted by the host. More importantly, legal norms are communicated and received with the same ease as the monetary transfers. But international aid produces further consequences.

*Lending legislation*

Those public entities who loan have a legislative bent. If money is to be given, whether at a current, low rate of interest, or simply donated, then assurances are expected. The lender does not contemplate the borrower will use the available funds for warfare against the lender. As a matter of fact, it seems natural to expect the borrower to have a similar view of social life as its lender. When we examine the various letters of understanding executed between international public lenders and sovereign borrowers, we discover that the lender requests commitments from the borrower which resound as proposed legislative bills issuing from parliamentary committees.

The borrowers are extorted, and they agree, to liberalize their financial markets; labor laws must become less rigid so that the economy will burst forth in robust vigor; promises are undertaken to construct a modern infrastructure; foreign investment is to be encouraged; guidelines are agreed upon to protect foreign investors. Expropriation without just compensation borders on medieval heresy and the borrower will be impaled on an immediate default clause.

The borrower is requested and obligingly agrees to undertake substantial legislative reforms in conformity with the letter of understanding. Typically, the borrower promises to promote economic growth through macroeconomic stabilization and a dedicated transition to a fully functioning market economy. A market-based economy is encouraged through privatization, legal reforms, price deregulation, trade liberalization, and bank restructuring. Budget expenditures should be curtailed. The wage bill of the state government must be slashed. Cut-backs in public investment not related to obligations to international financial institutions must take place. There is to be a reduction in purchases of non-essential goods and services.

Thus is lending confounded with legislation. Legislation becomes the non-repayable interest premium the borrower accepts. Of course, the modifications sought by the lender are but a mirror image of its own national creeds and beliefs. The major lenders are the industrialized nations. International aid furthers the globalization of Western law and the precepts of the major lenders.

But there is always an aftermath.

*There is profit in the carcass of debtors*

Another occurrence is fomented by international aid which tangentially, as it is not so apparent, renders legal globalization a reality. Besides imposing legislation, and encouraging the assimilation of legal norms, through the existence of default clauses, international aid from private lenders castrates the lender's sovereign rights and reduces the borrowing nation to a mendicant whose assets are its citizens' pension funds. Public international aid stimulates investment activity by the borrowing sovereignty. With the funds it receives from international institutions, some of it is applied to creating necessary infrastructures. But of course, public aid is not sufficient for all the needs. Once committed to modernizing its infrastructures, by opening its markets to foreign investors and seeking to stimulate its exports, the sovereign borrower procures outside private credit. Capital is raised in foreign markets by emerging countries through the issuance of bonds with the help and technical assistance of international finance advisers. One the one hand, the debtor nation has substantial funds in the form of a public institutional loan. Its other financing needs are from institutional buyers acting on behalf of the private sector.

It will come to pass, as many a story begins, that debtors sometimes default, and when they do, they are sued. If this happens, no matter who is the issuer of the bond, the debtor nation may find itself defending an action in a court, or an arbitration tribunal, far from its own jurisdiction, where other laws are applied.[9] Yet sovereigns have no assets. Their resources are those of their citizens. But it is not national laws which will be applied, but other legal norms being applied in faraway courts. The consequences can be devastating as when hedge funds purchase sovereign debts already in default at a substantial discount and levy on the debtor's assets within a particular jurisdiction.[10] So critical has this problem become that the International Institute of Finance, a leading association of financial institutions, has called for legal strategies to combat the effect of these so-called 'vulture funds'.[11]

Still, what arises from this morass of profit-taking from the corpses of imprudent nations is not the cleverness of the predator, but the subjection of nations to other laws based on a growing body of Western international commercial law. Private international credit becomes a mechanism for enlarging the ambit of the law of credit, the law being the lender's law. International aid and credit, public and private, demand a uniformity of legal standards, otherwise, surely regarding private credit, the bond market would collapse and credit would be eliminated. From this perspective, international aid corrals nations and their merchants into the Western system of jurisprudence, forcing nations to adhere to generally accepted standards of behavior which is technically designated the harmonization of laws.

This becomes even more evident when we consider a topic as obscure but primordial as accounting.

### *Be in harmony with yourself*

The institutional lenders, public or private, do not openly require the borrowers to harmonize their laws with those of the industrialized nations. Yet, this is the result and it can be studied in its micro-economic aspect through the prism of one indispensable, ever-present element. No responsible institution, nor coherent individual, loans money without reviewing the debtor's accounts. Nations have accounts. They are denominated public finances. They may be rudimentary; they may be erroneous; but accounts they are.

Nor do multinationals or entrepreneurs consummate contracts of any significant amount, or form companies with nationals from other countries, without an understanding of the finances of the parties involved which necessitates reviewing the accounts. Contrary to the popular adage, the oldest profession may be accounting. It is difficult to think of many human activities where numbers are absent. From eating to dying, counting quantities seems to occupy the human mind. It should come as no surprise, therefore, that international recognized accounting standards are a prerequisite for any borrower, be it an individual, a corporation, or a nation.

Additionally, development aid and private credit, which is a modern day necessity, has basically emanated from the developed nations, and the US is the world's largest donor.[12] Consequently, it is the US and its commercial *corps* which must be satisfied that 'the accounts are in order'. But for accounts to be acceptable there must be agreed-upon standards. And so, what seems simple enough unravels into that most difficult topic in which agreement is oftentimes elusive: harmonization of standards and laws, in this case accounting standards. We need not yet probe into details. Whether it is accounting or other international criteria serving as a reliable measurement such as the forms of documents, the standard clauses, the operative facts, the rote language, Western international accounting standards, derived in principle from the industrialized nations, vacuums into its orbit all irregularities.

Harmonization, a euphemism for Western legal standardization, begins to dominate the various human endeavors associated with international investment and harmonization applies a uniform model which is another facet of legal globalization.

*Supranational organizations exercise supernatural powers*

Even though the names are familiar, there is in formation a 'new generation'[13] of global institutions, interconnected by a network of experts sharing similar viewpoints, and the public lending industry is a pristine example. Customary organizations in the public eye are performing activities which deviate from their original charter obligations. The functions of the IMF and World Bank have changed. Lending and trade are the pretext for social policies.[14]

Additionally, the WTO is determining global commercial rules which contain legal precepts with significant social impact for the signatories such as open market for goods and services, the recognition of Western intellectual property rights in emerging economies, free capital markets, private investment rights, private competition with public services, and open government procurement bids. Finally, the movement towards legal globalization has now also attained the domain of international human rights with the anxiously awaited creation of the International Criminal Court.[15]

There emerges, therefore, from a study of supranational organizations, a different legal regime[16] removed from legislative and judicial control, but ruling by consensus. We can see clearly a trend towards larger public organizations and multilateral treaties or conventions to which multiple nations adhere. Everyday entities are the IMF, the World Bank, the WTO, the Bank for International Settlements, the Basle Committee on Banking Supervision, the OECD, the United Nations with its diverse organs such as the United Nations Conference on Trade and Development, the diverse regional development banks, the regional trade agreements, the Incoterms promulgated by the International Chamber of Commerce,[17] international insurance and accounting associations, to select the more obvious.

This process is often referred to as 'multilateralization'.[18] From such institutions, emerge rules and standards which create 'soft' law, standards which because of their political source are accepted voluntarily by others for fear of ostracism. Other nations are not obliged to comply with the discipline established, but then banishment from the international monetary community is inevitable. Note that the fear is not becoming a social pariah but rather a financial outcast. One needs not friends but a flow of income is vital.

Driving the creation of supranational organizations is the motive of power[19] which is always ancillary to dominion over capital. The major supranational organizations concerned with lending are controlled by the industrialized nations and the inspiration of many multilateral set of rules lies with the Western theorists from these jurisdictions. This is because the main pillars of international trade consists of multilateral rules under the domain of the WTO, a stable international monetary system under the tutelage of the IMF, and public international lending under the jurisdiction of the World Bank. All of these organizations reflect the predominant economic and social policies of the Western industrialized nations.[20]

Accordingly, if financial institutions in general, wherever situated, are being subjected to a process of globalization of regulations, then surely the consequences for international commercial law are significant. We cannot speak of harmonization of financial laws because it is not an obligatory or legislative process. However, the results are clear. One more sector, but a highly important one, is impelled into the general process of legal globalization. The globalization of laws affecting financial institutions, under the theoretical guidance of the industrialized nations, is achieved through various institutions, removed from any democratic plebiscite. Nevertheless, while there is a democratic deficit, the regulations in question are intended to prevent credit losses, specifically those of depositors. However, whatever political shortcomings such institutions reveal, whose discrete intervention emanates a supernatural atmosphere is fortunately compensated by the rule of 'wise and just bankers'.

Notwithstanding a reticent behavior, enough information is available to grasp the trend and consequences of international financial regulation and the future financial architecture.

### *So it must be*

International aid reveals itself to contain multiple sources of legal globalization. Dispute settlement with its legal precepts, the transfer of legal norms through foreign investment, and involvement with the borrower, legislation imposed on the borrower which frequently introduces legal standards, the subjection of the sovereign to distant national courts, the harmonization of many aspects of aid through banking supervisory organizations, these are some of the immediate, obvious consequences of international aid and credit.

International trade and international aid are indispensable collaborators in the globalization of the law. With the majority of trade flowing from the industrialized countries to the emerging nations, and with international aid following the same route, it does not surprise us that the globalization of the law in course is Western law as molded by modern American jurisprudence under the tutelage of the US, one of the greatest traders of our epoch and also its most significant lender.

## Notes

[1] See home page at of the Bank for International Settlements at <www.bis.org.>.
[2] Ibid and links to this organization.
[3] Richard Henry Tawney, Religion and The Rise of Capitalism, Pelican Books, (Penguin Books Limited), London (1938 Edition).
[4] See the brief, but illuminating article by Alan Beattie, *Investors voice concern over bank's role*, The Financial Times, 25 April 2002, at p. 5.
[5] Ibid.
[6] Currently there are discussion being held as to international public lenders agreeing to accept obligatory moratoriums from defaulting sovereigns, analogous to private companies who can seek court protection from creditors. This would be made possible under an International Bankruptcy Convention.
[7] On 10 October 2002, at p. 34 The Financial Times reported the stock exchange of Sao Paulo, Brazil continued to fall because of persistent fears of the ability of the Central Bank of Brazil to roll over a substantial amount of domestic debt soon to mature.
[8] Reduction of public expenditures, rise in taxes, end to subsidies on essential goods (bread is always the first), removal of tariff barriers, removal to foreign investment restrictions, as examples.
[9] Rosemary Bennett, *Crackdown on 'vulture funds' proposed by finance minister*, The Financial Times, 6 May 2002, at p. 6.
[10] Ibid, describing purchase of Peruvian bonds at a substantial discount and the hedge fund in question sued in a New York court for collection.
[11] Ibid.
[12] Scheherazade Daneshku, *Development aid down to $54.4 bn*, The Financial Times, 14 May 2002, at 6, reporting: 'The US became the world's largest aid donor last year for the first time in almost 10 years ...'.
[13] Manuel Escudero, *The world at a great crossroad*, El Pais, 10 August 2002, at p. 2.
[14] Alan Beattie et al., *IMF picks its way through Latin America minefield*, The Financial Times, 2 August 2002, at p. 5, reporting that after Argentina defaulted in December 2001 on its external debt, the prospect of the IMF becoming involved in containing a generalized monetary in Latin America was a reality.
[15] The treaty establishing the international criminal court was ratified by 60 nations on 11 April 2002 and entered into vigor on 1 July 2002, see Carlos Albino, *Crime e castigo, a partir de agora*, (trans. 'Crime and punishment, as of now') Diario de Noticias, 1 July 2002, at page 16. When it is feared hegemony may be jeopardized, then, even against the astonishment of long-time allies, adherence will be denied. The refusal of the US to ratify

the Rome Treaty establishing the International Criminal Court has placed this liberty-loving nation on the erroneous side of civil rights history.

[16] Supra, n.1.

[17] See <www.iccwbo.org> for an example of incoterms such as EXW (Ex works named place; FOB (Free on Board named port of shipment); and CIF (Cost, Insurance and Freight named port of shipment).

[18] Supra, n. 16.

[19] Ibid.

[20] Ibid.

## Chapter 10

# IMF Debtor Nations are Bribed into Globalization

*Controlling the purse strings, changing the social structure, cloning your culture*

From eating to drinking, from style to cinema, international trademarks and symbols identified with the Western industrial nations invade the daily life of the average citizen. Yet this encompassing culinary and cultural invasion surely pales before other bearers of social change. Commercial global aspirations are leading to common community habits.[1] As the law is but one more cultural expression of the communal spirit, such ambitions are also conducive to legal globalization. Were digesting, imbibing, dressing, and entertaining, the predominant vectors of globalization, its consequences would be more appropriately treated in a nutritional guide or confined to imaginative television advertisements of the happy and well-dressed consumer. Globalization might even pass for an irreversible trend towards obesity draped in a minimum amount of cloth.

However, there are other harbingers of globalization and acculturation less apparent or entertaining, even at times downright disheartening. Their consequences are more profound and lasting, as they put nations into permanent debt, modify the social structure of the borrower, cajole their citizens into becoming free market adepts, and finally subject them to a global system of commercial law under the aegis of the industrialized nations. This is done with a measure of goodwill, under the guise of international aid and credit, two distinct concepts but usually grouped together. By these means, the borrower is lured into the sphere of global commerce. But the road to international commerce and aid is ornamented with economic, social, and legal impositions which are a mirror image of the lender's philosophies. According to the efficient-market hypothesis, 'there are no free lunches' which reminds us 'nor is aid or credit given as tips'. Even if the loan comes at zero interest, it usually has attached conditions of social change imposed by the lender on the borrower.

A reflective moment on our part instigates doubts as to why international public organizations are created to lend money. After all, with war-ravaged exceptions, it is difficult to encounter nations which do not have a local network of banks. On a large scale, assistance is necessary because what aid channels to the nation or national lender is an international currency, such as US dollars, Euros, or Yen. The use of these currencies can only be to import goods or services produced by the countries emitting such currencies. Otherwise there would be no need of having foreign funds. Responding that these currencies assist the development of the infrastructure of the borrower through imported technology, begs the question. We do not know why an infrastructure is dependent on foreign currency for surely every nation has its local contractors and manufacturers, even if using less-sophisticated equipment, and in any event, transposing to an emerging country the latest optic fiber technology is probably an erroneous priority. Thus we can see the difference between aid and credit. Succor is assisting with benevolence; credit is a profit-making transaction, usually formalized in a loan even if masquerading as 'development support'.

If we search for answers disassociated from corruption, a great deal of the stimulation for sovereign borrowing comes from the prodding of public international lenders just as national banks strive to incite credit consumption. The IMF, the World Bank, the socially minded banks, the aid agencies, all tout their willingness to assist the development of the nations of the world. That the nations need to be befriended is undeniable, but by whom raises other questions. Perhaps the lenders see themselves as apostles of their own society and its commercial beliefs. With a dedication bordering on a religious conviction, international aid and credit organizations triumphantly announce the blessings and benefits of their largesse. Of course, for every web page describing the commendable destruction of slums to make way for social housing, there is left unstated that the construction usually needs imported cement. Whatever the reason, for the mercantile spirit can be tempered but it invariably bursts forth as do latent volcanoes, international commerce has spawned multiple aid agencies of all varieties. One of them is the IMF.[2] Due to its high profile, it merits a detailed review of some of its procedures and role as a legislator to all nations.

The IMF came into official existence on 27 December 1945, when 29 signatories signed its Articles of Agreement (its Charter) at a conference held in Bretton Woods, New Hampshire, USA, from 1-22 July 1944. The IMF commenced financial operations on 1 March 1947. Its current membership is 183 countries.[3] Its original function was to secure the fixed rate of exchange existing among the various currencies. Without sufficient reserves, one country could not maintain the fixed parity then in existence, for example, 25 escudos (Portuguese currency) to the US$. If the Portuguese Government did not have sufficient dollar reserves in 1945 it was not possible to meet its international payments. Today, the fixed rate has given way to floating rates and fixed rates have become a minor problem. But more significantly, the IMF now acts as a lender from industrialized nations to the emerging economies who find themselves in a state of poor economic development. The loans are a consequence of a variety of programs including structural adjustment policies (SAPs).[4] Within this technical expression, which sanitizes any implication of a political program, is the idea that the IMF will counsel the borrower as to how to modify its social and economic structure so as to join the global commerce club. Once this is done, or promised, a loan is granted. As one former chief IMF economist commented, 'Lose one function, invent another'.[5] To which we might add, 'The best method for achieving permanent organizational employment is to create a consumer dependency'. This is achieved by inculcating your borrower with the belief that 'markets by and large work well and that governments by and large work badly'[6] and these new markets offer abundant opportunities for the culture manufacturers.

Without question, there are good reasons why nations need aid, although, again, loans are a different concept. Yet loans denominated as aid achieve the same result since the public institutions do not distinguish between them carefully in their marketing, often calling credit 'aid', so the insistence on the distinction fades away in practice. Loans and aid are needed for the problems developing countries face which include deflation, a high unemployment rate, depreciation of national currency, inflation, erosion of real income, short-term cash-flow crunch, public sector wage increase, capital flight, and a growing public deficit. To confront these social dramas, countries need money. Emissions of the local currency could be increased, but this might debase the currency and in any event it does not generate foreign currency. Hard currency is needed to import necessary equipment to augment production. If the nation cannot product its own food requirement, hard currency is needed to import basic necessities. Without export markets, our emerging economy has to request either aid or an international loan.

Although international aid is available from various sources, the vast sums of money channeled to nations are dispensed by the IMF in the form of loans and require approval through voting. The founding nations believed that the IMF would function most efficiently and its decisions would be made more responsibly by relating members' voting power directly to the amount of money they deposited with the institution through their quota subscription. Those who contribute most to the IMF are therefore given the strongest voice in determining its policies. The US, the largest quota holder, now has more than 265,000 votes, or about 17.5 percent of the total. Between the US and the EU there is a majority of votes although these countries constitute a minority in terms of number of countries. The IMF has no reticence about its policy considerations.

> ... [B]efore the IMF releases any money from the pool, the member must demonstrate how it intends to solve its payments problem so that it can repay the IMF within its normal repayment period of three to five years (which in certain cases can be extended up to ten years). The logic behind these requirements is simple. A country with a payments problem is spending more than it is taking in. Unless economic reform takes place, it will continue to spend more than it takes in.[7]

Lending therefore requires economic reform. Since the borrower already has national policies in place, reform must mean casting them aside, or modifying them, for other philosophies. The loan is an extension of credit in exchange for various structural changes. However, separating social modifications from economic changes becomes impossible to discern. Driven by the fear of not belonging to the global community, coupled with the urgency in obtaining funds from the IMF, sovereign behavior is reminiscent of a breadline.[8] Incontestably, the notion of sovereignty, the underpin of international law, is undergoing change.[9] For countries not brandishing the investment benefits of US dollars, Euros, or Yen, sovereignty becomes an euphemism for a national language, local cuisine, social benefits (hopefully), and a few scattered tourist attractions. Waterfalls are particularly appreciated. The exigencies of international commerce cannot accept rigid concepts of sovereignty. During the capital flight crisis in Argentina, one of the conditions of the IMF for further funds was the alteration of a law previously enacted to prevent banking frauds and make them punishable as a crime.

While at first thought the law appears reasonable, the IMF wanted its revocation as a condition for further financing. Possibly the IMF did not want to see the law applied to international banks which are dominant in Argentina. However, the law was popular with various social classes as a means of protection against governments which improperly use the funds of the electorate. After a fierce debate in both chambers of the Argentine Parliament, the revocation of the law was passed by one vote in the Senate but only after the President of Argentina threatened to resign.[10]

Normally, the IMF at some point sends a mission to a country to determine the structural problems confronting the potential borrower. This is referred to as an Article IV consultation mission. In other words, first the IMF looks to see the economic and social structure of its borrower; recommendations are made and published, and eventually a letter of intent is sent to the IMF. It does not need great imagination to foresee that the letter of intent and the mission report complement one another.

As an example, although no letter of intent is yet published, the IMF Slovak Republic 2002 Mission[11] contains the following recommendations:

> 18. Promoting real convergence to EU living standards requires a concerted implementation of reforms to increase productivity in Slovakia. In addition to spending fiscal structural reforms that need to be accelerated for fiscal consolidation (primarily health and pension reforms), the government should focus on enhancing labor and enterprise flexibility, and strengthening further the financial sector …

By labor reforms is meant ease of hiring and firing; enterprise adaptability means bringing commercial law into harmony with Western legal principles; and improving the financial sector obviously means freedom of capital movement. Thus is the social structure molded by virtue of a forthcoming loan. Familiarity with IMF procedures leads to the conclusion that economic development and the availability of funds is dependent on host countries introducing specified social legislation approaching in spirit neoliberal market philosophies. With funds made available, many of the recipient countries will naturally be disposed to encourage foreign direct investment.[12]

A further practical grasp on the implications of the activities of the IMF and its social policies can be seen through the typical letters of intent sent by prospective borrowers to the IMF. They are fairly similar in content and they are like court pleas before the King by mendicants. While the most recent letters of intent are reviewed, they are usually preceded by earlier letters of intent.[13] The following is an edited letter of intent of the government of Armenia sent on 26 April 2001 to the IMF, but only with reference to some of the macroeconomic policies.

The letters usually begin the same way:

> Managing Director
> International Monetary Fund
> Washington, DC 20431
>
> Dear Mr … :
>
> We are committed to moving ahead with an ambitious and far-reaching macroeconomic and structural reform program …

Eventually, after recitation of various anticipated reforms, there is set forth the macroeconomic modifications:

> Armenia maintains a liberal trading system with no [sic] nontariff barriers (for trade protection purposes) and no export taxes. Most imports enter the country duty-free, while goods subject to import duties are assessed a uniform 10 percent import duty. The payments system is also very liberal with no current account restrictions and only a few minor capital account restrictions (most of which are imposed for prudential reasons). The government will maintain this liberal trade and payments system, which has served Armenia well, and strive to integrate further the Armenian economy into the world economy. In the very near future the government expects to adopt the remaining regulatory and legal requirements for WTO admission with the hope of completing Armenia's accession to the WTO in 2001. Furthermore, the government will redouble its efforts to attract foreign direct investment through a strengthened public relations campaign abroad and an improved business environment at home.

This commitment to a market economy is reflected in the Government of Armenia signing bits, for example, with the US[14] whereby any dispute between a foreign investor and the Government of Armenia is obliged to be submitted to international arbitration. There is thus constructed a self-contained legal system of market policies and international arbitration under the auspices of the authorities contained in the US-Armenian bilateral investment treaty. It is not an exaggeration to claim that the IMF, through its lending facilities, has induced the Government of Armenia into the wave of legal globalization, in this case, Western commercial law.

As the IMF loans are not given without a declaration of adherence to Western market values, this is tantamount to requesting allegiance to Western commercial law. If you, the Government of Armenia, intend to carry out privatization programs, inviting foreign investment, then of course, you, the Government of Armenia, are acknowledging the principle of private property which must have a legal foundation. Private property issues will be decided before an international arbitration tribunal in accordance with Western law precepts. It could not be otherwise. Sometimes, it is not necessary to seek the link between IMF loans and bits. The foreign investment law of the borrower is explicit. Thus, we can see a typical letter of intent dated 22 February 2000 from the Government of Lithuania to the IMF as the precondition for a loan.

After the usual salutations to the Director of the IMF, the Government of Lithuania declares its free market convictions:[15]

> The overarching objective of Lithuania's economic policies is to lay the basis for sustained economic growth through macroeconomic stabilization and a continuation of the transition to a fully functioning market economy … [The Government of Lithuania intends to accomplish this through] … a broad-ranging structural reform program aimed at establishing a market-based economy has been carried out, including privatization, legal reforms, price deregulation, trade liberalization, and bank restructuring … [Lithuania will implement] … (i) a freeze of the wage bill of the state government and extra-budgetary funds (which should have an important signaling effect to the private sector); (ii) an elimination of civil service bonus payments; (iii) a partial hiring freeze in the civil service; (iv) a reduction in subsidies (e.g., abolition of the VAT reimbursement on energy consumption combined with a targeted subsidy for poor households, and cuts in agricultural and transport subsidies); (v) a cut-back in public investment not related to Lithuania's obligations to international financial institutions; (vi) a reduction in purchases of non-essential goods and services; (vii) a streamlining of state government institutions and extra-budgetary funds; and (viii) a postponement of restitution payments for land and houses.

However, in contrast to Armenia, Lithuania need not rely on a bit to ensure its steady march towards embracing Western commercial law concepts.

Pursuant to its foreign investment law:[16]

> In case of investment disputes, foreign investors also have the right to apply to the International Centre for settlement of investment disputes since Lithuania is a member of the 18 March 1965 Washington Convention 'On the Settlement of Investment Disputes between States and Nationals of other States.'

Happily foreigner investors need not determine if their country of origin has signed a bilateral investment treaty with Lithuania. Their investment rights are protected by international arbitration. There is no requirement of any knowledge of Lithuanian law. Nor is any needed. It will never be applied. Examples as to the desired reforms can be multiplied. Thus in various letters of intent we find following the statements from the loan-seeking governments:[17]

> The **Malagasy** government began to implement market-oriented reforms in 1994. It liberalized the exchange, trade, and price systems;

eliminated restrictions in key economic sectors, such as petroleum, food, and transportation...; Or:

Since 1985, **Bolivia** has achieved a considerable degree of macroeconomic stability, and the steadfast implementation of structural reforms has helped remove most of the distortions that adversely affected the economy in the early 1980s. This strategy has been anchored by a strong fiscal policy, designed to avoid central bank financing of the combined public sector, and a comprehensive program of structural reforms aimed at dismantling the extensive state intervention in economic activity that had been built prior to 1985.

**Bulgaria** promises to liberalize trade and restore lands; **Chad** will establish an arbitration tribunal and develop the private sector; **Kazakhstan** will admit private ownership of land and look towards 'a high sustained private sector-led growth'.

The information is all posted on the web pages of the IMF.[18] The descriptions herein given have been shortened dramatically to economize space. In summary, an IMF loan is not only an commercial operation but a substantial reformulation of the social and economic policies of various countries. From **Albania** to **Zimbabwe**, a total of 70 letters of intent were signed with the IMF during the period 1999 to approximately March, 2000,[19] all containing conditions similar to the ones summarized above.

IMF loans, as do all public institutional grants, cause a surrender of sovereignty in the era of globalization. Yet what replaces national determinism are the legal precepts of the lenders destined to foment industrial growth. Everything remains in place. The confluence of corruption, an unreliable judicial system, elitism, deflation, dissociation of the majority from fertile lands, inaccessibility to education or health not to mention the tragedies of female serfdom and child exploitation.

Instead of requesting letters of intent from borrowers concerning favorable investment laws, the borrowers should be required to take serious steps towards democracy or at least something akin to it. Otherwise, IMF loans, as others, will only promote the opening of bank accounts in Switzerland.

### *The modern capitulation of sovereign states*[20]

The policies of the IMF are but an historical continuation of a long process of international relations which once bore the designation of 'capitulation'.[21] The term of war employed is apt. If sovereignty is akin to absolute power over all subjects within the territory, then a surrender of even partial jurisdiction entails a capitulation before either a powerful idea or entity.

Today, it is submission to both, the notion of joining the global, commercial society and the realization that without yielding up some aspects of sovereignty, commercial and eventually social isolation from the industrialized nations will be the realized threat. As such, IMF loans are only the modern version of capitulation inserted within a global movement towards the hegemony of Western international commercial law.

In the early nineteenth and twenty centuries, the US and European nations extracted capitulations from regions such as the Ottoman Empire,[22] Japan and China.[23] Essentially, the capital-exporting countries and their merchants did not want to be subject to the court jurisdiction of the non-Western nations and their laws. Those sovereign states which capitulated to this demand received the benefit of more trade from the capital-exporting countries. Much can be written about the history of capitulations and it superficially appears that capitulations and present day IMF loans have little in common. This is not true.

Behind the theory of capitulations and our current IMF loans are similar ideas about the nature of law. SAPs, as were capitulations, permit legal globalization to foment more trade and development. What occurs is not a negotiated harmonization of laws, between the industrialized nations and the emerging economy, but the offer of a loan in exchange for structural social changes. Calling them structural adjustment policies is a mere euphemism. Rather than a sincere compromise on social and legal elements, the lender, the IMF, imposes its philosophic theories on the borrower. Legal globalization thus becomes the historic capitulation extended beyond its original parameters.

Capitulation was originally limited to the sovereign, host nation agreeing to restrict its judicial powers on foreigners doing business. This was perhaps a modest concession to obtain much-needed foreign capital. SAPs reach beyond judicial boundaries. Political, economic, and legal modifications are promised to be implemented in return for IMF funds. This process reveals how legal ideas from one social community become extended in an ever-increasing social space. In the world of international commerce, the law is only an instrument of mercantile relationships, their formation, the rights and obligations of the participants, and their dissolution. The IMF SAPs present the borrowers with a system of law which will permit the traders of the lenders to comfortably invest and trade with the lender.

### *IMF governance and Western ideologies*

By tradition, the managing director of the IMF is European and the President of the World Bank is American.[24] Of course, one managing director, no matter how charismatic, is unlikely to enforce decisions without the support of the other IMF members. Although the IMF is composed of countries, each nation has a spokesman. For the IMF, it is the finance ministers and the central bank governors who represent their sovereigns.

What cause us concern, as social investigators, are the undeclared policy objectives of the IMF. An acute example is the massive failure of Baninter, a Dominican Republic bank. On 16 May 2003, The *New York Times* reported a US$2.2 billion bank shortfall had shaken the Dominican economy. Apparently Baninter kept two sets of books since 1989, and in this way it was possible to conceal a massive fraud. The bank's failure tabulated to 15 per cent of the Dominican gross domestic product which was 80 per cent of the government's annual budget. Fifteen government and bank officials were arrested, including the

Baninter president while the government seized 76 radio stations, four television stations, and the nation's leading newspaper.[25]

On 4 June 2003, the US Treasury announced it had no plans to loan any money to the Dominican Republic nor did it know of any request to the IMF.[26] Thereafter on 29 August 2003, the IMF announced it approved a $600 million dollar two year emergency loan to the Dominican Republic because of Baninter's failure.[27] Normally loans to countries are preceded by a letter of intent as to the macro-economic policies to be enacted. A search of the IMF web site only reveals a letter of intent concerning the Dominican Republic dated 22 October 1998[28] and there the causes were damages provoked by a hurricane. Of course, it is entirely possible, that the letter of intent, if one exists, was not published for an administrative reason.

Nevertheless, between May and August, it would appear a policy decision was taken at the IMF. A fortuitous news item reveals to us that on 8 July 2003, Scotiabank[29] entered into an agreement with the financial authorities of the Dominican Republic to purchase 35 branches of the defunct Baninter, as well as various other assets such as credit cards, personal, and commercial loans. Although the terms of purchase are not revealed, Scotiabank did announce the purchase would make it the fifth largest bank in the Dominican Republic.

Scotiabank is a mammoth Canadian premier financial institution. It is the fourth largest Canadian bank in terms of market capitalization. The main markets for financial operations are Canada, the US, and Western Europe. The bank has assets close to $300 billion.[30] Scotiabank serves over 10,000,000 customers and has operations in 50 countries employing approximately 48,000 employees. In 2002, its reported consolidated income was $1,797 million. From these few simple facts, the network of alliances between Scotiabank and international financial institutions is without question and omnipresent. We do not know if Scotiabank had any exchange of confidences with the IMF. But the coincidence leads us to infer what has been confirmed by another source:[31] decisions within the IMF are conducted along political objectives serving the international financial community. Perhaps not in this case, but, then, even if true, the salvation of depositor accounts and posts of employment merits our applause.

In general, the Baninter case is a recurrent example — the locals rob the national banks; the international financial community may or may not see a viable commercial opportunity; the international public institutions ensure the commercial venture has a working hypothesis; public institutions loan money to the government of the locale. Such a philosophy does not detract from the social benefits conferred in the case in question — the stabilization of the Dominican Republic banking system. However, it also emphasizes the long-arm of the neo-liberal market policies of the IMF which is further supported by the insistence on nations enacting laws which support this political vision. From the viewpoint of one who has worked closely with the IMF, the shift in the agenda of this international financial institution has been '... from serving global economic interests to serving the interests of global *finance*'.[32]

Whether or not we are confronting the situation of a 'bail-in' versus a 'bailout', that is the IMF was insisting on a private sector institution assuming the control of a failed bank before a loan would be committed, are enigmas only revealed within the financial circles concerned. What is clear is a consonance: promised assumption of control by Scotiabank followed by confirmation of a loan to the government.

There are earlier examples of the posture of the IMF towards ensuring the viability of banking systems erected on market fundamentalism. In February, 1999, the publication *Business in Thailand*[33] announced the government of Indonesia was injecting $477 million into twelve banks to revive the 'ailing financial sector' and which was intended to rescue the crippled banking sector.

In a letter dated 16 March 1999 to the IMF, the government of Indonesia declared:

> Banking reforms have entered a decisive stage. The resolution strategy has been elaborated, and implementation is moving ahead, in all the four major areas: (i) state bank resolution; (ii) private bank recapitalization; (iii) resolution of banks under ... control; and (iv) improvement of the legal, regulatory, and supervisory framework ...

On 25 March 1999, the IMF issued the following statement concerning Indonesia:

> Stanley Fischer, First Deputy Managing Director of the International Monetary Fund (IMF) said: 'I am pleased to announce that, in support of government's economic program, the IMF's Executive Board today approved the completion of the fourth review under the Extended Fund Facility (EFF), ... and release of the next SDR 337 million (about US$460 million) credit tranche ...'

The momentary solvency of Indonesia's banking system is stabilized by further advances under a previous program with Indonesia and the export of Western laws and their principles is confirmed by the letter of intent of the Indonesian government. Rebuilding a national banking system with the assistance of the IMF entails more than just injections of capital. It requires the adoption of legal banking principles as understood and sanctioned by the IMF. Both as regards Baninter and the IMF loan to Indonesian, we are dealing with what has been aptly denominated 'Epistemic Communities of Actors'.[34]

By this description our authors mean 'The epistemic community that steers financial regulation is a community of the North. Its most influential members are largely English-speaking. The ideas of this community now dominate the financial regulation of all states'.[35] Perhaps the most graphic revelation of the governance policies of the IMF are again to be found in our authors just cited, when, in support of their affirmation that the '... IMF has an explicit policy of fostering a public finance epistemic community', they quote from the IMF:[36]

> The idea is to develop a 'club spirit' among neighbors to encourage one another to pursue sound policies.[37]

By serving market-orientated economic interests under the dominion of the US and promoting global finance structures through its infiltration by the Wall Street lobbyists,[38] the IMF has established a political program without any legislative approval and a legal curriculum without an educational license. But whatever our social convictions, the general trends are unequivocal. Through policy implementations, the IMF, and other supranational organizations, reinforces the global spread of Western law just as effectively as bond default clauses requiring the application of New York law circulate in the international bond market.

## Notes

[1] John Micklethwait et al., The Financial Times, 27/28 May 2000.
[2] All information concerning the IMF has been obtained through the official web site <www.imf.org>as well as various links contained therein as of 10 May 2002. For a critical insider's view of the workings of the IMF, see Joseph Stiglitz, *Globalization and Its Discontents*, Penguin Books (2002).
[3] Ibid.
[4] See the home page of the IMF, supra, n. 2, which contains links to a variety of published papers on structural adjustment policies.
[5] O Publico, 21 February 2000, (Portuguese daily newspaper) Alan Waters, former chief economist of the IMF.
[6] Joseph Stiglitz, *Globalization and Its Discontents*, Penguin Books (2002) at p. 196.
[7] Supra, n. 2.
[8] Jan Kregel, *The Strong Arm of the IMF,* The Sunday Boston Globe, 18 January 1998, <www.levy.org/whatsnew/topic/strongoped.html>, accessed 12 May 2002.
[9] Mary C. Tsai, *Globalization and Conditionality: Two Sides of the Sovereignty Coin*, 31 Law & Pol'y Int'l Bus 1317 (2000).
[10] Thomas Catán, *Argentina urges IMF to hurry*, The Financial Times, 1-2 June 2002, at page 4.
[11] Reported on the home page of the IMF, supra, n. 2.
[12] As an example, Moldova has signed bits with 28 countries, including: the United States, Turkey, Poland, Germany, Romania, China, Switzerland, Ukraine, Uzbekistan, the Netherlands, Belgium, Luxembourg, Finland, Kuwait, Iran, Hungary, Bulgaria, Great Britain, Israel, France, Italy, Georgia, and Azerbaijan, www.moldova.org/business02>, accessed 22 May 02.
[13] From 29 September 1999 to 26 December 2001, Cambodia issued several letters of intent, see home page of IMF, supra, fn. 2, for links to Cambodia.
[14] For details, <www.bisnis.doc.gov/bisnis/country/000723legfrmwkarm.htm>, accessed 22 May 2002.
[15] Available on the IMF web site, supra, n. 2.
[16] The complete text is available at <www.lda.lt/investment law.foreigninvestment>, accessed 22 May 2002.
[17] All letters of intent can be seen on the IMF web site, supra, n. 2, under the country index.
[18] Ibid.
[19] Ibid.
[20] David P. Fidler, *A Kinder, Gentler System of Capitulations? International law, Structural Adjustment Policies and The Standards of Liberal, Globalized Civilization*, 35 Tex. Int'l L. J. 387 (2000). I am indebted to Prof. Fidler for his historical review of the theory concerning about capitulation. By his article, I have been able to think about globalization as an historical process with a longer past than I had imagined.
[21] Ibid, supra, n. 20.

[22] Modern Turkey is not as extensive as the ancient Ottoman Empire but the two terms are often used interchangeably.
[23] Fidler, surpa, n. 20.
[24] Stiglitz, supra, n. 6, at p. 19.
[25] www.americas.org/news/nir/20030529_massive_bank_fraud.asp, accessed 2 September 2003.
[26] <www.forbes.com/home_europe/newswire/2003/06/04/rtr9912047>, accessed 03 September 2003.
[27] Supra, n. 2, links to the Dominican Republic.
[28] Ibid.
[29] All information concerning Scotiabank can be found at <www.scotiabank.com>, accessed 5 September 2003.
[30] It is presumed the published 2002 annual report of Scotiabank is reported in Canadian dollars.
[31] Supra, n. 6, at p. 19.
[32] Supra, n. 6, at p. 195.
[33] <www.businessinthailandmag.com/archive/feb99>, accessed 5 September 2003.
[34] John Braithwaite and Peter Drahos, *Global Business Regulation*, Cambridge University Press (2000) at p. 123.
[35] Ibid.
[36] Ibid, at p. 124.
[37] Ibid, at p. 124 quoting IMF Managing Director Camdessus, IMF Survey, 6 October 1997, 294.
[38] Supra, n. 6, at p. 19.

## Chapter 11

# The World Bank is Becoming the World Justice Foundation

*It is not only money being dispensed*

Without doubt 'World Bank' is an appropriate name but bureaucratically misleading. Banks loan money but this particular public law international bank also counsels good governance, recommends clean government, suggests social safety nets and programs, instructs on knowledge transfer, and ponders cultural issues, including sewerage and roads. From its name, we might be lured into thinking we are describing a foundation established by one of the Digital Era-New Economy tycoons. However, it is the World Bank Group[1] (World Bank) which is figuratively running all over the world. In an apostolic spirit, funds are dispersed but so is much advice, particularly about judicial and legal reforms. Development apparently can not proceed unless there is transmitted from the lenders a bundle, not only of money, but a variety of reforms.

Consistent with the social logic of institutions, the World Bank's meritorious aim of contributing towards a more just international economic order is haplessly tainted by its interpretation of social justice. Blemished, because hierarchical organizations tend to replicate their creeds, otherwise designated as bureaucratic cloning. The World Bank, while extending a needed financial arm, does not hesitate to proffer morality. And since few of us undertake a systematic study of universal, social norms, the mores articulated are naturally a reflection of our own Western heritage. Perhaps the unintended slight to other cultures is not to be dramatized. Understandably, laws are merely moral messages, dispensed with a pat on the head with one hand as the other extends a check. If the recipient fails to become an acolyte, a law suit will not result. With time, the heretics will learn, particularly when the term of the loan matures and a renewal is sought. Yet, not all the World Bank proposes warrants economic cynicism. Zealotry is easily confounded with evangelism and the humanistic aims of the World Bank are not to be minimized.

Established in 1944, the World Bank is an important source of development assistance. In fiscal year 2001, the Bank provided US$17.3 billion in loans to various countries. It has programs in more than 100 economies. Each year an average of a billion dollars is committed to new loans. Admirably, it also contributes to combating the plague of HIV/AIDS with sums approaching two billion dollars.[2]

Not only is money arranged, for the World Bank also has ideas similar in creed to the IMF. Poverty is a lack of funds, but it is also an outcome of a faulty social and economic structure. In consonance with other epics and religious fervor, pauperism is not only about money supply. A profound ethical transformation of the mendicant is warranted. There is an *opus magnum* to be read and studied and then repeated in the loan application wherein the borrower indicates what economic and social reforms it will undertake. At least such is the viewpoint of the World Bank and its moral ally, the IMF. However, the organization of the World Bank is emphatically not dictatorial. With all its clients, the Bank is in close contact with government agencies, non-governmental organizations, government bureaus, civil organizations, and multiple vectors of the private sector. An attempt is made to hear the various viewpoints prevailing in a nation.

Unquestionably, the Board of Governors and staff of the World Bank are relentless in their pursuit of humanitarian objectives. Yet human justice is as elusive as a just loan. Still, undaunted by the challenges, understandably convinced of the need for development programs which address social injustices, the loans and advice of the World Bank are frequently accompanied by almost mandatory legal reforms. A loan application becomes a monograph on intended and promised economic and social reforms. This is to be expected for the advisers of the World Bank know well that an economic system is the substratum of visible social aspects, such as the ownership of assets, income distribution, citizen civic participation, protection of civil liberties, access to law, assurances of a just and impartial judicial system.

The orientation of the World Bank is manifest when we learn that the shareholders number more than 180 member countries whose views and interests are represented by a Board of Governors and a Washington-based Board of Directors. The decision-making power in the World Bank falls to the shareholders, the largest being the US. Through the voting system, there is clearly a dominance of the World Bank by Western nations, in particular the US.[3] For this reason, the World Bank's President is by tradition a national of the largest shareholder, the US.[4] Elected for a five-year renewable term, the President sits on the Board of Executive Directors and is responsible for the administrative management of the World Bank.

However, the World Bank is not a singular organization, but a group, comprising five entities. There is the International Bank for Reconstruction and Development (IBRD), which provides loans and development assistance to middle-income countries and creditworthy poorer countries near market rates. This is to be contrasted with the International Development Agency which provides long-term loans below or at zero interest to the poorest of the developing countries. With a different objective, there is the International Finance Corporation (IFC)[5] which promotes private sector investment, both foreign and domestic, in developing member countries. The IFC offers private sector advisory services to nations seeking to attract foreign investment. For this to be a reality, the IFC, in more then 100 countries, is advising on appropriate conditions for business operations, basic business law, and policies for foreign direct investment, among other topics.[6]

Complementary to the IFC, is the Multilateral Investment Guarantee Agency (MIGA). Foreign direct investment is critical to emerging economies. MIGA promotes foreign direct investment by issuing guarantees against political risk through insurance to investors and lenders. However, for the host country to be eligible for such a guarantee it must be a signatory to the MIGA Convention.[7] Finally, the World Bank group includes The International Centre for Settlement of Investment Disputes (ICSID)[8] whose importance is primordial in the adjudication of disputes under NAFTA and bits. The ICSID provides facilities for the settlement of disputes by conciliation or arbitration of investment disputes between foreign investors and their host countries.

*A World Bank dilemma: charter mandate versus human rights.*

The articles of agreement (charter) of the IBRD, the principal lending institution of the World Bank, are eminently clear.[9] The IBRD will ensure the loans are for reasons of economics and efficiency. Political or non-economic considerations are to be disregarded. The Bank and its officers are not to interfere in the political affairs of any member. Only economic considerations are relevant. Well, this seems quite straightforward. And now begins the confusion or perhaps corrective justice, depending on your ethics. The World Bank has no intention of adhering to its charter.

For decades following the financial crises of the 1980s, the World Bank's loan policies were heavily influenced by the principle of 'conditionality'.[10] This was the requirement by the World Bank that sovereign borrowers undertake financial reforms including correction of inflation, public deficits, liberalization of foreign commerce, and other topics such as land and tax reforms. Concomitant with this philosophy was the academic theory of 'modernization' which saw the developing countries as lagging behind in progress.[11] It was necessary for emerging nations to adapt to Western-style legal institutions.[12] Lawyers and economists working with international public organizations provided assistance and advice on the drafting of laws, constitutions, and the indispensable economic free-market models. Such efforts struck at the heart of the macro-social structure of the sovereign nation and of course altered the contents and purposes of national laws.

Today, the World Bank is an advocate of a comprehensive development framework.[13] Its published declaration of social principles leaves no room for doubt. All sectors of the borrower's society must be heard. Development is not only macro-alterations but also the details of the smaller social units. Accordingly, the World Bank has a 'holistic' approach to development in countries requiring its funds. But the World Bank is not relying on a statement of objectives. It intends to 'ensure the principles are put into practice'. From the viewpoint of the World Bank: 'Development is therefore about transforming whole societies'.

Moving beyond the financing of projects, the World Bank addresses broader issues such as 'human and social development, governance, and institutions.' This is translated by the World Bank into an agenda of 'good and clean government, an effective legal and justice system, a supervised financial system, and a social safety net and social programs'. Trade, labor conditions, gender discrimination, all form part of an inseparable whole and with bureaucratic enthusiasm the World Bank has launched its comprehensive development framework in over 11 countries, including nations as different as Bolivia and Ethiopia.

The World Bank, through its public communications, displays its determination to ensure economic development is accompanied by respect for the inherent rights of humanity. It is therefore entirely logical that the World Bank invokes with frequency the Universal Declaration of Human Rights,[14] a splendid document which consecrates popular democracy and recites exactly what are the inalienable rights of humanity. There are certain standards of moral conduct which are inherent to the status of a social being, such as the right to a life of dignity, freedom from serfdom even if denominated 'free labor', affordable housing, accessible education and health services, all subsumed in the expression 'respect for the human condition'. Such considerations reflect the highest aspirations of woman-mankind. Without question, were it capable of doing so, the World Bank would be remiss to concede loans without evaluating the performance of the borrower against the moral code of the Universal Declaration of Human Rights.

Thus, the dilemma of the World Bank. The clear economic dictates conferred by the World Bank charter are in collision with its moralistic perceptions. Instructed by its charter not to intervene in the affairs of the sovereign nation, the World Bank nevertheless reacts with apprehension, if not downright condemnation, of political practices in many of the borrowers' countries. So the ethical lending spirit becomes partially tainted by economics and charter dictates, attempts to remain partially virtuous, but consistency is lost from the experience understandably earned through decades of dealing with loans, governments, some honest, many corrupt, loans whose funds never trickle down to the citizenry of the borrower. The shanty towns grow larger. The foreign bank accounts swell from pilfered funds whose source the foreign bank feigns ignorance.

For the moment, the World Bank publicly has chosen the path of morality in contravention of its own articles and even in violation of the UN Charter which makes clear that each nation stands as a sovereign equal to the other. From the ethical vantage of the World Bank, sovereignty is missing a qualifying adjective. It is not naked sovereignty which must be respected, and stand equal, but a humane sovereignty. Naturally, concepts such as 'humane', 'just', 'benign', or even 'compassionate', compel us to take on judicial robes. To determine the content of such words we must rely on our own ethical standards and hence, once again, we judge others through the vision of a Western ethos. Naturally, the compassion felt by the staff of the World Bank for the plight of the masses can only encounter a solution in the spread of more Western ideas and Western laws. There is no escape from the influence of our own culture and obligating others to adhere if they wish our assistance. It is as natural as human nature.

### *With these laws, I thee wed*

The World Bank is clearly in favor of affirmative legal and judicial reform in the countries where it lends money:[15]

> The central mission of the World Bank is the alleviation of poverty, defined not only as a lack of resources, but as a sense of powerlessness and the absence of basic security as well. The latter two dimensions of poverty in particular are exacerbated when a nation's legal institutions perform poorly and the rule of law is weak or nonexistent. While the elite can often use wealth or connections to cushion themselves from the impact of a poorly performing legal system, these alternatives are not open to the poor. They are the ones most vulnerable when the rule of law is absent.

The World Bank underscores the critical importance of an effective legal and judicial system:[16]

> Without the protection of human and property rights, and a comprehensive framework of laws, no equitable development is possible. A government must ensure that it has an effective system of property, contract, labor, bankruptcy, commercial codes, personal rights laws and other elements of a comprehensive legal system that is effectively, impartially and cleanly administered by a well-functioning, impartial and honest judicial and legal system.
>
> Although legal reform efforts often involve institutional restructuring, rewriting old laws and drafting new ones remains a necessary component of most legal reform projects. Moreover, many development projects that do not constitute legal reform per se, such as administrative reforms, infrastructure projects, environmental initiatives, nonetheless require changes in the substantive law. Yet even in stable, democratic countries, creating sound laws and regulations is a challenge. In developing and transitioning countries, political interference, a lack of experience and resources, and the constraints imposed by weak enforcement agencies often make the job of law drafting even harder.

Surging as a natural conviction, or because lenders see borrowers as their mirror social counterparts, if not in fact then soon to be, credit given requires a moral acknowledgement of gratitude from the borrower and a declaration of faith. Varied are the proffered reasons, still the World Bank Group admist its various programs gives a substantial emphasis to its legal reform policies and it is the results which are of importance, not the motivations. In this singular approach, the World Bank plays a prominent role in divulging Western law concepts across commercial frontiers and is a significant force in fostering world-wide legal reform.[17] This initiative is not a result of idealistic concerns about concepts of justice.

They surely exist, but there are practical consequences for such preoccupations. The World Bank sees itself as responsible for harmonizing laws so that the foreign merchants and traders will be encouraged to invest internationally under a structured regime of laws.[18] It is not surprising, consequently, that the World Bank has embarked on a number of legal and judicial reform projects.[19] Extracting a few highlights: regarding Albania, the project will address the judicial/legal system; the

Argentinean project will establish alternate dispute resolution mechanisms; concerning Armenia, the objective will be to establish an effective, efficient, and independent judiciary, improve court administration, train judges and court personnel, as well as support the Ministry of Justice in enforcing court decisions.

For Azerbaijan the project includes strengthening the legal and regulatory framework and strengthen its capacity to provide efficient and effective dispute resolution; in Bolivia the project will render assistance to Judiciary for the implementation of the judicial career, including implementation of appropriate procedures for personnel recruitment, performance incentives, and periodic evaluation; Brazil will be trained in improving human resource management while the Dominican Republic will undergo a comprehensive judicial reform program. Judicial strengthening procedures will be taught in El Salvador, Guinea, Mexico, Morocco, Philippines, Sierra Leone, Sri Lanka, Thailand, Trinidad and Tobago, Ukraine, and Yemen.

The content and details of these programs are only meaningful within the details of the local culture but such disclosure is not presently necessary. What is of relevance is whether the World Bank is merely assisting foreign communities in making their local legal cultural accessible and efficient or if the World Bank is exporting to other nations a legal ethnocentric perspective. For the moment, the practice is that Western law principles exported by the World Bank are displacing local customs.[20]

The following anecdote is not attributed to the World Bank but to other centers of law reform assistance. What could be more wry then the description of a young Mongolian official who gratefully accepts a stack of documents concerning US securities laws from American experts in Ulan Batar on a short visit. After the group departs, the Mongolian explains that the texts are of dubious use in Mongolia but the other, blank side of the texts will help mitigate a shortage of quality paper.[21] The reasons for indoctrination are surely obvious. Legal systems represent the power structure at any one given epoch. Lawyers and development specialists reproduce the beliefs of their organizations.[22] They fly around the world bringing with them drafts of laws word for word to be delivered to their rural colleagues who need not securities laws but more access to local courts free from corruption.[23]

With even more nonchalance, a prestigious Western law scholar is reported to have assisted a post-communist Eastern European nation draft its new constitution by delivering a complete manuscript entitled 'Constitution of …' which in essence was a form book on Western economic freedom, rights, democratic representation and restriction on government powers. The sovereign beneficiary only had to insert the name of its country and proclaim the contents the 'Constitution of the Republic of …'.[24] No further consultations were possible since our academic was on a plane visiting another nation with his constitutional form book.

More efficiency, and time gained, could have been achieved if our mandarin had also added a further parenthetical instruction but in various languages, much like the operating manuals for electronic equipment, such as 'insert the name of your country'. While these two examples are not intended to impeach the impressive services rendered by the World Bank, in general its dedication to promoting law reform coupled with foreign aid and foreign investment development has an pervading, obvious practical consequence: the proselytism of Western, and more specifically, American law.

*New York, New York, is my town, right where the IFC wants to be*

Created in 1956, the other powerful affiliate of the World Bank, the IFC promotes foreign investment and development by investing in private enterprises.[25] Unlike the IBRD, its main instrument of assistance is by investment, not loans. Through its years of experience the IFC has counseled predominantly in the area of financial services and privatization. IFC has 175 member countries, which collectively determine its policies and approve investments. To join IFC, a country must first be a member of the IBRD. The members vote in proportion to the number of shares held and the Western countries predominate by a substantial majority.[26] The President of the World Bank Group also serves as IFC's president.

Although IFC coordinates its activities in areas with the other institutions in the World Bank, IFC generally operates independently and is legally and financially autonomous with its own Articles of Agreement, share capital, management and staff.

Article 1 of the IFC (Corporation) charter emphasizes its supplementary role:[27]

> The purpose of the Corporation is to further economic development by encouraging the growth of productive private enterprise in member countries, particularly in the less developed areas, thus supplementing the activities of the International Bank for Reconstruction and Development ...

Less explicit than the IBRD articles, as Article 1 does not expressly prohibit political activity, nevertheless the subsidiary role of the IFC mandates that it should not exceed its mentor in all things considered, particularly development theory. Still, we can envisage that the IFC does not stray far from the philosophical themes of the IBRD.

The IFC is not oblivious to its potential contribution to sustainable development,[28] a term with multiple meanings but in general indicating support for programs with humane consequences as opposed to financing merely for profit and gain. Sustainable development is an attitude towards the community and as such is susceptible to divergent interpretations. Fortunately, pressure from multiple non-governmental groups, as well as the IFC's declared philosophy of not contributing to projects which exploit child labor, or injure the environment, has had positive results with the commercial banks involved in project financing.[29] Various banks have agreed to adopt the IFC's social and environmental rules as a prerequisite to furnishing financing for private development projects.[30] Such an initiative is indeed laudable but of course implicit in obligating adherence to guidelines lies the unspoken power of establishing standards, even if, in this case, for the obvious community welfare.

But the authority exists. The commercial banks can dictate policy as they understand it. Loans are a cudgel. Hence, IFC investment practice contributes equally to legal globalization as does the IBRD. Policy-making is legislation in an informal setting. Moreover, the social guidelines of the IFC are subject to implementation through legal documents which often means the original intent will be diluted. This is because investments by the IFC require more legal instruments than a loan and are different in objectives. As soon as lawyers produce law records, technical questions arise and one of the most urgent is what law will govern relations between the IFC and the other foreign investors, including the sovereign wherein the investment is located which is the site of the project financing. With headquarters in Washington DC, and an investment in an African country, lawyers for all parties naturally confront complex questions as to the law which will regulate disputes.

We are advised[31] that IFC investments, being made in US dollars, are normally disbursed and repaid in New York. If a law suit were brought in New York, New York Courts would apply New York law. Legal counsel for the IFC prior to investment disbursement obtains a legal opinion from an attorney in the country where the investment is to be made that the legal documentation is effective and can be enforced in the foreign country in question. Naturally, some investments are secured by mortgages on assets in the foreign country and enforcement of such instruments would normally be according to the law of the situs, where the assets are located. However, this technical observation can not obscure what usually takes place. When there is a dispute, and it may not be at all about enforcing a mortgage or other security instrument, the law of the contract will be the law of New York, or other US jurisdiction where the contract and disbursement was effectuated.

This ostensibly cabal aspect of public financial aid has not gone unnoticed, either to lawyers[32] or the banking industry. In 1984 the State of New York enshrined its status as a world financial market, or perhaps it is more accurate to say, ensured its availability. By passing a law which obligated New York Courts to take jurisdiction and apply the laws of New York to contracts where the parties have expressly chosen the forum of New York for resolution of their legal problems,[33] New York assuaged the fears of international lenders, public or private. Now lenders do not have to worry if their loan contract to emerging economies might be subject to another 'foreign' law. Or that a New York judge might doubt the relevancy of an action in a New York court. No, just insert in the contract a clause accepted by all parties — abject borrowers normally do not object — electing to have any disputes heard and determined in New York and the globalization of lending laws is enshrined. Consequently, standards of international child labor as envisioned by the IFC and supported by commercial banks nevertheless must stand the scrutiny of New York law which in its turn raises questions of immense complexity. While the policies of New York courts will be certainly of an honorable standard, yet the guidelines, drafted in Washington, DC, meant to be exercised in a distant sovereign, are now subject to review by a municipal court. The road map of international financing is indeed tortuous.

Thus, shrouded from public scrutiny, but essential to the mechanics of investment and loan disbursement, the Western donors formulate legal documents to protect their interests in the language they best understand. Western law, particularly US jurisprudence, is bringing *Lex Americana*, New York legislation, as well as US aid to needy recipients who see in the donations, both monetary and legal, the sacred via to international commerce. The World Bank, and its affiliates, are establishing the World Justice Foundation. Or perhaps it should be called the New York World Justice Foundation, which, unlike its predecessor the New York World Fair, is destined to endure for decades.

## Notes

[1] See the official web site of the World Bank at <www.worldbank.org> accessed 25 June 2002 and link to 'comprehensive development framework questions and answers'.
[2] Supra, n. 1.
[3] Mark E. Wadrzyk, *Is It Appropriate for the World Bank to Promote Democratic Standards in a Borrower Country?*, 17 Wisconsin International Law Journal 555 (1999).
[4] On 28 May 2002, the President was James D. Wolfensohn, a naturalized US citizen.
[5] All information concerning the IFC has been obtained through the official web site <www.ifc.org> as well as various links contained therein.
[6] See home page of the IFC at <www.ifc.org>, accessed 1 June 2002, and links to private sector advisory services.
[7] See home page of the MIGA at <www.miga.org>, accessed 1 June 2002.
[8] See home page at <www.worldbank.org/iscid>, accessed 28 June 2002. The activities of the ISCID are discussed in Chapters 3 and 5, 'Finally Giving Citizens Everywhere Their Trade Rights' and 'The NAFTA Investor and Legal Globalization'.
[9] Supra, n. 3.
[10] Richard Cameron Blake, *The World Bank's Draft Paradigm Comprehensive Development Framework and the Micro-Paradigm of Law and Development*, 3 Yale Human Rights and Development Journal 159 (2000).
[11] Ibid.
[12] Ibid.
[13] See supra, n. 1. The topics discussed in this section are an abridgement of a published report entitled 'Comprehensive Development Framework Questions and Answers' available on the official web site of the World Bank. All material in quotations is from the published report.
[14] See home page of the United Nations, <www.un.org>, accessed 27 June 2002 and links to Universal Declaration of Human Rights promulgated on 10 December 1948.
[15] See home page, supra, n. 1 and links to judicial and legal reforms.
[16] Ibid.
[17] Joseph R. Thome, *Heading South But Looking North: Globalization and Law Reform in Latin America*, 2000 Wis. L. Rev. 691 (2000), for a lucid and comprehensive discussion of the role of the World Bank in promoting legal reforms in other countries.
[18] Ibid.
[19] All the national projects subsequently indicated can be found on the home page of the World Bank, supra, n. 1, under the topic of judicial and legal reforms.
[20] Supra, n. 3.
[21] As reported in Jacques de Lisle, *Lex Americana?: United States Legal Assistance, American Legal Models, and Legal Change in the Post-Communist World and Beyond*, 20 U. Pa. J. Int'l Economic Law 179 (1999).

[22] Sammy Adelman and Abdul Paliwala, *Law and Crisis in the Third World*, London, New York: Hans Zell (1993), reviewed by Richard Bilder & Brian Z. Tamanaha, Van Vollenhoven Institute for Law and Administration in Non-Western Countries, Leiden.
[23] J. Faundez, *Legal Reform in Developing and Transition Countries*, <www.worldbank.org/legal/legop/_judicial/ljr_conf_papers/Faundez3.pdf >, accessed 29 May 2002.
[24] Supra, n. 21.
[25] A typical example is when the IFC in June 1997 approved an African investment in Mozambique in the amount of $120 million for the Mozal Aluminum Company to construct an aluminum smelter, see Paul J. Crystal, *The International Finance Corporation: Encouraging the private sector in challenging conditions*, 165 The Courier ACP-EU, September-October 1997, pp. 45-47.
[26]The US has 24.16 per cent of the capital stock, see official web site of IFC, supra n. 5, with link to 'Statement of Capital Stock and Voting Power'.
[27] See home page of the IFC, supra, n. 5, and links to articles of agreement.
[28] Ibid, and links to sustainable development.
[29] Demetri Sevastopulo, *Four banks adopt IFC agreement*, The Financial Times, 07 April 2003, at p. 19.
[30] Ibid.
[31] D. L. Khairallah, *The Developmental Role of the International Finance Corporation*, 2-Sum NAFTA: L. & Bus. Rev. Am 3 (1996).
[32] Barry W. Rashkover, *Title 14, New York Choice of Law Rule for Contractual Disputes: Avoiding the Unreasonable Results*, 74 Cornell L. Rev. 227 (1985) arguing that the law in question was unconstitutional.
[33] New York Law of General Obligations, Title 14, Sections 5-1401 & 5-1402, posted on <www.senate.state.ny.us>, accessed 28 June 2002.

Chapter 12

# The Basle Bank Decrees Global Financial Regulations

*Banking is not about money and we introduce social monetary power*

Instead of telling the workers of the world to unite,[1] our fiery sociologists[2] should have counseled, 'Remove your bank deposits!'.[3] Without a monetary mass in circulation, government by consent in our industrialized nations is not possible. What was needed for 19th Century English social reform was not a revolution — but a banking boycott. Besides cash in deposits, there are also instruments of value such as shares, bonds, bills of exchange, promissory notes, letters of credit, varied non-tangible assets — and all are held somewhere in institutional custody. Add to this savings and investment by deposits, or through pension funds, insurance annuities, mutual funds, real estate investment trusts, share and commodity indexes, future contracts, option rights, bonds, government obligations; in sum, accumulation in a bewildering variety and function. The potential power of united depositors is indeed formidable.

Guarding these possessions, whether as receipts, or as administrators of funds, are financial institutions whose present day functions go beyond the receipt of cash deposits.[4] Thus, the vitality of the modern world economic system is predicated on financial institutions and this dependency will only augment. We only need to know that the major financial custodians, all from industrialized nations, control 85 per cent of the estimated $41,000 billion held by the banking industry in various forms of paper assets.[5] Global bank deposits as of December 2001 were $10,040.5 billion.[6] It is estimated the world's financial services market exceeds $18 billion in global securities and $2,500 billion in insurance premiums.[7]

The major 200 private financial institutions involved in the international financial markets are located primarily in the G-10 countries.[8] These countries hold 84 per cent of the world's bank assets, 86 per cent of the world's stock market capitalization, and 76 per cent of the world's debt securities as of 1999.[9] Regarding bank loans, the Bank for International Settlements reports[10] total international bank claims as of the 1st quarter of 2002 amounted to $11,453 billion. Of this amount, European banks held 62.1 per cent and US banks 7 per cent.[11] However, if we examine the category of the borrower, then in the same period the US banks increase their lending of the total to 18.7 per cent for developing countries; refined further to reflect a particular region, we then find indicated 17.9 per cent for Asia and the Pacific; and 27.6 per cent for Latin America and the Caribbean.[12] Hence the total credit of American bank loans approximates 21 per cent,[13] a significant figure for only one nation.

It is academic commonplace that there is a new international financial architecture now in place.[14] Services encompassing traditional banking, securities, insurance and other instruments are now international, merged under one corporate umbrella, and dominated by the mega-financial corporations. The only geographical frontiers are those self-imposed by the board of directors. The neighborhood bank or broker has become a monetary fossil. Yet what interests us is not pecuniary archaeology or the complexities of cyber-finance which makes global markets possible, but instead a more urgent and immediate preoccupation: the repercussions of financial institutions upon the social community. Suggesting labor unions to substitute aggressive postures by a banking boycott clearly emphasizes a different perspective. While our relationship to a mode of production surely conditions some of our conceptual premises, in fact the importance of this association is exaggerated. The consciousness of humanity may be molded temporarily by conditions of labor but social behavior are in direct proportion to material, today it is financial, independence, or the lack of it.

By accepting a restricted, functional, moderately-paid position in the productive process, the average laborer is forced to admit that access to the monetary circuit has been substantially denied. You then either cooperate and sell your labor or resort to violence. You unite in protest or you withdraw your bank deposit, neither of which is occurring in any significant degree. But the salient cause should not be clothed in presumptions that machines disaffect and alienate[15] the operator. This seems contrary to mankind's affection and addiction to technology. More likely any alienation, if it exists, is the result of truncated gain. Alienation is an immeasurable emotional state, a measurable scale is yet to be produced, and more likely the result of an underlying cause of deprivation of available community resources. The social representation of the individual through a material and social consummation is what pacifies the community. The law, then, solidifies this condition by way of its precepts of declared rights and wrongs subject to enforcement.

Instead of referring to alienation or social status, it may be more useful to denominate our field of investigation as the social monetary power of individuals. Social, because without a society, numerical representation, electronically or on paper, is meaningless. Monetary, because once a community is established, there is required a means of exchange of resources if violence is to be avoided. Power, because the means of exchange only exist to confer rights upon its possessors. The rights and obligations of each individual towards another is a community fiction encased in legal precepts and which permits or excludes its members from the circulation of resources. Accumulation affects our relationship to each other and to the governing organ. The deprived and dispossessed are only in this state when confronting another class or social group which is in possession. One solitary person on an island can have no social attribute. Such a category requires a human milieu.

Making possible accumulation, social monetary power by the general public is generally achieved through labor, bank loans, or recourse to other sophisticated corporate financial techniques. However, in modern societies, labor is the usual route to sustenance and is normally not sufficient to obtain consumer goods in any quantity. The availability of credit has become one of the hallmarks of industrial life and is the principal method for entry to resources.

International credit and its statistics demonstrate its pervasive existence and probable cultural repercussions. The present economic epoch is founded on the use of capital basically furnished through credit. Granted the enormous and ubiquitous presence of international loans, we are concerned to know if the financial institutions themselves are undergoing a process of legal globalization of banking regulations. Banks loan but nations and people borrow. There is a logic of community aftermath involved whose trail inevitably leads to the regulators.

If banks are restricted in their credit policies, there is a social fallout because governments are also debtors. Activities involving social expenditures such as health and education are affected. For the private sector, industrial expansion is curtailed and unemployment rises. Financial institutions cannot loan freely if their reserve requirements must be raised to meet international standards.

When credit lines are curtailed, the national economy retracts[16] and ultimately deflates. Currency runs are quite common and reserves are depleted to serve foreign currency debt service. The national economy stalls, if it does not collapse. Social chaos on the streets is frequently captured by the media.

Moreover, the availability of private credit is going to affect risk management in the form of who will get a loan amongst many potential borrowers, which in turn casts over into areas of research, capital expenditures, production, exports, and imports of needed technology, growth or not of the national infrastructure.

Thus credit, its availability, its rate, and the determination of credit worthiness are dependent on bank supervision. But behind the financial institutions acting as a primary source of living standards for a nation, lie the international regulators. This raises the complex web of international financial institutions and the sociology of supranational organizations which in this case are the international financial regulators. Nations and citizenry are subject to the politics of their national banks, which may or not be subject to a democratic accounting. Yet in all cases, the regulators and influence makers remain, for the most part, removed from public analysis and opinion. What regulators counsel, affects nations all over the world. Thus the eventual globalization of laws affecting financial institutions through the ubiquitous, indispensable loan market impacts on citizenry everywhere. International credit is as necessary as a municipal water system.

By the banking conduit, also a community fiction — for how can a building housing bits of paper with numbers on them have an existence other than a 'thing imagined' — we are able to realize our aspirations or see them impeded. Clearly, then, the availability of credit, and its terms, has a profound influence upon the lives of nations and their citizens. Nations borrow for infrastructures and individuals contract debt for investment and life style. Banking and borrowing are indispensable to the modern social life. If interest rates to borrowers do rise, consumption by the general public retreats. If interest rates to debtors are low, there is a constant stimulus to spend. This is a well-known fact and is described as 'monetary policy', there of course being others techniques such as 'fiscal policy'. This monetary program seeks the same objectives but through the rise or decline in taxes. Behind these facades of economic language lies the reality of monetary circulation and consumerism, both intimately dependent on financial institutions.

Social monetary power in our present epoch can only be conferred upon an individual by the financial industry. The effect of financial institutions upon the lives of ordinary people everywhere, from industrialized nations to emerging countries, conditions availability of credit for whatever purposes, certainly including investments, asset purchases, education, leisure, and retirement. It is no longer possible to accumulate capital of any significance without the presence of, and possession by, assets in a financial institution. Consequently, for most of us, our social universe is dependent on material objects which permit other goals. Therefore, the concepts we employ which express our social self are derived from a material basis. Mental images and myths are not a result of the means of production but dependent on access to the resource circuit.

The perpetual employee is condemned to discontent, not because of his/her rationalization of a particular social slot or a sense of alienation. Rather it is resignation. Bank credit not forthcoming or minor salary increases below the level of inflation does not permit a change or the possibility of material improvement. Consequently, bank credit in its varied forms also ultimately influences the mental content and imagery of our social relationships, all of which is expressed through social monetary power. It might be thought that such economic considerations, while certainly dramatic, nevertheless are confined to the commercial aspects of our daily lives and humanity is accustomed to arranging compartments, one for the flesh and the other for the spirit. Yet a closer examination reveals how social life shifts from one image to another, creating an integrated repository of what is at times denominated mores, custom, culture, community, or a nation. Quite simply, access to the monetary circulation requires an elaborate system of social and legal myths. There cannot be loans without an agreed upon system of property rights, contract law, company law, financial law, foreign investment law, bankruptcy provisions, tax law, and when we realize law school courses run from 3-5 years depending on the educational system, the list recited is indeed highly abbreviated.

Nor is this schedule exclusive but should suffice to confirm the inevitability of a complex system of jurisprudence which must support the modern day monetary societies. However, when we invoke the necessity of laws, cultural standards must be articulated, for the law is no more than a declaration of social beliefs. There cannot be property rights without an agreement on what is property, how it may be used, sold, rented, left to heirs, or made available for security. Thus the inordinate roster of legal precepts which are a constant feature of industrialized nations is also a catalogue of cultural precepts. Labor laws require a philosophical underpinning. Free market usually means termination of employment without cause and without indemnities. This contrasts with social capitalism which constricts management's rights to fire at will. In some jurisdictions, labor has a seat on the board of directors, in others such a presence is anathema.

Domestic law consecrates various ideas, many derived from tribal and religious sources, yet the present, prevailing mores of equal rights for all sexes in Western nations may collide violently with other cultures where male dominance is accompanied by female submission bordering on forced servitude. We cannot privatize public goods unless we adopt a system of private ownership based on a system of law. The elimination of corruption at an official level obligates a clarification of what is composed bribery and a resulting legal definition. Yet it is not difficult to grasp that in some societies people in power receive gifts as a token of respect and not solely as an inducement to corruption. What is involved, necessarily, is an agreed criminal precept which is no more than a codified cultural standard.

Financial services require legal myths and the more financial services are internationalized, the more the laws serving such institutions become global, for it would be commercially awkward to have complex legal principles inconsistently applied dependent on the jurisdiction. This would abort dramatically the growth of international financial services which is a necessary adjunct to international commerce. The dominant legal systems are those used by the main trading nations which restricts the choice to the common law or the European Civil Codes, the latter also applicable in the Latin American countries. While the Asian countries are seen as potential, significant markets, their laws have not influenced to any important degree the basic tenets of international commercial law which has developed from the industrialized nations and Western jurisprudence.

Of course, some differences are accepted. Efforts are made to accommodate local laws. Nevertheless, the usual is the contrary. Loans and banking services are facilitated when borrowers utilize language and myths readily understood by the lenders. The major borrowers and recipients of aid and investment have every motive to alter their legal concepts in conformity with the lenders and traders. Based upon these premises, it is a short walk to our conclusion. Laws which promote access to resources and enhance social monetary power are going to be embraced and will drive out other legal myths. Western law will triumph and become the standard bearer of international commercial law not because of its inherent value or cultural superiority but because the international monetary circuit is dependent on Western banks and in particular American banks. Out of the top 16 international custodian banks, eight of them are American.[17]

This being so, the internationalization of financial services should lead to a globalization of the underlying legal principles. *The Communist Manifesto*[18] should have been originally published under the title, *Citizen Power Through American Bank Deposits*, with the necessary contextual amendments. With a change of title, and Mr Karl Marx changing his office from the London British Library to the New York Public Library, the course of history would have been accelerated.

Confirming our initial thoughts, is a description of the power held by two Basle banks and which has been voluntarily conferred upon them by the international banking community.

### *The Basle Club membership application is not published on the internet*

Two major bankers' organizations in Switzerland contribute substantially to ensuring the globalization of financial services is accompanied by a common set of precepts. Were there a deliberate legislative intent, or even one conferred by treaty, we could speak of the harmonization of international financial law. But this is not the case, for harmonization refers to a concerted effort by dispersed groups to draft and promulgate laws where heretofore there has existed substantial diversity. Concerning our Swiss bankers, it is current, instead, to use the expression 'soft law'.[19] This phrase conveys the informality of the process and the voluntary character of the guidelines promulgated. However, the designation also emphasizes the moral obligations which are behind suggested codes of conduct, and which time commutes into custom; mercantile expectations create into commercial usage; and finally judges confirm as law. It is a familiar formula which has not been displaced by the plethora of legislative activity emblematic of industrial nations and is equally effective.

The two associations are the Bank for International Settlements (BIS)[20] and the Basle Committee on Banking Supervision (Basle Committee).[21] Both are located in Basle, Switzerland and it is BIS which provides the secretariat for the Basle Committee. However, do not confound recondite organizations and esoteric titles with bureaucratic anachronisms or a subterfuge for frolicsome bankers on Swiss ski slopes. The tasks and objectives of these two groups are staffed with highly professional technicians who have considerable global influence directly and indirectly,[22] affect the lives of populations everywhere, and contribute significantly to the globalization of Western financial law.

Originally established to effectuate wartime settlements due to German reparations following World War I,[23] the activities of BIS have grown considerably. Those original technical functions have been superseded by a more profound role. BIS began its activity on 17 May 1930 and by its own declaration is the '... world's oldest international financial organization'.[24] Its shareholders are central banks, composed of the banks from the industrialized nations. It is pertinent to note that the board of directors comprises the Governors of the central banks of Belgium, France, Germany, Italy, UK, and the Chairman of the Board of Governors of the US Federal Reserve System.[25]

While the statutes of BIS provide for election of other members to the board, this has been confined presently[26] to the Governors of the central banks of Canada, Japan, the Netherlands, Sweden, and Switzerland. There is no central world banking authority, so in theory each sovereign is free to regulate its own domestic banking affairs. However, any nation intending to engage in international commerce is not likely to be of any assistance to the local merchants unless the central bank in question is prepared to adhere to standards promulgated by BIS. Beyond its functions as a central settlement authority amongst central banks, or similar institutions, the mandate of BIS includes a forum to promote discussion in the international financial community, a platform for international monetary and financial cooperation, a center for research, and an agent and trustee for other banks.

Within its competencies, BIS holds 10-15 per cent of global monetary reserves in the form of deposits by other banks. Banks needing short term funds can borrow from BIS. More than 80 central banks from all over the world maintain deposits with BIS.[27] This is done so that the depositing central banks can earn interest on their surplus funds. In turn, BIS loans these deposits out at short-term rates. With a considerable store of reserves, BIS can step into a financial crisis. It often happens that while one international lending institution, such as the IMF, is reviewing its policies or waiting for instructions from its officers, BIS, akin in its lending philosophy to the IMF, can advance substantial short term funds to ward off a contagious financial crash. Known as bridging loans, this is precisely what happened with the critical debt situations of various Latin American countries.[28] The BIS is prepared to advance resources to the IMF on a short term basis.[29]

Besides establishing committees such as the Committee on Global Financial System or the Markets Committee (monitoring foreign exchange market activities) for forums of discussion and policy making, BIS allows its headquarters to furnish secretarial and executive services to the International Association of Insurance Supervisors and the International Association of Deposit Insurers. Naturally there are frequent exchanges of opinions and forums held amongst these groups and committees. Peer education is similar to continuing adult education required in many professions. Two further councils with obvious influence are the Financial Stability Institute, created by BIS jointly with the Basle Committee on Banking Supervision,[30] and the Financial Stability Forum established by the Finance Ministers and Central Bank Governors of the G7 countries.[31]

The Financial Stability Institute conducts seminars on financial sector supervision and regulation; holds regional workshops to permit a more detailed discussion of issues with local authorities; and provides supervisors with pertinent information on the newest supervisory developments. The Financial Stability Forum is an elite club by virtue of its membership. It has a total of 40 members.[32] There are representatives of the G7 treasury, central bank, and supervisory agencies. There are representatives of the IMF, the World Bank, the Basle Committee on Banking Supervision, and the OECD and well as representatives of the International Organization of Securities Commissions and the International Association of Insurance Supervisors.

If any further schedules are needed to display the potentate character of BIS, the creation in 1974 of the Basle Committee on Banking Supervision determines how powerful in reach and effect BIS has on ordinary citizens. The Basle Committee is a forum for setting standards for supervision of national banks and sensible reserve requirements. Its Governors are the representatives of the G10 central bank governors.[33] Thus in 1988, there was promulgated the Basle Capital Accord which was to achieve international acceptance on adequate capital reserves for banks. This is to be superseded within the near future by new capital adequacy requirements denominated Basle II. This has been classified as a monumental event in financial history and is expected to be implemented by 2006.[34]

So powerful is the moral authority of the Basle Committee that the German banks felt compelled through lobbying to obtain an exception to reserve requirements for loans to smaller German companies and the American banks procured a lesser reserve requirement for retail credit exposure, such as credit cards.[35] With the promulgation of the Basle II accord and rules issued by the BIS, the capital reserves of banks everywhere will be affected. Seemingly a technical aspect of banking, yet reserve requirements can discourage capital investment, lending, and, through alterations in the cost of borrowing, reshape the global economy. Investors and consumers in the most diverse jurisdictions will be affected in their standard of living. In 1992, the Basle Committee agreed on minimum standards for the supervision of international banking groups. It is anticipated the largest international banks will be rewarded with a 3-4 per cent reduction in capital requirements.[36] This has led one academic to conclude that the main beneficiaries of the Basle accord will be the international banks and this will permit them to purchase the smaller banks.[37]

Finally, for our purposes, the Basle Committee is a stimulant for discussion amongst various entities. There are conferences attended by the International Association of Securities Commissions,[38] the International Association of Insurance Supervisors,[39] and the International Accounting Standards Board.[40] Although removed from politics, even international accounting standards require committees to strive towards creating a consensus for international commerce.

Contrary to their titles, BIS and the Basle Committee are not exclusively occupied with banking matters, nor could it be. Finance is one of the bonds of social life. For the Basle banks, their influence is far more pervasive due to liason with other groups and to the topics embraced and policy decisions taken. Even this synthetic survey of what some of these groups undertake can lead to no doubt that the globalization of financial law is firmly in the grasp of the industrialized nations who govern BIS, the Basle Committee, and all the forums, seminars, and 'financial talk shows'.

So if BIS and the Basle Committee are not formally the world's central bank, they fulfill its functions. What the Basle Committee decrees as sensible becomes gospel. By law,[41] the US Federal Reserve Bank is entrusted with establishing reserve requirements for all US domestic banks. In 1988 when the Basle Committee issued an interpretation of the Basle framework for capital adequacy for banks, the Federal Reserve issued a press release stating it will '... make a determination as to how to implement the Basle interpretation with regard to US. banks after consulting with other federal financial institutions regulatory agencies'.[42] The creation of the European Central Bank has not encroached upon the powers of the national central banks who still retain jurisdiction over their reserve requirements.[43]

With the world's cash reserves held within the confines of banks scattered throughout a multitude of nations, it is indeed comforting to know that the Basle bankers are exercising control for the benefit of depositors everywhere, although there are no representatives of any populist groups. Nevertheless, composed of representatives from democratic nations, the influences of the Basle bankers and their colleagues are not subject to any public debate. There is surely no harmonization of international financial law because there are no formalized mechanisms for interested parties to submit a point of view. What is transpiring on an irreversible scale is the globalization of international financial law which is firmly within the domain and dominion of the G10 industrialized nations.

### *Not a new world, but just one with similar laws*

With the implantation of banks and financial institutions in all parts where there is commerce, with the preponderance of reserves and assets held by the industrialized nations, and due to the need for the emerging countries to solicit aid and investment from these sources, the 'new international financial architecture'[44] has its legal consequences.

For observers of international commerce and finance, it is apparent that private law must converge on the principles underlying the legal systems of Western Europe and the US. Due to its global reach, the US banks and financial institutions are the harbingers of this one legal world. It is not possible for international finance to proceed in expansion without a fully developed system of private law which must ultimately include private dispute resolution principles founded on uniform legal principles. Otherwise, investors will go forum shopping which produces the lamentable legal situation of creditors and debtors suing one another simultaneously in different jurisdictions. The plethora of appeals this produces normally becomes textbook material for law students.

Merchants require stability and legal prediction before committing funds to a venture. The liberalization of financial markets has brought cross-border capital flows, pension funds investing in overseas markets, insurance companies offering financial services in various, national markets, access to security exchanges all over the world available through internet, to mention some of the more obvious. This internationalization of capital markets requires international standards to be implemented by other agencies, such as the IMF[45] and the World Bank. Criticism has been indirectly leveled at the IMF for compelling adherence to the Basle banking standards by insisting the Basle conditions be incorporated in the terms of a loan.[46] This imposition has contributed to the attenuation of legal principles associated with socialist principles through the implicit legal framework supporting international financial standards.[47] Naturally, the embrace of capitalism by former socialist states will include conformity to banking standards. Behind all regulations or standards lie the principles of civil and commercial law. Even insolvency and bankruptcy procedures, associated in the lay mind with technical aspects hardly susceptible of influencing daily life, are imbued with a cultural dimension. One need only think of defaults on sovereign bonds and their consequences to realize that what happens to a nation obviously has repercussions on its citizens. Failure to pay can cause a capital flight which plunges the debtor nation into a significant recession.

For the moment, the development of 'soft law' through the imposition of international financial standards, promulgated by a non-legislative group, is reformulating international financial law.[48] Both Basle banks collaborate to achieving harmony internationally in supervision, capital requirements, risk management, transparency of markets, standards to ensure stability when there are major financial failures, and periodic maintenance of the guidelines involved.[49] What emerges from the concerted efforts of the organizations involved are certain core principles[50] which, while directed towards financial institutions, cannot help but have repercussions in the community. Capital to loan reserve requirements, credit card exposure limits, risk calculation, special treatment of small and medium enterprises, mortgage lending standards, accounting standards, currency market discipline, and institutional disclosure requirements, are modest, simple examples of consensual regulations which are commuted to the public. Disclosure requirements assume a sensitive area for it is intended that financial institutions reveal more about their financial solvency. In this way, it is anticipated potential defaults of institutions affecting the international investment community may be avoided as other lenders, both public and private, will know when to stop further funding.

Thus disclosure requirements will discipline national banks which, in turn, are a protective measure for the local citizenry. All the core principles could be also newly denominated 'banking social principles', for a sound financial architecture contributes to a healthy macroeconomic structure. Financial institutions which comply with the Committee standards will obviously find access to the IMF and the World Bank facilitated another benefit which should under normal circumstances transmit to the general public.

Before the awesome Delphic pronouncements of the Basle establishment, not even the giants of the banking industry can voice opposition. With new capital requirements about to be approved by the Basle establishment for implementation in 2006, and which may require banks to increase by 32 per cent their capital adequacy ratios to secure equity investments, one by one the world's large financial institutions are selling off their private equity operations.[51] Major financial institutions are scrambling to sell-off their private equity institutions because of their colleagues, the bankers from Basle. No legislature has ordered them to do so. No central bank has issued an edict requiring their banks to dispose of their private equity investments. Banking standards from the bankers' regulators is a sufficient alert; otherwise one is cast from the financial community. The proposed regulations are the private laws of the banking community.

Private international law will surely be shaped by American and Western international financial legal principles. Otherwise, there will be no loans. If the boys and the banks from Basle are heeded, depositors' funds are safe and the precepts of Western financial standards are enshrined. Without monetary support, there will be no commerce of any quantitative significance. Without trade, the world will plunge into recession. The dominion of trade and finance by the industrialized nations can only result in their total capture of global legal imagery.

## Notes

[1] Karl Marx & Friedrich Engels, *The Communist Manifesto*, London (1848).

[2] '... [M]any younger thinkers now are willing to accord Marx his rightful place among the giants of sociological thought', George Ritzer, *Sociological Theory*, 2nd ed., McGraw-Hill Publishing Company, New York (1988).

[3] This is less provocative than the recent declarations of the Argentine Senator José Luis Barrionuevo, 'go and destroy the banks' reported by Thomas Catán, *Argentine Legislators 'asked for bribes to stall tax law'*, The Financial Times, 30 August 2002, at p. 5.

[4]The top ten world financial custodians hold over $35,000 billion in assets, see Tony Tassell, *Custodians taking over the back office*, The Financial Times, Global Custody Survey, 5 July 2002, at p. 1.

[5] Ibid.

[6] Statistics published by Bank for International Settlements, see official web site and links to international financial statistics <www.bis.org>, accessed 7 July 2002.
[7] Lawrence L. C. Lee, *The Basle Accords as Soft Law: Strengthening International Banking Supervision*, 39 Va. Ja. Int'l Law 1 (1998).
[8] Wendy Dobson et al., *World Capital Markets: Challenge to the G-10*, a summary of which is available at <www.iie.com/press/worldcapitalmarkets>, accessed 8 August 2002. The G-10 (but the authors in question list 12) countries are: Belgium, Canada, France, Germany, Italy, Japan, the Netherlands, Sweden, Switzerland, the UK, the US, and Spain.
[9] Ibid.
[10] BIS Press release Ref. No. 15/2002E (Consolidated Banking Statistics) <www.bis.org>, accessed 8 August 2002.
[11] Ibid.
[12] Ibid.
[13] (18.7 per cent + 17.9 per cent + 27.6 per cent)/3=21.39 per cent.
[14] Joseph J. Norton, *A 'New International Financial Architecture? — Reflections on the Possible Law-Based Dimension*, 33 Int'l Law 891 (1999).
[15] Karl Marx described the distortions of the human personality through the conditions of labor imposed by a capitalist society as 'alienation'.
[16] Raymond Colitt, *Brazil plans loans to troubled companies*, The Financial Times, 13 August 2002, at p.1, reporting the Brazilian central bank is committed to assisting 'embattled Brazilian companies'.
[17] Supra, n. 4.
[18] Supra, n. 1.
[19] Supra, n. 7.
[20] The home page of BIS is <www.bis.org>, accessed 9 July 2002.
[21] Information concerning the Basle Committee is found through the home page of BIS, supra, n. 13. The Committee members are Belgium, Canada, France, Germany, Italy, Japan, Luxembourg, the Netherlands, Spain, Sweden, Switzerland, UK, and US. As of August 2002, the Chairman of the Committee is Mr. William J. McDonough, President and CEO of the Federal Reserve Bank of New York.
[22] Doug Cameron, *Banks urged to hit terror funding*, The Financial Times, 18 April 2002, at page 4, reporting the Basle Committee is addressing the problem of terrorist funding and the need to '... work towards a global policy framework'.
[23] Marlo Giovanoli, *The Role of the Bank for International Settlements in International Monetary Cooperation and its Tasks Relating to the European Currency Unit*, 23 Int'l Law 841 (1989). Dr Giovanoli is presently (10 July 2002) General Counsel to BIS, see home page of BIS, supra, n. 13.
[24] Supra, n. 19 and links contained on home page.
[25] Ibid, as of 10 July 2002.
[26] Ibid.
[27] Ibid.
[28] Ibid.
[29] Ibid.
[30] Supra, n. 19 and links to Financial Stability Institute.
[31] G7 countries are Canada, France, Germany, Italy, Japan, UK, and US, See <www.fsforum.org>, accessed 13 July 2002.
[32] Supra, n. 13 and links to Financial Stability Forum, membership posted as of 14 July 2002.

[33] G7 nations France, Germany, Japan, UK, US, more Canada and Italy. Inducing confusion is the so-called Group of 10 (composed of 11 countries) to which must be added Belgium, Netherlands, Sweden, and Switzerland.

[34] James Mackintosh et al., *Basle accord set to change banking landscape*, The Financial Times, 10 July 2002, at p.8 where it is announced a new set of banking rules soon to be promulgated known as Basle II accord which will restructure the banking industry and reshape the global economy.

[35] Charles Pretzlik et al., *Deal on bank reserves in sight*, The Financial Times, 11 July 2002, at p. 8.

[36] Ibid.

[37] Ibid (quoting Prof. Avinash Persaud, global head of research at State Street Bank).

[38] See home page at <www.iosco.org>, accessed 10 July 2002.

[39] See home page at <www.iais.org >, accessed 10 July 2002.

[40] See home page of Financial Accounting Standards Board at <www.fasb.org>, accessed 10 July 2002, for history of origins of IASB.

[41] Depository Institutions Deregulation and Monetary Control Act of 1980, 12 U.S. C. 226, Section 1 of the Act of March 31, 1980 (Public L. No. 96-221).

[42] Federal Reserve Press Release, October 27, 1988, posted on <www.federalreserve.gov/boarddocs/press/general/1988>, accessed 11 July 2002.

[43] Nout Wellink, *The role of national central banks within the European system of central bank — the example of De Nederlandsche Bank*, 13-14 June 2002, available at <www.bis.org/review/n020620a>, accessed 11 July 2002.

[44] Supra, n. 8.

[45] Y. V. Reddy, Deputy Governor of the Bank of India, *Legal Aspects of International Financial Law*, at the International Seminar on Legal and Regulatory Aspects of Financial Stability, sponsored by the World Bank, the IMF, BIS, and the Financial Stability Forum, at Basle, Switzerland, on 23 January 2002, available at BIS internet site, supra, n. 13.

[46] Ibid.

[47] Ibid.

[48] Ibid.

[49] Supra, n. 20.

[50] The Core Principles of the Committee, amounting to approximately 25, are available on its web site at supra, n. 4. On 10 July 2002 the members of the Committee agreed upon the new capital rules to be applied to the supervision of banks.

[51] Peter Smith, *Banks re-examine economics of private equity*, The Financial Times, 20 March 2003, at p. 17.

# Chapter 13

# International Financial Services and Monetarized Sovereignty

*Money is sovereign*

Whether we are dealing with industrialized nations or emerging economies, the integration and internationalization of capital markets has monetarized sovereignty and brought with it a globalization of, firstly, financial laws and, secondly, services traditionally associated with the financial industry such as insurance, securities, and accounting. We can refer to those performing these services as the informal regulators who normally form associations to govern their industry or profession. These cooperative associations are powerful adjuncts to the weakening of sovereignty everywhere and have resulted in a standardization of financial law principles. More than ever, sovereignty is dependent on financial markets and their support services. Yet, it must not be forgotten the consequences spill over into all aspects of community life. Overwhelmingly, the paradigms emanate from the Western economies.

Not subject to any effective public, democratic scrutiny the informal regulators afford a crystalline example of network technocracy operating independently from sovereign control or any public constituency.[1] No one elects the regulators nor do they have to account to the public for their decisions. While the regulators may be appointed by a democratically elected government, the tendency to reward the faithful with semi-official jobs needs little documentation. Moreover, the professional associations — from securities organizations to accounting bodies — similar to the OECD — are a closed club of technocrats and professionals who promulgate standards by consensus. Yet, what the informal regulators accomplish is as effective as if there were a world financial parliament. Such is the nature of informal peer regulation and the inability of sovereign nations to contest effectively this parallel power.

With the differences between banks, securities firms, and insurance companies in their loan and investment functions rapidly disappearing, there is an informal international regulatory convergence emerging. The results are discernible in multiple aspects, firstly on a broad scale and then affecting specific sectors. The principles of public international law, founded on the inviolate integrity of national sovereignty, are withering before the emergence of multiple supranational and industry organizations, the mobility of capital and services, and, on a micro-scale, the regulation of these services by their own elite. As standards of public share exchanges or proper financial company reporting are formulated, with a view to an economic objective such as fairly representing the assets and liabilities of a company, the professional organizations create their norms as to what is just and reasonable. Insurance companies, securities firms, accounting boards, bar associations, all those serving the financial markets in one capacity or another, converge on principles deemed at once rational and functional.

Of course, the origin of these technical gauges is a reflection of the composition of the organizations, for associations are an effort of women and men. Indoctrinated by their own cultures, such groups are a conduit for personal philosophies, particularly in the area of economics, but not only so. Economics cannot be separated from social life. In fact, economics is an eminently social activity, as any trip to a supermarket or bazaar will confirm. In any event, and quite simply, capital is power and, for example, the accounting standards to which a company must adhere affects its entire corporate structure. Debits can not be adequately determined if there is not a comprehensive internal reporting system with checks and counter-checks for errors. Thus the internal structure of a corporation must conform to an analytical vision otherwise proper accounting is impossible. Job descriptions are created. A hierarchy is established. The economic actor is modified. Although not apparent at first when viewed from the micro-level, nevertheless, the regulation of the insurance or accounting industry creates a separate parallel power structure to the nation in so far as it affects the economic units, nor actors. Sovereignty is being tethered, if not castrated, by the international regulators.[2] This is, in the generality, what can be critically studied in the particular. For these reasons, the global spread of the multinational is partially the result of rationalization of accounts and management.

Broadly speaking, and concerning international banking, we have seen some aspects of the main architects in this process through the activities of the Bank of International Settlement[3] and the Basle Committee on Banking Supervision (Committee).[4] However, there are a number of international financial societies such as the International Organization of Securities Commissions (IOSCO),[5] the International Association of Insurance Advisors (IAIS),[6] accounting federations, such as the International Accounting Standards Board[7] in the UK, or the many US associations such as the Financial Accounting Standards Board, Independence Standards Board, International Accounting Standards Board,[8] and, of course, a wide-ranging, diverse group of private institutions and *ad hoc* committees.[9] The dominion of the financial sector over the social structure of a nation is uncontestable no matter what our academic approach, whether the power associated with lending, the economic changes wrought by informal regulators, the rating given to a sovereign by credit analysts, or the private rights now given to investors to hold the sovereign liable before an international arbitration board.

When considering the international aspect of informal regulation, the consequences for national sovereignty are debilitating. International loans and finance have eliminated geographic frontiers. International capital and its sponsors are a globalizing force and no nation escapes its influence. Witness the political fact that the international financial community also forms part of the non-resident, non-citizen, and non-working class of the electorate[10] of a nation. The local voters are too disenfranchised to influence the exchange markets. Capital flight by non-resident investors has become the new form of emigration. The information conveyed by telecommunications technology and computers has more immediate effect than the deliberative decisions taken in a national assembly. The financial markets, the insurance industry, and the accounting associations take a vote on the political economy of a nation and its professional standards even if they are not registered voters. The insurance associations set parameters as to the type of pension plans to be offered; the accounting boards decide how the financial health of the insurance company will be evaluated; the securities industry creates products which link pension plans to index performances; the law profession constructs the policies which determines the responsibilities and liabilities of their insurance clients. The consumer-voter's intervention in this process is, if not zero — why exaggerate? — close to nil.

Factually, the sovereign nation can no longer regulate capital movements across national frontiers nor is its influence very substantial in the related industries.[11] If the legislators pass laws to regulate an industry, such as the insurance market, it is in the generality. The details and specifications which result in a final consumer product are based on standards developed by the particular industry. As a result, one of the nation's main functions — control of its financial industry and related, support services — is determined by professionals and not by legislators. The details are everything. For the most part, the broad legislative principles are window-dressing. Traders and professionals in distant share exchanges and offices, where often the language of the sovereign under scrutiny is not even spoken, determine the method for doing business in multiple nations. Nowadays, mass migrations caused by the unemployed seeking a better future are minor when compared to capital fleeing devaluation on the foreign exchange markets;[12] or regulations decided upon in New York or London which set accounting standards across the world. More dramatically, the opinion of the foreign exchange markets as well as industry policies is based on Western economic judgments,[13] not whether particular governmental policies are socially useful.

Governments cannot implement national policies without acknowledging their international impact.[14] In 1995, the Australian dollar was lowered on the foreign exchange markets due to concerns over Australia's external international debts.[15] The Brazilian real in 2002 faced devaluation pressure as foreign investors feared a socially-minded candidate might win the presidential elections.[16] It is indeed the iconoclastic nation which can remain indifferent to foreign capital and investment; the obligation to reduce tariffs and eliminate protectionism; the demand for the entry and flow of capital with minor regulation; the need for a convergence towards international standards on all matters affecting the banking and financial laws of a nation; its insurance industry; its stock exchange regulations; and its accounting profession. The law profession has escaped global regulation but it is an illusion. The law profession serves the informal regulators and, as in any whirlpool, their skills swirl around their clients drafting the documents which encapsulate the desired economic objectives.

International capital, with its accompanying services, thus becomes simultaneously the cause of diminished sovereignty, impregnating the concept of sovereignty with monetary values, but also the catalyst for social transformations, at times denominated industrialization, progress, modernization, technological advances, all descriptions which reflect an ethical bias, but which fairly can be summarized as the global effect of Western culture on other nations. This hegemony of Western culture is a process which began in the 1500s through the European colonizing process in North America, South America, the Indian continent, Africa, Asia, and the Middle East.[17] It has culminated with the triumph of modern technology created and nurtured first in Europe and now in the US, once colonized but now the mother of all colonizers with its enormous fountain of available capital. The turnover of capital produces the somersaults of social history. However, if international capital is available for lending it is also channeled through various organizations which we have grouped under the term informal regulators.

*The house the financial architects built*

Financial crises are not confined to the solvency of banks. Monetary defaults reflect directly in the gross domestic product of any nation, devaluing not only its currency but its standard of living.[18] Financial supervision of banks and their kin has been in existence a respectable amount of time, with statutes on insurance supervision in the UK dating back to 1774.[19] Comfortably secure from public accountability on technical aspects,[20] are the Basle banks and their central bank brethren across the world. Equally discrete, but no less significant in their cumulative effect upon the lives of nations are organizations such as the IOSCO,[21] IAIS,[22] and the ubiquitous accounting firms.[23]

We have stressed the central role of the Basle banks.[24] Consultations, encounters, and development of policy issues frequently transpire between the Basle banks, IOSCO, and IAIS. IOSCO has 100 members ranging from Albania to Zambia[25] represented by the securities and investment supervisors from these counties. IAIS also has 100 members, represented by the insurance supervisors from the member nations.[26] From the various meetings between the groups involved is the drafting of Memoranda of Understandings (MOUS)[27] which represent the collective view on sundry aspects of financial architecture.[28]

Turning to specifically IOSCO and IAIS, we find similar forces towards globalization, although with a different emphasis. Investor and insured protection standards, efficient and transparent markets, reduction of risk, fair practices, enforcement procedures, and international cooperation are a moderate selection of the many topics. From the globalization of investment and insurance laws is transmitted a uniform standard for investors in all their variegated forms worldwide, a welcome development for the proponents of global markets. The institutions involved are under the guidance, influence, and policy judgements of the industrialized nations. If there are no international financial institutions with powers to enforce compliance everywhere there is a bank, an insurance company, a stock exchange, an accounting firm, and finally the law profession. The financial industry, through all its agents, beyond its national frontiers, is self-regulating. Being self-disciplined, there is a firm tendency in practice towards uniformity, and not exceptions. Without neither legislative authority nor laws decreed and published, there is little room for legal counsel and others to devise avoidance strategies. Consensus is the most sensible platform. The services strive to accomplish to objectives within the consensus so as not to disrupt the ground-rules.

If we were to consider only the professions, the accounting and auditing professions wield enormous influence. The power of the multiple accounting associations and auditing firms is unquestionable. A simple reading of the home page of one of the many US internet references[29] indicates the wide, international pervasiveness of the accounting associations. If Albania and Zimbabwe are to host foreign investment, the international accounting associations are there to assist in constructing numerical standards to be followed.[30] The reports filed by public companies everywhere are cast within international accounting standards. No entrepreneur can possibly hope for recognition without producing results which are considered drawn by international measures. As a glaring example of the informal regulation a profession can exercise, accounting regulators in various nations have signaled their intention to adopt standards drawn up by the International Accounting Standards Board.[31]

As a further sign of the informal global harmonization of accounting standards, the UK International Accounting Standards Board and the US Financial Accounting Standards Board signed a memorandum committing these two power peer organizations to a long-term collaboration with a view towards professional convergence on rules and guidelines for their industry.[32] Typical areas of concern will be revenue recognition, business acquisitions, and financial performance,[33] all areas which affect profoundly how companies are internally organized. But perhaps one of the more dramatic phases of the global thrust of accounting standards comes from the US in the form of the Sarbanes-Oxley Act of 2002.[34]

Under the US Sarbanes-Oxley Act, and in a highly abbreviated summary, a Public Company Accounting Oversight Board (Board) is created whose function, among others, is to adopt ethical and technical standards for public auditors preparing and signing financial statements for companies subject to the jurisdiction of the US SEC and require the auditors to register with the Board. While the supervision of US auditors by American regulators surely has a laudable purpose, the authors of the Sarbanes-Oxley Act also declared the jurisdiction of the Board extended to any foreign accounting firms auditing US companies subject to the SEC wherever located. This long-arm jurisdiction has caused a minor transatlantic skirmish. The EU has even issued a warning. It will retaliate against the 'Americans' if any attempt is made to extend the Sarbanes-Oxley Act to European auditors.[35] Without commenting on the many complex issues raised by the Sarbanes-Oxley Act, it is clear that the authors of the bill intended the global presence of US multinationals to be accompanied by the regulation of their financial statements even when prepared by non-US auditors. Whatever will be the protests, the results are unlikely to alter the steady march of US laws in consonance with its economy. And the non-US auditors are unlikely to protest too long. Just or unjust, the Sarbanes-Oxley Act is not going to prevent the auditing profession from its traditional role of being an indispensable ally of capital. The regulation of non-US auditors will eventually be accepted and US financial laws under the Sarbanes-Oxley Act will have a global presence.

What is a sensible and fair system of standards can only be determined by the experience and judgment of the participants. Of course there are no debated, published, voted-upon social standards put to the public. They emanate from the participants who are the actors. There is no definable legislative or constitutional declaration as to what are the wishes of the community. It is the objectives of the industrialized nations, represented by the cadre of professionals, trained in these countries, which determine the content of the suggested core principles. Compliance must rest upon general principles and are enforced by financial ostracism. An institution which fails to honor disclosure requirements and then is subsequently declared insolvent is unlikely to be a welcome candidate for further public international lending.

Domestic regulators of international banks will of course adopt the orientation of the Basle banks.[36] The Basle banks influence the professional associations and organizations. These in turn through peer consensus construct further standards. So the new financial architecture now in place contains the imperfections of a consensual process which are the early stages of the globalization of financial laws and related services.

As money is sovereign, the globalization of financial laws of course has its merits. But it also brings further cracks in the wall of sovereignty, reducing its foundations to the will of investors.

*Sovereignty is a currency peg*

The last resort of sovereignty is a nation's currency, the strength of one complementing the other. But so powerful are the effects of international capital movements that even the US$ — more concretely the formidable, indomitable 'greenback' — has had to face some humiliating facts. Asia has become the most significant purchaser of US treasury debt.[37] General Motors, the icon of US industrial power, has implored the US government to request Japan to stop intervening on the foreign exchange markets to support the yen. General Motors wants a weaker 'greenback'.[38] Yet if sovereignty means independence then US sovereignty, in all matters except military force, is becoming a hapless onlooker before the economic prowess of others. According to the US Federal Reserve, US financial markets, in particular the purchase of US treasury bonds, are subject to the whims of China, Japan, South Korea, and Hong Kong.[39] The irony of the currency markets is that depreciated Asian currencies make it possible for US consumers to continue their buying spree thus adding to the imbalances of the US current account.[40] Should Asian central banks decide to sell their US$ surpluses on the foreign exchange market, a massive depreciation of the US$ would occur, driving up interest rates in the US in order to attract foreign buyers of US debt. The result is domestic monetary and fiscal policies are conditioned upon the decisions of central banks of other nations, with their own objectives, which are, of course, a consequence of geo-commercial strategies as well as political aims.

With global integration of financial markets, sovereignty is thus reduced and restricted. Freedom of capital movement now means domestic policies are conditioned by events over which the electorate has no power. The captains of industry of other nations muse as to whether or not it is appropriate to devalue or appreciate the US currency. Of course the IMF is concerned. It can easily be replaced by the Asian Monetary Fund (AMF). Financial markets and sovereignty have become incompatible.

## Notes

[1] Kanishka Jayasuriya, *Globalization, Law and the Transformation of Sovereignty: The Emergence of Global Regulatory Convergence*, 6 Ind. J. Global Legal Stud. 425 (1999).
[2] For a general discussion on markets and human rights, See Frank J. Garcia, *Humanizing the Financial Architecture of Globalization: A Tribute to the Work of Cynthia Lichtenstein*, 25 B.C. Int'l & Comp. LO. Rev. 203 (2002).
[3] See home page at web site <www.bis.org>, accessed 20 August 2002. Material concerning the Basle banks is found in the Chapter 12 entitled 'The Basle Bank Decrees Global Financial Regulations'.
[4] See home page at web site <www.bis.org>, accessed 12 August 2002, with links to the Basle Committee on Banking Supervision.
[5] See home page at web site <www.iosco.org>, accessed 13 August 2002.
[6] See home page at web site <www.iaisweb.org>, accessed 12 August 2002 and whose activities are discussed further in this chapter.
[7] See home page at <www.iasb.org.uk>, accessed 13 August 2002.
[8] For a list of many such associations in the US, <www.bluefield.edu/library/subguides/account.htm>, accessed 7 April 2003.
[9] See Joseph J. Norton et al., *The Ongoing Process of International Bank Regulatory and Supervisory Convergence: A New Regulatory 'Partnership'*, 16 Ann. Rev. Banking L. 227 (1997). A typical example furnished is by the US Commodity Futures Trading Commission and the UK Securities and Investment Board which issued the Windsor Declaration of May 1995 (on file with the International Financial and Tax Law Unit, Centre for Commercial Law Studies, Queen Mary and Westfield College, University of London). This Report addressed the exchange of information between regulatory authorities concerned with securities transactions and was produced from the participants present: Australia, Brazil, Canada, France, Germany, Hong Kong, Italy, Japan, Netherlands, Singapore, South Africa, Spain, Sweden, Switzerland, US, and the UK.
[10] Gordon Walker, *International Regulations in the Information Age: The Political Dimensions of Globalization*, Journal of International Banking Law, 10(11), 463-465 (1995).
[11] Ibid.
[12] Allan H. Meltzer, *Back to Bailouts*, The Wall Street Journal Europe, 8 August 2002, at p. A8, describing how the IMF had to extend credit to Uruguay because of a 'run' on bank deposits by Argentines unable probably to obtain funds from their deposits in Argentina because of a monetary crisis there. The IMF extended a credit line of $3.8 billion, more than $1,100 per capita. Mr Meltzer aptly states the citizens of Uruguay have mortgaged their future. One can also add that the interest rate should be paid by the Argentineans.
[13] Chris Giles, *Markets rise on Brazil's IMF deal*, The Financial Times, 9 August 2002 at p. 2, reporting all candidates for presidential elections in Brazil have accepted terms of a proposed IMF loan in the amount of $30 billion provided there is a commitment to a 2002 budget surplus of 3.75 per cent of gross domestic product. As some of the candidates are campaigning for more social benefits, the extraction of this promise curtails their social net programs.

[14] Ibid.
[15] Ibid.
[16] Raymond Colitt et al., *Investor fears of leftwing poll win disturb fragile confidence in Brazil*, The Financial Times, 10/11 August 2002, at p. 1.
[17] John H. Mead, *Supranational Law: How the Move towards Multilateral Solutions is Changing the Character of 'International' Law*, 42 U. Kan. L. Rev. 605 (1994).
[18] See statistics cited in Huw Evans, *International Financial Architecture: Learning the Lessons of History*, Journal of International Financial Markets 3, 70-79, (2000).
[19] Ibid.
[20] The public furor or preoccupation over central bank tight or loose fiscal policy seldom concerns itself with capital reserves or credit parameters established by a central bank. The public is interested in its immediate reward, interest calculations, at times forgetting that the policies which transpires to the journals is the end result of technical guidelines emanating from as far away as Basle.
[21] Supra, n. 5.
[22] Supra, n. 6.
[23] Supra, n. 8.
[24] See supra, n. 3 and reference to Chapter 12.
[25] See home page of IOSCO, supra, n. 5, for full list.
[26] See home page of IAIS, supra, n. 6, for full list.
[27] Supra, n. 4 and links to topic.
[28] A consultation of the home page of BIS at supra, n. 4, reveals the extensive organizational network with other entities and, by way of illustration, including multiple international accounting standard committees.
[29] Supra, n. 8.
[30] Ibid.
[31] Lucy Smy, *Accounting rules find global favor*, The Financial Times, 12 February 2003, at p. 19.
[32] Andrew Parker, *Accounting standards move towards compatibility*, 30 October 2002, at p. 6.
[33] Ibid.
[34] Public Law 107-204, July 30, 2002, 116 Stat. 745.
[35] Francesco Guerrera et al., *US warned over auditor laws*, The Financial Times, 6 March 2003, at p. 1.
[36] Connie M. Friesen, *The 1998 Basle Committee Supervisory Initiatives and Their Potential Consequences of International Banking Activities*, J.I.B.L. 14(2) 55-61 (1999).
[37] Jenny Wiggins, *US bonds face gloomier future as selling continues to increase*, The Financial Times, 8 September 2003, at p. 17.
[38] James Mackintosh, *GM calls on US to lobby over yen*, The Financial Times, 11 September 2003, at p. 19.
[39] Päivi Munter, *Foreign holdings of US treasuries hit record 46%*, 11 September 2003, at p. 20.
[40] Alan Beattie, *Asia is a threat to recovery, says the IMF*, The Financial Times, 19 September 2003, at p. 1.

# Chapter 14

# Insolvent Sovereigns and Global Insolvency

*In the beginning there was a sovereign*

For anarchists, there is, at last, cause to rejoice.

Prior to the oil revolution of 1973-74, there was an unprecedented economic growth in the industrialized nations.[1] The major petroleum companies had not anticipated this expansion. As a result, the oil producing nations failed to make the required capital investments. Even if there had been no embargo by the Arab cartel, OPEC, one-third of the major Saudi oil reserves would have been shut down anyhow for technical reasons thus sponsoring a spiraling price rise. Accordingly, probably as fast as the oil spurted forth from wells, the slush of petroleum dollars generated by the revolt of the oil cartels were judiciously deposited in Western banks. Few bite the hand that feeds them. Overseas branches of US banks were a favorite choice by the OPEC exporters.

By making short and medium term loans with interest rates adjusted frequently and periodically to an agreed index, such as the London Interbank Offering Rate (LIBOR), the Euro dollar market flourished and profit was awash thanks to the innovative floating interest rate mechanism. Sovereign borrowing was poised to expand dramatically. With the birth of the Euro dollar, there was a surplus waiting to be invested. The IMF, dominated by US policy makers, was, and still is, considered a safety net for US investors as well as US banks. Bailouts by the IMF in the form of emergency loans for sovereign debtors are a constant news feature of financial journals. Possessed of a significant surplus, the banks scurried to loan out their excess funds to any sovereign without regard to its financial stability — with an eye over their shoulders at the Washington-based IMF — so long as it was short term. Short term was needed to avoid any possible future inflationary interest trends. On the other hand, the same periods are disadvantageous to borrowers since they are subject to sudden inflationary trends. But this obvious threat deterred few sovereigns. Moreover, the choice of sovereign borrowers by US banks was part of larger US institutional lending abroad, stimulated for various reasons.

Concurrently, the American Overseas Private Investment Corporation (OPIC) had been established in 1971.[2] A self-sustaining agency of the US, OPIC insures, among other things, against political violence such as war, revolution, insurrection, terrorism, civil strife, and sabotage. Since its inception, OPIC has insured American investors abroad in the total amount of $138 billion dollars.[3] This clearly stimulated US banks to loan funds for investment in foreign countries since the main risks associated with foreign investment debts — war, civil strife, revolution — were now covered under OPIC insurance. The global reach of US capital in emerging economies supported the movement for sovereigns lending since the sovereign who hosted foreign investment were seen as good risks.

Complementary to the insurance offered by OPIC, US corporate expansionism abroad was taking place at the same time, fostered by American tax policy. Under US tax legislation, banks and multinationals operating overseas and subject to a foreign tax are able to claim a credit against existing US tax liabilities.[4] Thus, available US insurance against usual sovereign risks combined with US tax policies favoring US banks operating abroad, created the conditions ideal for global US multinational expansion and a plethora of international loans to sovereigns. It meant good business for US banks to be abroad. Euro dollars, or petrodollars, depending on your grammatical honesty, were plentiful and in search of application.

With foreign branches of US banks oscillating between sovereign nations and US multinationals, the international banking system fomented the era of Euro dollars. Unfortunately, with reserves sloshing about in accounts but not earning revenue, the banks did not act like prudent lenders.[5] The result could only be, and was, a brewing sovereign debt crisis which would eventually require the international public lending institutions to intervene.

### *Sovereign immunity and sovereign insolvency*

The hoary, legal doctrine of sovereign immunity should be renamed the doctrine of modern sovereign irresponsibility. Whereas once the proverbial soup line was a symbol of individual desperation, its contemporary equivalent is the governmental letter delivered to the IMF, humbly requesting relief from insolvency. Normally the dispatch of the letter assists in the remission of insomnia for the official obliged to write the missive. In the area of international economic law, theory has melodiously accompanied mercantile profit. The middle age doctrine whereby the King could do no wrong, eventually grafted onto the nation state's general exemption from all liability, is now defunct. While for some there may be hesitation as to criminal accountability for heads of state, answerability for commercial acts is present conventional doctrine.

As a typical example, 45 states of the US as well as the US Federal Government, now recognize a sovereign can be sued for a variety of acts including commercial activities.[6] Of course, the change in legal doctrine is a result of economic forces. The insatiable need of funds by nations and the imprudent lending by international banks in their frenzy to obtain above market interest rates have combined to dethrone sovereign immunity. When it comes to international loans and the raising of funds by sovereigns, therefore, the academic debates are not whether a sovereign nation can be sued. Surely borrowers in the private capital markers can have no immunity and courts have readily found liability for sovereigns attempting to seek refuge in the sovereign immunity doctrine.[7] Legal doctrine eventually adheres to practical economics.

Rather, presently, scholastic interest is focused on to what extent there should be international rules governing sovereign insolvency and what these regulations should be. Various proposals have been ventilated, some attracting even media attention[8] for what is usually considered the exclusive turf of legal scholars. Yet the social consequences of global insolvency procedures for the sovereign and its citizens remain largely either not considered or not deemed relevant. That the normative effects are clearly more significant than the insolvency formalities under discussion requires a comprehension of the international sovereign bond market.

Initially most lending to sovereigns in the 1970s was effectuated through syndicated bank loans.[9] This technical term applies when a reduced amount of international banks pool resources to obtain funds for borrowing nations. However, by the 1990s the composition of lenders changed considerably. Bond and equity issues became the dominant form of raising capital in international markets, replacing significantly the syndicated bank loans. This shift in how sovereign loans were arranged resulted in the proportion of outstanding public external debt owed to private creditors in the form of bond purchases to rise from 13 per cent in 1980 to 60 per cent in 2000.[10]

The situation is even more dramatic when we consider the sovereign debts of the world's poorest nations. Total debt from heavily indebted poor countries (HIPC) as of 1999 was $106 billion.[11] However, of this amount $12 billion is owed to the US Treasury Dept., $19 billion to the public finances of Germany, and $31 billion to that of Japan.[12] Although the US is only the third largest individual creditor yet its attitude and actions are more significant in consequences. This is because it dominates the major public lending institutions, the IMF and the World Bank, which is the principal source of bailouts and emergency loans.[13] Of multilateral total debt, as of 1999, from HIPC to the IMF there was owed $12,345 billion and to the World Bank $60,835 billion.[14] The US directly or indirectly controls 85 per cent of HIPC debt as of 1999 if we assume de facto control of the IMF and the World Bank. Critical to legal globalization is that a majority of third world debt is owed to US banks.[15] In 1991, third world debt approximated $1.3 trillion.[16]

Where there is borrowing there are defaults. The credit-rating agency S&P's calculates that over the last two centuries 90 sovereigns have either defaulted or rescheduled their debts and some more then once.[17] Sovereign borrowing and sovereign defaulting, potential or actual, will continue. What has changed, however, is the nature of the international bond market, the players, and the response to potential sovereign defaults. No longer are we dealing with a restricted amount of sophisticated bank lenders prepared to negotiate new terms with a sovereign in distress. In the 1980s, 85 per cent of a country's debts could be resolved by convening 15 creditors to a crisis conference.[18]

The market of emerging market finance has changed dramatically since the debt crisis of the 1980s. Capital markets are more integrated, and thus globalized, and countries have turned to bond issues rather than syndicated bank loans as their principal means of raising finance. Sovereign borrowers now issue debt in a range of legal jurisdictions, using a variety of instruments, to a diverse and diffuse group of creditors. Moreover, the majority of holders of present day sovereign bonds are private investors,[19] with diverse interests, often owning sovereign bonds through funds or other financial instruments, with no motive in a continuing relationship with the sovereign, and less interested in rescheduling for the sake of fostering a propitious working climate.

Faced with recurrent sovereign crises and unresponsive investors, the international financial community, represented by the IMF, has responded to assuage the potential cascading effect of a sovereign default rippling through the transnational banking community. Relief emergency loans to sovereigns are now part of the portfolio of the IMF. Nevertheless, by altering in practice its original statutory purpose, that of ensuring countries were able to meet their foreign exchange obligations, the IMF has been chastened and branded as fomenting a moral hazard.[20] If the IMF will always step in and salvage the insolvent nation, lenders have no reason to take seriously credit reviews.

Notwithstanding, the IMF, in conjunction with the US, has intervened as a lender of 'last' resort. Although these initiatives can be characterized as the market system reacting to save its own philosophies and economic objectives, the fact is that sovereigns on the brink of insolvency with violent disruption to community life imminent, have been rescued. In the late 1980s when the threats of possible sovereign defaults appeared real, the US Treasury cajoled US bank creditors and sovereign debtors to reschedule bond maturity dates. As this plan was conceived of and supported by the then US Secretary of Treasury, Nicholas Brady, the new, rescheduled bonds became known as 'Brady bonds'.[21]

The first Brady bonds were introduced in 1990. Brady bonds are repackaged, defaulted commercial bank loans. In the mid 1990s there was an outstanding stock of $150 billion.[22] These are financial instruments encouraged by the US Treasury whose objective is to exchange default bonds for new ones with lower interest secured by US Treasury 30 year securities that the debtor-nation purchases. Moreover, the Brady plan allows banks to write off sovereign debts and lend further to help amortize existing debts. The US, through its internal revenue service, provides tax advantages to US banks participating in the Brady plan. Unexpected, draconian results have been banks selling back to countries at a substantial discount loans in default; or debt-equity swaps; debt for debt exchanges; and debt for nature swaps. There is no lack of financial imagination or complicity existing between foreign debtors and US creditors.[23]

As recently as 1997, the Brady bond program was buttressed by the creation of an IMF Supplemental Reserve Facility (SRF).[24] The SRF enables the IMF to confront a sovereign debt crisis within a relatively short period by making short term loans at above market rates. But it is the bond markets which have spurred efforts at devising global solutions to insolvent sovereigns. The Brady bonds were sold by banks to other private investors thus reducing their banking reserve exposure.

Being sold to various investors, the sovereign bond and the domestic commercial bond markets face similar problems, such as the need to harmonize creditor responses; the necessity for the debtor, company or sovereign, to be able to continue doing business; the appointment of creditor committees to review proposed plans of reorganization or rescheduling of debts; the ability of creditors willing to accept new terms to be able to bind and preclude other creditors from taking legal action. These are some of the more common themes which occupy insolvency scholars. However sovereigns and commercial creditors are not twin brothers.

A sovereign borrower is distinguished from its private counterpart by a critical distinction. The assets of a private company can be liquidated and monies obtained on a forced sale. Except by war and plunder, the values of an insolvent nation are unreachable. There can be no liquidation of national assets. To enforce a creditor's lien would require the consent of the sovereign's courts. It is neither a conceivable nor a probable reckoning. The solution is to achieve through legal formalities what is sometimes done by the sword.

As we are dealing with a global sovereign bond market, what is required are global insolvency procedures. The reasons are the urgency in avoiding multiple law suits; creditors in a race to be the first to the court house; a standard procedure to permit rescheduling of debts and binding all creditors; a method so that a sovereign can continue with its imports and investment plans without fear of judicial actions which disrupt normal economic activity. In short, sovereigns, similar to private companies, need a degree of legal certainty within which to proceed. This would benefit both debtors and creditors, and it will contribute to, one might wistfully conclude, a perfect market economy.

### *Sovereign debt default and the International Creditors' Court*

There is no international convention establishing the orderly restructuring of unsustainable sovereign debts when creditor action becomes imminent.[25] Currently, a creditor of a sovereign debtor in default either pursues its remedies in a court or, in conjunction with other creditors, reschedules the debt with the sovereign debtor. There is substantial unanimity among academicians, the IMF, and the various private trade associations[26] that efficient international legal procedures must be constructed to bring order into the sovereign debt bond market. Without any international insolvency regulations, creditors, when faced with impending sovereign defaults, attempt to garner advantages over one another; some refuse to reschedule a sovereign debt, hoping other creditors will pay them off in full to forestall legal action; while other creditors are ready to buy defaulted bonds at deep discounts so they can sue and reap substantial profits; while still others, armed with a court execution, attempt to seize assets wherever they can be found.[27]

Constant throughout the published discussions are the various proposals which discuss the relevance or not of using the US bankruptcy regulations[28] as a model to apply to sovereign debtors, scattered, as they must be, all over the world.[29] Thus, disregarding the social and economic origins of the bankrupt law paradigm invoked, various chapters of the US Bankruptcy Code are touted as offering a workable framework for, variously entitled, an International Bankruptcy Court, International Bankruptcy Agency, or International Debt Restructuring Agency.[30] One proposition includes a contractual approach involving more ambitious use of collective action clauses in sovereign bond. Such a clause limits the ability of dissident creditors to stand in the way of a widely-supported restructuring. With the proper legal language inserted into a sovereign bond, buyers are put on notice that unanimous creditor action is not needed to effectuate a rescheduling but only a predefined super-majority.

Other recommendations include an international convention which could establish formal procedures before an international bankruptcy court; or whether the IMF should have its articles amended to permit it to supervise insolvency procedures supported by the power of a super-majority of creditors to impose their will on all other creditors; or whether instead of a court or the IMF, compulsory private negotiations supplemented by arbitration[31] are a sensible, practical solution.

For those favoring the present status, where bankers and sovereigns attempt to reschedule debts voluntarily, it is advocated market forces should determine what actions prevail or fail. If negotiations fail, the adoption of procedures similar to those used before the ISCID,[32] an arbitration center dependent upon the World Bank and which hears disputes between sovereigns and private citizens, offers a sensible framework when debtor-creditor settlement prove futile.

However, the various insolvency designs presented in detail are invariably from the viewpoint of the creditor. Mechanisms for binding all creditors, techniques for ensuring a smooth transition to a rescheduling, having creditor claims heard before an arbitration board, requiring the debtor to proceed in good faith (but not the creditors), priority financing, staying creditor claims so as not to precipitate a default, these are some of the usual themes discussed in public.[33]

Throughout the discussions, even in the proposal for a name, the plight of the sovereign debtor is rarely taken into consideration. In fact, it seems more appropriate and accurate to denominate the international supervisory authority to be created by an international convention, the International Creditors' Court. No matter in most cases it is creditor misbehavior, plain, simple loan avarice, which is the basic problem. An improvident lender is as responsible as a penurious sovereign debtor. Yet there is rampant, imprudent bank lending; disregard for the elementary practices of credit analysis, for deposits must be lent out and anyhow the IMF will keep the sovereigns in cash. Time and time again the IMF has come to the rescue of governments who do not maintain credible policies; private property rights are altered in conformity with the profit interests of the ruling classes; destructive policies imposed on the citizenry ensure that those in control of the economy will obtain revenue whatever the crisis.[34]

The list of misfeasance can be lengthened to include the willingness of many international banks to accept sums whose amount indicates they are the pillage of the sovereign treasuries by chiefs of state and which impedes the sovereign from subsequently honoring its bond maturity dates; funds served in dollop by the financial community so that the debtor sovereign eventually has more interest to serve than principal to repay. And if this were not enough the debtor sovereign is now expected to adopt, no matter what international scheme, procedures based upon the general principles of Western bankruptcy law, specifically those derived from the principles of the US Bankruptcy Code.

The conclusion is inescapable that the primary object of the IMF and the US Treasury has been to assure security and mobility of capital. In 1995, the then US Treasury under-secretary rescued Mexico from default with an IMF emergency loan reinforcing bond investor conviction as to the safety of sovereign bonds.[35] Latin American sovereign bond issues thereafter quadrupled from $9 billion to $37 billion.[36] By 2001, official emergency loans to economies in distress amounted to $250 billion.[37] Ultimately, the powerful exporters of capital, the US banks, are thrown IMF lifesavers when the tidal wave of sovereign default threatens US shores. The present international financial system is based on the unrestricted and unregulated movement of capital. The banking system is the triumph of pursuit of profit and naiveté over common sense.[38] Without doubt, subjacent to all discussions as to the appropriate forum for hearing sovereign insolvency claims are broad social issues, which are presumed to be the correct formula for judging and hearing sovereign insolvency issues.

But it is apparently the unpaid creditor which predominantly monopolizes scholastic interest.

## *The social aspects of international sovereign insolvency*

The basic social premise, which is often characterized as a legal issue, is whether insolvency procedures applicable for private parties can be applied to sovereigns.[39] There are approximately 200 nations.[40] It is not logical, nor correct to employ one word to characterize the aggregation of rights and obligations surmised under the expression 'sovereign'.

The characteristics which confer sovereignty to the United Kingdom have little in common with the nature of a sovereignty, for example, based upon tribal law with its clans, kinship, right of redress for vengeance, and where order is perhaps based on a matrilineal society.[41] Even recognizing the rare appearance of such extremes, it cannot be denied that the social and economic structures of industrialized countries do not find a mirror image in many sovereign nations throughout the world. Urban nations and rural sovereigns present distinct and different cultural contours.

The first consideration of any insolvency procedure must be to decide is the object of the procedure. Most authors assume it is relief to the debtor and eventual payment to the creditor. However, there are other legitimate concerns. Satisfaction of creditors is but one of many, such as fomenting general economic rehabilitation; savings jobs; ensuring a transfer of knowledge from one generation to another; not losing export markets needed for a source of foreign currency; preserving access to housing, health, and education. Furthermore, often economic conditions have changed radically due to the creditors' economies and not the debtor, such as devaluation of the creditor's currency so that emerging nation exports are hindered or deflation grasps the creditor's economy and consumption is depressed. Ironically, the monetary zero hour is transferred to the debtor who anticipated servicing principal and debt out of exports.

But even if we were able to pass over this essential premise as to the objectives of an insolvency procedure, we are confronted with an equally important dilemma: a definition of insolvency. To be an insolvent sovereign requires a standard. Many exist, but none are utilized since it would probably include most of the industrialized nations of the world. There can be a current account deficit in the balance of payments, sometimes denominated the gross external financing gap, when imports exceed exports which the debtor cannot satisfy within the near future. There can be an exaggerated amount of budget deficit to public revenue.[42] Or the public deficit may exceed 60 per cent of the gross national product which may be considered excessive.[43] There are also the traditional measures of the health of a nation such as gross domestic production, private consumption, capital investment by the private and public sector, and government consumption.

One could with equal reason argue that insolvency cannot be determined by reference alone to the debtor but to the world economic conjuncture. With capital markets integrated globally, and international commerce the prevalent activity, sovereign insolvency makes no sense without reference to a list of international indicators. Measures for a malaise of generalized insolvency are world share and commodity indexes; rate of bankruptcies; brusque exchange alterations in currency markets; industrial production; consumer price indexes; business inventories; employment statistics; non-farm payrolls; jobless claims; and of course consumer sentiment. The usual statistics which are published to monitor the economic activity of a particular country can be utilized to construct a world economic indicator. In other words, sovereign insolvency is intimately related to world commerce. If many of the nations of the world are undergoing deflation or stagnation, the international banking community has a responsibility beyond the collection of receiving its principal and interest.

Private entities receive temporary relief from creditor pursuit on the theory that insolvency may only be a temporary aberration in the economic cycle. The same reasons seem more imperative when discussing sovereign nations. Of course, such assertions will meet scant reception, deviating as they do from the prevalent mercantile spirit. Rather, supporters of an international convention see a moral purpose in establishing a uniform, supervised procedure.[44] Taxpayer's money is saved since the IMF is not needed for emergency bailouts. Within the confines of regulatory procedures, conditions can be imposed on the debtor in the nature of legal or economic reforms. An international convention minimizes moral hazard since all creditors know they must adhere to the convention procedures.

Nevertheless, there is official recognition that sovereign debt restructuring must be accepted as part of the consequences of international commerce and it is not just an isolated event whose principal actor is the sovereign nation.[45] It is a social event although characterized as an economic crisis. It will come as no surprise, therefore, that the IMF, a global bank without a banking license, and whose depositors-shareholders are limited to sovereign nations, proposes a sovereign debt restructuring mechanism for its members when a debt becomes unsustainable.[46]

We are not informed what unsustainable means, but the IMF expounds a minimum definition, even if vague and sparse, that it is identifiable as there would be 'no feasible set of sustainable macroeconomic policies'[47] to enable the crisis to be resolved immediately without a reduction of the debt. In other words, borrow more money, reduce principal maturing, and reschedule a new amortization program. Since the money must ultimately come from the citizens, there has been declared an augment of taxes without parliamentary discussion, presuming the nation in question possesses such an organization.

The IMF report shows a genuine compassion for the plight of the debtor sovereign, while its apparent concern with a four-point program reveals a sensible analysis of creditor problems:

- collective creditor action so as to bind dissenting creditors
- a stay on creditor enforcement of claims in court
- the protection of creditors by procedures designed to preserve sovereign assets and avoid payment to non-priority creditors
- a mechanism to stimulate further borrowings through priority financing.

Yet the basic solution lies elsewhere. Once a sovereign debtor either suspends payment or is on the threshold of doing so, presumably we are confronting an unsustainable debt, and then the sovereign debtor is expected to collaborate with the IMF.[48] The IMF will propose an appropriate economic framework for the sovereign debtor.[49] Of course this will include a fiscal and 'external adjustment'[50] path which means no more nor less then further official financing accompanied by social and economic changes advocated by the IMF. The language of the report is the IMF will establish 'certain parameters'[51] for a viable restructuring.

One scholar[52] has set forth another four-point outline which could be supported by the IMF:

- the IMF establishes a global standard for sovereign bonds which contains a collective action clause: a majority of creditors is sufficient to establish new bond terms
- for pre-existing bond issues by developing nations, the IMF should assume the fees for conversion of old bonds into new long-term bonds with the proposed standards, including of course a collective action clause
- other sovereigns incorporate the proposed collective action provisions into their bonds or pay a 3-5 per cent surcharge when an emergency loan becomes necessary.

We thus return to what has always been the leitmotif of the IMF: a carrier of Western social beliefs and economic principles. The IMF adheres to the doctrine of the 'establishment of universal treaty obligations'[53] rather than 'through the enactment of legislation in a limited number of jurisdictions'.[54] But the IMF's preference for a bold bankruptcy solution is apparently derailed for the moment.[55] Universality is to be preferred over diversity. Official doctrine is to be imposed regardless of cultural variety. There is no clearer example of the globalization of Western law. For sovereign debtors, similar to their commercial, private counterparts, suffer from the same infirmity. One does not dispute with the savior the morality of its commandments.

The avalanche of sovereign borrowing has substantially weakened the traditional concept of sovereignty. Freedom of capital movement has integrated the sovereign nation into the intricacies of the financial world. Sovereign bonds are traded as easily as corporate obligations. But while the circulation of capital and services may grant independence to the proprietors, the same cannot be said of the sovereign nation. Sovereign insolvency brings fears of a 'contagion effect' whereby investors will withdraw their funds from a particular country. Then there is the threat of 'systemic risk' which will cause major international financial institutions to collapse. Finally, cementing these thoughts together are economic concerns about a 'moral hazard' whereby investors make decisions based on the knowledge potential sovereign defaults will be avoided by the IMF in conjunction with other entities.[56] This is, of course, contrary to the precepts of a free, unfettered, unregulated market economy.

Clearly, debt creates obligations and the sovereign nation, now a major debtor, has had to capitulate before the forces of capital and accept the social precepts which underlie its circulation. Law reflects social ideas and the more debt the sovereign accumulates, the more it is obligated to accept the mores of the triumphant West. No doubt the final resolution of sovereign insolvency will be the enactment of an international convention with international arbitration as the dispute resolution process. Such a convention has the support of distinguished scholars.[57]As international loans are a phenomena of the Western industrialized nations it is logical that the laws regulating the failure to pay will require the sovereign debtor to proffer, besides interest, homage to the laws of those countries.

More than other areas of the law, such as the law of contract or company law, international bankruptcy law, an oxymoron since none yet exists, will impart to sovereigns dependent on international capital concepts which appear merely technical, but which are essentially social beliefs. The object of a bankruptcy proceeding; the accountability of the debtor and its public functionaries; the rights of creditors towards the sovereign and toward each other; the power vested in a bankruptcy arbitrator or judge; the legal references international arbitration will invoke and the contents of same; these crucial themes involve economic theories and social beliefs.

Sovereign insolvency opens the path to legal globalization under Western law concepts as the Westerners are the creditors and the rest of the world is in debt.

## Notes

[1] The material in this section is indebted to the exposition by Jerome I. Levinson, *The International Financial System: A Flawed Architecture*, 23-SPG Fletcher F. World Aff. 1 (1999).

[2] See home page at <www.opic.gov>, accessed 07 January 2003.

[3] Ibid.

[4] Supra, n. 1.

[5] Ibid.

[6] While there is a vast legal literature on sovereign immunity, a condensed, schematic, description of the origins of the doctrine can be found in www.smithphillips.com/law/presley, accessed 06 January 2003.

[7] See Allied Bank Int'l v. Banco Credito Agricola de Cartago, 757 F.2d 516, 519 (2d Cir. 1985) where a US federal court held the government of Costa Rica liable on a commercial debt in spite of a general regulation by Costa Rica suspending external debt payments.

[8] Allan Beattie, *IMF's plan for bankruptcy gaining favor*, The Financial Times, 18 September 2002, at p. 6.
[9] The brief historical review which follows is based upon Anne Krueger, *The Evolution of Emerging Market Capital Flows: Why We Need to Look at Sovereign Debt Restructuring*, <www.imf.org/external/np/speeches/012102>, accessed 05 January 2003.
[10] Ibid.
[11] These statistics are available at <www.jubilee2000uk.org>, accessed 03 January 2003.
[12] Ibid.
[13] See voting procedures established by statute at <www.imf.org> and <www.worldbank.org>.
[14] Supra, n. 11.
[15] Brett H. Miller, *Sovereign Bankruptcy: Examining the United States Bankruptcy System As A Forum For Sovereign Debtors*, 22 Law & Pol'y Int'l Bus. 107 (1991).
[16] Ibid.
[17] Supra n. 9.
[18] Ibid.
[19] Lee C. Bucheit & G. Mitu Gulati, *Exit Consents In Sovereign Bond Exchanges*, 48 UCLA Rev. 59 (2000).
[20] Steven L. Schwarcz, *Sovereign Debt Restructuring: A Bankruptcy Reorganization Approach*, 85 Cornell L. Rev. 956 (2000).
[21] Ibid.
[22] Mary D'Ambrosio, *Ten Years of the Brady Markets*, Emerging Markets Investor, 6 (10), November 1999.
[23] Supra, n. 15.
[24] Supra, n. 9.
[25] Anne O. Krueger, *Preventing and Resolving Financial Crises: The Role of Sovereign Debt Restructuring*, International Monetary Fund, Latin American Meeting of the Econometric Society São Paolo, Brazil, July 26, 2002, <www.imf.org/external/np/speeches>, accessed 03 January 2003.
[26] See remarks by Michael M. Chamberlin, Executive Director, of the Emerging Markets Trade Association, *Revisting the IMF's Sovereign Bankruptcy Proposal and the Quest for More Orderly Sovereign Work-Outs*, before the Institute for International Economics, Washington, DC, April 2, 2002, available at <www.emta.org>, accessed 10 December 2002.
[27] Supra, n. 9, describing legal action against Peru brought by a creditor in an attempt to extract full payment from the sovereign by threatening to lien payments on the restructured debt, rather than by trying to seize its assets. The existence of such a legal threat makes otherwise cooperative creditors more reluctant to participate in a restructuring.
[28] All bankruptcy procedures in US are regulated by Title 11 of the US Bankruptcy Code, see 11 U.S.C. § 101 (1988). Title 11 of the United States Code is colloquially known as the Bankruptcy Code. The relevant chapters of the Bankruptcy Code most discussed are Chapters 7, 9, and 11. Chapter 11 procedures relate to commercial companies while Chapter 9 applies to municipalities. Chapter 9 permits groups such as unions or debtor employees to be heard. Furthermore, under Chapter 9, there can be no interference with the political process of debtor. It is the factor of no interference which attracts some scholars as using Chapter 9 for a model for insolvent sovereign debtors.
[29] Christoph G. Paulus, *Some Thoughts On An Insolvency Procedure For Countries*, 50 Am. J. Comp. L. 531 (2002).
[30] Kenneth Rogoff & Jeromin Zettlemeyer, *Early Ideas on Sovereign Bankruptcy Reorganization: A Survey*, International Monetary Fund, WP/02/57, March 2002.
[31] Supra, n. 20.

[32] For information concerning the ICSID see the home page of the World Bank at <www.worldbank.org/icsic>, accessed 09 January 2003.
[33] See IMF report at <www.imf.org/external/NP/pdr/sdrm/2002/021402>, accessed on 05 January 2003.
[34] Allan H. Meltzer, *New IMF loan will not solve Argentine crisis*, The Financial Times, 13 January 2003, at page 11.
[35] Adam Lerrick, *A bankruptcy court without credit*, The Financial Times, 11 April 2003, at page 13.
[36] Ibid.
[37] Ibid.
[38] Sara Silver, *Guatemalan 'Peace Bond' causes alarm*, The Financial Times, 08 January 2003, at p. 22, reporting that the Guatemalan government has been accused by the President of the Guatemalan Chamber of Commerce of being '... corrupt and inefficient ...' Nevertheless, the Guatemalan sovereign bonds are readily purchased by private investors because, in the words of a sovereign research bond broker, the sovereign bond market '... is so cash-rich ...'.
[39] Supra, n. 30.
[40] Ibid.
[41] See the discussion of the matrilineal society of the Trobiand Islanders in North Eastern New Guinea as reported by Bronislaw Malinowski, Sex and Repression in Savage Society, Meridian Books, New York (1927).
[42] The European Union requires its members to adhere to no more than 3 per cent of gross national product.
[43] Ibid.
[44] Supra, n. 20.
[45] IMF report entitled, *A Sovereign Debt Restructuring Mechanism-Further Reflections And Future Work*, dated 14 February 2002, available at <www.imf.org/external/NP/pdr/sdrm/2002/021402>, accessed 05 January 2003.
[46] Ibid.
[47] Ibid.
[48] Ibid.
[49] Ibid.
[50] Ibid.
[51] Ibid.
[52] Supra, n. 35.
[53] Ibid.
[54] Ibid.
[55] Alan Beattie, *Uruguay provides test case for merits of voluntary debt exchange*, The Financial Times, 23 April 2003, at page 3, describing Uruguay's proposal to renegotiate its bond debt service with a new issue of bonds. The decision to accept the rescheduling will be entirely dependent on the favorable opinion of market forces, specifically the investment bank bond holders and other segments of Wall St.
[56] General Accounting Office (US), *International Financial Crises — Efforts to Anticipate, Avoid, and Resolve Sovereign Crises*, (1997), GAO/GGD/INSIAD/-97-168, available at <www.gao.gov>, accessed 14 January 2003.
[57] Supra, n. 20.

# Chapter 15

# Sponsoring Global Law by International Alliances

*A road infrequently traveled*

Our present journey takes us through material as diverse as statistics, international alliances, legal documents, economic objectives, and power structures. Yet the ultimate aims, after such meandering, are to display how commerce strives to dominate; to reveal how alliances are assembled with the objective of preserving power; to substantiate how legal documents are tools for preserving authority. When we conclude our exposition of current law practice underlying international alliances, the social aspects will be considered. At least in the area of economics, the law continues to reveal itself as a tool for constructing and manipulating power. Ultimately, some will wonder if this is not true for all facets of community life and whether or not social exchange is essentially extracting privileges with an agreed game of rules consecrated with the symbol 'laws'. But we must not extrapolate and, now, turn our attention to a winding road and start out.

*The incomplete statistics of foreign direct investment*

Behind the closed mahogany doors of your typical investment bank, at any moment of the day in all the major capitals of the world, are being executed spiraling mounds of documents whose social consequences will have repercussions elsewhere. There is nothing neither sinister nor conspiratorial about this documentary architecture. Business as usual is being conducted. Your bank is assisting the financing of mergers and acquisitions as well as other types of international alliances.

The value of mergers and acquisitions, national and international, measured by assets or capitalization of the companies involved attains gigantesque numbers[1] They are a valid indicator of transnational[2] corporate influence with its social consequences.[3] However, other important statistics alert us to further, specific activity which informs us more completely. The category is foreign direct investment and its all-pervasive effects are not to be ignored. Foreign direct investment occurs when an investor in one nation purchases an asset in another jurisdiction, the latter usually denominated the 'host' country. Assets of course include equity participations in other enterprises.

Although this simple definition is not without its critics,[4] the general meaning is sufficient for our purposes, that being to grasp, graphically, the full impact of foreign direct investment taking place all over the world. Further statistics are revealing. In 1995, foreign direct investment inflows obtained $315 billion.[5] Of this amount, in 1996, 37 per cent of foreign direct investment went to developing countries while the rest was between the developed economies.[6] Still relevant for our present analysis is that 95 per cent of foreign direct investment consisted of transactions involving multinationals and their affiliates.[7]

Moreover, recently published statistics reveal a further dimension of the social reality. According to a 2002 world investment report,[8] there are 65,000 transnational corporations who have 850,000 affiliates in different parts of the world. In 2001, these affiliates employed 54,000,000 people.

The top 25 non-financial transnational corporations all come from the industrialized nations, with the US representing 25 per cent of the total. Foreign affiliates of the transnational corporations account for one-tenth of world gross domestic product and one third of world exports. Sales from these transnational corporations attain $19 trillion per year.[9] Cross border merger and acquisitions in the amount of $8.4 billion were reported during the week of 21 October 2002.[10] The industries involved were extremely diverse composing sectors such as mining, insurance, sporting goods, air freight, and of course telecommunications.

A prudent pause is merited. While there is reported a correlation between transnational investment and affiliates, we are not instructed as to what is meant by 'affiliate'. In fact, statistics concerning foreign investment are replete with apparently technical terms yet textual explanations are frequently omitted. Terminology is often a suspicious endeavor and the effort is not always commensurate with the results. However, in the case of foreign direct investment, there are meaningful insights to be garnered from this labor. We will want to understand better terms such as *affiliate, subsidiary, associate, associated group,* and *influence*. These are some of the notions which are a daily part of the practice of international alliances and which make the statistics meaningful. Moreover, their understanding reveals a commercial world normally curtained-off from our daily lives.

### *The random terminology of international alliances*[11]

According to one authoritative definition, by *affiliate* is intended an enterprise in another jurisdiction, the host country, where the foreign investor, for example our multinational, owns at least 10 per cent of the capital.[12] References to a minimum percentage platform are often encountered in definitions where the objective is to quantify influence or control. There are good reasons for this. Control, the ability to influence a legal entity, is seen as the primary tool by which commercial objectives laudable, or not, may be obtained, often by parties with an apparent minority interest. By way of illustration, in competition law, the notion of 'control' is one of the elements which decides if there has been accumulated a dominant position which may lead to market abuse.[13] There are good reasons for preoccupation with control, for, as in a community, so in company life, the ability to command guarantees access to resources.

However, accounting considerations aside, recognizing control only when there is at least a 10 per cent capital ownership is misleading and contrary to the practices of the entrepreneurial community as well as the law profession. No matter what legal conditions are established for definitional purposes, confining them to mathematical formulae is doomed to fail, or at least be out of harmony with business practices. This is demonstrated simply when we turn to subsidiaries. This is a common form of international alliances and has been defined as one company having at least 50 per cent of the voting power of another enterprise.[14] Yet this requirement is satisfied if the foreign investor can remove the majority of the board members of the subsidiary.[15] Even with minority participation, this can easily be achieved through various legal means. Considering a concept such as an *associated group*, this has been defined as two or more persons acting together to exercise an 'influence' over management[16] or an enterprise in which there is control of between 10-50 per cent of the shares eligible to vote.[17]

Control, therefore, is manipulated to the realities of business life and arithmetic is not fiat. Moreover, it is folly to distinguish an affiliate from a subsidiary from an *associate* by the percentage of participation. A reduced minority position in a company may still be able to have a veto power of a wide range of corporate board decisions which grants a substantial influence in the corporate decisions to be implemented. Far more critical is the element of control and less important are definitions which are unable to confront commercial realities.

We thus see that various definitions in addition to numerical concepts also include situations such as 'influence' or control'. The difference between control and influence has yet to be satisfactorily explained but presumably control means the ability to act without collaboration from others while influence requires an element of cooperation. Of course, influence is another aspect of control. Without control, there are no consequences for someone, and without end results foreordained, influence evaporates with its verbal command. It does seem as if control without influence is a grammatical puzzle. Nevertheless, there persist in legal literature frequent references to either one or the other.

Such an attitude is demonstrated by supranational competition authorities.[18] Competition boards early learned that regulating mergers or acquisitions so as to prevent unfair competition or impede a dominant position in the market could not be done by mathematical concepts. In the practice of European competition law, it is imperative to be familiar with the concepts of 'lasting control', 'decisive influence', or 'substantial influence'.[19] Yet it is not only competition law which illustrates the pervasive recourse to influence or control. It is all of commercial law, particularly company law. Control can be accomplished in many ways and were one to allow a client with a 99 per cent ownership of capital to agree that 1 per cent will have the right to nominate the entire board of directors, we surely would concur that 1 per cent effectively 'controls' the corporation or can 'decisively influence' it.

This unrealistic, draconian example[20] can be modified and expanded into many areas of corporate law where there are sound commercial reasons for a yielding of power. A frequent motive is the need for cash flow which requires a new shareholder. But the new shareholder, realizing the investment in the alliance carries risk demands, veto power over a range of corporate acts. With an abundance of legal devices available, what determines whether or not there exists an affiliate, subsidiary, or associate in the plain sense of the words resides more than not in a concept such as control. Through a multitude of legal documents it is possible for an entity with a modest equity position to construct a substantial influence over an affiliate.

From the understanding that affiliates and their kin do not require an apparent majority position, should come the realization that what the statistics are really describing are all sorts of international alliances without regard to an entrepreneurial concept. Whether the compiler of statistics is thinking in terms of 10 per cent or 50 per cent, without the legal documents in hand to study, the actuality of the alliance escapes the observer. Additionally, to render even more suspect the statistics, no technical description of an international alliance exists. Words tend to melt into sentences and phrases and at times we do not stop to consider what is the information being conveyed. International alliance is one of them. Certainly an international alliance includes affiliates, subsidiaries, and associates. But also contemplated by our international capital venturer are international joint ventures and strategic alliances, collaboration between entities with a lasting commercial objective.

With this perspective, a concise definition of international alliances academically acceptable is unobtainable. There are just too many varieties of legal structures obtained through the decades of experience by international practitioners. A reasonable schedule would require a specialized lexicon, only to become outdated rather quickly. Nevertheless, rather than constructing an exposition on a multitude of definitions, all of the objectives intended by the statistics and terminology can be grouped under the expression 'international alliances'. It really doesn't matter on a broad scale the precise nature or legal structure of the international alliances being studied. The information sought to be transmitted is the foreign direct investment and its consequences. The end results will be substantially linked to forging methods of control. It is more understandable to envision what is taking place as does the entrepreneur. Business from one jurisdiction is moving to another. Collaboration will be undertaken. It can have many forms, and we will certainly examine some, but what is pretended is an economic collaboration. To the merchants and their investment banks, an international alliance is being constructed, whether it be through an acquisition, international joint venture, or a consortium, any of which fall within the classification of an subsidiary, affiliate, or associate.

International alliances, therefore, is an elusive category. Yet the comprehension of the underlying spread of transnational corporate power through alliances is not to be sought by grappling with semantic problems. The key word is 'control' or 'substantial influence' and how this is done. It is the daily practice of international alliances which illuminates how transnational corporate power spreads through international alliances and what are the consequences. As the invasion is only possible with the use of legal concepts, the economic domination of US multinationals on an international scale invariably carries with it the subjacent legal principles.

*Capital remuneration through power*

International alliances are both a legal and social endeavour. The two cannot, in practice, be separated. But the sociological consequences exist, in abundance, and can be grouped and studied under the theme of capital remuneration through power utilizing the share corporation structure. The modern share corporation, modeled along Western legal concepts, has contributed immensely to the maintenance of Western corporate power and its legal concepts.

However, the study of capital remuneration through power and its effects globally cannot be disassociated from some aspects of company law. Although the material initially appears fraught with categories and complexity, it need not be so. A general initiation in alliances is indispensable for a comprehensive introduction to this topic. There is the foreign investor, the party with the capital, and there is the host investor, or partner, knowledgeable in the ways of the foreign jurisdiction. They form international alliances with the purposes of increasing market shares through complementary skills. A lateral consequence is a further contribution to the construction of a global law. There are valid reasons for these phenomena.

The proposed international alliance will use a legal form known to the international investors and lenders. No foreign investor is going to accept an unfamiliar legal structure. A transfer of an important patent right from an English company to an Angolan subsidiary is going to utilize a contract form and technical legal language thoroughly mastered in all aspects by the English advisors. No other alternative is even contemplated. Those who want capital have to be prepared to accommodate themselves to the legal concepts of the major exporters of capital. The need for Western capital confers on the traditional Western legal model an undisputed choice. This naturally has global consequences.

Again, thinking of international alliances, foreign investment is seldom made in an individual name in a foreign jurisdiction. The possibility of an individual being subject to the laws of another jurisdiction is not conducive to foreign investment. International alliances are preferred through a company structure as this achieves limited liability for the investor. Responsibility is limited to the alliance assets. Noted for its flexibility and adaptability to innovative ideas, inevitably the legal form chosen is the share corporation.

Moreover, for foreign capital to be attracted to another nation in the form of an alliance, there usually are offered incentives. This is made possible by foreign investment laws. Such laws are adopted by the host countries because institutional lenders such as the IMF require these laws to be enacted. The IMF knows, as does any institutional lender, that foreign investors require promises of advantages. A loan will not even be considered without the proposed borrower, by letter of intent, addressed to the IMF, indicating the major lines of economic and social reform to be enacted. Unsurprisingly, international alliances are stimulated by favorable foreign investment laws. The reason is obvious. Alliances are encouraged by incentives, particularly fiscal. Sovereigns enact laws which will attract foreign investment, often in the form of international alliances with the local citizenry. Investment laws adopt economic and social philosophies conducive to attracting capital. It does not require any undue persuasion by the IMF to secure promises of favorable legislation. Of course laws without ideas are impossible. The penchant for international alliances founded with transnational corporations stimulates the enactment of favorable legislation modeled on Western economic and legal concepts.

Additionally, international alliances create a complex web of corporate networks which maintain the power of decision distant from the local alliance. When we are dealing with transnational corporations, it is customary for affiliates to be interlocked with the parent corporation through various techniques, one of which is the familiar holding company. The Portuguese Bank Banco Espirito Santo with consolidated assets of over 37.4 billion Euros is controlled through the holding company ESFG[21] located in Luxembourg. A common method is to have on the board of directors of the affiliate an officer from the parent company. The persistence of Western economic doctrines throughout the trading world owes a debt to the various interlocking mechanisms normally created, resulting in major decisions emanating from the centers of capital. This is made possible through the flexibility of the share corporation.

Furthermore, international alliances frequently reveal a minority domination of an affiliate even though the other, local partner has a majority capital interest. Through minority tyranny, for it is no less than this, the foreign investor protects and furthers the power of the capital investment. Few legal forms permit the minority to have substantial influence over the enterprise as does the share corporation. This is an efficient legal technique which permits transnational corporations to expand throughout various jurisdictions using international alliances and moderate capital investments. Even with a minority participation in the capital structure, the international alliance, if properly formulated, can obtain control over a network of companies in which the foreign investor only has a minority interests.

This is a modest list of what is the possible agenda of the transnational corporation doing business through an international alliance. In all these situations, the element which links one possible practice to another is the extent of control achieved through careful incorporation documents and ancillary agreements. While the concept of legal control is normally a topic reserved to attorneys, some of the mechanics of achieving control or influence are of importance to sociologists and political scientists. It is not possible to unravel the behavior patterns of transnational corporations without a broad view of control and its colleague, substantial influence.

It is 'control' which in great measure sponsors the legal globalization now in course. Control makes possible capital remuneration through power with all its derivatives, from economic policies to maintenance of a centralized management. It is economic imperialism very well disguised. Yet an understanding of control requires a further conceptual step. Control is dependent on the form and the method used to form an alliance. The law is not unresponsive to this methodology. Establishing a subsidiary is not the same as forming a consortium. The selection of certain forms of alliances, and the methods chosen cannot be a matter of indifference to the social scientist.

Finally, are the topics which are normally the subject of detailed draftsmanship and involves a substantial amount of specialized knowledge. Share structure, voting rights, quorum requirements, and purchase options, all are examples of material which can be used to augment or dilute power. Nevertheless, these concepts are substantially influenced by the legal form of the alliance. There are many valid reasons for this necessity of control. The international alliance rotates around the axis of power because the participants seek to expand their influence in all areas, from profit-making to economic and social ideas. It is not necessarily aggression in commercial form. It is just the nature of business.

If we begin with the reasons why there is foreign investment, it will render more meaningful why power is required. There is no unified academic theory as to why corporations expand internationally through alliances. The simplest explanation appears to be one of capital remuneration through power which is one of the consequences of centralized management and control through the share corporation form. Nevertheless, the lack of an acceptable theory as to international alliances, will not be a deterrent to understanding the general background against which international alliances are structured as how the alliance is used by exporters of capital. The methods used by transnational corporations will permit us to understand the popularity of alliances. The essential characteristics of any one legal form and its importance to the foreign investor will reveal to us the obscure side of the power struggle and why it foments the legal globalization process.

### *Egoism and foreign direct investment*

Transnational corporation alliances focuses our attention on foreign direct investment which is what takes place when an investor based in one country acquires an asset in another country with intent to manage the value acquired. Traditional reasons exist why companies seek international alliances. As various theories exist, it is reasonable to assume that there is no one single cause. They range from microlevel explanations to general sociological theories, from cost to imperialism, from skills to the implantation of the American Republic.

High labor and related expenses are frequently cited as a reason why companies establish affiliations abroad. In countries where social benefits are non-existent, manufacturing costs as a percentage of the sales price can be reduced substantially. 'Denationalize your product' advocates this theory and augment your profits accordingly. Instead of going West, go abroad. Additionally, many products are sold internationally. Trade mark reputation has to be protected. This also means quality control and frequently after-sales service. Overseas independent distributors are not prepared to maintain quality control or may not have capital resources for after-sales service. Normally, a distributor purchases and resells. It makes sense to form a local subsidiary with the distributor or establish an affiliate in a nearby jurisdiction.

Moreover, a great deal of international commerce is conducted under the category of transfer of technology. Technology includes a wide range of topics. Besides patent rights, the most obvious, there are industrial processes and trade secrets. Trade secrets are more difficult to control. The subject matter is more subjective. It may be something as simple as a client base. Licensees vary in their commitment to honoring contractual clauses of secrecy. Establishing a licensee-affiliate ensures the technology transfer obligations or trade secrets will be fulfilled; that customer lists will not be snatched away to competitors; that the expertise of the licensor will not become common-knowledge.

Assurances of much-needed raw materials or semi-finished goods are another determinant for forming alliances. This reason can be classified as the transaction cost theory. When the costs become too high to obtain needed goods or services from external parties, it is more sensible to internalize the item. This may require an alliance abroad for an added reason. The wise importer of raw materials surely wants to avoid becoming dependent on an avaricious supplier. This can be accomplished by the purchaser and supplier establishing an export company in the foreign jurisdiction. This also prevents the supplier from profiting from inside information as to the market in question.

Finally, in order to do business in a particular jurisdiction it may be necessary to have a local partner. Although less frequent because of the world movement towards liberalizing trade and movement of capital, there are still jurisdictions where a company cannot be owned 100 per cent by a foreign entity. This requires the foreign investor to form an alliance with a national.

These are some of the micro-level reasons which explain the popularity of international alliances. We can glance at other, more philosophical theories that regard the expansionistic nature of capitalism as inherent to this model; dominant companies in a sector wanting to maintain their privileges in a world-wide industry, such as pharmaceuticals; or the need to establish a firewall against other newcomers, a theory known as strategic entry deterrence so that newcomers to an industry cannot easily obtain a market share; the need for new markers as national consumer consumption is saturated; the dominion over natural resources needed for national survival, such as petroleum.

For all of the reasons proffered, whether at the micro-level or philosophical sphere, glaring disclaimers can be offered. The statistics already cited indicate that the majority of foreign direct investment is between economically developed nations.[22] While the media image of the exploited child factory worker in a village hut producing shoes for city dwellers corresponds to fact, most of the alliances are between enterprises from advanced economies. Therefore the delight of the production manager in finding low labor costs abroad is not a sufficient explanation for the significant amount of foreign direct investment between developed industrial economies. Cheap labor may result in alliances in the underdeveloped host country but it probably involves manufacturers in an industry of simple technology. The popular theory of transaction costs should be contrasted with the failure rate of alliances published daily in any financial newspaper. A moderate inquiry into published material on how to make a merger or acquisition viable is testimony to the high transaction costs in seeking a solution through the creation of an international alliance.

Surely there are many circumstances where the transaction cost theory is warranted, but then multitudinous are the failures and without doubt the corporate chairmen are aware of these figures. Yet the alliances and mergers continue. There persists the notion of other reasons offering a better explanation or at least being included in the academic schedule. As to the theories of commercial empire visions or expansion inherent in neoliberal economic theories, the catalytic destruction of the capitalist model has yet to prove verifiable. If anything, the irresistible lure of foreign direct investment has lowered trade barriers everywhere.

The consequences attributed to historical or philosophical motives can be explained by a more discoverable ideology. As in other areas of the social sciences, field studies are particularly instructive. In this respect, the study of international alliances from a documentary source will lead us to fruitful conclusions. Without an elementary discernment of the basics of international alliances the fusion of theory and practice will remain difficult. Academic analysis and commercial ways are graphically illustrated through snap-shot case studies. From apparently odd results are discerned techniques, allusions to other avenues which must be studied and explained by the social scientist.

The study of international alliances deciphers an important element for its popularity. Beyond market convenience, quality control, labor expenses, and transactions costs, the international alliance permits the expansion of power of the enterprise through the relatively simple guise of an international alliance. One reason for the popularity of international alliances may reside in its providing easy access to markets, capital, assets, personnel, and local knowledge with a modest investment (understood as such by the foreign venturer) and yet being also able to conduct business through familiar moulds which permits centralization of authority and capital remuneration. Rephrased, international alliances are a device by which capital remuneration persists and is extended geographically.

A cogent theory of international alliances must therefore consider to what extent the commercial enterprise, in its need for survival, seeks to extend its domain over markets through the control of other companies. Case studies are the most probable source for verification of this hypothesis. This requires only a general grasp of various legal concepts. What the random case studies demonstrate, and their examples could be multiplied without logical limit into a textbook on 'corporate control', are how the share corporation and the international alliance, whatever its form, expands the power of one group over others. This can also be commuted into one legal culture exercising its influence on the international commercial markets.

### *The riddles of international alliances — Swedish spirits*

According to business reports issued March 2001, the Swedish company Vin & Sprit paid $270 million dollars for access to the US Jim Beam bourbon distiller Fortune Brands, Inc. distribution system. The price also purchased a 49 per cent percent stake in Fortune Brands LLC, a US joint venture company to be formed between the two entities.

Additionally, Vin & Sprit invested $97 million to become an equal partner in Maxxium, a joint venture established in 1999 by Jim Beam Brands, Remy Cointreau, and Highland distillers. From these few, but essential and typical facts, the researcher will have some perfectly reasonable inquiries. Vin & Sprit paid a considerable sum for only a 49 per cent interest. Ordinarily, a 49 per cent is as effective as 1 per cent. It is a minority interest, ostensibly subject to always being outvoted.

Moreover, we are informed Vin & Sprit will spend $97 million to become an equal partner. Equal partners should mean the same amount of representatives for each party of the board of directors. It appears $97 million has purchased endless impasses. Surely counsel to the parties could have devised a more hopeful scenario for their clients. Whatever the techniques selected by counsel and the economic rationale of other advisers, our doubts would vanish if we knew the parties had negotiated limitations on the majority voting partner, probably on a topical basis.

This could be enhanced by conferring on the minority Vin & Spirit certain rights exceeding their nominal voting strength, and, finally, devising solutions for deadlock situations. Examples would be the annual budget requires the approval of Vin & Sprit, ignoring the 51/49 division of capital. Minority rights could be protected further by stipulating that each partner will have the right to appoint a defined number of members to the board of directors, again ignoring the 51/49 division of capital; and deadlocks can easily be avoided by having a qualifying vote in the President of the board of directors, which office must be rotated on a term basis.

All of these solutions are possible through the execution of legal instruments apart from the legal structure of the alliance. However, besides independent juridical documents, the incorporation clauses of the average share corporation representative of Western legal thought contain sufficient flexibility so that the articles of incorporation of Fortune Brands LLC could simple state that a qualified majority of votes on the board of directors is needed for a particular item.

Vin & Spirit, with such a clause, can drink a toast to the flexibility of the American stock corporation.

### *The riddles of international alliances — Italian bravo*

A recently reported business failure illustrates either excessive enthusiasm or confidence, traits normally self-destructive in commerce. The financial journals reported in late 2001 that Molineux Brandt, the French maker of household appliances, had filed for bankruptcy protection. Buried in the details of the company's history, is the fact that while El.Fi, an Italian group, owned de facto control of Molineux Brandt, it only had four members on the board of directors out of 13 seats. El.Fi abdicated its natural right as majority owner to control the board of directors.

The reversal of roles, whereby the majority owner reduced its voting power to approximately 21.5 per cent, contradicts the normal statutory provisions of companies. A 'major mistake' a source close to El.Fi, is quoted as saying. No doubt this major mistake cost a law firm a good client or a promising law clerk lost his job. Again, the solution probably lies in documents executed by the parties apart from the formal company structure in which they are shareholders. Another possibility is that the articles of incorporation of Molineux Brandt limited seats on the board of directors to a fixed amount for any group of shareholders without regard to percentage of ownership.

*The riddles of international alliances — Japanese ceremony*

Nomura, a Japanese broker, paid $75 million for a 3.75 per cent of the capital of Thomas Weisel Partners, a US financial investment counselor. The percentage purchased is a high price for minimal influence. Yet we learn that Nomura is to have one seat on the board of directors. Thomas Weisel Partners get substantial cash and Nomura a prestigious, if ceremonial, nomination. However, most likely this was only made possible by agreements operating between the parties whereby the majority partners of Thomas Weisel Partners agreed to surrender, in part, their normal prerogatives to nominate the entire board. Without special provisions in the articles or side agreements, 3.75 per cent is not sufficient to nominate even a member to the board of directors. The presence and use of multiple agreements which modify normal legal consequences attendant upon percentage of ownership is a development intimately associated with the American legal profession and which has been adopted with varying degrees wherever American capital has constructed international alliances.[23]

*The riddles of international alliances — French ingenuity*

In October, 2001, it was reported that Vodafone, a UK mobile company, wanted to take control of Cegetel, a French company. Vivendi, another French company, owns 44 per cent of Cegetel. Cegetel owns 80 per cent of SFR, a French mobile operator. Therefore, control of Cegetel obtains dominion of SFR. SFR is a French mobile operator and dominates the French market.

The other 56 per cent of Cegetel is owned 15 per cent by Vodafone; 26 per cent by British Telecommunications (BT), and SBC with 15 per cent. BT and SBC are reportedly willing to sell their shares. Vodafone wishes to increase its stake in Cegetel but so does Vivendi. Under normal circumstances, shareholders can sell their shares when and to whom they want. However, Vivendi has a right of option on any sales by either BT or SBC. Moreover, Vivendi has a preemption right which allows it to buy SBC's ownership at a 13 per cent premium above the Vodafone offer.

Any offer made by Vodafone which a shareholder of Cegetel wished to accept, is thus subject to a right of first refusal by Vivendi over the BT sale price, more a 13 per cent increase over the SBC sale price.[24] Rights of options, sometimes categorized as rights of first refusal or rights of preference, are standard clauses in corporate charters. Very often, agreements have to be drawn to modify these clauses, particularly if the alliance is constructed on an acquisition and thus there already exists a company charter. The unusual rights conferred upon Vivendi through prior agreements is intended, and well conceived, to secure to Vivendi continuing control of its investments if it has the capital to match competitive offers.

All these case studies serve to illustrate or offer an insight into the practice of international alliances. The theories of international alliances have in general been heretofore confined to the law profession. What is additionally needed, is a methodology for a study of international alliances encompassing social aspects.

## *The methodology of international alliances*

A complete methodology of international alliances can not be constructed here. It is too vast an undertaking and can only be undertaken in parts. What follows is intended as an inauguration, more in the way of an example, or a path if you prefer.

Alliances can be created by the method of an acquisition. But then the same result can be achieved by the formation of a subsidiary. Both are a method of constructing an international alliance. Yet there is still a further incognito. The form of the international alliance can vary. Methodology does not forcibly lead to the formation of a partnership, or share corporation, or private limited liability; all susceptible to being established. What must be studied besides the method of the alliance is its final form, and the advantages/disadvantages each offers to the foreign investor. Methodology and form are a permanent axis.

The final form of the international alliance is frequently referred to by practitioners as the 'joint venture vehicle'. The introduction of this new phrase need not discourage us. Joint venture or international alliance, they all describe an economic collaboration. However, concentrating on the form is not an idle academic endeavor. Deciding upon an acquisition or establishing a subsidiary still leaves open the decision as to what will be the configuration within which the collaboration will function. The law recognizes many forms, from the individual doing business, partnerships, consortiums, share corporations, holding companies, to strategic alliances, and of course many other forms exist.

From the method-form-advantage/disadvantage axis there can be seen how power is accessed. Anticipating the conclusion, and with the intent of furnishing immediately a better comprehension, those international alliances founded on the method of subsidiaries resulting in a share corporation offer the widest latitude in creating and maintaining power through control. Method and form blend together gracefully in corporate subsidiaries and without question this is the preferred international alliance.

The most familiar methods for achieving an international alliance are acquisitions, subsidiaries, and unincorporated joint ventures, also denominated consortiums. Of course, there are many other forms of alliances such as limited partnerships, investment trusts, franchises, distributorships, agency representations but some would contest the genre of alliance for all these categories and in any event it is not possible to compile an exhaustive list.

Each alliance with its method/form axis presents advantages and disadvantages in the muted power struggle of collaboration. As an inducement to further research by social scientists, there is offered a general view.

### *Acquisitions*

An acquisition is the purchase of the totality or part of the capital interests of another entity. An interest is sold and purchased. However, the rights and obligations of the various owners remain unknown. Often, independent agreements, not recorded for public purposes, affect critically the legal interests of the participants.

As the comparison of the benefits and drawbacks in an acquisition involves many elements, a summary may be helpful. Once the comparison is understood, it become readily apparent why acquisitions are not so popular as the formation of subsidiaries in the quest for international alliances. There is not so much flexibility in the use of power or creating devices of control.

The advantages to a purchase of an interest in a corporate or other entity include its existing economic history, personnel, assets, and market knowledge. As an acquisition can be for a partial interest, the materialized return on the investment can be increased in nominal terms, provided this condition was foreseen. For this to happen, it is only necessary to purchase more shares. On the other hand, an acquisition permits a withdrawal from the investment and of course this is possible through a sale of shares. Acquisitions belie the prudent foreign investor. With an acquisition is associated a 'wait and see' approach.

The disadvantages include the necessity for considerable accounting examination of the existing company and a possible unsatisfactory legal structure which resists change. Existing partners do not like to have legal clauses with which they are familiar altered. Moreover, in an acquisition there exist vested personnel interests which it is not easy to dislodge. The foreign investor may wish to have direct administration over a department, such as corporate finance, and there is already occupying the position a local financial director. While these personnel issues can be overcome, they are normally troublesome.

Acquisitions do not permit the foreign investor to saturate the alliance with its own economic and managerial philosophies and are less used by capital exporting companies when investing in underdeveloped or countries or emerging economies. The preferred route is the formation of a subsidiary.

### *Subsidiaries*

Probably the most frequent method of forming an international alliance is by the creation of a local subsidiary, whose legal outlines, capital structure and managerial aspects is negotiated between the parties. Forming a subsidiary means establishing a new company. Normally, in international alliances, the foreign investor, for example a capital sufficient corporation, will establish a subsidiary with a local entity located in the host country. The subsidiary, in theory, is distinct from its shareholders, or partners.

The main advantage of forming a subsidiary is that it reflects the objectives and intentions of all participants and is therefore an harmonious legal structure. Specific objectives can be tailored to the will of the parties and thus through a subsidiary it is easier for a minority investor to secure special privileges in return for the capital injected.

The main disadvantage is that the formation of a subsidiary requires extensive financial and legal efforts. Everything must be determined from the beginning. This normally requires lengthy negotiations if the owners will be from different jurisdictions, such as a foreign investor and a local host country national. Nevertheless, subsidiary formation is the most popular form of doing business abroad in the form of an international alliance as it permits the power structure to be modeled along the lines of the predominant capital partner.

*Consortiums*

A consortium is a temporary alliance of entities to achieve a common purpose and is often referred to as an unincorporated joint venture. A contract establishes the consortium. There is no perpetual corporate identity. The contract defines the rights and obligations of each party and their capital contribution; their ownership interests; and the contribution each will make to the success of the consortium.

The unincorporated joint venture and the general partnership share many legal characteristics in common. However, in a general partnership, there is not set forth any dissolution at a specific time. Not so with the unincorporated joint venture. Its existence is temporal. It is agreed in the original contract it will end, e.g. when the damn is built. A consortium is accredited as a satisfactory way of doing business for short periods. Its existence is temporary, in that a specific task is confronted by multiple parties with a view towards completing the job within a specific time frame.

This form is often thrust upon the participants because of public bidding requirements. A foreign construction company is obligated to associate itself with a local entity by the conditions of the public tender. Of necessity, being of temporal existence, its importance as a method for globalizing the law is restricted. Consortiums, for all their popular references in daily financial news sources are not a preferred form for international alliances where a lasting presence is intended.

Form, our joint venture vehicle, requires careful deliberation. Many elements are relevant. But without a detailed list, *a priori*, the foreign investor will choose a form which insulates it from local liability, provides devices and mechanisms for control, permits the decision-making process to be difficult to discover, if not concealed, facilitates obtaining a larger portion of a profitable alliance, or a quick exit for a failure, and admits of private agreements which do not inform the public as to the complete extension of authority or lack of it.

Nothing occult or evil is intended. Casinos do not exist for the population to earn a windfall. On the contrary, it is the casino which hopes to lull the public into the magic sphere of luck. So with the international alliance. It is not founded on altruistic considerations. The object is profit which is achieved through power which is related to control. International alliances permit the spread of power and it can be occulted from public view through private agreements. The share corporation exists to return to its shareholders a dividend on capital invested and was not formed for the social weal, although evidently it was not established for the contrary.

When deciding on what form to utilize for an international alliance, the foreign investor, or counsel, will consider at least nine elements which affect considerably the power manipulation of the investor and which indicate areas in need of social theory.

*Essential points on the power axis*

Our foreign investor is going to ponder carefully various, for the moment arbitrary, elements, with the sole objective of determining how they can be manipulated for purposes of capital remuneration through power. The general categories are social concepts involving distant ownership, occult documents, veto power, social organization, and professional standards concerning management hierarchy and accounts. And these are only a selection for purposes of exposition:

- profit withdrawals
- management structure
- financial engineering flexibility
- effect on private agreements of form chosen
- how ownership interests are represented and transferred
- restriction on sale of ownership interests
- subsequent reporting requirements
- monitoring the investment.

There are other intangible aspects to be considered. But for the moment this modest list will emphasize how power is created and used by a careful conjugation of these variables. This is not intended to be a schedule of all the elements to be pondered involving an international alliance. Each one chosen, however, deserves a succinct description from the viewpoint of the entrepreneur as borne out by experience. We can demonstrate, in part, their utility, without any pretensions of limitation. The schedule is not designed as a list created by a lawyer for lawyers. It is intended to indicate to social scientists material for investigation and to what extent the law facilitates or hinders the expansionary forces of capital and the possessors of same through the share corporation. The inventory should convince others why the multinational is normally a share corporation and how this is possible.

International alliances are formed to realize profit as quickly as possible and then withdraw them. While concerns of general liability rank high in the list of relevant topics for managers, ease of profit-withdrawals are of enormous importance. However, some legal forms permit profits to be received in a more advantageous manner than other forms. This is true of the share corporation. By having different classes of shares, a foreign investor can insure the right to a dividend, denominated a preferential share. For this reason, share corporate subsidiaries are a preferred form for the foreign investor. Structured from the beginning, the various participants can agree on a hierarchy of shares with distinct rights. The right to dividends is normally associated with majority voting rights and a declaration of dividends at a general assembly. But this is not obligatory. Preferred shares circumvent this requirement.

Profitable ownership is dependent on efficient management. Different legal forms have various manners of authorizing management. There is considerable overlapping among the multiple legal models and management functions can be designed in conformity with the expressed intention of the parties. It is also affected by the laws of the foreign jurisdiction with a great variety of possibilities. Nevertheless broad valid generalities do exist.

A share corporation is governed by a board of directors with a well-defined hierarchical system where management prerogatives are clearly delineated. Management structure also determines how control is exercised. From the board of directors to department heads there is a clear line of command. It is easy to limit the powers of any one individual or unit. In a share corporation, authority must be exercised through powers of attorney and thus absentee owners can have themselves represented. This is an important consideration for the foreign investor who often has headquarters far from the affiliate. The share corporation, coupled with imagination, makes it possible for the foreign investor to design a management structure bearing all the hallmarks of the Western enterprise.

The form chosen will ultimately affect access to financing which is essential to the survival of an alliance. A private individual, even if permitted to incorporate, will not have the same flexibility as other traditional forms of company. But the concern of obtaining financing also goes beyond a simple credit request to a bank. Augments of capital, the issuance of new shares and bonds, the retirement of capital, the creation of holding companies, are more easily achieved through one form than another. In this respect, the share corporation affords substantial financial engineering. The enormous flexibility share corporations afford in terms of obtaining funds is not equaled by other legal forms.

More relevant to our discussion of power, the financial engineering inherent in a share corporation permits capital markets to be tapped in locale far removed from the site of the international alliance. It often happens that one of the partners, usually the foreign investor, may secure a loan from its home office on favorable terms to the local subsidiary. When exercised within reasonable terms, such a loan arrangement is beneficial to all parties. But it is also a device for extracting funds from an otherwise profitable subsidiary. Unfair interest rates, a term too short, a requirement to be repaid in a particular currency, are common examples of subsidiaries manipulated by the foreign investor.

The end result is a captive subsidiary and the international alliance is beholden to the foreign investor. It cannot survive without grace periods as to due loans. Labor unrest must be stilled for fear of causing an acceleration of a debt already due. While other examples come to mind, this should suffice to indicate how financial power, exercised discretely, ensures adherence to various economic and social objectives.

There are many different types of agreements accompanying international alliances which find expression in other instruments yet which are crucial to the maintenance of power. Agreements contain obligations and, as an illustrative list, we have promises derived from joint venture agreements, which can be compared to a constitution. There are shareholders' agreements wherein the shareholders make promises to one another. Such documents are often not revealed to the public but can have significant influence over the alliance. For example, a shareholders' agreement might provide that no other shareholder will purchase any interest of another partner without first without consulting the other partners. This keeps the alliance a 'closed' corporation.

Then there are agreements between members of the board of directors. This is an obligation which establishes how much of a majority is needed for any issue which comes to a vote at the board of directors. It can augment substantially the power of the minority interests by requiring unanimous vote for a particular topic, such as augments of capital or dividend declarations.

How ownership interests are represented and transferred weights significantly in the choice of legal form for an international alliance. The share corporation in most jurisdictions world-wide facilitates both possession of ownership through a paper title which also serves for its transfer or even pledge for a debt. Complementary to ownership is the right to transfer ownership and here the share corporation permits restrictions on the sale of ownership rights, whether by rights of preference or other devices which ensure the original homogenous ownership interests, normally the closed corporation, are not disturbed by the entry of unknown partners.

Finally accounting requirements and the monitoring of the international alliance are immensely facilitated through the share corporation form. This has been the form preferred by public auditors. It is the legal form most used for public companies quoted on public exchanges. Moreover, the high degree of accounting standards demanded of public companies has made its incursions into the small and medium corporations not traded on exchanges.

While this may seem a lengthy list, in fact it is modest in comparison with a typical constellation of agreements affected to an international alliance. Yet even this brief review should make it obvious that through the share corporation a multitude of rights and duties can be settled which contradict the normal consequences of the law; permit capital owners to extend their influence beyond the nominal value of their ownership; retain control or at least influence substantially the subsidiary in question; create a complex network removed from ordinary public observation.

### *The allies*

Whatever is the theory which appears more correct and revealing, the fact is that the transnational corporation is a formidable force in the construction of international alliances. Cause and effect in the social milieu are usually circular and not linear. To Hegel and Marx we are grateful for this insight. However, insights are not theory, as the demise of Marxism demonstrates. What do seem clear are the consequences of international alliances through the transnational corporation for the development of global law. The various legal devices which make it possible for exporters of capital to create interlocking directorships; assume minority positions while still influencing magisterially the affiliate; impose a managerial style removed from the local culture; devise techniques for ensuring profits return to the foreign investor; prevent dissident investors from selling to others without first offering their shares to a particular group; and this list is susceptible to much further extension. The share corporation facilitates these legal devices which permit control to be exercised from a distance.

Globalization owes a debt no one wants to repay to the share corporation and the American innovations imposed on this legal form through the centuries. With Western industrialized nations dominating international commerce, and with the Western legal models the only ones ever considered in the significant international alliances, it is not too much of a desperate thought to imagine that the share corporation along with foreign capital dislodges local law in the field of international cooperation.

Were these phenomena only confined to the subject matter of international alliances, the impact might be acceptable. But the laws of international alliances are more than company laws. Every corporation is also a social enterprise. In many parts of Europe, a company is conceived as a social pact and capital interests are described as 'social parts'. From the corporate structure and its existence as a corporate citizen flow aspects affecting the lives of laborers; the right of the corporation vis-à-vis the sovereign nation; the insulation of the alliance from local courts through bits; and more profoundly the image the local citizenry obtains of what the law is.

At first, the right to discharge employees without cause may be seen as a horrendous capitulation by the host government to the dictates of the alliance. With time, a new generation sees this law of labor as part of the legal consequences inherent in the share corporation model. It is not questioned whether or not the labor law is a product of the share corporation or whether one concept can be separated from the other. This is how share corporations function. The managerial functions, far removed from the local site, dictate what are to be the consequences of the yearly budget.

Legal principles implemented in a corporate organization affect the social structure of the community. Of necessity, labor rights have repercussions in society, for without sustenance the communal existence can not continue. Through power manipulation in the business community, social consequences are wrought. The importation of legal ideas, crafted onto local economic units, if important in their contents, mould and alter social relations. The final victory is when the legal imagery of the local population changes and new legal concepts become part of the vocabulary of jurists. A nation distant from the Chicago headquarters of our multinational permits a global network to strangle independent local corporate progress through legal devices of quorums and vetoes as it may foster too much competition and prevent the maintenance of a world-wide price structure.

This is what is meant by the globalization of the law through international alliances. Form shapes content. Yet we know the empty vase can be filled with water or wine. Before the superior flexibility of the share corporation which permits the accumulation of power and then wealth, the social options are contracting. On the other hand, the hegemony of Western corporate law is expanding.

## Notes

[1] Lina Saigoi, *Deutsche takes top slot in M&A*, The Financial Times, 3 October 2002, p. 23, reporting that for the first nine months of the year 2002, DeutscheBank advised on mergers and acquisitions with a total value of $36 billion. These figures represent the activity of one bank in one country. The Financial Times publishes once a week a selection of international merger and acquisitions activity. Assets involved are often reported in the US billions.

[2] Transnational should mean one enterprise has affiliations in different parts of the world while multinational should mean one enterprise is present in various jurisdictions. However, the terminology is imprecise and journalistically interchangeable. For our purposes, transnational is accurate because it focuses on affiliations.

[3] Mergers and acquisitions can affect thousands of employees. When America Online, Inc. acquired Time Warner over 80,000 functionaries were absorbed into one company, reported in the Portuguese newspaper Expresso, 15 January 2000.

[4] Foreign Direct Investment, Development and the New Global Economic Order. A Policy Brief for the South available at <www.southcentre.org>, accessed 13 May 2002.

[5] Ibid, citing statistics gathered by UNCTAD.

[6] Ibid.

[7] Ibid.

[8] World Investment Report 2002 published by UNCTAD with excerpts available at <www.unctad.org>.

[9] Ibid.

[10] The Financial Times, 21 October 2002, at p. 24.

[11] For a legal exposition, see Ronald Charles Wolf, Effective International Joint Venture Management: Practical legal Insights for Successful Organization and Implementation, M.E. Sharpe, New York (2000); also Ronald Charles Wolf, A Guide to International Joint Ventures, Kluwer Law International, London, (1999).

[12] For a variety of definitions, see the survey printed by the US Dept of Commerce, entitled, Annual Survey of US Direct Investment Abroad – 2000, available at <www.bea.gov>, accessed 3 October 2002. This is the definition followed by Sylvia E. Bargas, Direct Investment Positions for 1999 Country and Industry Detail, July 2000 Survey of Current Business.

[13] For a national illustration, in Decree Law No. 371/93, Article 9, the Portuguese law of competition defines a concentration of enterprises where, among other things, there exists the possibility of exerting a decisive influence on the activities of the enterprise.

[14] Anna M. Falzoni, Statistics on Foreign Direct Investment and Multinational Corporations: A Survey, 15 May 2000, available at <www.cepr.org/research>, accessed 3 October 2002. The guidelines published by her are based on the standards adopted by the IMF and OECD.

[15] Ibid.

[16] Supra, n. 12, definition by US Dept of Commerce.

[17] Supra, n. 14.

[18] Supra, n. 13. The subject of control is the object of legislation by the EU as exemplified by the Merger Regulation of 1989. Control constitutes one of the more difficult conceptual areas for regulation by the EU.

[19] Supra, n. 12 and the Mergers Regulations of the EU.

[20] See Norman Cohen and Andrew Hill, *Governance issues lie behind Simon/Taubman battle*, The Financial Times, 14 February 2003, at page 19, reporting that a shareholder, Taubman, with about 1 per cent ownership of shares had management control of over 33 per cent of the corporate board of Taubman Centers, an owner of shopping malls in the US.

[21] Report published on <www.biz.yahoo.com>, accessed 22 September 2002.

[22] Supra, n. 4.
[23] This is an empirical affirmation from professional experience. The published legal literature and continuing professional education programs, both in the US and Europe, attest to the popularity and need for expertise concerning supplementary agreements adjacent to international joint ventures.
Any doubts subsisting can be ameliorated by glancing at the contents of a 18-19 November 2002 conference in London entitled 'Joint Venture Agreements' posted on <www.hawksmere.com>, accessed 4 October 2002.
[24] Robert Budden and Martin Arnold, *Vivendi may take Cegetel stake to foil Vodafone*, The Financial Times, 18 October 20002, at p. 15.

# Chapter 16

# International Alliances and Tape Worm Tactics

*The table of international alliances*[1]

The surge of international commerce which has brought industrialized capitalism to many parts of the world owes a significant debt to international alliances. An international alliance is a legal form whose description tends to be carelessly applied. Names such as 'joint venture vehicle', 'strategic alliance', 'joint partnership', 'international acquisition', or 'international joint venture' are often utilized.

But scant theory will be gained by wandering through the distinctions and differences possible with this nomenclature. For our purposes, it is sufficient to know an international alliance results when a foreign investor intends to do business with an entity in another country, normally through a corporate structure. International trade has been substantially aided by this legal model which has no easily identifiable specific form and yet is commercially omnipresent.

The study of international alliances can of course be approached from many aspects. Many social science insights are possible once it is understood how control is achieved by foreign investors in their expansionist activities abroad. It is a fascinating journey but one which requires an initiation into fundamentals. It is possible the groundwork produces yawns, if not downright fatigue. Yet once understood, other horizons, dependent on the researcher's interests, are within reach. A highly occult facet, except to the practitioners of this material, is the various techniques which enable a foreign investor with only a minority participation in an international alliance, to augment their influence beyond the nominal voting power of their shares. The object is to obtain a decisive influence upon the 'alliance'.

Whether denominated as decisive influence, substantial influence, or control, the underlying facts bear a similarity. Through a variety of legal mechanisms it is possible for foreign entrepreneurs, such as our transnational corporation, to invest in an overseas company with a modest equity position. This implies the transnational corporation will not, under ordinary circumstances, have a majority of the votes. But this is of no importance. This is what the transnational wishes: a modest capital investment but power in excess. The transnational corporation wishes to obtain a foothold in the alliance. Once an equity position is achieved, and provided it has become accompanied by the necessary legal mechanisms, the influence of our investor becomes substantial. The technique lies in the method and manner by which international alliances are constructed. It is possible, with a minority position, to have a substantial influence over a subsidiary provided legal precautions have been taken. By such stratagems, the transnational corporation can conserve its capital, achieve remuneration, and expand its influence into a variety of alliances in various jurisdictions. Through the mechanisms to be described, it becomes possible to construct a network of alliances without inordinate resort to capital proper. The transnational corporation is a legal model of how clauses to protect the minority in reality choke the majority.

Nor need we be concerned with the documents attorneys use, or the language necessary to obtain the objectives to be discussed. Our attention is directed exclusively as to how control is exercised by the transnational corporation through various devices seldom reported except in journals for the law profession. What follows is a preliminary schedule of mechanisms as to how control may be achieved in an international alliance by a minority partner. Excluded are others necessary to protect the foreign investor. Thus the schedule is incomplete, for all investors have rights. Nevertheless, our interest is minority control, a specialized legal field which is in dire need of social description.

In the ensuing discussion, the expression 'company' is referring to the legal form representing the international alliance without particular characteristics in mind.

### *No changes, please*

Prior to the foreign investment, the exiting company articles, or those intended to be used, make clear they cannot be subsequently changed except by a supermajority vote exceeding the voting capital of the majority partner. This prevents the diluting of any rights receiving special protection in the company articles which will take effect upon the formation of the alliance. As the foreign investor intends to establish special rights in the company articles, this tactic prevents the majority from later eliminating such benefits by calling for a general assembly to alter the company articles. A supermajority of votes, which must include part of the voting partner of the minority owner, ensures complete protection.

The result is that nothing in the company articles can be altered without the minority owner's consent. The apparent simplicity of this device belies its effectiveness. Most participants in an international alliance will initially agree as to no further changes. It sounds reasonable. Unfortunately, time brings disillusionment and then the dissident partner realizes changes which should be made, cannot, unless all others agree. The disagreeable aspect of minority power surges forth: a pay out for a substantial premium.

### *Know all means to see all*

Many jurisdictions confer upon shareholders the right to demand access to all sorts of information regarding the international alliance. However, this may require a minimum equity interest, such as a 20 per cent ownership. In all events, such rights are general and limited to the most basic financial information. To expand this privilege, the appropriate legal document is drafted to confer substantial rights to all partners, no matter what their equity ownership.

The minority shareholder will now want unfettered access to all financial details; minutes of board of directors meetings; inter-department communications; access to all computer held information; in short, should the minority owner desire to do so, it can conduct a complete and exhaustive legal and accounting investigation. While appearing a reasonable request, it can often be used for harassment purposes by minority owners who demand to see extensive information. It permits knowledge over details which are normally confined to a majority owner. It dilutes the secrecy veil which majority owners possess.

*Not even bankruptcy will impede the distribution of dividends*

Normally, shareholders only receive dividends at the discretion of the board of directors when there is an annual surplus which warrants this distribution. But other legal mechanisms can insure that what passes for a royalty is in fact a dividend. It is quite common for patent licensors or other possessors of technology to purchase a modest participation in an overseas company. Simultaneously, there is executed a transfer of technology contract between the licensor, who is also a minority shareholder, and the international alliance.

There is stipulated a royalty or other licensing fee which in so far as the minority shareholder is concerned is really its dividend. The corporate financial department of the licensor will calculate what royalty rate is necessary to compensate for the capital invested more than the cost of the technology transferred.

Should the alliance prove to be unsuccessful, the transnational corporate transferor of technology is treated as a creditor and not an equity owner who has lost its investment. Technology transfers and their royalty payments represent a substantial segment of transnational corporate activity. A large part of the profits from transnational activity is subsumed in royalties so as not to have the international alliance (the licensee), realize that royalties have been substituted for dividends.

*A place in the sun, guaranteed*

Various are the techniques for insuring that a minority shareholder will have an assured seat on the board of directors, or more than one. Such an agreement can be contained in numerous legal documents as well as be part of the rights adherent to a special class of shares. However, the transnational corporation is not interested in merely being a member of the board of directors. It will want to ensure that its representation is sufficient to block any adverse action to its interests. This is achieved through the voting right of the members of the board.

This power can be general, that is, a specified number of votes is necessary for any vote, which number must include the votes pertaining to the minority shareholder; or it can be selected, confined to important material, such as augmenting the capital of the company, or the creation of a special class of shares.

It is inappropriate to describe here the various legal documents which prevent a nominal majority owner from exercising total power. Such documents are the province of lawyers.

Yet the premise is easily described. By legal means, give a minority owner power to veto the acts of the majority.

*Democracy is respecting the will of the minority*

In theory, a member of the board of directors should exercise independent judgment. In practice, most directors are beholden to their nominees, the shareholder who elected the officer in question. Just being on a board of directors does not mean the interests of the principal are adequately protected. It is legally possible to arrange mechanisms so that on important issues, such as augment of reserves or disposition of income surplus, a specific majority is required, not just a numerical one.

The same is true for the general assembly, the annual meeting of shareholders who, in many jurisdictions, are the ultimate decision-making authority for various issues. For example, a two-thirds majority vote may be needed to vote for a merger. But although one shareholder owns two-thirds of the capital, through the company articles of special agreements, it is established that, on specified issues, a 75 per cent majority vote is required. The result is that more than one block of votes is needed. This technique goes by the names of qualified majority, supermajority, or necessary quorum. Here, majority does not mean majority. It means majority plus minority, who may or may not cooperate.

With simple mathematical calculations, a minority shareholder will strive to require a quorum of votes on issues of interest to it. The same theory and technique used in the board of directors is transposed to those provisions concerning voting in the general assembly of shareholders. Jurisdictions vary on what powers are conceded to the board of directors and what powers reside in the general assembly. From the viewpoint of the transnational corporation, it does not matter. Both organs of the alliance must have the necessary protection. The reasons are quite obvious. By such tactics, the minority becomes an indispensable ally to the majority.

*No budget, no alliance*

No company can operate without an annual budget. Yet this accounting exercise can be used to deplete the resources of a company or make worthless a minority interest. However, the converse is true. With sufficient control, a minority partner can use the annual budget to impede further development of the company and bend the majority owner to its corporate will. This is done by establishing a platform beyond which a qualified majority is needed.

By requiring a specified quorum of the board of directors for approval of an annual budget, the minority owner can ensure that the international alliance proceeds towards the objectives of the minority partner. Otherwise, it will not receive approval for the budget. Without the concurrence of the minority partner's vote, the majority capital interest will eventually become a fragile asset and the alliance founders in its objectives. Approval of the annual budget defines the scope of the alliance's activities and if the minority partner's concurrence is necessary, compromise and conciliation are the order of the day.

### *Keeping honest accounts has its rewards*

Many international alliances result from acquisitions. The company in which an interest was purchased may have a rudimentary accounting system designed to ensure the non-payment of substantial taxes in the host country. Nevertheless, transnational corporations will insist on transparent accounting practices. Not necessarily out of a desire to see the taxes paid, but rather for fear that what is hidden from the fiscal authorities may also be concealed from an absentee minority shareholder.

Moreover, international accounting standards imposed by a minority shareholder also integrate the alliance into other international standards, such as maintenance of reserves, normally to the benefit of the minority shareholder. Revealing the true extent of cash solvency may mean the alliance needs a capital augment which the majority shareholder cannot afford. If the corporate finances reveal an augment is necessary by law and the majority partner cannot afford further purchases of capital, the minority shareholder, our transnational corporation, increases its participation with substantial ease.

The importance of accounting standards is never contested by entrepreneurs, even those who detest its transparency. Yet, numbers bring with them more than credits and debits. Proper accounting methods require an adequate company structure whose activities can be monitored. It also means personnel are accountable for their acts. The proceeds of budgets must be adequately described. Collusion and financial chicanery become more difficult when proper accounting standards are installed.

In short, the accounting profession is a cultural model and is responsible, along with the law profession, for displacing local customs with international standards, whose origin is normally identified with the industrialized nations. When our minority partner requests the international alliance to agree upon international accounting standards, the request is difficult to refuse.

### *Managing your partner*

Similar to transfer of technology contracts, a minority partner can have the alliance execute a management contract with itself, giving it the right to either manage the alliance or at least an important department. Besides acting as a substitute for dividends, such a contract provides substantial control over the various departments of the alliance. Often, personnel from the transnational corporation are transferred to the alliance but put on the alliance payroll. Provisions are enacted to ensure that the personnel in question supervise a particular department, such as the corporate finance division.

Should the alliance result from an acquisition, the company will have employees. Personnel assigned to the alliance from the incoming minority shareholder will normally have other ideas than the current staff. This requires a purging of labor ranks. The transnational corporation will strive for the right to nominate or have the right to agree as to the appointment of key personnel. Besides improving efficiency in the alliance, new loyalties are created. The power structure shifts. The majority owner is not the only entity to hire or discharge.

*No profit in the sale*

One of the most common clauses in international alliances is establishing that each partner has the right to purchase the other's shares upon an intended sale. While the provisions vary substantially, the object is the same: no sale without the consent of the other partner. The reason usually given is that the international alliance was formed upon a degree of trust amongst the parties. Altering the composition changes the motive for the international alliance. This may be, and the parties may be convinced of their motives. But the result is that a majority partner wanting to dispose of its interests cannot easily do so. Mechanisms are created to discourage any sale and it tends to produce accommodating partners.

The sale is too difficult and it is easier to compromise with the minority partner; just sell the interest to the minority partner.

*Never say goodbye*

When business turns sour, it is necessary for the transnational corporation to be able to exit. The sensible investor plans this before the formation of the international alliance. From continuation of the business by one of the investors to the disposition of assets, the minority shareholder will seek to ensure agreement is reached before the international alliance is consummated. Very often a dispute issue is what will happen to the assets, such as the company name or distribution networks. By setting up elaborate provisions which ensure the minority partner has a substantial role in termination and disposition of assets, the majority partner is again cajoled into a more flexible attitude.

A termination of the international alliance does not offer a feasible, lucrative exit. While the same limitation can be imputed to the transnational corporation, the financial consequences are less felt. Thus an unhappy alliance may result in the assets of the alliance collapsing into the coffers of the minority partner.

***

From the succinct description offered above we can understand how a modicum of capital allied to management prerogatives ensure the transnational corporation will have a substantial influence over the international alliance. By only investing a minimum amount of capital, the transnational corporation is able to achieve a global reach. Even this brief survey permits us to offer some suggestions as to the probable consequences.

How to constrict control has plagued many a competition authority and multiple are the laws which attempt to define control and circumvent its use. All to no avail. The resourcefulness of the law profession exceeds the prolixity of legislators. This has been aptly referred to as the 'ingenuity gap'.[2] Competition authorities, competition attorneys, and their clients have constructed a complex, imaginative network of merger and competition rules which invariably shifts the emphasis not to compliance but legal avoidance. The imaginative use of control has permitted the transnational corporation to expand throughout the commercial world with relative ease. The consequences of this social phenomena clearly call for more investigation by the social sciences.

With control assured, the transnational corporation needs not to invest substantially. The alliance can seek funds for operating purposes from the local banks. Thus substantial control or influence permits resource to the funds of third parties. The transnational corporation is able to conserve its capital. Similar to a bank, where approximately ten per cent of deposits are actually held as reserves, yet enormous amount are loaned on paper transactions, so too, the transnational corporation. Its influence extends beyond its total, global capital investment.

By controlling, or at a minimum manacling, the local alliance, the transnational corporation ensures it is not fomenting a competitor. Markets can be divided more easily without calling attention to the competition authorities. The competition authorities tend to concentrate on the initiatives to expand. But there are also the invisible barriers which prevent competition. Every time the alliance wants to expand into other markets, not enough votes can be mustered on the board of directors. Such inaction easily passes muster by the competition authorities.

Carefully planning acquisitions, even with minority participation, makes it possible to construct a network where other alliances of our minority partner have interests. In some, it may have a majority interest. Favorable contracts are drawn. The minority partner in the international alliance may be willing to lose money in one foreign investment provided vital raw materials are obtained.

Examples could be multiplied. Yet, they might be more appropriate for law students. Nevertheless, there are decidedly social issues which surge forth. Any international alliance where control is effective must bring to the alliance a new culture, whether legal, managerial, or entrepreneurial. That is what control means: imposing, if not by conviction, by legal means, a point of view. International alliances are a cauldron of social exchange and with control the foreign investor's cultural background infiltrates into many aspects of the alliance, from simple labor issues to internal corporate structure. This is why the foreign investor wants control: to effect such changes. When the appropriate alterations are in place, legal followed by cultural attitudes, the conquered become the victors.

Consequently, minority control, or influence if you will, can be studied through the various changes caused throughout the international alliance field. Influences, like tape worms, once installed, are difficult to eliminate.

## Notes

[1] This chapter is a logical complement to Chapter 15, 'Sponsoring Global Law By International Alliances'. However, for ease of reading it was thought best to constitute a separate chapter on how control is created in international alliances. For a complete, legal exposition, see Ronald Charles Wolf, *Effective International Joint Venture Management: Practical Legal Insights for Successful Organization and Implementation*, M.E. Sharpe, Inc., New York (2000) and Ronald Charles Wolf, *A Guide to International Joint Ventures With Sample Clauses*, 2nd Edition, Kluwer Law International, London (1999). In these books, the material was written from a different aspect as it was directed to lawyers and other specialists in the area of international alliances.

[2] Merger Control 2003, *Global Competition Review*, London (2002).

# PART 3
# INTERNATIONAL ARBITRATION AND THE GLOBALIZATION OF WESTERN LAW

# Chapter 17

# Investment Treaties Disputes Will Make You Wonder

*The basic tenets of public international law are ...*

Bits, through clauses invoking international arbitration, constitute an important source of the private rights of an investor against a sovereign. By the concession of allowing individuals to arbitrate claims against a nation, thus piercing the shield of sovereign immunity, bits have substantially advanced the role of private international investment law. With recourse to bits for international arbitration a frequent occurrence, there is unleashed the principles which permit the globalization of Western law: vague award supported by the invocation of customary international law which invariably turns out to be the all-too-familiar precepts of Western law.

Multitudinous are the international arbitration cases determined each year. Varied are the sources and jurisdictions. International arbitration disputes are happening every day. Some awards are published; many are not. The parties to the arbitration take this decision. Material is therefore scarce in comparison with the obligatory publication of municipal law cases.

Short of compiling a year book on the obtainable results, such as choosing cases reported by the ubiquitous international arbitration boards, one insightful alternative is to present a selection of cases from a public organization which offers us a vision into the day-to-day issues of international arbitration affecting a large sector. Bits and their ensuing awards are an excellent paradigm. The assortment of sketches which follow are confined to arbitration cases as reported by the ICSID based on jurisdiction under the bits or the NAFTA treaty. The principles of law as enunciated will provide a perceptiveness into material normally of interest only to lawyers. Yet the results may leave sociologists bemused and throw into relief material of sociological concern. Society is governed by consensus principles but the source of these generalizations and how they are generated is pristinely revealed. At the end, we will dismally conclude that public international law; the interpretation of treaties; the resort to customary international law, is not evidence of law but something else.

In 1987, the ICSID was solicited to arbitrate the typical provisions of a bilateral investment treaty. Due to the importance of the decision for principles of public international law, the attorneys and parties consented to have the complete arbitration decision made public. Although the interpretative principles set forth by the arbitration board were an appeal to the rules affecting nations, yet the underlying cause of the claim was a commercial claim. The claimant sought damages for the destruction of a shrimp farm in Sri Lanka. The facts of the case now presented have been extremely truncated, with many condensations and omissions.

The claimant was a Hong Kong investor in a Sri Lanka company. The arbitration was conducted in Washington, DC before the ICSID. The World Bank has the tutelage and administrative responsibility for the ICSID. Our interest is not in an exhaustive examination of the law principles and how they were applied. Rather, this case illustrates the latitude and discretion which is conferred upon arbitrators. From the arbitration board's analysis and invocation of law principles we will find ourselves cast out upon a sea of homilies and generalizations. What emerges from this case is guidance for future arbitrators; the principles to orientate their decisions; and the sources of the law to be applied. We lawyers will be surprised and our sociology colleagues dismayed for, after reading the commandments, we are no more clarified than, undoubtedly, was the loosing party.

In *Asian Agricultural Products Ltd. (AAPL) v. Republic of Sri Lanka*,[1] there is related how Sri Lankan security forces on 28 January 1987 destroyed the installations of AAPL while routing Tamil rebel forces. Thereafter, AAPL sought compensation under a bilateral investment treaty between Sri Lanka and the UK When compensation was not paid, AAPL requested arbitration before the ISCID pursuant to the terms of the Sri Lanka-UK bilateral investment treaty.

Much of the debate centered on the interpretation of various words in the Sri Lanka-UK bilateral investment treaty, such as 'full protection and security' and 'adequate compensation'. While the response of the ISCID arbitration board sets forth public international law interpretative principles, as bits are agreements between nations, nevertheless the precepts enunciated deal with commercial facts; the rights of private investors; the doctrines which will define the obligations of a country towards entrepreneurs.

Clearly, then, if private individuals are to have rights — an inauguration under public international law created by the ubiquitous bits — the frontier between public and private international law becomes nebulous. Listening to the maxims proffered by the ISCID arbitrators leaves no doubt that the public law principles when applied to private commercial arbitration cases makes possible the foundations of a global law, applicable to commerce, which is free from municipal or national legal restrictions.

This becomes apparent when reading the directives of the ISCID board in reaching its conclusion. The *Asian Agricultural Products Ltd. (AAPL) v. Republic of Sri Lanka* case illustrates well the interplay between private commercial rights, treaty interpretation, and public international law, all used to arrive at compromises of national sovereignty since the ideas annunciated have no objective content.

Summarizing the decision, the basic rules to be followed by the board were, in its opinion, established in 1888 — recourse to antiquity is often equated to a moment when ideal justice reigned and nasty dissidence was absent — where it was laid down that when interpreting treaties, reference must be made to the law of nations and international jurisprudence.[2] Consequently, when two nations speak to each other they use the language of nations.[3] This dialogue is articulated through a series of rules which if not pronounced by an arbitration board would border on the theatre of the absurd. The arbitration board neatly formulated various quixotic rules whose veracity our heroic Don Quixote might have doubted.

Rule A is the first general maxim of interpretation. It is not permitted to interpret what has no need of interpretation.[4] From this astounding premise we continue. Rule B is that there should be no serious deviation from treaty language unless there is a very strong reason.[5] From platitudes we do not dissent. Rule C is that when there are ambiguities, appeal must be made to the spirit of the treaty.[6] In other words, jurists are asked to get into the 'spirit of things'.

Further, Rule D states that in all cases there must be recourse to the rules and principles of international law for a comprehensive construction of the treaty.[7] There then follows Rule E which dictates that clauses must be interpreted so as to give, rather than deprive, them of meaning.[8] Cruel, jurists are not. Then there is Rule F which advises arbitrators to review earlier, similar precedents for guidance.[9]

Less generalized, but hardly overwhelmingly helpful, are other rules. Rule I requires a party having the burden of proof '... to convince the tribunal of their truth ...'. Moreover, the '... international responsibility of the State is not to be presumed'.[10] As to rules of evidence, extreme flexibility is counseled. Rule K dictates that international tribunals ' ... are not bound to adhere to strict judicial rules of evidence'.[11] As a general rule, the 'probative force of the evidence presented is for the Tribunal to decide'.[12]

To the joy of international counsel everywhere, the arbitration board concluded with Rule M that: 'In cases where proof of a fact presents extreme difficulty, a tribunal may thus be satisfied with less conclusive proof, i.e. prima facie evidence'.[13] In street language, this can be rephrased as 'we'll do as we please'.

To satisfy our curiosity, if any is left, the final arbitration award[14] was reached by awarding the claimant a substantially reduced claim on the grounds of the applicable treaty which held the Sri Lanka government responsible to provide 'full protection and security'. Disallowed was the claimant's argument, and which was accompanied by a demand for over $8,000,000, that the Sri Lanka Government deliberately destroyed the premises in their efforts to squash the rebels.

Of course the case represents a compromise and most arbitration claims do. Everyone receives something. But *Asian Agricultural Products Ltd. (AAPL) v. Republic of Sri Lanka* tells us something about the inner mechanisms of the arbitration process. We are indeed fortunate for the publication of this report. What emerges is an appeal to generalizations whose application gives no guidance. Not offering any orientation, each and every arbitrator will decide for her/himself when a claim has met the proof of 'satisfaction'. The rules formulated are statements without content. From the precepts announced it is impossible to construct rules of application.

And indeed, therein lies the problem. Cast against public international law principles, the assertion of private international law rights must rely on the moral 'sense' of the arbitrators which is, if anything, not objective. Nor could it be, since what the layman usually calls 'morals' is rightly and academically designated 'political economy' when referring to property rights. Such catechisms will no doubt remind some readers of the observation by other scholars that international law is not really 'law'.[15] As we will see, not much has changed since the *Asian Agricultural Products Ltd. (AAPL) v. Republic of Sri Lanka* case.

*When all else fails, there is bound to be a botanical solution*

As the NAFTA provisions explicitly authorize the ISCID to hear and determine disputes under this regional trade agreement, it is natural that much of the global law being forged in the Western hemisphere emanates from arbitration.

In *Metalclad Corporation v. The United Mexican States*,[16] the broad legal principles involved illustrate how regional trade agreements,[17] in combination with the dispute settlement procedures of the ICSID, forge social, commercial norms which may collide with local, citizenry interests. What is disclosed to the observer of this case is that NAFTA law will supercede municipal law interests, whether in Mexico, Canada or the US.

The facts divulge a clash of cultural interests. *Metalclad*, a Mexican company which was a wholly-owned subsidiary of an American company, initiated a process to build a hazardous waste landfill on a site containing, unknown to the company and probably to most of the local inhabitants, rare Mexican cacti. From 1990-97, Metalclad, with the full support of the Mexican government, and various technical agencies of the government, sought permission to construct and operate a hazardous waste landfill. This was against the manifest opposition of the municipality of Guadalcazar who steadfastly refused to issue a local permit, apparently also a requirement. So vocal was local opposition that on opening day, after the national licenses had been granted, demonstrators '... blocked the entry and exit of buses carrying guests and workers ...'.[18] At this stage of the process no mention was made of cacti.

While the mass protest succeeded in temporarily preventing the opening of the landfill, *Metalclad* went steadfastly through further governmental steps to achieve its goal of installing a plant. Eventually *Metalclad* obtained again the consent of all the needed authorities, although the local municipality still refused to issue a license for the plant construction. *Metalclad* also made various promises of training local workers, and contributing sums of money for social purposes. When confronted with the persistence of *Metalclad*, the local municipality of Guadalcazar went to court to obtain an injunction against *Metalclad*. After the local city council failed in its judicial initiatives, the plight of the local municipality appeared hopeless.

Desperation was not the mettle of the Governor of the province of Guadalcazar, who, three days before the expiry of his term, and prior to the opening of the plant, in gallantry surely without parallel — three days was probably enough time to escape from his pistol-wearing superiors — issued '... an Ecological Decree declaring a Natural Area for the protection of rare cactus. This area [the cacti site] encompasses the area of the landfill'.[19]

In the face of this masterful stroke of ecological conservation, and believing further administrative steps were no longer productive, *Metalclad* abandoned its project. An action was brought for damages against the sovereign Mexico as being responsible for the acts of lesser public agencies, such as that decreed by the

Governor of Guadalcazar, under the provisions of NAFTA, requiring arbitration before ISCID.

Mexico was ultimately ordered to pay damages. *Metalclad* was compensated for its failed investment. The reason, according to the arbitrators, is to be found in the NAFTA preamble[20] which states clearly that the parties agreed to 'ENSURE a predictable commercial framework for business planning and investment'.[21] Moreover, the arbitral board pointed out that a NAFTA provision[22] provides that each of the signatories (parties) will '... accord to investments of investors of another Party treatment in accordance with international law, including fair and equitable treatment and full protection and security'.[23]

The wily act of the Governor to encounter a solution to preserve the interests of a local municipality aligned against the determination of the investor and its Mexican Governmental allies was considered a breach of the NAFTA treaty.

Although the decision of the arbitrators certainly is consistent with treaty interpretation,[24] disturbing legal questions still hover over the facts. The arbitrators did not consider the plain truth that if the decree in question was legal, if *Metalclad* did not secure all its permits, and if the Governor encountered a solution, then the Governor is to be complemented for his originality. The law demands thoroughness from all parties, including *Metalclad.*

More importantly, the reference of the arbitrators to 'international law' is not a reference to the laws concerning the interpretation of treaties. This the arbitrators already did when striving to understand the general purpose of the NAFTA treaty.[25] Rather, the arbitrators were referring to a standard of social norms known as 'international law' although its contents are never identified. The social norms invoked must be that the local community may have its cacti but its government must pay for this botanical solution. The reason can only be that NAFTA was intended to promote investment at a sovereign level and local interests must be subordinated. *Metalclad* was awarded as damages approximately US$ 17,000,000.

The *Metalclad* case is not so much an indication of treaty interpretation but rather of social norms. The arbitration board weighed the social interests of the local citizenry in opposition to the grandiose commercial scheme of NAFTA and dismissed the significance of the Governor's decree to a meaningless legal corner. The arbitration board could easily have decided the contrary. The solution decreed by the Governor was legal, if serendipitous, and therefore was not an affront to NAFTA.

Hopefully, the cacti, worth on the rare flora market US$ 17,000,000, are still there.

### *Once again, south of the border*

In another case involving rights under NAFTA, the ISCID arbitrated claims in *Robert Azinian and others* v. *United Mexican States.*[26] Here, the claimants invoked rights as shareholders in a Mexican enterprise, DESONA, which had held a concession for the collection and disposal of solid waste in the municipality of Naucalpan, a suburb of Mexico City.

The claimants sought damages resulting from the annulment of the concession by the municipality. The annulment had been declared on the grounds that the concession was either void due to misrepresentations or rescindable for failure of performance. DESONA unsuccessfully sought the reversal of the concession's annulment before the State Administrative Tribunal and its Superior Chamber, and then before a Mexican federal circuit court. All Mexican courts agreed the annulment was well-founded.

The arbitration tribunal could not avoid ruling on a conflict between national law and the provisions of the NAFTA treaty. According to the arbitrators, the fact that the Mexican courts found the annulment in accordance with Mexican law did not absolve the Mexican state from its liability under NAFTA if a substantive obligation of Chapter 11 of NAFTA had been breached.[27]

In the view of the ISCID arbitrators, such obligations included minimum standards of treatment under international law and expropriation standards as formulated by international law criteria. The arbitration tribunal found that the evidence before it could not support any such finding of Mexican law violation and dismissed the claim entirely. Before the ISCID was therefore an extraordinary set of legal facts. An arbitration board not formed by the Mexican government was being asked to pass upon various aspects of Mexican law as contravening some of the treaty provisions of NAFTA. The tribunal, in upholding the Mexican court's actions, did so because the arbitrators found the Mexican court had not breached the principles of international law.

The ICSID Tribunal then made the following observations:

> The only conceivably relevant substantive principle of Article 1105[of NAFTA] is that a NAFTA investor should not be dealt with in a manner that contravenes international law. There has not been a claim of such a violation of international law ...[28]
>
> The responsibility of the State for acts of judicial authorities may result from ... different types of judicial decision.
>
> The first is a decision of a municipal court clearly incompatible with a rule of international law.
>
> The second is what it known traditionally as a 'denial of justice'.[29]

Concluding, the ISCID found that before a violation of NAFTA could be determined it was necessary that 'the Claimants must show either a denial of justice, or pretence of form to achieve an internationally unlawful end'.[30] None was found.

No doubt the judges of the Mexican courts moaned with relief. Their municipal law system was still intact. As legal scholars well know, such satisfaction is temporal. What was put in cause was an evaluation of Mexican law by others and this power by the arbitrators was not questioned. In the next conflict, the sighs could easily turn to cries of desperation.

*What a difference twenty years makes!*

A Costa Rican corporation, Desarollo, controlled by American shareholders, filed a claim against the Republic of Costa Rica demanding damages because of an expropriation.[31] Desarollo purchased land for tourist development in Costa Rica in 1970 for $395,000. In 1978, Costa Rica expropriated the land due to its scientific value for existing 'flora and fauna' and offered to pay $1,900,000 compensation to Desarollo. Desarollo disagreed, alleging the land was worth $6,400,000. In economics this difference is dryly designated 'capital gains'.

As might be expected, this significant discrepancy caused delays and 20 years passed in sporadic attempts by the parties to reach an agreement. No doubt, more decades would have passed except that the Costa Rican government was anxious to receive a loan of $175,000,000 from the Inter-American Development Bank. The loan could not be approved because of US legislation, the Helms amendment,[32] which prohibits financial aid by international financial institutions to a country where the property of a US citizen was expropriated without just compensation. With the obvious intent of complying with the Helms requirement of compensation, Costa Rica agreed to arbitration before the ISCID as both Costa Rica and the US were signatories to the ISCID Convention.

The arbitrators awarded $16,000,000 to Desarollo, calculated by giving a value of $4,150,000 to the land when it was expropriated in 1978 plus compounded interest to the date of the award in 1998. Deducting the compensation due from the loan Costa Rica now hoped to receive (a mere 1 per cent loss), this still makes a positive cash balance for Costa Rica and there seems no reason to comment further on the facts — except for some disturbing principles of international law enunciated by the arbitral board.

Costa Rica argued that under its law compounded interest was not appropriate. In its reasoned opinion, the arbitral board pointed out that other international arbitration awards recognized compounded interest,[33] compounded interest was awarded in the Iran-US Claims Tribunal Reports,[34] supported by writers of 'high authority',[35] and by a Reporter for the UN International Law Commission.[36]

In other words, Costa Rican law on awarding simple interest versus compound interest was not deemed relevant. The municipal law had to submit to the standards prevailing in international law doctrine.

*The American Marijuana syndrome*

Lest scholars conclude NAFTA is basically a US investment device to cudgel its Southern neighbor, there are no lack of disputes against the US or Canada.[37] The most recent involves a Canadian company, Kenex Ltd., which has filed a claim under NAFTA against the US alleging illegal acts preventing importation of hemp into the US. Apparently, the Drug Enforcement Agency of the US believed the content of marijuana found in imported hemp might be chemically extracted for opiate users.[38]

Whatever the final result, the giant as well as the small economies must now submit to investor complaints that their laws are not in conformity with NAFTA standards. Since the NAFTA canons are generalized, there is created a new legal ethos for international commerce. As eloquently stated in Chapter 11 of NAFTA:[39]

> Each Party shall accord to investments of investors of another Party treatment in accordance with international law, including fair and equitable treatment and full protection and security.

We will probably never be certain as to the interpretations to be given to the NAFTA treaty provisions. In a recent case,[40] the ICSID was called upon to interpret the meaning of the word 'expropriation' in the NAFTA treaty. The case involved a claim against the Mexican State. In its search for guidance, the arbitration board found it natural that the meaning under customary international law would be clarified in the treatises of the American Law Institute, Restatement of the Law, Third. Apparently Mexican sources do not qualify as evidence of international customary law. Or perhaps, the prestige, justly deserved, of the American Law Institute, is not to be by-passed.

We are thus full circle to the Greek chorus of *Asian Agricultural Products Ltd. (AAPL) v. Republic of Sri Lanka*, the only difference being more than a decade has elapsed but the background chanting continues. Further cases and arbitral dicta could be referenced, but all at the expense of the ennui of the reader. With the occasional exception, the reported cases on the ICSID web site make clear the influence of US jurisprudence or will we claim the lack of interest in the theories of other nations. With every case, there surges forth as froth on the crest of rolling waves the economic inspired arbitration decisions of NAFTA and the creeds of the ISCID. The shores of municipal law are receding before the billows of international commercial law, whatever 'international law, including fair and equitable treatment and full protection and security' comes to mean.

A simple solution would be to have the tenets of the American Law Institute's Restatement of the Law, Universal edition, enacted as law in the legislatures of those nations wishing to trade with the West.

## Notes

[1] *Asian Agricultural Products Ltd. (AAPL) v. Republic of Sri Lanka*, 30 I.L.M. 577 (1991).
[2] Ibid, at paragraph 39.
[3] Ibid.
[4] Supra, n. 1, at paragraph 40.
[5] Ibid.
[6] Ibid.
[7] Ibid with a citation to article 31 of the Vienna Convention on the Law of Treaties which by its terms refers to all the principles of international law applicable to the parties.

[8] Ibid.
[9] Ibid.
[10] Ibid.
[11] Ibid.
[12] Ibid.
[13] Ibid.
[14] Supra, n. 1. The original claim for US$ 8,067,368 (which included projections as to goodwill, future profits and intangible assets) was reduced by the arbitration board to US$ 460,000 plus interest.
[15] David Palmeter, *The WTO as a Legal System*, 24 Fordham Int'l L. J. 444 (2000), in the introduction states:

> H.L.A. Hart in 'The Concept of Law' observed that primitive law and international law are foremost among the examples given of doubtful cases when the question 'What is law' is asked.

[16] This case is reported on the ISCID web site, <www.worldbank.org/icsid>, Case no. ARB (AF)/97/1, accessed 22 January 2002. Date of award is 30 August 2000.
[17] In this case, it is NAFTA.
[18] Supra, n.16, at paragraph 46 of the reported dispatch.
[19] Supra, n. 16, at paragraph 59 of the reported dispatch.
[20] Supra, n. 16, paragraph 71 wherein the arbitrators cite the relevant NAFTA treaty language.
[21] Ibid.
[22] Article 1105 (1).
[23] Supra, n. 16, paragraph 74.
[24] Supra, n. 16, paragraph 70:

> The Vienna Convention on the Law of Treaties, Article 31 (1) provides a treaty is to be interpreted in good faith in accordance with the ordinary meaning to be given to the terms of the treaty in their context and in light of the treaty's object and purpose.

[25] Ibid.
[26] The case is reported on the ISCID web site <www.worldbank.org/icsid>, Case No. ARB(AF)/97/2), accessed 1 February 2002. Date of award is 18 October 1999.
[27] Supra, fn. 26, par. 85, referring to the articles of NAFTA:

> Article 1110(1)
>
> No party may directly or indirectly nationalize or expropriate an investment of an investor of another party in its territory or take a measure tantamount to nationalization or expropriation of such investment (expropriation) except:
>
> (a) for a public purpose;
> (b) on a non-discriminatory basis;
> (c) in accordance with due process of law and Article 1105(1); and
> (d) on payment of compensation in accordance with paragraphs 2 through 6.
>
> Article 1105(1)
>
> Each Party shall accord to investments of investors of another Party treatment in accordance with international law, including fair and equitable treatment and full protection and security.

[28] Supra, n. 26, at paragraph 92.
[29] Supra, n. 26, at paragraph 98.
[30] Supra, n. 26 at paragraph 99.
[31] The case is reported on the ISCID web site <www.worldbank.org/icsid>, Case no. ARB/96/1, accessed 1 February 2002. Date of award is 17 February 2000.
[32] Section 527 of the 1994-1995 US Foreign Relations Authorization Act.
[33] Supra, n. 31, at paragraph 99.
[34] Supra, n. 31, at paragraph 100.
[35] Supra, n. 31, at paragraph 101.
[36] Supra, n. 31, at paragraph 102.
[37] See <www.cyberus.ca/~tweiler/naftaclaims.html> for a review of various cases.
[38] Case reported in The Financial Times, January 17, 2002, at p. 3. Also cf. links on the web site supra, n. 33.
[39] See <www.nafta-sec-alena.org>, accessed 6 March 2002 for details as to NAFTA clauses.
[40] Marvin Roy Feldman v. Mexico, the case is reported on the ISCID web site <www.worldbank.org/icsid>, Case no. ARB/91/1, accessed 14 April 2003. The date of the award is 16 December 2002.

# Chapter 18

# WTO Trade Disputes are Still Power Politics

*A gathering of the clans*

Without procedures for resolving disputes and then enforcing the awards, the most laudable of multinational organizations can only muster a political posture. As absurd as it appears, after approximately 50 years of voluminous GATT panel decisions and multitudinous agreements, the superseding 'Agreement Establishing the World Trade Organization' (Agreement)[1] only manages to ensure that the WTO nation members will not discriminate against trade, whatever that means,[2] in all its variegated facets. Our preoccupation is not with tariff disputes, nor the grid classification of products, nor the implementation of export credits, as important as these topics are, but rather the essential principles which constitute the pillars of the free trade as envisioned by the WTO. Our concern is with the political economy upon which the WTO is founded. For the WTO Agreement is a constitution and not a legislative act.

The much heralded and believed rule of trade law now enshrined by the WTO Agreement has proved to be, if not folly, a misplaced confidence. The existing legal structure of the WTO ensures it will perform no better than GATT in resolving trade disputes.[3] Although constituted to foment international trade, the WTO has no power to formulate international trade regulations.[4] Indeed, its title 'An Agreement' makes clear its modest contractual aspirations, and, as such precludes, *a priori*, any enforceable adjudicative powers with serious, social consequences. Even considered as a contract, the WTO Agreement is bereft of most of the rights and obligations attendant to such a legal concept.[5] Politics, rather than legal principles, exhale from its text[6] and is a perceived reality by WTO members or those dealing with the organization.[7]

Lacking any substantial, regulatory authority, the WTO only presents a threat to national sovereignty if attempts are made to extend or amplify its present contractual status.[8] But then, as granting any regulatory authority to the WTO would render it unaccountable to citizens everywhere,[9] such an enhancement of powers is precluded. Precisely what its social critics claim — a democratic deficit — would be the result if the WTO Agreement were an enforceable legal instrument containing 'jurisdictional rules', in contrast to 'customs' or 'laws' which are based on consent.

Of course, if all parties agree, it is possible to amend a particular provision or even alter substantially the 'Agreement'. Yet, such an eventuality is remote, and, unlike a parliament where political forces may forge a majority, the unanimity requirement provisions of the WTO Agreement impede this tactic. The fear of each member of loosing the traditional attributes of sovereignty is an insurmountable obstacle.

Far from striving to be a constitution therefore, purporting to define the basic rights of international commerce which will be binding and enforceable, the agreement instead emphasizes an *esprit de corps*. The WTO will promote the framework 'for the conduct of trade relations'[10]. Its function will be a 'forum for negotiations among its members'.[11] Moreover, manifesting its broad, collaborative economic spirit, the WTO declares, it will cooperate, when appropriate, 'with the International Monetary Fund and with the International Bank for Reconstruction and Development'.[12]

Were these the only references to WTO objectives, it would be difficult to understand the storm of social criticism and activist demonstrations often associated with its creation and meetings. Yet, the WTO did inaugurate an innovation in international trade relations by incorporating, within its terms, by reference to an annex, the Understanding on Rules and Procedures Governing the Settlement of Disputes (DSU).[13]

This apparent, adjudicative power of dispute settlement — oh, the guile of words! — raises the specter of trade policies becoming enforceable laws through the decisions made possible by the DSU. Such a conclusion fomenting anxiety in the activist population is a premature and considerable exaggeration. In fact, other truths surface and are discernible. By its terms, both the WTO and the DSU reveal its hapless legal status and inevitable convergence with prevalent, mercantile philosophies.

As already indicated, the terms and rules of WTO international trade are to be 'negotiated'. The relevant legal instruments establish no mechanism for enforcement of decisions other than voluntary payment of damages, or the retaliation of one county against another in the form of aggravated tariffs or suspension of trade benefits. There exists through the WTO the declared will to further the goals of free, unfettered trade but the means are similar to those of a council of tribal chiefs: an appeal to the common sense of the economic warriors.

Thus the DSU states unequivocally that the purpose of the dispute settlement mechanism is 'to secure a positive solution to a dispute'.[14] However, the adjudicative organ created, denominated the Dispute Settlement Body (DSB), with its dispute panels and appellate bodies 'cannot add to or diminish the rights and obligations' of the various, sovereign signatories.[15] Such an affirmation can only mean the nation members have not relinquished any of their powers to the WTO. For this reason, we cannot speak of a WTO constitution, but rather a contract, or gentlemen's agreement among governments.[16] Nowhere is there in the WTO Agreement even a partial delegation of sovereign powers. The agreement only reflects a political consensus as to the wise and just standards of international trade.[17]

This is apparent within the text of the DSU because when the DSU refers to a 'positive solution to a dispute' it means a solution 'mutually acceptable to the parties'.[18] Voluntary compliance and not mandated obedience is the social milieu of the trade club. Members of the WTO are exhorted to utilize 'good faith' in the resolution of disputes.[19] When consultations and conciliation fail, then hearings will be conducted. Should a complaint be justified and a party be found in default under a WTO obligation, then compensation may be voluntarily paid,[20] failing which the offended member may refuse to grant to the offending nation a typical WTO obligation such as the most favored nation principle.[21]

Various trade law scholars have questioned the efficacy of voluntary payments going so far as to say that the record on implementation is mixed.[22] Some members refuse to comply; others make cosmetic changes to their domestic laws. The conclusion is that the efficiency and integrity of the WTO dispute settlement process is being challenged[23] and at other times, ignored. Moreover, if the recalcitrant nation believes itself wronged, it will obviously retaliate, imposing tariffs or other onerous duties on its once former partner. If no nation voluntarily implements the guidance of the WTO dispute panels, the recourse is to muted, economic war.[24] This is hardly the stuff meriting the designation of a legal instrument.

Without question, the Agreement has few of the aspects of a legislative instrument despite its massive text and infinite encyclopedic length as a result of the annexes and prior GATT references. However, while a substantial amount of trade law is restricted to technical aspects of tariffs, duties, dumping, subsidies, and occult protectionism measures, there are significant social issues brought before the WTO dispute panels which do have material human consequences.

WTO panels have and can be expected to hear and consider such areas as environment; public services, where private rights are asserted against the common weal; measures concerning genetically modified plants; and, probably, in the near future, genetically altered animals as well. It thus matters a great deal whether we are going to deal with an international trade organization beholden to politics or to the rule of law.

## *Of customs, laws, rules, and regulations*

While there is a natural, generalized belief that the WTO Agreement is based on the laws of international trade, an understanding of the present course of the WTO and its future evolution necessitates distinguishing between customs, laws, rules, and regulations. While such categories are amorphous, still a general appreciation of their differences is attainable and helpful in delineating the actual role of the WTO as a trade policy organization and what it can successfully accomplish.

Excluding territorial conquests of war, where the victors impose their social will on the vanquished, custom clearly precedes law in the history of a human community. Common sense dictates that people do not accept conduct with important social consequences as being democratically acceptable by them through mere legislative fiat. Sullen silence is not to be confused with concurrence. For this reason, the strident aspersions as to the legitimacy of the WTO and its perceived objectives are the results to apparent legislation which has not been preceded by community discussion. But as many social anthropologists have described in multiple field studies,[25] written, codified laws are not necessary for social legislation. What is required are the general principles of behavior, recognized and accepted as pertinent and valid. Custom, then, is a moral statement about social conduct, which seems, to a particular society, in a specific epoch, as pragmatic rules of comportment.

Thus, it is with good judgment and based on the propensity of mankind towards consensus that the WTO admits to be guided by 'decisions, procedures, and customary practices' which were followed by the member nations to its predecessor, GATT 1947.[26] By customary practices, of course, we are referring to the trade principles accumulated through approximately 50 years of commercial disputes under GATT 47. In the same vein, the DSU also recognizes the importance of custom as a source of both permitted and expected conduct.[27] But while we can speak of and even resort to using a concept such as custom, we will not lose sight of its fundamental characteristic which distinguishes it from law. It is more accurate to say 'state law', for that is the implication.

Custom needs to be proved, demonstrated to exist as socially admitted and properly applicable to conduct between the parties.[28] There is conducted a search by the judicial authorities to determine the prevalence and social acceptance of a norm of behavior. Not so with a law. Whatever its origin, and in less socially complex societies it surely was custom, laws are already known, in theory, by the average member of a community to be relevant in a particular fact situation, or at least by their counsel.[29]

Thus, we cross the frontier between custom and law when we leave behind discussions as to the existence or not of prescribed social behavior and instead ask if any particular act has or not been committed and for which the law defines a norm to be followed. When we are confronted with a principle of law, we do not inquire if such a norm exists. Rather, our inquiry is to whether or not the principle of law is applicable in the particular fact situation. Phrased differently, we stop searching for a model standard of behavior, as we are satisfied it exists, and instead we pass to the determination of its application. Customs are preceded by an investigation, an endeavor of social scientists, no matter if they are ordained judges or lawyers, to determine a truism: if the existence of a *modus operandi* is generalized or not. Custom has no certain content by definition. It is a concept still in formation.

A law does not have a *modus operandi*. Proven custom, or judicial interpretation, or a legislative act, has decreed its existence. But a further element is necessary to contrast custom to law. Without means of enforcement, laws are not distinguishable from custom for they both have the same origin and the same function. Both are seen as sensible patterns of conduct. But there is a critical factor which separates custom from law and that is the degree of enforceability. An eminently practical division is how obedience is secured, coaxed, which is the result of the WTO structure, or compelled by a third party entity, a common element of modern societies.

Enforcement thus looms as the significant feature of a 'law'. If law is to have a separate classification, its own category different from custom, than this must reside in the means of enforcement a particular society has devised to compel obedience to its norms. With custom as the dominant mode of settlement, a consensus is achieved through a political dialogue. The warriors are counseled by their chiefs. Social ostracism is a probable form of enforcement in tribal societies. On the other hand, confronting laws, a judicial sentence commands a wide range of mechanisms wresting compulsion. While the difference is one of degree, it is a qualitative separation. Of course, between custom and the law there will be gray areas. The study of the law is not a science, nor an art, but a humane vision upon which is imposed the rule of reason.

Separate from custom and laws are the interstices of a judicial system. Rules are but the deductions derived from laws. From a law, we can deduce a rule, such as if consent is a sine qua non of a contract, than such consent must be manifested. A law carries with it, *a priori*, rules. And of course, the condition of consent may come to be further refined by requiring consent in a particular factual setting, such as real estate transactions, to be demonstrated in writing. Rules are the logical development of a law, whether by inference or deduction. This is the flourishing art of the counselor at law. Regulations are but the procedures and formalities surrounding the exercise of any right. While their existence is often the first encounter with a legal system by citizens, they are not the reflection of serious social ideas. Regulations are the engine oil of the motor of the law, such as the pleading which must be delivered to the court house.

Viewed in this fashion, the WTO is not a legal system, but rather a consultative body for affirming or denying the existence of a custom. We cannot say 'law' because, even with the large body of trade disputes preceding the WTO, a satisfactory system of enforcement was and is still lacking. True, the history of GATT disputes will reveal multiple decisions concerned with the vast range of trade topics, ranging from tariffs to trade behavior. However, under GATT, no dispute settlement sentence was possible without a unanimous vote by the members. No further analysis is needed to inquire if we were then dealing with customs, laws, rules, or regulations. Since GATT required the exercise of political will, it is not possible to coherently systemize the GATT trade sentences. Lacking a binding system of precedent, there cannot be law. Under GATT, with a requirement of an affirmative, unanimous vote by all members as to the terms of a sentence, it was not possible to create a system of binding precedents. One recalcitrant nation member renders the concept of binding precedents ludicrous.

Fortunately, the requirement of a prior political consensus was reversed under WTO. Now, a panel decision will be valid unless a majority of the WTO members vote to the contrary. However, while this means it is now theoretically possible to think of a continuum of dispute panel sentences leading to permanent judicial trade jurisprudence, the absence of an enforcement mechanism dilutes this prediction and renders without content the rule of law in the WTO. If enforcement of trade dispute panel decisions must rely on voluntary enforcement, then there is a strong impetus for such decisions to strive for politically acceptable solutions when the issues before a panel are laden with social import. The dispute settlement process of the WTO invariably will result in decisions which propose a consensual solution and which confronts the realities of international commerce. This means recognizing that the present major economic powers will not with grace voluntarily accept panel decisions deleterious to their interests. The political process is cabalistic by nature and seeks in the corridors of power compromise solutions.

From this postulate it is a short step to acknowledging that the WTO panel decisions of broad significance, lacking any enforcement mechanisms, will render their opinions in conformity with reigning economic principles, careful not to offend sovereign rights. Otherwise, compliance by the offending nation will not be forthcoming. Such practices are but a political vehicle for the globalization of the legal principles contained within the political economy of international commerce. Social theorists who correctly see in the WTO a threat to humanistic objectives are misunderstanding the adjudicative powers of the WTO. The WTO is anything but a judicial forum. It is a gathering of nations struggling to find the most common denominators of trade practices and custom.

This being so, a reversal of any trend towards the primacy of political economy over human rights[30] requires either reformulating the WTO Agreement so as to contain specific laws protecting human rights, which is surely utopian, or establishing a mechanism whereby private parties can be heard.[31] In the absence of these two alternatives, we are once again returned to the forum of power politics[32] which characterized the GATT.

### *From power politics to the rule of law*

Reversing an earlier stance, the WTO has now confirmed that *amicus curiae*[33] briefs, legal opinions on the dispute by parties interested in the outcome but not a party to the pleadings or hearing, may be sent directly to the WTO without being annexed to a litigant's submissions,[34] the latter having to give its permission. This is a welcome innovation but which also brings a disadvantage. While the ability to submit briefs makes it possible for human rights, or other groups to assert their opinions before the WTO, it is also true that those opposing such concepts can do the same.

With the shift to permitting *amicus curiae* briefs, we therefore leave open to political capture the dispute settlement structure of the WTO. This will aggravate further the idea held by some that the WTO represents a democratic deficit,[35] or more accurately, a democratic absence, since the panels of the WTO are not accountable to any citizen through the electorate process. It is only the member governments who participate in WTO panel hearings. Unless private parties are allowed to represent their view directly before the WTO, the political initiative offered by *amicus curiae* briefs befalls to those most informed and aggressively inclined.

A parallel movement distinct from *amicus curiae* briefs would be to allow a member sovereign to retain and be represented by private counsel, instead of an attorney representing a government member, such as the Attorney General. This is different from *amicus curiae* briefs as in theory it is representation of a participant with a legitimate interest and private counsel may, it is not a hopeless conclusion, be expected to bring a larger vision which permits, if indirectly, issues relating to other groups to be raised. A private counsel representing a sovereign can include arguments on behalf of private groups, while in theory an Attorney General might feel constrained to enlarge his protected interest group. The WTO has allowed member governments this right of legal representation.[36]

Nevertheless, neither *amicus curiae* briefs nor private counsel for member nation participants is going to alter significantly the glaring fact that WTO is hardly different from the GATT in its dependence on power politics. Unless there are textual changes to the WTO Agreement in the near future, which appears as probable as amending the US Constitution in the same time period, WTO will prove to be as anchored to the will of nations as GATT, except for one fact which could alter this panorama substantially: granting private parties standing before the WTO. The only viable solution to the present unfortunate impasse is to grant private parties the right to appear before the WTO when there is alleged a violation of a provision.

Permitting private interests to bring cases before the WTO frees the WTO from political capture through lobbies exercising their pressure on governments and at the same time ensures complaints will be brought without regard to political consequences. Moreover, with the appearance of private parties, which will surely necessitate the formation of lower and possibly intermediate arbitration boards prior to reaching the WTO, there is created the beginnings of a system of precedent which is fundamental to any rule of law. Even without automatic enforcement, private parties have no reason to mask their opinions; nor are they reluctant to take their arguments to the public square; nor is there any reason to withhold publication of the award.

Reported, arbitration awards will naturally exercise their influence on subsequent cases. It can be envisioned that opening international trade law issues to private litigants will result in a deluge of claims. Aside from the fact this is hardly a reason for refusing to create a proper system of justice, the same argument could be made for any national jurisdiction. Yet citizens of countries expect their governments to provide a forum for their alleged wrongs.

Finally, private parties whose commercial interests have been confirmed by arbitration boards as being prejudiced can seek enforcement of these awards through various international arbitration conventions with suitable amendments to those legal instruments or in their own national courts. Thus, the devastating absence of enforcement now characterizing the WTO can be overcome. Naturally, many items need to be analyzed in more detail ranging from the hierarchy of such a system to defining by a supplemental agreement to the WTO the elements which grant a private party the right to invoke a WTO violation. Nevertheless, unless this formidable task is studied and eventually undertaken, the hopes that the WTO will be a legalistic system and not one of economic power conflicts will prove to be in vain.

The anticipated trend from the power relations of GATT to the expected rule of law of WTO will not be consummated. For the moment, we must contemplate what the present will mean to the future of international trade law. International trade has always generated its own social units, from the maritime merchant community to the stock exchange clubs. What begins as the practice of gentlemen, transforming into custom, then crystallizing into a law, illustrates at a micro-level the macro-dimensions of international trade. The present amorphous nature of the

WTO has prompted numerous scholars to question the role of the WTO — whether it has a duty to promote human rights; whether it has an obligation to ensure support policies and rules which translate into benefits for the world population, and not just commercial entities.[37] While the merits of such academic contributions will no doubt influence policy-makers, for the moment, numerous panel decisions attest to the elusive nature of the WTO — consensus is lacking as to broad objectives. In the meantime, the importance of trade suggests the WTO will adopt conduct which avoids confront to sovereignty while issuing proclamations in support of collaboration.

Inevitably this means that international trade, far from being only a compendium of tariff rules and regulations, is instead a social system dominated by the dynamics of sovereignty and consent. But such eminently, courtly manners bring certain consequences. When a social system is subject to the rules of volition, the voluntary granting of consent, then, of course, the realities of power become the silent background for the stage of international trade.[38] Presently, regardless of the WTO Agreement and its 21 annexes, there is no manner of enforcing WTO panel decisions other than international opinion and sanction. WTO members who do not accept the result of a WTO panel report are liable to trade retaliations by their partners.

Nevertheless, when the partners involved dominate international trade, the threat of sanctions is the nip of the gadfly. Trade sanctions imposed by a minor player in international commerce bring no consequences. There can be no political pressure exercised by injured economic groups. The stark truth of the WTO adjudicative machinery reveals its dependency on the voluntary cooperation of its members. This being so, the natural tendency will be for trading partners to accommodate themselves to the economic philosophies of the dominant traders. Knowing in advance that an adverse WTO panel decision which is prejudicial to large economic groups will only raise the possibility of interminable sovereign conflict, there is exacted a considerable pressure to find a common ground of convergence between the trading partners. Ludicrous will be trade sanctions by struggling junior partners whose only hope of survival in all its aspects is to attract foreign investment.

As the WTO dispute process is substantially dependent on sovereign consent, the customary practices sanctioned by WTO panelists must take into account the realities of power politics. With customs preceding laws in the evolution of social groups, the international trading community, clearly a communal unit, is steering towards jurisprudence influenced and ultimately dominated by the economic powers. Any contrary trend will not meet with success and if there is anything abhorrent to a merchant, it is bankruptcy, whether financial or spiritual.

With no other choice available, the WTO contributes to the globalization of Western law as practiced by the economic giants of our present epoch. If the WTO is merely announcing prevalent commercial customs, and not laws, then voluntary compliance will only be forthcoming in the majority of the cases when the norms decreed are seen as acceptable. Since the WTO has numerous members but a restricted club of industrialized countries, what is reasonable must reflect the dominant precepts of the major law merchants, also known as the *lex mercatoria*, mercantile principles utilized in the major trading blocs such as the US and the EU.

This is because the customs enunciated must find a comprehensive responsive by those responsible for international commerce. It is the merchant community class exercising its political pressure in the various member nations which will render voluntary compliance by a disobedient nation a fact or not. The WTO customs, similar to the tribal wisdom of grassland councils,[39] fortify and propagate the dominant ideologies of an epoch which mirrors the globalization process wrought by international commerce. For the moment, the Western democracies are the economic *los conquistadores* and the WTO their forum.

Economics is capital. Capital is Power. Without independent, judicial enforcement supported by seizure mechanisms, arbitration awards are moral platitudes. Anyone doubting this affirmation should take cognizance of a $4 billion sanctions award by the WTO against the US in favor of the EU, which the EU hesitates to apply for fear of loss of transatlantic trade; an award in favor of Ecuador in the amount of $200 million sanctions against the EU which Ecuador can not utilize for fear of damaging its local economy; and Canada's refusal to apply an award of $220.5 million in sanctions against Brazil, no doubt for similar reasons.[40]

Determined to separate political economy from international obligations, many countries, including the US, are reported to be now negotiating separate bits with various trading partners who will substitute fines for sanctions.[41] While apparently confined to bits, the same philosophy will most likely be extended to regional trade agreements.[42] Behind this change in trade philosophy is the desire of the worlds' traders to opt for fines when commercial profits are put at risk. This is in accordance with US various business lobbies which have long argued that WTO trade retaliation dispute mechanisms do not work because they can be ignored.[43]

The inability to enforce obligations through judicial mechanisms leaves the WTO subject to political pressures exercised in the familiar corridors of power. The brief history of judicial decisions under the auspices of the ISCID demonstrates how effective arbitration is in compelling compliance with treaty obligations in contrast with the power politics still rampant in the WTO. The WTO is condemned to the debility of its sanctions unless the signatories in question establish effective mechanisms for enforcement. Such a possibility is more than remote.[44]

The inability of the WTO to enforce its decisions will have consequences for the course of legal globalization. Without judicial or arbitration mechanisms capable of enforcing WTO panel decisions, commercial norms will invariably emanate from the main trading partners and every attempt made other trading partners to secure compliance through compromise. Precisely through this social mechanism — negotiation followed by resolution — lies the history of harmonization of commercial standards which is the precursor to legal norms. In the absence of effective WTO enforcement procedures, legal globalization will continue to be under the aegis of the Western nations.

## Notes

[1] For terms of text, see official web site of the WTO at <www.wto.org>, accessed 6 April 2002. The agreement also includes the 21 annexes treating topics as diverse as agriculture, government procurement, patents, plant health, pre-shipment inspection, textiles and clothing, trade-related investment measures, technical barriers to trade, rules of origin, subsidies and countervailing measures, to name a few.
[2] John O. McGinnis et al., *The World Trade Constitution*, 114 Harv. L. Rev. 511 (2000), Introduction, second paragraph, 'It [the WTO] merely polices members' laws to ensure that these laws do not discriminate against foreign trade'.
[3] James Salzman, *Labor Rights, Globalization and Institutions: The Role and Influence of The Organization for Economic Cooperation and Development*, 21 Mich. J. Int'l L. 769 (2000); Guy de Jonquières, *WTO no better than GATT in ending EU-US trade disputes*, The Financial Times, 13-14 April 2002, at p. 3, citing study by Marc L. Busch et al., *Transatlantic trade conflicts and GATT/WTO dispute settlement*, no date given for the study.
[4] Supra, n. 2.
[5] Under common and civil law jurisdictions, a contract presupposes a remedy for its breach whose enforcement can be compelled through a variety of legal techniques, e.g. attachment of assets.
[6] J. Patrick Kelley, *The WTO and Global Governance: The Case for Contractual Treaty Regimes*, 7 SPG Widener L. Symposium. J. 109 (2001).
[7] Raymond Colitt, *US seeks WTO intervention on biotech, takes battle to Brazil*, <www.cropchoiceom/leadstry.asp?recid=1769>, dated 20 June 2003, accessed 24 September 2003, reporting on the lobbying efforts by the US government with Brazil to support a claim filed with the WTO against the EU regarding the latter's refusal to allow imports of US geneticially modified foods.
[8] Supra, n. 2.
[9] Supra, n. 2.
[10] WTO Agreement, Article II, Paragraph 1.
[11] Ibid, Article III, Paragraph 2.
[12] Ibid, Article III, Paragraph 5.
[13] Ibid, Article III, Paragraph 3.
[14] Understanding on Rules and Procedures Governing the Settlement of Disputes, (Understanding) Article 3, Paragraph 7, available on WTO web site, supra, n. 1.
[15] Ibid, Article 3, Paragraph 2.
[16] Supra, n. 6.
[17] Ibid.
[18] Understanding, Article 3, Paragraph 7.
[19] Understanding, Article 3, Paragraph 10.
[20] Understanding, Article 22.
[21] Ibid.
[22] Timothy C. Brightbill, et al., *International Legal Developments in Review:2000*, 35 Int'l Law 407 (2001).
[23] Sue Ann Mota, *The World Trade Organization: An Analysis of Disputes*, 25 N.C. J. Int'l L. & Com. Reg. 75 (1999), Conclusion, second paragraph: 'One weakness of the dispute process, however, is the relative unenforceability of the WTO's decisions. This can escalate into trade war among the parties'.
[24] Guy de Jonquières, *Europe hopes to 'hit the White house where it hurts'*, The Financial Times, 26 March 2002, at p. 2, reporting that after more than four years from an adverse ruling the EU has still failed to comply with a WTO ruling holding restrictions on meat

imports illegal. See also Edward Alden, *Transatlantic tensions set to escalate*, The Financial Times, 20-21 April 2002, at p. 4, where EU is suggesting they will target specific US exports, such as citrus fruits, with trade sanctions, so as to hurt political support of Pres. Bush.

[25] Max Gluckman, *Politics, Law and Ritual in Tribal Society*, Basil Blackwell, 2nd Edition, Oxford (1967). Also, Max Gluckman, *Custom and Conflict in Africa*, Basil Blackwell, Oxford (1963); also Sally Falk Moore, *Law As Process*, Routledge & Kegan Paul, London (1978).

[26] WTO Agreement, Article XVI, Paragraph 1

[27] Understanding, Article 3, Paragraph 2.

[28] WT/DS26/AB/R: EC — Measures Concerning Meat and Meat Products Panel Decision and Appellate Body Report, January 16, 1998.

[29] Ignorance of the law is hardly ever a valid defense in either civil or criminal law suits in Western jurisprudence.

[30] Marjorie Cohn, *The World Trade Organization: Elevating Property Interests Above Human Rights*, 29 Ga. J. Int'l & Comp. L. 427 (2001). Some of the material indicated by Ms Cohn suggests other interpretations but there are listed various topics meriting further investigation about the possible subordination of human rights to economic interests by the WTO.

[31] Michael Laidhold, *Private Party Access to the WTO: Do Recent Developments in International Trade Disputes Really Give Private Organizations a Voice in the WTO?*, 12 Transnat'l Law 427 (1999).

[32] The European Union won a WTO approval for permission to impose as much as $4 billion in duties on US goods as damages for a US law allowing income earned abroad by American companies to be excluded from US reporting requirements. However, the enforcement of the WTO ruling is dubious as the EU trade commissioner faces pressure from European companies not to impose the penalties. European companies are anxious not to ruin transatlantic trade worth $60 billion a year, see 'Top Financial News' of 30 August 2002, <www.bloomberg.com>, accessed 30 August 2002.

[33] Normally referred to as 'friends of the court' whereby a third party makes known its views to a tribunal as it is interested in the resolution of the case. For example, in the case of WTO panel disputes, a non-government organization might wish to submit a brief in support of an environmental issue.

[34] WTO Appellate Body, United States — Import Prohibition of Certain Shrimp and Shrimp Products, WT/DS58/AB/R ()ct. 12, 1998).

[35] Supra, n. 31.

[36] European Communities-Regime for the Importation, Sale, and Distribution of Bananas, WT/DS27/AB/R (Sept. 9, 1997).

[37] Padideh Ala'i, *A Human Rights Critique of the WTO: Some Preliminary Observations*, 33 Geo. Wash. Int'l L. Rev. 537 (2001); Jeffrey Atik, *Democratizing The WTO*, 33 Geo. Wash. Int'l L. Rev. 451 (2001); Adelle Blackett, *Whither Social Clause? Human Rights, Trade Theory and Treaty Interpretation*, 31 Colum. Human Rts. L. Rev. 3 (1999).

[38] John Gledhill, *Power and Its Disguises*, Pluto Press, London, Boulder, Colorado (1994).

[39] Gluckman, supra. n. 25.

[40] All reported in Francis Williams, *WTO arms Europeans with weighty weapons*, The Financial Times, 31 August/1 September 2002, at p. 2.

[41] Edward Alden, *US proposes fines instead of sanctions in trade disputes*, The Financial Times, 25 October 2002, at p. 7.

[42] Ibid.

[43] Ibid.

[44] The cost of WTO non-compliance is a schedule of uneforceable sanctions:

> In 2002, the WTO awarded US$ 4 billion against the US in its tax rebate law favoring US exporters dispute with the EU.
>
> In 2000, Canada was awarded US$ 220.5 million in a trade dispute with Brazil over aircraft subsidies.
>
> In 1999, both the US and Canada were awarded substantial amounts, over US$ 300 million, in trade disputes with the EU over a ban on hormones.

# Chapter 19

# International Arbitration Without International Arbitration Law

*International arbitration but no international arbitration law*[1]

International arbitration is based on the merchants' conviction there is a universal standard of justice upon which disputes may be resolved and this is best achieved by avoiding the municipal court system. Viewed from this mercantile premise, arbitration, in the comfortable rooms of a institute where coffee is served and the perennial delays of a court room normally absent, is but an unceremonious procedure to arrive at the truth. Otherwise, logically, international arbitration would only be an informal substitute for diverse legal precepts and formal procedures reigning in different countries. But, no, it is precisely the imagined multiple, inconsistent legal principles the average merchant seeks to avoid. Or, if you prefer, the merchant's aversion to decisions of law contrary to common sense.

By virtue of this reasoning, international arbitration propels its participants towards a globalization of the law under the sway of the industrial nations, their entrepreneurs, and counsel. It matters not if the motive for arbitration is based on premises which do not exist: there is not a solid core of commercial principles applicable to all disputes. The impulses of the client are to to circumvent the sometimes ironic consequences of legal reasoning thought to be characteristic of municipal court procedures.

Were the arbitration process to be impeded, total legal and judicial confusion would reign. International commerce would come to a halt. The reason is known to the cadre of lawyers engaged in international litigation. Municipal law, with its scattered jurisdictions enshrining their own national laws and conflicting principles, cannot grant the degree of certainty international trade requires. Litigation results are often the outcome of the jurisdiction chosen by one party to a law suit; the search for a forum with the more favorable legal principles. This is a common maneuvering on the part of plaintiffs' attorneys. More credit is given to an attorney by his client for his choice of forum than for his subsequent endeavors in developing the case.

The merchant class is aware of this and accordingly there is an unrelenting request for arbitral dispute settlement.[2] Unfortunately, there is no international arbitration law. But this observation largely escapes the international entrepreneurs. Yet, this understandable arbitration trend, now so firmly entrenched in international commerce, leads inevitably to policy confrontations. We witness sovereign power versus the individual will; private law prerogatives over against public law policies; national law adverse to delocalized arbitration;[3] territorial limits opposite a virtual arbitration world;[4] national law systems in conflict with arbitral independence.

As with any organization, law courts do not like to see their power diminished. Arbitration is a threat. The sovereign authority to judge and determine is undermined. Sovereign control is lost over distant arbitration procedures. Arbitrators apply principles not anchored to a particular jurisprudence. The resolution of disputes through arbitration drifts towards legal globalization for the frontiers are limitless, the principles to apply confined only by the imagination and deductive powers of the arbitrators. The business sense of merchants and counsel is to arrive at compromises and solutions accepted in as many sites as possible. Legal principles which appear to satisfy the largest common denominator to judicial systems will be seized upon for valid reasons. Such an attitude makes less criticism possible from national courts who may have to review or enforce the arbitration award. This attitude leads inevitably to pronouncements by arbitrators of broad application. The generality suffices to hide the specific deviation. All this in the name of international arbitration clamored for by the entrepreneurs.

Naturally, the importance of international arbitration to world trade has long been recognized. Arbitration is not a recent phenomenon. As long ago as in 1961 an investigator reported that of 250 commercial associations involved in international trade and surveyed in the US, 81 per cent used arbitration.[5] Presently, the Netherlands Arbitration Institute reports that 80 per cent of private international contracts have clauses providing that disputes will be settled by arbitration.[6]

In this interval of forty years, the trend internationally is clear. The International Chamber of Commerce at Paris reports[7] that in 1999, 529 requests for arbitration were filed with the ICC. Of these requests, 1,354 parties were from 107 countries and arbitration was conducted in 48 different countries.

The Asian countries, aware of the need for arbitration facilities, have also inaugurated their own mechanisms. China has the China International Economic and Trade Arbitration Commission (CIETAC).[8] Hong Kong and Australia have adopted versions of the UNICTRAL[9] Model Law concerning international arbitration. Kuala Lumpur, Malaysia is the site of the Regional Centre for Arbitration.[10] The fecund source of arbitration includes the World Intellectual Property Organization (WIPO), the London Court of International Arbitration (LCIA), the Japan Commercial Arbitration Association (JCAA), the American Arbitration Association (AAA), the Stockholm Chamber of Commerce (SCC), the Chamber of Commerce and Industry of the Russian Federation (ICAC), the Belgium Centre for Arbitration and Mediation (CEPANI), and this selection is a mere sampling.

Then there is the augmenting use of international arbitration through its incorporation into the countless bilateral investment treaties with their references to the International Centre for the Settlement of Investment Disputes (ICSID)[11] as well as other trade-orientated conventions such as the WTO,[12] although the latter is confined to public law disputes, at least in theory.

Moreover, including arbitration clauses in international commercial contracts is routine and commonplace. Such clauses are the standard language of typical international contracts prepared by counsel. Both merchants and their advisors have obvious motivations. Transnational corporations and merchants engaged in international trade are reluctant to have potential disputes resolved in foreign courts. There is a distrust of the unfamiliar and the unknown. Trade rests upon one of the basic maxims of investment, intimate knowledge of the milieu. Foreign laws are an anathema. Attorneys cannot advise their clients with confidence. Arbitration clauses permit the parties to choose the law to regulate any future conflict. That they often fail to do so is beside the point. The option does exist.

Furthermore, investors fear foreign courts may have an inclination against non-nationals. Unaccustomed foreign court procedures aggravate the natural dislike of protracted, costly procedures. And of course, the simple incomprehension of a foreign language is a strong deterrent to submitting to the scepter of another authority. Nor should we forget that normal prudence and skeptical views on the laws of other jurisdictions are exaggerated by businessmen when a sovereign nation is one of the contracting parties. In a world of tribal loyalties, a nonpartisan political, legal, and judicial atmosphere is a preferred forum. Rightly, or not, international arbitration is seen as being informal and satisfying the requisites of international impartiality.

Little imagination is needed to see that the decisions emanating from international arbitration boards are global occurrences. With the surge in international commerce every year more apparent and statistically verifiable, it is natural there has also been a rise in recourse to international arbitration. But unlike national legal systems, which are rooted in centuries of growth and legislative history, arbitration has no nationality. It does not belong to any legal system. There is no supranational arbitration law. Understandably, this has caused arbitration activists to search for a substitute. It is denominated the *lex mercatoria*, or the new law merchant. This doctrine reclaims the right to emit arbitration awards founded on general principles of law and particularly commercial law which reflects the consensus of the world traders.[13] The doctrine has its origins in the customs and traditions of medieval English merchants which were accepted as constituting binding rules of conduct between the participants to commercial transactions. An odd state of affairs, when we recognize that the application of the *lex mercatoria* today is far removed territorially from the pastoral setting of the yeoman English countryside.

### *International arbitration but no international enforcement procedures*

Not all is as it appears, nor is arbitration the holy grail of dispute resolution. The despair at high legal costs in either court or arbitration procedures is only exceeded by the incredulity of victorious arbitration claimants when they discover enforcement of a favorable arbitration award is no assurance the underlying award will be collected.

Unless there is a voluntary implementation of an arbitration award, only the power and enforcement procedures of a sovereign court can compel compliance. Arbitration tribunals do not have enforcement mechanisms.[14] The police and judicial power of the sovereign is not an adjunct to the arbitration tribunal. This requires other lawsuits and courts to enforce the favorable arbitration award, critical considerations which involve complex analysis of various areas of the law.[15]

The response of national courts to the preference of commerce for arbitration has met mixed responses.[16] Frequently, the national courts when asked to enforce an arbitration award review all aspects of the dispute. This naturally reinforces the conviction that the arbitration process was a futile exercise[17] and that the courts are an impediment to sensible commercial alternatives. Nevertheless, the sovereign response is within the authority and determination of the judicial system. There are regional trade agreements with reciprocal obligations concerning arbitration.[18] There are a wide variety of multilateral conventions regarding international arbitration.[19] However such conventions require specific conditions to be met and while litigation attacking arbitration awards has perhaps diminished, the possibility of further court procedures is a real deterrent to an efficient international arbitration system. In any event, such conventions do not establish an international arbitration law but instead an international arbitration enforcement body of law.

The more judicious use of international arbitration is in the multiple bilateral investment treaties executed between nations as references to ICSID are references at least to the legal guidelines set forth in the ICSID articles. But private foreign investment is a fraction of the total activity falling within international commerce. International trade is not only foreign investment. There are multiple areas of international disputes involving delivery of goods, breach of warranty, claims for monies owed, construction disputes — varied and complex are the endless topics possibly subject to an arbitration clause. The enforcement of the overwhelming majority of arbitration results are dependent on the natural antagonists who are also the collaborators, the law courts.

It is only the national courts who can legitimize the legal theories upon which international arbitration awards are based. Unless the parties voluntary accept to implement the arbitration award, the enforcement must be sought in a national court. There is clearly reluctance on the part of many courts to give effect to international arbitration awards if the arbitration award is seen as contrary to public policy or contrary to the legal principles of the local judicial system.

Consequently, a global legal order is dependent on a consistent, growing body of international arbitration law which finds approval by local courts. The xenophobia which motivates many jurisdictions to permit litigation attacking the validity of arbitration award acts as a formidable spur for arbitrators to appear as if they are decreeing awards based on universal principles. Phrased differently, the rebels must learn to speak the language of those they wish to dethrone.

### *Law without precedents*

The distinguishing feature of international arbitration is the possibility for parties from different jurisdictions to have applied a law which is seen as neutral. Neither the law of New York nor the law of Nigeria. With manufacture of goods in New York, delivery in Paris, but resold in Milan, and then a defect discovered upon use in Spain, a choice of the applicable law to govern any dispute becomes a complex search for rules of law which is described as a conflict of laws issue.[20]

Municipal courts have no choice but to follow their own internal guidelines denominated, in legal terminology, the conflict of laws doctrine. However, private parties when executing a contract, can stipulate recourse to arbitration and simultaneously choose the municipal law they deem appropriate, or as often happens, direct the arbitrators to judge according to 'good faith and equity'. Or, perhaps the arbitration clause is silent. No mandate or reference to legal standard is evoked. The arbitration clause merely recites the obligation to, and the procedures for, arbitration. The arbitrators will then have to elect on what basis the dispute must be decided.

And therein lies both the problem and the opportunity. An arbitration decision must be rendered and the arbitrators are forced to seek a source of authoritative law. However, with no legislative or other defined standards, international arbitrators are forced to resort to pronouncements wrapped in unassailable language — 'the principles of civilized nations', 'equity and justice' — which of course are not very helpful legal precepts. It is the rare collectivity which will assume with pride the description of being 'unjust' or 'uncivilized'. But the utilization of allegoric language permits the arbitrators to appear to follow traditional legal systems while issuing awards based on commercial practice.

When arbitrators therefore receive a case for resolution and are not given a specific municipal legal system to follow, they do what any well-meaning person would do. Awards are rendered based on statements of justice, equity, general principles of law, the laws of civilized nations, internationally accepted customs, in short, the arbitrators invoke the idealism of human thought to reach a conclusion.

Hence, references to phrases such as 'justice and equity', or arbitration clauses which are silent as to the applicable law, delegate to the arbitrators the power to subjectively determine what is the law to be applied, by personal reason, unfettered or conditioned by rules of municipal law. Yet if this reasoning permits the thesis of the emergence of a global legal order based on international commercial customs of course immediately we will what to know what are its precepts and who established them. The answers must be from those and by those who command international trade.

This conclusion can be reached by a different logic. Awards are frequently announced by international arbitrators which are stateless, not anchored to any legal system, a purported restatement of universal commercial law principles which aspire to justice, fairness, and equity. If arbitral awards are not founded on any sovereign legal system, they are 'stateless' awards.

But 'stateless' awards are impossible because justice makes no sense unless it is inserted within a system of laws that are held to be 'just'. When faced with no dictated standards, sincere, reasonable arbitrators are obviously going to adopt the principles of the world with which they are familiar, in other words, their own value judgments. Nothing else makes sense, to them.

The hegemony of Western law, and in particular, American law, emerges as the intellectual framework for arbitrators since the arbitrators are citizens of the industrialized nations whose market economy and political theories are in substantial congruence and are the victorious commercial ideologies. Given that international trade is dominated by US companies and that the US has a preponderant influence in the supra-national organizations, the principles of law of the US, manifestly founded on an egalitarian ethos, is seen as a natural source for the laws of civilized nations. Thus, the *lex mercatoria*, or new law merchant, is a verbal tool within which Western legal precepts are inserted and then diffused globally through international arbitration.

By Western law is meant precepts emanating from those countries dominating world trade, substantially under the influence of either the common or civil law of the US and Europe, respectively; nations possessed of a parliamentary democracy; social units whose political economy acknowledges the consensual basis of society and the primacy of individual liberties. Furthermore, such republics are themselves substantially under the commercial sway of this century's major economic power — the US — so that the principles of Western law which emerge as a global order cannot be in contradiction to the basic tenets of American law. The more important international, commercial jurisprudence may complement American laws, or even amplify them, but the world's largest international trader establishes the paradigms.

Consequently excluded, although not because of any logical defect or cultural impropriety, are all the ideologies of those nations and their laws who are recipients of Western trade and services. Precisely because world trade is between or from industrialized societies to others, the flow of social ideas, in particular legal concepts, is heavily unilateral.

### *The social nature of the lex mercatoria*

Certainly, the diffuse implantation of American neoliberal economics in most parts of the world has made common law principles familiar to European and Asian jurists. Contrary to popular imagination, 81 per cent of America's direct investment overseas goes to high-income countries.[21] With American investments totaling billions in such countries, it is a survival necessity to understand its laws and commercial principles. The understanding of the influence of American law becomes even more acute when it is realized that countries such as China, India, Brazil, and Mexico only account for 5 per cent of total global exports.[22]

Moreover, as it is the entrepreneurs of capitalism which are circulating the legal documents for signature, we would not expect the contracts in question to contain references to legal systems foreign to one of the major participants. It is difficult to imagine a major American electronic manufacturer doing business in Iran to submit to arbitration according to the principles of Islamic law, although the latter may be eminently suited to the dispute.

Rather, the penetration of American, or if you prefer, industrialized nation economics into the far corners of the world has brought with it the complement of arbitration and with it, either a reference to the general principles of law and justice, or instead, to one of the major arbitration institutes in the Western world which is the same thing. Selecting an arbitration institute is not choosing a system of law. Understandably, the arbitrators cannot be expected to have an allegiance to any particular nation state but rather to their mandate, to judge according to justice.

Yet while everyone would agree with this conclusion no one can explain the content involved.

For the most part it has been the application of familiar principles of law known to the arbitrators which is generally their own legal system. Invariably, this means Western legal principles, plus a generous portion of private opinions as to what is equitable. International trade promotes a convergence towards acceptable legal precepts by the majority of the traders. Often such jurisprudence is described as Western law, a convenient but imprecise label which needs further clarification to be useful.

Nor is the globalization of American law the result of deliberate actions by the US Government or US multinationals in their quest for economic dominance. The forces at work are varied, subtle, dispersed, disorganized. In fact, many of the elements contributing to the diffusion of Western global law are not even American in source or identity, although obviously under its influence. We import from China but we know little of its laws. We sell to Tunisia but we are indifferent to its local legislation. We ship to Ecuador but the bill of lading with binding legal terms emanates from Spain. International trade, dominated by the West, conducts trade on its terms, its legal documents, its jurisprudence.

Consequently, the business of America and other Western nations is not only business, it is also 'corporate lawyering', bringing juridical notions everywhere there is trade, stockpiles of legal documents transferred digitally all around the world to legal correspondents who modify without substance the American legal concepts to sound as if they were home spun out of distant native soil. Dominated by Western technology and commerce, the global society being constructed by many factors is apt for the reception of a global legal order based on its jurisprudence.

Moreover, the globalizing of markets has created a demand for global legal instruments.[23] The domination of international commerce by American companies, has been accompanied by the rise of the mega-American law firms with their complex, detailed contracts.[24]

In this way, the foundations are laid for the emergence of a global law, without any municipal law allegiance, founded on Western legal principles, and the results vary in accordance with the subjective interpretations given by the various arbitrators. Without clear standards, it is to be supposed that international arbitrators will seek tutelage in the various policy statements of international organizations, conventions, treaties, and many other diverse legal instruments, all under the influence of Western law.

When the favorable arbitration orientation of public international institutions is combined with the avalanche of international commerce demonstrated by statistics, and the realization that such volume is bound to generate disputes, the role of international arbitration is seen to be of primordial interest in fomenting the arrival of a global system of law which, besides being heavily influenced by Western legal principles, admits of much individual determinism by arbitrators.

Yet, the lack of any generalized, agreed-upon principles of international arbitration will not deter its future growth. It is associated with the rise of the multinational corporation and transnational merchant. International arbitration is an auxiliary motor for international commerce and capital. These are the imperatives of our century. It is the power of capital which will dictate structural changes to the international arbitration legal order.

The law is an artifice to satisfy the collective beliefs and needs of the community. It has no other function. But before the final results there are the usual hiccups. The present state of international arbitration is one of them.

*Prof. Shapiro has a Socratic question*[25]

Following the argument to its logical consequences, we have arbitration without settled principles of law and therefore how can we speak of the globalization of a law(s) when all is in movement, fluid, principles announced in conformity with the arbitrators chosen. One possible answer is we are living in a legal ambient being constructed whose atmosphere is dependent on international commercial practices as understood by entrepreneurs, regulatory bodies, advisory organizations, private law forms, academic opinions, and of course the multiple international commercial organizations with their diverse model forms and contracts. We cannot authoritatively point to the contours of this law(s) as it is under construction by an eminent architect whose design is not yet complete: the American firm of International Commerce & Its Adherents.

## Notes

[1] For a scholarly, panoramic survey of international commercial arbitration, see W. Laurence Craig, *Trends and Developments in the Laws and Practice of International Commercial Arbitration*, at <www.coudert.com/practice>, dated 1995, accessed 26 August 2002.

[2] Ibid.

[3] Arbitration allegedly subject to neither the procedural nor substantive laws of a sovereign nation, a concept much contested by various authors and the subject of acerbic academic debate. The expression 'deanchored' or 'stateless' is also often used.

[4] If we admit the possibility of delocalized arbitration, then the arbitration tribunal has no fixed locale, other than where it is. Every arbitration has another site. In fact, in one arbitration procedure, for the convenience of the participants the locale may change several times.

[5] Sonia Mentschikoff, *Commercial Arbitration*, 61 Columbia Law Review 846-849 (1961), cited by Alessandra Casella, infra at fn. 6.

[6] Alessandra Casella, *Arbitration in International Trade*, Working Paper No. 4136, p. 1-43, National Bureau of Economic Research, Cambridge, MA (1992).

[7] ICC at <www.iccob.org>accessed 14 December 2001.

[8] Details available at <www.arbitration.org.cn>, accessed 28 August 2002.

[9] See home page of UNCITRAL at <www.uncitral.org>, accessed 22 August 2002. The model law was the result of many member states, intergovernmental organizations, and institutions with considerable arbitration experience, such as the International Chamber of Commerce, see Howard M. Holtzmann et al., *A Guide to the UNCITRAL Model International Commercial Arbitration: Legislative History and Commentary*, Kluwer Law International (London, 1989).

The UNCITRAL model law is not a convention. It is intended as a guide for other nations to emulate, when they either amend their own arbitration laws or enact new legislation.
[10] Details available at <www.klrca.org>, accessed 28 August 2002.
[11] For more information on the ICSID see their home page at <www.worldbank.org/icsid>, accessed 28 August 2002.
[12] For details, see home page at <www.wto.org>, accessed 28 August 2002.
[13] A survey of the doctrine of *lex mercatoria* merits a separate review and this is done in the chapter 'International Arbitration: The Global Customs of Merchants'. The delay of this discussion does not affect the ideas considered in the present chapter.
[14] Many jurisdictions permit arbitration boards to apply to the national courts for a necessary court order, but the arbitration board does not possess any police authority. An arbitration award is comparable to a United Nations resolution. There is moral authority but no mechanisms for compulsive obedience.
[15] A court, when asked to enforce an arbitration award, may review the procedures utilized, the completeness of the arbitration document, the underlying subject matter, the public policy aspects, the law applied to the controversy, the relationship of the arbitration site to the legal document in question. Each of these categories raise further inquiries.
[16] For an admirable collection of essays on many aspects of international arbitration, and to which this chapter is indebted, see Thomas E. Carbonneau (ed.), *Lex Mercatoria and Arbitration*, rev. ed. (1998) Juris Publishing, Inc. (Oxford) and Kluwer Law International (London).
[17] See Oil & Natural Gas Commission v. Western Co. of North America, excerpts printed in13 Y.B. Com. Arb. 473 (1988), the case reported in W. Laurence Craig, supra, n. 1.
In this case a dispute was settled by arbitration between an Indian company and an American enterprise. The American company sought compliance in a New York court. The Indian company sought to vacate the award in an Indian court. Eventually, the Indian court granted an injunction restraining the American company from further procedures in New York.
Without examining the merits of the dispute, it is easy to imagine the frustration of the parties when confronted with multiple law suits and costs subsequent to the arbitration.
[18] See arbitration provisions of Mercosur (Argentina, Brazil, Paraguay, and Uruguay, with associate members Bolivia & Chile) available at
<www.mac.doc.gov/ola/mercosur/mgi/dispute> accessed 27 August 2002.
[19] See 'Inter-American Convention on the Extraterritorial Validity of Foreign Judgments and Arbitral Awards', 18 I.L.M. 1224 (1979) (among OAS member states). See also New York Convention On the Recognition and Enforcement of Foreign Arbitral Awards available on <www.iccwbo.org>, accessed 14 October 2002.
[20] The search might begin with the United Nations Convention on Contracts for the International Sale of Goods (1980) executed in Vienna, Austria, and usually referred to as the 'Vienna' Convention for International Sale of Goods (CISG). For details on the Vienna Convention see the official web site of the United Nations at <www.un.org>, accessed 29 August 2002.
[21] Survey, The Economist, September 29-5 October 2001, *The Case for Globalization* at page 6, table 1.
[22] Ibid, p. 11.
[23] Martin Shapiro, *Globalization of Freedom of Contract*, pp. 269-298, footnotes pp. 361-363, in Chapter 9 of *The State and Freedom of Contract*, Ed. Harry N. Scheiber, Stanford University Press (1998), at p. 272, 'Globalizing markets lead to global contracting'.

[24] More than once, there crossed my desk, contracts forwarded to me from my American colleagues whose contents exceeded 100 pages.

[25] In a letter to me dated 15 August 2003, Prof. Martin Shapiro, James W. and Isabel Coffroth Professor of Law, University of California, School of Law, inquiries if we have law without law do we want to 'call it globalization of law?'.

# Chapter 20

# International Arbitration: The Global Customs of Merchants

*Silence is golden but also a problem*[1]

Reviewing international arbitration, we uncover how centuries of commercial activity are being frustrated by continual confrontation with applied legal theory. Contrary to the expectations among entrepreneurs, court decisions are often a technical application of a legal principle. If at times the business community believes itself deceived by the rigidity of the law courts, this is an inevitable consequence of a system of secular law built up through centuries of rationale, inference, deduction, deference to past decisions, and a self-imposed limitation on judicial activism. Nevertheless, it is the conflict between law practice and merchant rationale that has permitted the globalization of Western law through international arbitration.

Without a stable corpus of international arbitration law, and this does not yet exist, the recourse to arbitration by the business community confers on each arbitration board an ad hoc legislative power. Stateless arbitration awards emit principles of commercial law which need not be bound by deference to past decisions — indeed, this is almost an oxymoron since most arbitration awards are not published. In simple terms, it is every woman/man, or, more accurately, 'every arbitrator' for her/himself to judge according to individual principles and legal preferences. This becomes apparent when we examine the arbitration process from the inside.

Merchants often execute contracts involving more than one jurisdiction. Goods are ordered from Zambia, to be refashioned to specification in Germany, and then delivered to Algeria. This is denominated in Western law a plurilocal contract. The recited legal acts have reasonable contacts with various jurisdictions. Such contracts frequently have clauses calling for arbitration between the parties in the event of a dispute. As frequently occurs with such instruments, they do not indicate the applicable law to regulate their mutual obligations in case of breach by a party. It is as if due performance is naturally to be expected and a breach appears distant and improbable. Unfortunately, the litigious side of humanity is never far from eruption.

Normally prepared by lawyers anticipating legal conflict, the arbitration clause in international contracts should mean less recourse to protracted legal procedures. Yet any momentary intellectual relief is not prolonged. The legal problems arbitration engenders are no less complicated than the underlying controversy. If the arbitration contract refers to the applicable law, it may be the procedural law of the site of arbitration, for example, the arbitration will be conducted in accordance with the arbitration rules of the International Chamber of Commerce; or it may be the substantive law of a particular jurisdiction, such as the 'laws of New York'.

But then, if asked to enforce the eventual award, we do not know if the courts of the jurisdiction where the arbitration takes place will recognize either possibility. Nor is the locus of the arbitration necessarily where enforcement will be sought in the absence of voluntary compliance. It is quite common for arbitration to be held in London, UK but enforcement of the award sought in San Francisco, California where the defendant has assets. Such questions direct us to conventions or treaties[2] where various nations have agreed beforehand to recognize arbitration awards granted under a specified number of conditions, all of which normally generate more litigation with legal entanglements exceeding the underlying claim.

Our perplexity and the complexity of analysis is further compounded when we subsequently learn that normally arbitration clauses are silent as to the applicable law to be applied in the event of a controversy. It is the silence, or vague phrases which are its equivalent, which provokes even more uncertainty and turns what the merchant client thought was a simple business dispute into a legal decision to be cited and studied in law courses on international arbitration. When the law of the contract is not indicated; when the arbitrators are not told what law to apply; when there is no clear reference to the controlling jurisdiction and its legal precepts; the arbitrators are then obliged to frame their own solution.

Such discretion invariably pits courts against arbitration boards. Courts are used to sentences based on clearly defined legal precepts. Arbitration awards are often couched in general, hoary language. So many alternatives exist as to the choice of law for arbitrators that only one skilled in the recondite specialization of conflict of laws, essentially what body of law should apply to plurilocal contracts, could hope to dominate the material. There is the possibility that the law of the jurisdiction where the arbitration takes place will be applied. While this appears at first thought to be reasonable, it permits 'forum' shopping. The litigants strive to start procedures in a jurisdiction known to be favorable to a particular point of view.

On the other hand, the law of a jurisdiction may have specific rules as to how to determine what is the applicable law, denominated a conflict of laws issue. But this doctrine, founded on rules as to what facts will determine what is the relevant law, is replete with difficulties and attendant erudition, and unless the arbitrators are legal scholars, attempts at understanding are abandoned: far simpler, to issue an award with a citation to 'justice'. Or perhaps, and with understandable reasons, the arbitrators when faced with contractual silence will forgo technical, enlightened applications of what is a abstruse area of the law, and seek recourse in the general accepted principles of international trade law. This then becomes a search for what is known variously as custom, trade practice, usage, universal commercial practices and the like. After all, such an approach is what the merchants' desire.

Such a possibility is even more probable when it is realized that many arbitration contracts permit the arbitrators to judge *ex aequo et bono* or as *amiable compositeur*, both meaning 'in justice and fairness' or also understood as seeking the best solution for all the parties. In other words, the arbitrators seek not a technical solution but one grounded in reasonable standards of justice as understood by the mercantile community.

If summary, there is a lack of clear, definable legal standards to which arbitration awards must adhere. No wonder, then, that arbitrator, judges, legislatures, drafters of model or uniform laws, academicians have sought refuge in finding a universal, acceptable general theory for international commercial arbitration which will make the aspirations of merchants for efficient arbitration a reality.

### *Hail, merry England, and an introduction to ye olde* lex mercatoria

Although the controversy as to the existence of an international commercial law is truly of a more vast scope involving subsidiary issues, in fact, for the most part, this disagreement has been expressed as to whether or not there exists a core of international trade law usages known as the *lex mercatoria*, or the new merchant law, which may serve as a valid reference for arbitrators. For the most part, the emergence of this doctrine is facilitated when there are no clear references in the legal instruments as to what law will be applied in the arbitration.

The doctrine of *lex mercatoria* presumes that through the centuries exporters and shippers developed a basic core of sensible commercial practices and, equally importantly, legal principles derived from such customs. Proponents of the *lex mercatoria* doctrine cite current codification of these principles in trade documents, various conventions, model and uniform laws, legislation, and judicial as well as academic doctrine and naturally custom and usages which are entitled to judicial recognition.[3]

It is the recourse to community conduct or standards which seems the least contentious among other sources as an affirmation of the *lex mercatoria*. This reference to custom, usage, or trade practice, is a familiar standard to jurists. The terms are not often used with precision and it serves no utility to draw fine distinctions when usually none are drawn by judges or arbitrators. We are of course referring to principles not codified but which are acknowledged by most members of a particular community as being representative of their behavior. It would therefore appear quite reasonable to grant usage, or its equivalent, an honored place as a judicial reference. It is not possible for all legal instruments to foresee all contingencies and when there is a lapse, or an omission, it appears sensible to have recourse to usage or custom for a harmonious resolution.

However, for some legal commentators, it appears logical to go a step further. Usage, or custom, is a reflection for a wider norm, known as the *lex mercatoria*. The doctrine is not only a statement of solutions by default when faced with arbitration clauses which give no guidance. The *lex mercatoria* is present at all times and is in parity with other doctrines of the law, such as equity or unjust enrichment. Continuing the argument, centuries of international commerce have generated a wide range of rules, or patterns of conduct. These rules constitute a corpus of law regulating the comportment of merchants. Such a corpus is a valid reference when there is an arbitration clause which fails to select a municipal law system, or makes reference to a standard which is so vague and general as not to constitute an identifiable source. To those scholars who are adepts of the *lex mercatoria*, international commerce is founded on an identifiable core of principles which is seeing a wider diffusion and surge of application due to the global expansion of commerce. Hence the argument for a recognition of the *lex mercatoria*.

There is an opposing school of academic thought which is highly skeptical of the existence of any body of laws to be confined within the designation *lex mercatoria*. Custom, usage, expected rules of conduct, are so general and varied in application, that to grant them a particular status does not enhance the decision-making process. Custom and usage are one element out of many tools available to the arbitrator. For these critics, a reference to the *lex mercatoria* is as valid as a reference to the general principles of law and justice. It emphasizes an ideal or aspirations if you will, but reveals nothing of the details.

The resolution of this debate has substantial repercussions for international trade. Application of the *lex mercatoria* permits arbitrators an abundant freedom in the decision-making process. Arbitrators bound to apply a municipal law system must exercise due care in their search for a just solution. There is always the possibility of a reversal in a court of law. Arbitrators seeking a standard in custom can justifiably believe they are on sure ground. Custom has no specific, unique meaning and one arbitrator's judgment as to custom is as good as that of a judge. Every year a selection of arbitration awards are published. Some of the results spark academic comment. They demonstrate the award latitude possessed by arbitrators in their search for the applicable legal principles and are simultaneously examples of how law is formulated.

### *Sporadic cases demonstrating the erratic customs of the arbitrators*

International arbitration prefers recourse to international trade usages and practices because arbitrators are often familiar with the usage of particular trades from their own personal experience. However, what is a usage is not necessarily what is just.

Care must be exercised when dealing with the custom of the country. The *Deutsche* case[4] is an example of allowing custom to substitute fundamental justice. Arbitrators in Germany were asked to reduce damage claims on the grounds that had the injured parties paid the briberies which were customary in Iran, all delays would have been surpassed. The arbitrators agreed and the German courts refused to overturn the arbitration decision.[5] If the mercantile custom is to pay bribes, then subordination has another cultural significance which can not be ignored by the arbitrators.[6]

The dubious flexibility of the arbitrators is to be contrasted with the stern approach taken by the Lesotho High Court. The court found a Canadian engineering company, Acres International, guilty of bribery in an $8 billion World Bank project to supply water from Lesotho to South Africa.[7] Apparently the Lesotho High Court did not have the practical experience of international arbitrators for Acres, in brazen defiance, issued a statement, declaring the Lesotho decision was setting a dangerous precedent. If allowed to stand, the threat continued, companies faced greater risk in doing business overseas.[8] The Lesotho

High Court, undaunted, eventually imposed a fine of $2.2 million on Acres for bribery.[9]

The *Norsolor* case[10] further exemplifies the debate and illustrates a legal nightmare which no self-respecting law professor would invent for exam purposes on the grounds it would not be a realistic case. A French company established an agency contract with a Turkish representative but the arbitration clause did not indicate a choice of law. Declining to apply a municipal law, the arbitrators sitting in Vienna, Austria found in favor of the agent on the basis of the good faith principle of the *lex mercatoria*. When the Turkish agent sought to enforce the award in France, the French company opposed the enforcement procedures arguing that the application of the *lex mercatoria* by the arbitrators was incorrect and the arbitrators should have sought a legal principle founded on a municipal law. Although the arbitrators had not been given the powers of *ambiales compositeurs*, the French court sustained the arbitration award.[11] In other words, the arbitrators were free to make the choice of law they deemed applicable, including the general principles of commercial law.

As a living example of the complexity possible with international arbitration, a parallel pleading in the same case was presented to the Austrian court to invalidate the award. After successive appeals, the award was confirmed. The Supreme Court of Austria held that the arbitrators applied a general principle of law — good faith — underlying all systems of law. This principle is nothing more but the *lex mercatoria*.[12] We will never know if the agent was paid but we can image the most likely outcome was the French principal went into bankruptcy.

A further realistic and typical example is recited by a well-known arbitrator.[13] A European subsidiary of an American corporation engaged a Scandinavian subcontractor for a large construction project in a Middle East country. The subcontract provided for arbitration in Geneva but the procedural and substantive law of New York was to be applied. The ensuing dispute concerned failure of the contractor to make timely payments and one of the issues raised was interest for late payments. Forbidden under Islamic law, the operative contract did not contain a provision for such interest. The European debtor argued that the New York State rate of interest, at the time 6 per cent, should be used since this was the substantive law of New York and the contract provided the law of New York was controlling. The Scandinavian subcontractor argued that it was inconceivable interest should not be paid in a claim involving two Western parties and further claimed the rate of interest should be the Libor (London Interbank Offered Rate) rate which at the time was 15 per cent.

The arbitrators, an Englishman, a Canadian, and an American, agreed that interest should be paid. Late payments without interest would be commercially unreasonable. We are not told what interest was finally negotiated. However, the case demonstrates dramatically that even with a municipal law reference, arbitrators feel free to impose principles which are acknowledged in international commerce to be 'usual', 'customary', and in 'usage'. Interest has an ancient pedigree in commerce.

The *Sapphire* case[14] contributes to this debate. Sapphire, a Canadian Company, and the National Iranian Oil Company (NIOC) entered into a dispute. NIOC had executed an agreement, similar to others, which provided for the application of 'principles of law common' to Iran and the investor's country, or '... in the absence of such common principles, then ... in accordance with principles of law recognized by civilized nations in general, ... as may have been applied by international tribunals'.[15] The *Sapphire* agreement further provided that the parties would carry out their obligations in accordance with the principles of '... good faith and good will and to respect the spirit as well as the letter of the agreement'.[16]

In construing various provisions of the *Sapphire* agreement, the arbitrators found it was '... perfectly legitimate ... not to apply the strict rules of a particular system but, rather, to rely upon the rules of law, based upon reason, which are common to civilized nations'.[17] Decisions, such as in the *Sapphire* case, which are devoid of any municipal law standard, are construed by scholars to be authority to invoke the *lex mercatoria*.

The tendency to rely upon the *lex mercatoria* to explain arbitration awards at times encounters ambiguous results. A series of notorious cases involving oil concessions to private companies in Libya, demonstrate the confusing attitude often accompanying arbitral interpretation. In the *Topco* case,[18] the arbitrators stated the governing law was 'international law' and not the 'general principles of law'. It is impossible to garner easily the meaning of this distinction but presumably the arbitrators meant that the *lex mercatoria* is confined to cases involving international commerce. But one cannot be sure. On the other hand, in the *BP Exploration* case,[19] and the *Liamco* case,[20] the arbitrators held that Libyan law would apply but only to the extent that it was consistent with general principles of international law. In the event, of a conflict, the general principles of civilized law would prevail. In all instances, we are dealing with extremely vague standards and useful distinctions are not evident. The attentive reader will observe that references to 'international law', 'general principles of law', and 'civilized law' are not made with academic precision.

Another oil exploration example is the *DST mbh* case[21] where an English Court of Appeal upheld an award to be governed by Swiss law according to 'internationally accepted principles of law governing contractual relations'.[22] A further example is the *Spp* case.[23] In this dispute the parties had failed to select a judicial system to regulate their rights. The arbitral tribunal decided that as the law of Egypt furnished no answer to the questions posed, the arbitrators had to apply international law to arrive at a just solution.

Of course, it is rare for any municipal law system to offer a solution to all questions and normally results are achieved by deduction or comparison with similar cases. Consequently, the allusion to international law is merely a legal crutch to invoke a supposed general principle of commercial law which by its turn serves as a vehicle for a cultural determination: what is just, reasonable, or civilized.

Various academicians have championed the cause of the real and vibrant existence of the *lex mercatoria*. Thus, we have affirmations such as, 'The transformations in the global community and the economic interdependence of states have rendered the concept of territoriality obsolete'.[24] Moreover, 'A new legal order needs to be fashioned that takes new realities into account'.[25] The implications are substantial. 'National law is not being evaded; it is being redefined as the foundation of a 'supranational' commercial law process'[26] and '[T]he new law merchant is as real and as discernible as public international law'.[27]

Another legal scholar[28] also confirms the existence of the *lex mercatoria*. 'Certainly, where arbitrators have the authority of *amiables compositeurs*, they may settle the dispute according to legal principles they believe just'[29] Equitable justice becomes subsumed in the *lex mercatoria*. 'Arbitrators empowered by contract to decide disputes on the basis of "general principles of law" or "equitable consideration" will frequently base their awards on the *lex mercatoria*'.[30]

The evolution of the *lex mercatoria* is similar to the process of judicial precedents creating law in the early stages of the English common law. 'Many international commercial arbitrators believe, nevertheless, that a *lex mercatoria* in the form of generally accepted, [sic] uncodified, international commercial usages and trade practices, seems to be building up ... This practice seems to spill over into the substance of the dispute and is beginning to generate a body of arbitral case law, in much the same way as the common law was originally formed.[31]

For those scholars[32] supporting the existence of a *lex mercatoria*, the *lex mercatoria* is an 'autonomous legal system'[33] '... which may compete with national law.[34] The *lex mercatoria* '... should be recognized by national legal systems as customary law and, ... as one of the four main sources of the national law itself'.[35] In this view, legislation, precedent, equity, and the *lex mercatoria* are the four warriors of social control.

*The periodic table of the* lex mercatoria

Quite naturally, it is desirable to know the composition of the *lex mercatoria* in the view of its supporters. The contents of the *lex mercatoria* have been described as including at least the following:[36]

- *Pacta sunt servanda*, or contracts should be enforced according to their terms.
- *Rebus sic stantibus*, or substantially changed circumstances can justify a revision of contract terms.
- *Abus de droit*, or unfair and unconscionable contracts should not be enforced.
- In a contract of sale, an ambiguous agreement is to be construed against the seller.
- All legal relationships are founded on good faith.
- Bribes render a contract void or unenforceable.
- A state may not evade its obligations by denying its own capacity to make an agreement to arbitrate.
- The controlling interest of a group of companies is regarded as contracting on behalf of all members.
- Parties should negotiate in good faith if unforeseen circumstances arise.
- One party may be released from its obligations is there is a fundamental breach by the other.

- Force majeure, that is, acts of God excuse a person from the performance of a contract, such as an earthquake destroys a building the subject of a real estate sale.
- No party can be allowed by its own act to bring about a non-performance of a condition precedent to its own obligation.
- A tribunal is bound by the characterization of the contract ascribed to it by the parties.
- Damages for breach of contract are limited to the foreseeable consequences of the breach.
- A party which has suffered a breach of contract must mitigate its losses.
- Damages for non-delivery are calculated by reference to the market price of the goods and the price at which the buyer has purchased equivalent goods in replacement.
- A party must act promptly to enforce its rights, lest lose them by waiver.
- A debtor may set off his own cross-claim to diminish his liability to a creditor.
- Contracts should be construed according to *ut res magis valeat quam pereat*, or a law should be interpreted with a view of upholding rather than destroying it.
- Failure to respond to a letter is regarded as evidence of assent to its terms.
- 'Gold clause' (special rights) agreements are valid and enforceable, for example in privatization sales where a sovereign, although a minority partner, retains a special privilege of ownership.

The list contains a schedule of Latin and French phrases which puts stress on our library resources; principles of basic contract law; equity; erroneous layman common sense (unanswered letters are deemed consent which is not true in most jurisdictions); and a reference to privatization law. With fear of being critical in excess, it might be argued that such a short list of legal principles of law can hardly serve to found a legal order of even a reasonable body of rules.

However, as trenchantly noted by another scholar[37] when commenting on a similar list, it is perhaps '... a rather modest haul. I suppose that could be said of the Ten Commandments or the American Bill of Rights as well'.

Clearly, a substantial part of the academic debate revolves around those who see the *lex mercatoria* as a merchant's bill of rights and those who see refuge in the *lex mercatoria* as a road to arbitral private norms and personal prejudices. Attempting to conciliate the various conflicting views of legal scholars as to whether or not there is a *lex mercatoria* leads to multiple debates splashed across the pages of innumerable law review journals. A resolution can be more satisfactorily achieved through a resolution of another problem which has perennially perplexed the formalists. The social nature of the law must be confronted.

With a realistic appreciation as to the origins of the law, we will encounter a more pragmatic solution to the alleged existence of the *lex mercatoria* or not, and which simultaneously will reveal a new social order on a transnational scale. The issue of the existence or not of the *lex mercatoria* will depend on what we understand by the law. Thus the debate is false in its premises. Unless there is agreement on the corpus of the law there can hardly be any discussion as to its various characteristics. To confront the attributes of the law we must be prepared to admit the multifarious origin of social norms.

The *lex mercatoria* is a valid repository of international commercial norms and its use permits mercantile custom to be elevated to the status of a legal norm. Given the economic dominance of the Western nations, the *lex mercatoria* allows Western merchant usage to formulate global laws through international arbitration.

## Notes

[1] Dário Moura Vicente, Da Arbitragem Comercial Internacional, [On International Commercial Arbitration] Coimbra Editora, Portugal, 1990. This outstanding text is written in Portuguese.

[2] For example, the Convention on the Recognition and Enforcement of Foreign Arbitral Awards, June 10, 1958, 21 U.S.T. 2518, 330 U.N.T.S. 38; Inter-American Convention on the Extraterritorial Validity of Foreign Judgments and Arbitral Awards, 18 I.L.M. 1224 (1989).

[3] A collection of essays concerning the *lex mercatoria* has been assembled under the tutelage of Thomas E. Carbonneau ed, *Lex mercatoria and Arbitration*, rev. ed. Juris Publishing, Inc., Oxford and Kluwer Law International, London (1998). References to this indispensable work hereafter will be cited as 'Carbonneau collection' with appropriate page citation.

[4] [1979] Deutsche Rechtsprechung auf dem Gebiete des inernationalen Privatrechts No. 2A, cited on page xxiv, n. 6, in the Introduction to Carbonneau collection.

[5] Ibid.

[6] Low level bribes in Nigeria are not considered unethical but part of accelerating paper-work, see Michael Peel, *Squaring up to something rotten*, The Financial Times, September 12, 2002 at p. 8.

[7] James Lamont, *Lesotho bribery case warning*, The Financial Times, 18 September 2002 at p. 8.

[8] Ibid.

[9] Ibid.

[10] Award of October 26, 1979, Case No. 3131 (1983) Revue de l'arbitrage 525, English translation in (1984) Y.B. Com. Arb. 109, cited in Carbonneau collection at p. 67, n. 38.

[11] Supra, n. 3, March 4, 1981, 108 J. Dr. Int'l-Clunet 836 (1981), at p. 67, n. 39. In the opinion of the court, the arbitrators applied the 'law designated by the rule of conflict which they deemed appropriate' as required by the ICC rules of arbitration (article 13-3).

[12] Supra, n. 3, F. Dasser, Internationale Schiedsgerichte und *Lex mercatoria*, in Carbonneau collection at p. 67, n. 40.

[13] Andreas F. Lowenfeld, *Lex mercatoria: An Arbitrator's View*, pp. 71-91, at pp. 82-83 in Carbonneau collection. No date is indicated for the arbitration procedure.

[14] *Sapphire International Petroleum Ltd. v. National Iranian Co.*, 35 I.L.R. 136 (1963) (Award of March 15, 1963), cited by Georges R. Delaume, *The Myth of the Lex mercatoria and State Contracts*, pp. 111-132, at p. 116, n. 21 in Carbonneau collection.

[15] Ibid, at p. 116, n. 22.

[16] Ibid at p. 117, n. 23.

[17] Ibid, at p. 117, n. 23.

[18] *Texaco Overseas Petroleum Co. v. Libyan Arab Republic*, 17 I. L. M. 1 (1978), 53 I. L. R. 389 (1979) (Award of January 19, 1977).

[19] *BP Exploration Co. v. Libyan Arab Republic*, 53 I. L. R. 297, 329 (1979) (Award of October 10, 1973).
[20] *Libyan American Oil Co. v. Libyan Arab Republic*, 20 I. L. M. 1, 35 (1981) (Award of April 12, 1977).
[21] Deutsche Schactau-und Tiefbohrgesellschaft mbH v. R'As al-Khaimah National Oil Co. [1987] 3WLR 1023 cited in Ray Goode, *Usage and its Reception in Transnational Commercial Law*, pp. 3-36, at p. 30, in Jacobs S. Ziegel, (ed.), New Developments in International Commercial and Consumer Law, Proceedings of the 8th Biennal Conference of the International Academy of Commercial and Consumer Law, Hart Publishing, Oxford, 1998.
[22] Ibid.
[23] Supra, n. 21, *SPP v. Arab Republic of Egypt*, ICC case no. 233 of 1992, at p. 31.
[24] An affirmation of Professor Carbonneau, in Carbonneau collection, at p. 30.
[25] Ibid.
[26] Ibid, at p. 34.
[27] Ibid, at p. 36.
[28] William Tetley, *The Lex Maritima*, pp. 43-51, in the Carbonneau collection.
[29] Ibid, at p. 48.
[30] Ibid, at p. 49.
[31] Ibid.
[32] Harold Berman et al., *The 'New' Law Merchant and the 'Old': Sources, Content and Legitimacy*, pp. 53-69, at p. 64, in Carbonneau collection.
[33] Ibid.
[34] Ibid.
[35] Ibid.
[36] See list prepared by Andreas F. Lowenfeld, *Lex mercatoria: An Arbitrator's View*, at p. 89, in Carbonneau collection. Also references to n. 66 and 67 in same article; see excellent compilation by Jarrod Wiener, *The Transnational Political Economy: A Framework for Analysis*, University of Kent at Canterbury, cited at <www.ukc.ac.uk/politics/kentpapers> with no date, although posted on internet as of August 2000.
[37] Supra, n 35 on p. 89 of Lowenfeld essay.

# Chapter 21

# International Arbitration: The Documentary Evidence Abetting Legal Globalization

*The sociological drift of documents*

In their quest for commercial freedom and legal assistance, the merchant community has pursued an independent route to avoid national laws. How facile this is with the proper document, which needs only to be written with an ordinary pen, and it is agreed the contract will be subject to arbitration. Contrary to the predictions of digital advocates, we still live in a world of paper documents, stacks of them, with multiple objectives, all available through the mail, free for distribution at commercial associations, the stock-in-trade of chambers of commerce everywhere. One common element reproduced in this mass of paper is the arbitration clause requested by the mercantile class.

Employing the forensic profession, the international traders use legal expertise to circumvent the source of legal power: national courts. By doing so, the territorial limits of municipal law are cast aside by the growing use of international arbitration where there is frequent recourse to doctrines whose content is neither clear nor easily definable. Due to the growth of international arbitration without a consistent corpus of international arbitration law, arbitrators confront a testy dilemma. For the moment, the practice of businessmen is deemed a convenient yardstick. What is commercially sound, must, *ergo*, be legally correct. As international commerce is substantially dominated by the Western nations, the results are foreseeable. The inexorable spread of Western legal principles in the generality continues while arbitrators cast aside reliance on precedent in the specific. It could not be otherwise, as arbitration awards are in the majority not published, being considered private procedures whose divulging requires consent.

The universal use of legal and model commercial documents throughout the commercial sector fosters this conclusion. There exists a symbiotic relationship between documents, arbitration and the globalization of the law. It is not immediately apparent as the ostensibly separate areas of study are not easily unified with a common denominator. Yet the material is at hand. Private mercantile and legal documents are a source of rules, a stockpile of social norms defining what is commercially reasonable in a particular transaction. International trade utilizes myriad documents of the most diverse character and nature. The terms and standards formulated contribute a body of norms accepted by a particular trade community or profession.

International arbitration is replete with the interpretation of documents. When litigation arises involving a particular sector, either documents may form part of the dispute or they serve as a reference for the arbitrators. It is a rare arbitral case which does not have to interpret a document, at the very minimum the operative contract between the parties. If, as it often happens, the arbitration agreement part of the document fails to indicate the applicable law, there are theorists who argue that the new law merchant, or *lex mercatoria*, is the proper law of the contract. In this context *lex mercatoria* is referring to a body of norms regulating international commerce which has existed as long as there was commerce. It is a source of commercial norms not dependent on legislative edicts. Since the trade ships slipped out of their wharves, it is the behavior merchants expect from one another. It is denominated new, because the *lex mercatoria* which was part of the ancient medieval English common law is now being applied to present international commerce.

The question naturally arises as to the source of this mercantile law, proof if you will of its existence, and among other sources, trade documents loom as a sensible repository. After all, trade is best understood by the merchants engaged in it, and it is the businessmen who are seeking to resolve a dispute. Such an approach is different from that of a national court asked to pass upon a mercantile argument involving international issues. In theory, there can be no doubt as to the law, for presumably it is there for the judge to discover or decipher. While the judiciary may have recourse for interpretation to practices in a sector, few judges will forego a developed case analysis of past decisions in favor of embracing lofty concepts of 'justice or equity', the announced guidelines of many arbitration decisions.

Unlike arbitration tribunals, national courts are subject to the law of a nation. Recourse to mercantile practice is in *extremis*. Municipal law analysis requires a scholastic review of legal principles and their derived principles. This is to be contrasted with arbitration procedures. Arbitrators decide by the rule of commercial reasonableness for that is why they were chosen. The law courts are bound by precedent and decades of theory. Arbitration is what happens; the law courts what should be. Faithful to its origins, arbitration strives to be in harmony with mercantile expectations. To the contrary, there seem few reasons for choosing an arbitral forum.

Through documents and the autonomy of contract law — the right of parties to express their mutual rights and obligations — arbitration clauses are inserted. With contractual liberty, parties to international trade contracts can agree on how their disputes will be resolved and where. For most merchants, the choice selected is arbitration, a conscious, deliberate effort to circumvent the power of national courts. By use of an arbitration clause, the parties can negotiate not only purchase and sale terms, but their choice of the applicable law; the forum; the legal standards to be used; and the criteria to guide the arbitrators.

However, the admirable desire of simplicity spurring arbitration requests has its threats. Unfortunately, with the common thought that arbitration is all that is necessary, arbitration contracts, particularly those contained in industry-wide documents, are either often silent as to the applicable law or only contain broad references to idealistic concepts such as 'civilized principles of law' or merely a phrase such as 'justice and equity'. Faced with such lapses, scholars and practitioners have surged forth, with a body of scholars arguing nothing more than silence is needed. A clause calling for arbitration is sufficient. In their view, there is a large body of non-legislative, ex-judicial, international merchant law designated the *lex mercatoria*. This reservoir of trade custom is a reliable source of hoary mercantile practices adopted and considered sensible rules of behavior by the international trading community to which documents containing arbitration clauses will invoke.

Others have steadfastly refused to acknowledge its existence. One of the most virulent critics[1] of the *lex mercatoria* has succinctly stated: 'There cannot be a contract which is governed by no law at all'. Furthermore,[2] 'If it is a law, from where does it draw its force?'. What is meant is that the accumulation and accretion of words to be considered a contract requires a law which makes it so. Of course, such an observation is conditioned on what is meant by 'law'.

As in many debates, not all the participants are even agreed as to what is, or what could be, the contents of the *lex mercatoria*. Still, it can be said that there is general agreement that at least custom merits recognition and legal scholars are prone to accord to usage and traditional practices the dignity of being described as the *lex mercatoria*, without feeling the necessity of confronting the nature of law as a philosophical issue. This is in accord with the development of norms which become eventually recognized as a law. The customs of a trade become sufficiently generalized and accepted to be the expected conduct. The expectation translates into a reasonable standard of behavior. From custom, then, the industry maxims are transposed into documents.

### *The autonomy of documents*

In part this uncomfortable sequel of arbitrators being forced to define the applicable law when the arbitration contract is silent has been ameliorated through the wide use, and some might say, abuse, of documents in a variety of forms. By this method, one of the significant sociological events of the past century has been the emergence of rules dependent on neither legislation nor court sentences but rather on internal, group standards. From a variety of sources, law is created by clusters of social units whose collective will often takes a written form. Our concern is with documents as used in trade.

Private contracts, industry model consumer forms, commercial organization rules, civic association edicts, professional parameters,[3] joint venture and other typical international agreements which establish a transnational alliance,[4] cooperative rules, sport club regulations, military coteries, are some of the more obvious documents creating their own norms. In this fashion, there has arisen a body of rules governing social conduct not dependent on legislative action or judicial pronouncement.

With such a source of norms, the concept of justice for international trade is slowly being reformulated without reference to a national jurisprudence.

Documents are not confined to a particular nation. Similar to capital, they circulate everywhere. The countless documents reflecting the vision of various social blocks in any industry are no more than custom becoming privately codified. Documents, then, are fertile soil for commercial norms and social cohesion. A brief glimpse into the usual unfathomable paragraphs reveals the extent of documentary influence.

Institutions of the oddest sort issue documents affecting the wide range of community life.[5] From the African Seed Trade Association to the National Biodiesel Board to the World Food Summit, organizations are involved in dissimilar human endeavor but all permeated with the objective of creating reasonable standards for their industry. From these affiliations, stream forth recommendations on trade usage and acceptable patterns of business normally accompanied by recommended documents to regulate legal relationships. Instruments, therefore, far from being a strident cacophony passed onto paper, reveal the beliefs of a particular community. If we define the *lex mercatoria* as a source of settled, autonomous principles affecting a substantial part of the commercial community not dependent on national laws, then, numerous are its sources, clearly identifiable and definable. Scandalously, contrary to our expectations, the *lex mercatoria* is codified.[6]

How evident this becomes when we consider the various institutions and associations wielding enormous influence in myriad international markets. Such organizations are a veritable source of law and give credence to the existence of one sector of the *lex mercatoria*. A typical example comes from the farm labor of our North American neighbors.

Thus, the North American Export Grain Association (NAEGA)[7] was founded in 1912. It is the national association for US grain and oilseed exporting companies and cooperatives. The NAEGA membership includes all principal US and multinational companies engaged in the export of US grains and oilseeds.[8] Millions of tons of corn and wheat are exported by the US to other countries, reaching a value of $40 billion a year.[9] The grain industry is one of the largest export commodities of the US. It supplies 75 per cent of the world trade in these commodities.[10] Sales require contracts and the NAEGA furnishes a standard use contract for purchases of bulk grain, corn, rice, soybeans, and oilseeds called the NAEGA standard contract no. 2. It contains innumerable clauses covering the essentials of a contract, definitions of technical terms, and, for our purposes, consecrates an arbitration clause.[11] Under the NAEGA standard contract, any disputes concerning grain contracts will be settled by arbitration in the City of New York under the rules of the AAA.[12] Due to the importance of grain associations in international commerce, it merits reproducing the arbitration clause of the AAA:[13]

> Article 28
>
> The tribunal shall apply the substantive law(s) or rules of law designated by the parties as applicable to the dispute. Failing such a designation by the parties, the tribunal shall apply such law(s) or rules of law as it determines to be appropriate.

> In arbitration involving the application of contracts, the tribunal shall decide in accordance with the terms of the contract and shall take into account usages of the trade applicable to the contract.

Immediately our attention is drawn to the power of the arbitration tribunal to take into account the usages of the trade.[14] This is a reference to the multiple definitions and standard practices set forth in a particular sector such as that exemplified by NAEGA. The standard contract clarifies and imports understanding for multiple procedures adjacent to grain contracts and their terms, such as free on board (FOB), cost and freight (CNF), cost, insurance, and freight (CIF), 'flat price', strike clause, drafts, bills of lading, all for illustrative purposes. Within the confines of the NAEGA standard contract, the *lex mercatoria* is a reality.

But the NAEGA is not the only grain association nor are standard contracts its sole province. There are similar organizations such as the Grain and Feed Trade Association (GAFTA).[15] GAFTA also has a standard contract form and counsel arbitration.[16] This association has 1000 members in 80 countries.[17] There hardly exists a major industry which has not promulgated its standard contract form. International air transport is substantially regulated by the International Air Transport Association (IATA)[18]. The clauses regulating air travel are agreed-upon by the airline companies. Marine insurance policies, cargo clauses, policy forms, salvage agreements and other marine insurance topics are the subject of a variety of institutional supervision and advice.[19] FIDIC, the International Federation of Consulting Engineers, promulgates standard contracts and agreements for its members.[20]

Then there are silk, cotton, oil seeds and fats,[21] illustrative of the wide range of human commercial activity, some ancient, and others quite recent such as internet and the information society,[22] which propel their participants into social groupings to defend their interest and dictate standards. From this juxtaposition of usage and trade terms there is identified the commercial nucleus of the *lex mercatoria*. But there are other documentary sources which are justifiably part of the *lex mercatoria*.

Due the same recognition as industry documents, the standard model contract, whether drafted for consumers or by attorneys for clients, is positive law no less than legislation. The standard model contract defines and binds. It is a reference for all affected by a specific branch of international commerce and it is a significant area, circumscribing the entire world. So diffuse is the use of the standard model contract confronting the average consumer, including sales contracts for electronic products, warranties, service agreements, repair contracts, credit loans, utility covenants, that many nations have enacted legislation to protect the citizen signatory from its inequities.[23]

With such contracts requiring arbitration under official auspices, the arbitration awards are entirely dependent upon the various mercantile principles which are the habits and customs of the merchants codified in the form of standard contracts. Thus documents and legal instruments constitute a parallel source of law, without the parliamentary debates preceding legislation. Only, in this case, the edicts are conceptualized under the classification of the *lex mercatoria*. Nevertheless, there is no need to usurp Latin phrases to sanctify acts as having the force of law. Suffice that the associations serving the mercantile industry in their collective acts, recommend a practice. It will transpose and give meaning to what is a reasonable standard of conduct which renders it as effective as legislative fiat. That it is legislation emanating from private associations, such as the International Chamber of Commerce (ICC)[24] can not detract from its moral authority. The ICC is a paradigm of a private association establishing legal standards for an industry.

The ICC was founded in 1919. Its activities are global, with thousands of member companies and associations from over 130 countries. From this organization there has emanated the well-known ICC Incoterms which are a compilation of standard terms to be used in a variety of legal matters. The ICC incoterms define the responsibilities of the customers and the suppliers. In this way, a substantial amount of dispute is avoided through a clear definition and allocation of risk.

Phrases such as 'Act of God', 'All Risk', 'Collect Freight', 'Delivered at Frontier', 'Ex Works', 'Free alongside', 'Free carrier', find their content given precise meaning by the publication of these terms by the ICC. Moreover, the recommended standard forms by the ICC have the effect of forging a model so that arbitrators, when searching for what is reasonable and customary, turn to these compilations in the relevant circumstances. Moreover, the ICC also issues rules for combined transport. Such rules have gained world-wide recognition and been incorporated in several widely used typical transport documents such as the transport bill of lading.[25] Their terms have been incorporated into other standard transport documents such as the International Federation of Freight Forwarders (FIATA) transport bill of lading.[26]

The rules are available to international trade for world-wide application and are acceptable to the international banking community who become involved because of credit transactions based on documents. Such rules are intended to be fully compatible with the latest revision of the ICC Uniform Customs and Practice for Documentary Credits (UCP).[27] The UCP rules are adhered to by banks everywhere, from Algeria to the United States to Zimbabwe, and set forth the contents letters of credit and other banking instruments should contain. Such standards are incorporated by banks into the documents they issue to their clients or on behalf of their customers.[28]

While these documentary references appear esoteric and of apparent remote interest, in fact their existence affects a significant part of international commerce. Aside from the conventional mortar and brick offices which cater to international traders in all aspects of commerce, there has sprung up internet sites devoted to the same need. Thus, as a partial list, forms for shipper's export declarations, shipper's letters of instruction, drafts, ocean bills of lading, customs and export forms are all available with a 'click' and the delivery of a compact disk (CD) with the necessary software.[29]

*Documents and the nature of the law*

When we think of the law and then contrast our ideas with merchant custom, contradictions arise. Classical, common contract law holds that in the face of an unforeseen event, a party may be discharged from its obligation. The *lex mercatoria* appears to delay performance in an attempt to preserve the underlying commercial relationships.[30] We would expect the same result from an arbitration award which normally seeks to preserve commercial expectations instead of having recourse to technical legal principles. In this example, law and custom appear to be in conflict. A brief introduction into the nature of the law can alleviate the apparent tension between what is thought of as the law and commercial norms. But it can never be entirely eliminated.

No doubt, much of the criticism and academic denial of the *lex mercatoria* has been based on the impossibility of locating with any exactitude the situs of the *lex mercatoria*. International trade requires certainty, predictability and order. Unlike national courts, the authorities utilizing the *lex mercatoria* have no fixed domicile. During one arbitration procedure, the tribunal may change its locale several times in order to obtain the necessary evidence. Likewise, the *lex mercatoria* for many academicians is additionally unattractive because it is no more than substituting the arbitrators normative preferences for the properly applicable law. With no national authorities defining the contents of the *lex mercatoria* the familiar attributes of law are glaringly absent. Gnawing within such doubts, of course, is the elusive idea of the nature of law.

Others[31] argue that recourse to any alleged *lex mercatoria* is not necessary. Arbitrators should seek solutions through the methodology of jurists which clearly means applying the principles of the conflict of laws no matter how complex the task. In this view, anational arbitration neither exists nor is it needed. What is demanded is more academically prepared arbitrators. In the same vein, it is claimed all arbitration depends for its existence on a legal order. Arbitration requires law to regulate the agreement; to govern the arbitral process; and apply a precept to the substance of the issue. Opponents to the *lex mercatoria* cannot reconcile themselves to the reality of an anational law:[32] '... the *lex mercatoria* ... remains, both in scope and in practical significance, an elusive system and a mythical view of a transnational law of state contracts'.

The debate concerning the *lex mercatoria* obligates a modest introduction into one aspect of social anthropological investigation into the customary laws of tribes, an area of research which has been profoundly researched and discussed in multiple publications. A reconciliation of the tension between law and norms is only possible through a cultural prism of the nature of the law and the realization that society is not a single set of laws but constellations of standards accepted by particular groups, fluid, changing, evolving towards practical solutions. Valuable contributions to the nature of the law have been made through field investigations by social anthropologists with particular emphasis on custom. One general theory is that there is a piecemeal development of law, with an attempt to formulate a logical system, which evolves over a period of centuries.[33] Such an evolution cannot reflect a consistent core of social values because history is not logical. Law is a convenient term to distinguish between what can be enforced by a political authority and the rules of local groups, or corporations, another common designation of social units. The study of human behavior reveals partial order and partial control. In between is a gray area of change and opposition. Chaos is often imminent.[34]

Additionally, the law is an expression of parallel, social groups, or fields, interacting with one another.[35] There is a substantial amount of overlapping in what lawyers call jurisdiction so that these social fields often are in confrontation. Corporation law grants substantial rights to shareholders as a class. Yet the law also grants a certain autonomy to the board of directors. These concentric circles of social activity intermesh and often there are conflicting rules. The board of directors must exercise a prudent management, which may mean withholding dividends for reinvestment; but at the same the shareholders have a right to profits.

Whereas many scholars have sought to establish the various universal truths supporting the concept of law, some social anthropologists argue that laws address specific categories of social groups and if the law of leases may favor the landlords, the laws of share corporations may favor the shareholders. The law addresses social relationships. As a deterrent to social behavior it has a limited, partial success.[36]

Some of the various definitions[37] described by anthropologists and jurists concerning the nature of the law reveal the most profound divergences:

- Law is the use of physical force.
- Law is a rule of conduct likely to be enforced by the courts.
- Law is social control through a political entity with the power of enforcement.
- Law is social norms enforced by legal institutions with executive power.
- The law exists when there is an obligation plus adjudication.
- The law is composed of corporations-groups-which are the framework for the law.
- Law is a statement of social relations. It is not distinguishable from social control in general.
- The law is a symbolic representation of the ethos of a social group.

And certainly we must advance a further suggestion: the law is also a grammatical artifice serving a variety of objectives, mostly occult. From physical force to myths, from adjudication to consent, from decree to beliefs, the nature of the law oscillates. Certainly documents of the most varied source exhibit what a social group thinks over a particular topic, from seed regulations to bills of lading. Law is thus seen to be social life, rules, values, ways of life, symbols, procedures, authority, group norms, and of course documents which define with exactitude operative terms and conditions. The law is so varied in content that it escapes a single, unitary definition. Accordingly, the nature of the law is that it has no specific character. Unfortunately, it is inherent to the human mind to conceptualize its environment. All experience needs to be identified with a name. What receives the classification of 'law' is nothing more than behavior seen as reasonable in a variety of situations. Under this panorama, the *lex mercatoria* revealed through the trade usages printed in documents is entitled to the same status as a law(s) as legislative decrees.

To insist on police enforcement as an indispensable attribute of law is to equate justice with force and is contrary to a multitude of social anthropological studies. Executive force makes certain compliance with the dictates of justice but its absence does not erase its existence. The idea of what is right and what is wrong is always dependent on a moral conviction. Being an inherent part of humanity's emotional component, justice and the law requires a fluid, unstructured approach. Understanding the legal form of a society in this fashion corresponds to the realities of daily life and recognizes that the *lex mercatoria* has a contribution to make, albeit not with the significance its supporters decry.

With documents as a potential provider of legal norms, international arbitrators are more inclined to utilize the concept of *lex mercatoria* as a justification for arbitral awards not anchored to any particular national legal system. Instead awards are predicated upon the customs and ordinary documents in use in a particular industry. This makes possible arbitration awards founded on the documents preferentially used in international trade. For the moment, Western organizations and institutions have easily established their hegemony. Thus, Western formulated documents invade the arbitration tribunals and, no longer restricted to national frontiers, the laws of the industrial nations are adrift, globally.

Entitled to the same honors as custom as a proper source of commercial norms, are the documents of mass production and the computer-generated contracts. Simultaneously with the conference call which announces on its mini-screen what client is calling, it is only necessary to open the computer archive and the relevant document is immediately retrieved and displayed. If this is not possible, an email to the local industry organization will produce the same results.

## Notes

[1] Mustill, *Contemporary Problems in International Commercial Arbitration: A Reponse*, 17 Int'l Bus. Law 161 (1989) at p. 162.

[2] Ibid, at p. 163.

[3] The various national accounting associations and regulatory boards have an enormous influence upon what is considered reasonable and necessary to be reported in statements. Such edicts are a reference for judicial authorities when disputes arise. Yet, judicial authorities are not consulted prior to their adoption.

[4] Such as the international joint venture, cross-border mergers and acquisitions, horizontal or vertical integration, and international franchises. For a complete discussion, see Ronald Charles Wolf, A Guide to International Joint Ventures With Sample Clauses, 2nd Edition, Kluwer Law International, London (1999).

[5] See web site of <www.grainnet.com/info/site>, accessed 9 September 2002. In a lengthy, illuminating list, we find grain, milling, seed, bakers, port authorities, chemical engineers and sugar organizations indicated.

[6] This view is confirmed in Dario Moura Vicente, *Da Arbitragem Comercial Internacional*, Coimbra Editora, Portugal (1990) at p. 139, presently only available in the Portuguese language.
[7] For details of this association, see web site <www.uswheat.org>, accessed 4 September 2002.
[8] Ibid.
[9] Ibid.
[10] Ibid.
[11] Ibid.
[12] For details see web site home page at <www.adr.org>, accessed 4 September 2002.
[13] Ibid.
[14] See the comments of the law firm of Holman Fenwick & Wilan, <www.hfw.com>, accessed 5 September 2002, where it is stated, '... Many international sale of goods transactions use standard form contracts published by Trade Associations' in IT&C Newsletter, Issue 1, July 2001.
[15] For details see web site home page of <www.gafta.com>, accessed 5 September 2002.
[16] Ibid.
[17] Ibid.
[18] See web site home page of <www1.iata.org>, accessed 9 September 2002.
[19] See web site <www.admiraltylawguide.com/insurance>, accessed 9 September 2002.
[20] See web site <www.fidic.org/federation/>, accessed 9 September 2002.
[21] Supra, n. 6 at p. 144, n. 2-5, inclusive.
[22] See links created at <www.qlinks.net>, accessed 9 September 2002.
[23] See supra, n. 6, pp. 142-143 for multiple references.
[24] For details on all ICC material, see <www.iccwbo.org>, accessed 9 September 2002, and links to topic of interest.
[25] Ibid.
[26] Ibid.
[27] Ibid.
[28] Ibid.
[29] As a typical example, see <www.unzco.com/storefront>, accessed 10 September 2002.
[30] Jarrod Wiener, *The Transnational Political Economy: A Framework for Analysis*, University of Kent at Canterbury, at <www.ukc.ac.uk/politics/kentpapers> with no date, although posted on internet as of August, 2000.
[31] Hans Smit, *Proper Choice of Law and The Lex mercatoria Arbitralis*, pp. 93-110, in Thomas E. Carbonneau (ed.), *Lex mercatoria* and Arbitration, rev. ed. Juris Publishing, Inc., Oxford and Kluwer Law International, London (1998).
[32] Georges R. Delaume, *The Myth of the Lex mercatoria and State Contracts*, pp. 111-132, at p. 132, in Thomas E. Carbonneau (ed.), *Lex mercatoria* and Arbitration, rev. ed. Juris Publishing, Inc., Oxford and Kluwer Law International, London (1998).
[33] In her collection of essays entitled *Law As Process*, Routledge & Kegan Paul, London (1978) and the published results of her investigation of the Chagga people living in Kenya at the foot of Mt. Kilimanjaro in a book entitled *Social Facts & Fabrication: Customary law on Kilimanjaro 1880-1980*, Sally F. Moore presents numerous facts in her analysis as to the nature of the legal process as well as a summary of the theories of other investigators.
[34] Ibid.
[35] Ibid.
[36] Ibid.
[37] Ibid.

# Chapter 22

# From Treaties, Conventions, Uniform Rules, and Arbitration, to Global Law

*The unconventional aspects of treaties and conventions*

With international commerce straddling continents, trade cannot be subject to the idiosyncrasies of the various world legal cultures. When faced with divergent juridical systems, the international merchant feels hesitant and fearful. Foreign laws appear awesome and contrary to commonsense. From treaties to uniform rules, from public efforts to private initiatives, the world-wide legal community is striving to develop laws specifically for trade. Resulting from this concerted labor are the multiple treaties, conventions, uniform and model laws whose ultimate consequence is wresting from the nation control over the substantive interpretation of international trade law.

Foremost in notoriety are the various international treaties and conventions. Such nomenclature, apparently redundant, causes us initial consternation. We are told on august authority[1] that '... "treaty" means an international agreement concluded between States in written form and governed by international law, whether embodied in a single instrument or in two or more related instruments and whatever its particular designation'.

Happily the definition corresponds to our expectations but then it is a convention — The Vienna Convention on the Law of Treaties — which is the primary source of the law of treaties. Moreover, a multitude of what appear to be treaties are denominated 'conventions'. The distinction eludes us. Perhaps our imagination is still captive to early English law when a convention was an extraordinary assembly of the houses of lords and commons without the consent or summons of the sovereign.[2]

Treaties and conventions are powerful weapons in the globalization of the law because the signatory is a sovereign nation. But treaties also internationalize a topic. Municipal courts are bound to the plain meaning of the treaty in question. Treaties and conventions are signposts on the highway of transnational law being constructed. Surely, the objective of multiple treaties and conventions is to work for the unification of private international law. The reasons for a treaty or convention on any topic of law can only be to come to an agreed-upon solution and interpretation to a law topic and its vexing subtleties, such as the execution of an international will.

Treaties and conventions circumvent to a limited extent the legislative process of nations. They are normally drawn by legal experts and then submitted to their governments for execution and ratification. Theoretically there is a legislative review but often the technical aspects of the material preclude any prolonged discussion. One of the influential voices in non-legislative globalization is the Hague Conference on Private International Law (Hague Conference).[3] The First Session of the Hague Conference on private international law was convened in 1893 by the Netherlands Government, so the present laudable toil has its remote antecedents. The Seventh Session in 1951 marked the beginning of a new era with the preparation of a 'Statute' which made the Hague Conference a permanent intergovernmental organization. The Statute entered into force on 15 July 1955. Presently,[4] there are 61 members, with very different legal systems, such as Brazil, China, Egypt, Latvia, Sri Lanka, and the US. Naturally, the industrial nations are well-represented.

From the Hague Conference has come over 40 conventions, regarding topics as varied as the law applicable to succession, protection of children, conflict of laws regarding marriages, law of trusts, law of adoptions, matrimonial property regimes, and service of summons abroad.[5] The treaties and conventions are of interest not merely for their legal content. In the quest for simplifying trade and creating uniformity, the legal instruments in question also make an important contribution to the unification of international trade law. Many scholars concede to treaties and conventions the distinction of evidencing the much lauded but also decried body of international trade law known as the *lex mercatoria*, or the new law merchant. The *lex mercatoria* has already been defined[6] as a body of custom and usage applicable to international commercial transactions which may or may not be codified in published texts but is nevertheless understood by international merchants as binding on their contractual behavior. Of necessity, the definition is broad and vague because there is an acerbic academic debate whether such a body of rules even exists.[7]

For those who support the existence of the *lex mercatoria*, documents are evidence of custom but only one example of a multitude of commercial norms which have always regulated, if informally, international trade. They are a modest part of a large body of trade canons derived from other sources. Professional debate has frequently concentrated on one convention which has had large acceptance among nations and has also been hailed as a primary source and repository of the *lex mercatoria*. This is the Vienna Convention on Contracts for the International Sale of Goods (CISG) signed at Vienna on 11 April 1980 and which now has over 60 ratifying nations.[8]

### *As 60 nations believe in international trade customs, so must we*

The CISG regulates international transactions affecting the sale of goods. It has been aptly stated that the purpose of the CISG, in part, was to recognize the customs of international trade regarding the sale of goods and encourage municipal courts to apply them.[9] For some authors, the CISG is intended to restate the customs of the *lex mercatoria*. A complementary objective is achieved with the construction of a global legal order due to the treaty's large adherence. As it is a convention with substantial signatories, the CISG conveniently provides a body of law applicable to international trade. Some brief excerpts are illuminating.

Article 9(1) and (2) of the CISG[10] provides:

> (1) The parties are bound by any usage to which they have agreed and by any practices which they have established between themselves.
> (2) The parties are considered, unless otherwise agreed, to have implicitly made applicable to their contract or its formation a usage of which the parties knew or ought to have known and which in international trade is widely known to, and regularly observed by, parties to contracts of the type involved in the particular trade concerned.

These provisions of the CISG are not without their results. Various authors have argued that such explicit language of the CISG consecrates the *lex mercatoria*.[11] Moreover, the nations which have adhered form a diverse, representative sector of the global community, as 60 nations must indeed do.[12]

While the title of the CISG appears to be only the sale of goods, its ambit is far greater than the designation used. Thus, by virtue of Article 3 of the CISG, a sale also includes goods to be manufactured and services such as technical assistance or the transfer of know-how. The CISG is a prime example of an international convention intended to apply broadly to international commerce. Provided there is a reasonable link to one of the national signatories to the convention, the CISG can also be elected to be a source for parties to a contract in the event of litigation.[13] Private traders and their counsel are thus provided with an opportunity to circumvent what they perceive as restrictive national laws.

This is described as 'party autonomy' and in connection with other international conventions, encourages international merchants to seek more practical solutions to their trade disputes than presently offered by municipal law courts.[14] Nothing could be stated more clearly than that proffered by the terms of the CISG:[15]

> (1) In the interpretation of this Convention, regard is to be had to its international character and to the need to promote uniformity in its application and the observance of good faith in international trade.
> (2) Questions concerning matters governed by this Convention which are not expressly settled in it in conformity with the general principles on which it is based or, in the absence of such principles, in conformity with the law applicable by virtue of the rules of private international law.

Was this the pronouncement of one isolated, perhaps even iconoclastic legal scholar, we might interpret such statements as inspired visions of a world legal order still far distant. Yet over 60 nations do not make for eccentric singularity. Here we have 60 nations declare their willingness to be bound by the rules of private international law whose source and contents continues to be the subject of academic polemics. If there exists a substantial corpus of international commercial law, then, it must be the *lex mercatoria*. The wide diffusion of the CISG has thereby lent substantial support to those scholars who see in the CISG a codification of some of the rules of the *lex mercatoria*, a diminution of the role of the nation state in adjudicating international trade disputes, and a substantial advance in the creation of a solid core of international trade law.[16] The legal character of this convention is not founded on the laws of any particular nation. The CISG was intended to satisfy the requirements of international businessmen and their counsel. The numerous technicalities developed by municipal law courts were to be avoided. The application of the CISG was to be by plain language and therefore sensible application.[17] Commerce is the objective of the CISG, not legal nuances. Of course, one treaty does not reformulate international trade law.

There is no lack of conventions to study for their effect upon international private law.[18] The Council of Europe (Council)[19] was formed on 5 May 1949, as the first European political institution. With 39 member countries,[20] the Council is the European organization with the widest geographical representation, exceeding even that of the EU. The Council was set up 'to achieve a greater unity between its members for the purpose of safeguarding and realizing ... common action in economic, social, cultural, scientific, legal and administrative matters ...'.[21]

The Council endeavors to synthesize policies and adopt common standards and practices in member states. Over 155 European conventions, the equivalent of over 75,000 bits treaties, provide the basis for member states to amend and harmonize their domestic laws. Subjects range from obligatory insurance against civil liability; to technical aspects of bearer securities in international circulation; nationality; human rights and biomedicine; liability of hotel keepers; the protection of computerized data, mass media issues. The Council strives to modernize and harmonize national legislation. There are special programs of cooperation with emerging democracies, including cooperation and assistance programs with central and eastern European.

While the overwhelming majority of nations adhering to and ratifying the treaties are members of the Council, non-member states have signed some of the treaties. Thus the US has signed the Criminal Law Convention on Corruption while Australia has executed the Convention on Laundering, Search, Seizure and Confiscation of the Proceeds from Crime.[22] Although constituting a body of law for ratifying European members, the conclusion is inescapable that such conventions represent the considered thoughts of jurists and legislators from a variety of jurisdictions. As such, these treaties are a source of knowledge and precedent for jurists everywhere. Without question, the conventions are a valuable, potential contribution to the *lex mercatoria* of international trade and civil law.

The cumulative effect of conventions is to increase the distance for decision from the analysis of municipal courts. The relevant law premise determined by the principles of a convention represents the combined efforts of many scholars. Many of the conventions are not drawn from any one legal system, neither with a background in the civil law or common law. For an understanding of the purpose of each convention, it is necessary to consult its history.[23] Yet it is precisely this academic determination to encounter a legal consensus on the correct principle which is the main impulse towards the globalization of the law. Conventions such as the CISG and those published by the Council form a body of law which serves to harmonize law principles globally.

*The model and uniform citizens UNIDROIT and UNCITRAL*

Diversity in culture derives from community isolation. It should be of no surprise, then, that as internationalization of products and services becomes the dominant motif of our epoch, efforts spring forth to also internationalize the law and dilute differences in legal cultures. The oracle of uniformity is economic necessity and not legal imperialism. In this respect, internationalization is distinguished from globalization. Internationalization is the transnational circulation of goods or services. Globalization in the law is one juridical umbrella from the storms of conflict. In the name of efficiency, legal models are adopted or copied for specific purposes, for example, the enactment of a law to regulate electronic commerce, a relatively new concept imported from the industrialized nations. Emerging nations are not likely to commence de novo with a law for electronic commerce. Such an assumption would be equivalent to testing every scientific principle before beginning with an experiment.

The globalization of the law strikes at the mythical structure of the host society. What appears just and reasonable takes on new content. The legal illusions of the affected society change. Globalization is the absorption, substitution, or significant modification of one legal culture, or part of its main tenets, by another. Of course, the two processes, internationalization and globalization, are intertwined and difficult to separate. When capital markets become transnational, it is difficult to determine whether we are dealing with internationalization or globalization. All definitions have their limits.

The emerging economies in their need for foreign capital are quite willing to adopt whole foreign laws concerning securities and bonds even though their financial markets are as absent as water in the empty desert wells. Yet, globalization implies a voluntary, conscious adoption of other values by a social unit, no matter such consent is given under economic duress. What is intended is not to cast aside other legal concepts in order to accommodate the needs of economics, but to seek a body of principles to which other nations or social units can adhere concerning frequently arising legal issues.

Precisely in this aspect, in the cooperative and collaborative efforts of many scholars from diverse countries, can be found the movement to harmonize and unify various aspects of the law. After all, a moment's reflection will suffice to realize that the ubiquitous franchises seen everywhere must have a common legal foundation. Behind the similar logos, decoration, styles, and prices are legal mechanisms to enforce such conformity. To facilitate the incorporation of standard legal precepts to ensure comparable results, are the model and uniform laws. The model laws are promulgated to serve as guidelines to legislators in diverse parts of the world.

The uniform laws are those enacted by various jurisdictions to ensure certainty in the various municipal law systems, such as in the US where the Uniform

Commercial Code is operative in the various states. Uniform laws, often times designated as restatements of law, are the results of conferences and exchanges of scholastic ideas between lawyers, academicians and other interested professionals. One of the more determined initiatives to harmonize law internationally comes from the International Institute for the Unification of Private law, with the well-known acronym UNIDROIT.[24] Originally established in 1926 as an auxiliary department of the League of Nations, the Institute was resurrected again in 1940 on the basis of a multilateral agreement, the UNIDROIT Statute.[25] Presently UNIDROIT has 59 member states and they include nations from the five continents representing diverse cultural, and thus varied, legal backgrounds.[26] Nations as different as Australia, Iran, Pakistan, Tunisia, the US, and Uruguay are constituents.[27]

The objectives of UNIDROIT are quite clearly stated. They are to study the methods for '... modernizing, harmonizing and co-coordinating private and in particular commercial law as between States and groups of States'.[28] Similar to the Hague Conference, UNIDROIT has also spawned conventions. The list is indeed impressive.[29] As an illustration, there is the 1973 Convention providing a Uniform Law on the Form of an International Will; the 1988 UNIDROIT Convention on International Financial Leasing; the 1988 UNIDROIT Convention of International Financing; and the 1995 UNIDROIT Convention on Stolen or Illegally Exported Cultural Objects.

Probably one of the more influential legal texts has been the UNIDROIT Principles of International Commercial Contracts, (Principles)[30] which is not a convention but a set of principles intended to be applied to international commercial contracts. We are thus dealing with a model contract, and not a convention. Moreover, the team which collaborated to produce the Principles reveals the varied juridical expertise and diverse cultures involved, including individuals from Italy, Canada, Egypt, US, China, Russian Federation, Japan, and Singapore.[31] The Principles have been hailed as the restatement of the law of international commercial contracts.[32] 'The UNIDROIT Principles seek to articulate rules that are common to most legal systems and which seem best adapted to the special requirements of international commerce'.[33]

As an example of the diversity of material consulted to arrive at the restatement, there was considered the US Commercial Code, the Algerian Civil Code of 1975, as well as Chinese, Dutch and Quebec legislation, amongst many others.[34] This restatement of private law '... may reduce considerably, perhaps eliminate, the difficulties thus far encountered in the attempts to 'denationalize' the legal regime of cross-border transactions'.[35]

UNIDROIT publishes comments to the Principles and they reveal the extent to which international legal scholars have assaulted the insularity of municipal courts by offering an alternative to their national jurisprudence. The comments make it quite transparent that local national courts are not the suitable forum for issues of international commercial law. This being so, then the only other alternative is arbitration. This preference is not stated as an obligation in the Principles, but nothing else could be intended since the Principles are replete with suggestions for arbitrators.

These Principles might also be entitled 'A Hymn in Honor of the *Lex Mercatoria*' since anyone reading the Principles is convinced of their reasonableness and utility in international trade contracts. Recognizing this allegiance, the drafters of the Principles intended the various articles to serve as a body of law which would be a reference for the *lex mercatoria*. 'Hitherto, such references ... has been criticized ... because of the extreme vagueness of such concepts'.[36] To mitigate this problem, the Principles substitute language intended to be more explicit,[37] 'The parties are bound by a usage that is widely known to and regularly observed in international trade by parties in the particular trade concerned except where the application of such a usage would be unreasonable.'

If the Principles express linguistic doubts or verbal imprecision, the distressed arbitrator, admonished to distinguish between *lex mercatoria* and 'usage' is told ' ... it might be advisable to have recourse to a systematic and well-defined set of rules such as the Principles'.[38] But no matter the grammatical confusion. Faced with the intransigence of law courts in adhering to precedent and the insistence on ignoring the large body of international commercial behavior, the Principles counsel drafters of international commercial contracts to chose rules of law other than national laws on which to instruct arbitrators.[39] Thus eminent colleagues and practitioners alike urge the international merchants, and by extension their attorneys, to avoid national courts, accept international custom as a reasonable pattern of reference, and emit arbitration awards which are based on the 'general principles of law'.[40]

Equally active in promulgating model laws is UNCITRAL, established by the United Nations on 17 December 1966.[41] Besides having promulgated a model law on international arbitration,[42] it has been stated that UNCITRAL is seeking to establish a new international economic order.[43] The reason for this affirmation lies with the model laws drafted and published by UNCITRAL which include projects such as the UNCITRAL model law on electronic signatures (2001), cross-border insolvency (1997), procurement of goods (1993), international credit transfers (1992), liquidated damages and penalty clauses (1983).[44]

The publication of a model law does not guarantee its enactment. It is of interest to have an idea of adhesion, what nations adopted the various model laws. Without attempting an exhaustive list, the UNCITRAL model law on international commercial arbitration has received significant adoption with over 30 nations adopting similar legislation ranging from countries as diverse as Egypt, Greece, Iran, Nigeria, United Kingdom, various states of the US, and Zambia.

Were we only interested in compiling tables, our survey could pause here. But the significance of model laws is not only in their attempt at uniformity. The effort at harmonization, the search for the model which will satisfy various legal systems, requires a consideration of what is common and just for a majority of nations. A model law attempts to achieve a global standard of justice on a particular topic. Besides striving for a global reach, the UNCITRAL model arbitration law also harmonizes a significant area of international commercial law. Arbitration is not only procedure, it is also what laws will be applied to the dispute. In this respect, the UNCITRAL model law on commercial arbitration consecrates and grants an honorable place to international usage and custom in the settlement of disputes.

The UNCITRAL model law on international commercial arbitration permits the parties to choose their law; allow the dispute to be governed by the rules of *ex aequo* or as *amiable compositeur*,[45] and finally 'In all cases, the arbitral tribunal shall ... take into account the usages of the trade applicable to the transaction'.[46] Of course, international usage and custom is the primary source for the principles of the *lex mercatoria* and so there can be no doubt that the UNCITRAL provisions are intended to delineate and clarify the contents of this doctrine. But there are more consequences and they are indicated in the explanatory notes to the model law.[47]

UNCITRAL views its provisions as '... acceptable to States of all regions and the different legal or economic systems of the world'.[48] It is quite clear that legal globalization is the intended objective. This is because '... domestic laws are often inappropriate for international cases'.[49] Domestic laws are undesirable because with municipal courts '... the unfortunate consequence is that traditional local concepts are imposed on international cases and the needs of modern practice are often not met'.[50]

The other model laws proposed by UNCITRAL have been received with less enthusiasm than the arbitration model. Nor do the other model laws contain arbitration clauses. But this is understandable since a nation undertaking to adopt a UNCITRAL model law would be aware if its arbitration counterpart. With a present limited success which will no doubt be amplified through the years, UNCITRAL model laws seek to extend legal globalization of the chosen topics through an appeal to the harmonization of international trade.

### *From Spanish to Russian, speaking one language, the jus commune of trade*

International law associations represent the collective thought of professionals consecrated to the highest standards of law and justice. No matter how vague and difficult it is to articulate the contents of these ideas, they remain a constant challenge to scholars. The organizations dedicated to the promotion of justice and its realization through laws are varied and dispersed throughout the world. From the Asociacion de Abogados de Buenos Aires (Lawyers Association of Buenos Aires) to the XXIst Century Lawyers Association (Russian Federation), approximately 100 can be easily located.[51]

And there are many more, sometimes associated with universities such as the Center for American and International Law affiliated with Southwestern University in Houston, Texas and its emphasis on transnational arbitration law. There is the Max Planck Institute for Comparative Public Law and International Law in Germany and its many scholarly publications. The International Law Institute in Washington, DC has trained thousands of lawyers from all over the world.

While each institute and professional organization has its statutory objectives, the cumulative effect of the high degree of professional activity concerned with international law invariably leads to a consensus on universal standards. The dominance of international trade in the mercantile sphere of our epoch requires an adequate response. This can only be achieved through an international *jus commune*, the common law, or law of right, a body of law derived from multiple sources but free from municipal law interference. As in the field of arbitration, where the national law courts have had to relinquish their exclusive jurisdiction, so international trade will eventually rest on a transnational law containing its own jus commune.

From conventions through model laws counseling arbitration, the cumulative body of precepts will not denigrate concepts recognized by municipal courts but instead strive to find common principles and practices current in international trade. These will prove to be none other then our dubious *lex mercatoria*.[52] From the pyre of the *lex mercatoria* arise the flames of legal globalization whose attraction does not extinguish its adherents but facilitates their international trade. The moths die in the heat while the merchants thrive.

## Notes

[1] Vienna Convention on the Law of Treaties signed at Vienna, Austria on 23 May 1969, see web site at <www.unsystem.org>, accessed 18 September 2002.

[2] See *Black's Law Dictionary*, Fourth Edition, West Publishing Co. (1954), under 'convention'.

[3] See home page at <www.hcch.net>, accessed 18 September 2002.

[4] As of 20 August 2002. See supra, n. 3, and relevant links.

[5] A full list of the conventions can be found at the web site of the Hague Conference, supra, n. 3 and relevant links.

[6] See chapter on 'International Arbitration Without International Arbitration Law'.

[7] Essays concerning the *lex mercatoria* have been assembled under the tutelage of Thomas E. Carbonneau (ed.), *Lex mercatoria* and Arbitration, rev. ed. Juris Publishing, Inc., Oxford and Kluwer Law International, London (1998), hereafter referred to as the 'Carbonneau collection'.

[8] For the terms of the Convention and an extensive collection of material concerning the CISG, see web site of Pace University at <www.cisg.law.pace.edu>, accessed 18 September 2002.

[9] For a comprehensive review of the international law consequences of the CISG, see Bernard Audit, *The Vienna Sales Convention and the Lex Mercatoria*, Chapter 11, in the Carbonneau collection.

[10] For complete text of the convention, see supra, n. 8.

[11] Supra, n. 7.

[12] Supra, n. 9.

[13] Supra, n. 8.

[14] Ibid.

[15] Article 7 of the CISG, supra. n. 8.

[16] Supra, n. 9.

[17] Ibid.

[18] For a comprehensive review, see discussion in Peter H. Pfund, *United States Participation in Transnational Lawmaking*, Chapter 13, in the Carbonneau collection.

[19] For a discussion of the competencies of the Council of Europe and a complete list of treaties sponsored by this organization, see <www.convention.coe.int/treaty/EN/cadre principal>.

[20] Ibid, the 39 members are Albania, Andorra, Austria. Belgium, Bulgaria, Cyprus, Czech Republic, Denmark, Estonia, Finland, France, Germany, Greece, Hungary, Iceland, Ireland, Italy, Latvia, Liechtenstein, Lithuania, Luxembourg, Malta, Moldova, the Netherlands,

Norway, Poland, Portugal, Romania, Russia, San Marino, Slovakia, Slovenia, Spain, Sweden, Switzerland, 'the Former Yugoslav Republic of Macedonia', Turkey, Ukraine and the UK.
[21] Ibid.
[22] Ibid.
[23] Supra, n. 18.
[24] See the web site home page at <www.unidroit.org>, accessed 15 September 2002.
[25] Ibid.
[26] Ibid.
[27] Ibid.
[28] Ibid.
[29] The home page of UNIDROIT, supra, n. 24, publishes list of all conventions, details as to their terms, and list showing nations which have ratified the convention and the date.
[30] Supra, n. 24.
[31] Ibid.
[32] Michael Joachim Bonell, *UNIDROIT Principles and The Lex Mercatoria*, Chapter 16, Carbonneau collection.
[33] Ibid.
[34] Ibid.
[35] Ibid.
[36] Supra, n. 24 and see link to UNIDROIT Principles of International Commercial Contracts, 1994, Comments.
[37] Ibid, Article 1.8 (Usages and practices).
[38] Ibid.
[39] Ibid.
[40] Preamble to the UNIDROIT Principles, supra, n. 24.
[41] See web site home page of UNCITRAL at <www.uncitral.org>, accessed 21 September 2002 and links to model arbitration law.
[42] The model arbitration contract is published on-line at supra, n. 41.
[43] Ferenc Madf, *Codification of Commercial Practice in Eastern European Countries: Lex Mercatoria From a Hungarian Perspective*, Chapter 15, Carbonneau collection.
[44] Supra, n. 41, and links to arbitration.
[45] Supra, n. 41, Article 28 (3) of the UNCITRAL Model Law on International Commercial Arbitration.
[46] Article 28 (4), UNCITRAL Model Law on International Commercial Arbitration, supra, n. 41.
[47] Supra, n. 41.
[48] Explanatory note to the UNCITRAL Model Law on International Commercial Arbitration, supra, n. 41.
[49] Ibid.
[50] Ibid.
[51] See links at web site <www.findlaw.com/06associations/foreign>, accessed 20 September 2002.
[52] Vratislav Pechota, *The Future of the Law Governing the International Arbitral Process*, Chapter 17, Carbonneau collection.

# Chapter 23

# Laws are not the Subject Matter of the Law

*The intrepid search*[1]

Imbued by many with magical qualities, yet declared by its participants to be a science, the study of the law confronts this semantic paradox. While the logic of the mind presses for an answer as to the essence of the law — its unique attributes; its indispensable qualities — responses elude the pursuers. Undoubtedly, a science of the law appears remote. Yet without a consensus as to the nature of the law, there can hardly be a discussion as to its globalization.

By 'law' we are referring to broad principles, oral or written, which we understand as regulating the many facets of social life but which impose obligations on individuals. The recognition of law is not solely dependent on regulation. There is a reciprocal response of moral obligation, understood to be reasonable. These responsibilities are recognized as such by the majority of members of the community, be it miniscule as a neighborhood sport association or gigantesque as a nation. The law is therefore not about what is often denominated 'laws'. Club rules, traffic ordinances, lottery regulations, treaties, international conventions, corporate by-laws, pharmaceutical label requirements, municipal housing conditions, UN model laws, the US Uniform Commercial Code, the membership requirements for Bar Associations, English common law, the Civil Code of Portugal, the Penal Laws of the State of New York, the voting rights affecting the IMF — the list can continue indefinitely.

There are as many laws, rules, regulations, ordinances, administrative codes as there are human institutions. Since the range and variety of community units is probably limitless, it is impossible to ever compile a schedule of the laws of a country. Nor does it seem prudent to undertake encyclopedic summaries of the basic laws of all the civilized as well as the unfairly denominated uncivilized nations of the world. No matter how erudite our redaction, it will be faulty for custom is also law; yet the customary can only be garnered from local cultural immersion.

But it is also a truism that wherever there is a community, there is law. Law therefore has various expressions or modalities. Sometimes written, other times verbal tradition, affecting fundamental issues such as family or ownership, or regulating highway traffic, yet the omnipresence of the law has not facilitated a comprehensive definition of what is the law. Scholars and their readers continue with doubts. Some postulates can be hesitantly advanced.

The concept of the law certainly implies a duty, if nothing more than the moral onus of obedience. When a person has an obligation, another must have a duty, for accountableness cannot exist outside of a social community. Law without a citizenry does not exist. Where there is law, there is always social restraint. Intimidation is a necessary property of the law. Such coercion takes many forms, ranging from social ostracism to forcible implementation. The origin of these constraints we will defer momentarily and we will write about the law as if it were a fact in our search for its reality. This is not as irrational as it appears since every field science proceeds from an assumed reality. Excluded from our examination are the rules of bureaucracy, the mechanics of legal procedures with their varied forms, the study of doctrine already formulated, enforcement procedures devised by the state or its subdivisions, legislation in its many forms, from the grandiose conventions to the mundane parish ordinances.

All these categories are exempted as being secondary sources which depend for their vitality upon the substrata of social life known as the 'law'. They are the details of the law derived from general principles, practical solutions, technological state of the art, historical accidents, community necessity, and, of course, social engineering. Our search for the law begins with many difficulties. There is no physical, identifiable object to study. So many descriptions are possible. An incomplete list indicates it is compensation for perceived wrongs, enforced by an authority; it is human morality, part of our genetic constitution; it is a charter of basic human rights; it is the ethical expression of our natural inheritance, unfettered by historical incidents; it is a verbal summary of social values; it is the prevailing customs of the community or any of the many mini-units of the same society; it is what the legislature promulgates; it is what a court recognizes as the law; it is what a dictator and his coterie declare it to be. Admittedly, we have created a short list out of the many explanations propounded through the centuries.

Additionally, any realistic recognition of the phenomena known as the law must concede that in any community multiple levels of law exist. There are the laws of the church, the laws of the nation, the laws of other sovereigns, and finally the law of humanity.[2] Furthermore, the law affects people and therefore the understanding and compliance with the law begins with its perception. Court clerks, lawyers, judges, law schools, and academicians make their contributions to the proper comprehension of the law, in conjunction with other scholars from related disciplines such as sociology, economics, and political science. To all this uncertainty, there is a further handicap. It is doubtful if there can even be achieved agreement as to what is the proper subject matter being examined. There is the morality of the law; the jurisprudence of law; the function of the law; the sociology of the law; and even, for some, the ultimate purpose of law.

In addition to these broad, ill-defined areas of discussion, there are multiple, further subdivisions which could be made, such as the mechanisms for legal enforcement; the processes of change, which must include alterations to the law; the organization of a legal system; and, of course, the classification of the law. Opportunely, the study of the law has undergone a radical transformation from the time when any analysis was basically constructed on arm chair theory alone to the present moment when there are abundant field studies by social anthropologists of 'law in action'. We have gone from the pronouncements of Greek philosophers to the field studies of social anthropologists.

A selective panorama is required in order to present a more complete picture without becoming encyclopedic and pedantic. It is usual to classify contributors to legal theory as being adherents of one 'school' or another. Such an attempt raises a subsidiary contention: are the classifications correct? This leads to the often acrimonious scholarly debates in which substance becomes secondary to the primacy of logic — a defect often exhibited by the law profession. For ease of illustration, and an appreciation of the imagined objectivity of the law, a general review of varied, and often, contradictory insights provide an illuminating journey. But, firstly, the voyage.[3]

*Be philosophical*

The obvious defect of philosophical theories is that they are neither provable nor refutable. They constitute concepts only rarely confronting concrete facts. Philosophical insights contain a mixture of idealistic doctrine, legislative opinions, sociological impressions, and moral assumptions.

For a long period, English legal doctrine advocated the moral basis of law. The Middle Ages needed no dynamic, conflict-orientated interpretation of the law as it was a period of social stability heavily influenced by the religious orders. The dominant belief was that God wills only reason and the law is but a reflection of this design. Detailed studies of English medieval society have demonstrated the fusion of law and morals in the English manorial life. All law was seen as having a religious origin and moral purpose. Justice was that which articulated the correct moral truth. The search for law thus became a methodology for interpreting the various religious doctrines. The rise of capitalism wrenched law away from morality and eventually urged that the realm of conscience was to be distinguished from the market place. But before this victory, the law and morals were fused.

Within this mantra, the law and justice are synonyms. As stated eloquently by the medieval church, morality invades and permeates society. The whole universe is governed by divine reason. Hence the plan of governing things as it exists in God, the ruler of the universe, has the character of the law. Law and divinity cannot be separated. American law has also been substantially affected by the early English doctrines of the amalgam of law and morals. From the American continent, we have the contention for a moral basis to the law as being the natural outcome of human development. The law is seen as evolving slowly from a state of controlled warfare to freedom of contract. The growth of the law is commensurate with the moral development of a particular society.[4]

The law proceeds from self-help to administratively enforced rules. The clan is eventually replaced by a supra-corporate organization such as the state. Public law gives way to private law. Contract and equity become dominant over criminal sanctions. From a rigid interpretation of local customs the law moves towards welding certainty with equity.

Continental thinkers have lent their articulate voices. Many have seen in the law a manifestation of the divine element in the human psyche. The quest for justice is but a reflection of the eternal justice which reigns. One continental school declares law is what is possible and morals what ought to be. The law is the unfolding of the idea of human morality. Legal history is a record of how the idea of right has realized itself progressively in the human experience of the administration of justice. Progress in human society will be achieved by closing this gap between law and morals. What is 'just' is 'law'.

Much can be criticized of equating law with morality. All we are doing is replacing one vague concept with another. It tells us nothing about why laws emerge other than by allusions to morality. It is an austere, remote view of human life told on a grand scale assuming there is a moral purpose to humanity's existence, a conviction reluctantly abandoned. Afflicted by the spectacle of social misery on a grand scale, this vision sees humanity presently held in chains by economic necessities. At a distant future replete with justice, the mortal spirit will flourish in its entire splendor.

No irony is intended in our description. Such aspirations — are they more than that? — deserve our applause for, while it does not describe any practical aspect of law in any society, the references invoked are admirable. We might restate the general tenet. What is not just should not be obeyed. This still will not tell us very much about law, but rather standardize civil disobedience and when it is necessary. Additionally, the approach offers little methodology. We are told what the law is, or why it exists, but when we are through reading such expositions it tells us nothing about how law is in everyday life. There is not revealed to us a science of law. We are given broad, general statements predicated on study and thought but, unfortunately, in most cases, not related to specific facts. It is a method for seeking the origin of the law in man's nature and history, revealing a general trend towards an egalitarian, equitable society. In these terms, law becomes only another spiritual tool although the church temple is replaced by the marble floors of the court of justice.

*Think positively*

Another view holds that what is legislated is the law. Legislate and *ergo* you have created law. Perhaps the legislators have a moral basis to their debates but eventually this ethical component is transposed to a statutory edict and we pass from morality to law. What is pronounced in the Parliaments and is printed in the legislative journals is the law. Lawyers study statutes and the courts interpret their precepts.

Restrictively, this school advocates that the law is a codification of the complete and exhaustive body of legislative law. In this way, all laws can be known and thereafter interpreted. Although the legislative body can make pronouncements there will always be a margin for interpretation. Whenever legislative omissions exist, courts apply a modest ethical judgment in their interpretation and so, slowly, but resolutely, morality edges the development of the law forward. However, as a science, the study of law must be confined to what is legislatively enforceable and morality is largely a private matter, often times opposing a particular current legal precept.

The legislative school of thought differentiates between the philosophy of the law, which is a system of criteria of social values, and the sociology of the law which seeks to discover the rules of regulation of any human group. Predicated on a denial of human nature, the legislative school thus argues that the science of the law is the study of social control through an appeal to common cultural values made enforceable by the executive branch of a government. Of course, when we understand the main source of the authority of the legislative school we at once comprehend its merits and its defects as a tool for analysis.

There seems little doubt that the legislative school of legal analysis owes its emergence to the growth of the industrial state and the rise of parliamentary democracies. However, in this view, without edicts there can be no laws and hence in societies where the form of parliamentary government is non-existent or very fragmented, one is forced to conclude there is no law but something else — perhaps customs, or codes of conduct. At times mores are enforced, other times they are not. The human condition can and should be marked in a genome of regulations. The proper combination will create social peace and material progress.

Once again we find ourselves in an intellectual labyrinth because if we define the science of law as being synonymous with studying what is printed in the legislative halls we probably eliminate for analysis the overwhelming amount of human activity. We have to argue that the latter is not law but self-regulating conduct internalized by citizens. The average person would not consider this a sensible distinction. The existence of the law can hardly be made dependent on it being written or even enforced. Whether the result is a collection of laws or a compendium of legal language, the revelation of what law is still eludes us.

Moreover, legislative references such as the elements of due care, standards of fair competition, the obligations of a fiduciary, good faith, just compensation, equitable relief, and the standard of the reasonable man compel recourse to the collective beliefs of the community. Such concepts are not susceptible to parliamentary definition which will withstand scrutiny for long. The most substantial development in the study of the law and affording the more significant insights into the legal process has come from the sociological approach although the groundwork for this advance was preceded by the historical school.

### *Be retrospective*

Philosophy and history blend elegantly with the declarations of jurists who saw the origin of the law in the divine inspirations of humanity and culminate in the ethnographic anthologies. These compendiums of ancient customs, if they err as being as mere catalogues of the diversity of human culture, at least laid the foundation for the modern sociology of the law. Philosophy and ethnography complement one another, seeing in the movement of history a purpose. In simple societies, the individual is submerged in the whole. Criminal law is prior in time to civil law as the human social group has evolved from a uniform identity to individuality.

Social reality is infused with collective values and symbols, ideas shared by a contained social organization. Beneath these values lies a collective consciousness.

The law is disciplinary. It compels adherence to institutionalized values and hence the general collective psyche. However, this dependency on a collective consciousness raises the study of law to a metaphysical level. The psychological premise entails a search for the essence of the human mentality, modified by group behavior. The history of the law can be seen as a transition from group units to individual units. [5]

Customs are cultural affirmations and the law is one of the assertions. But there is a trend which is discernible. There is a movement from clans uniting to protect their members, paying as a group 'blood money' for a supposed injury, to the emergence of contract law, where the individual assumes his own responsibility.

Such general premises enunciated by continental thinkers find similar echoes in American scholars.[6] The law progresses from group law which is finally transferred to a public organization. Legal sanctions are withdrawn from kin groups and enforced by elected corporations, such as a government. Early American Indian society was an aggregation of families. Today the industrialized world is a cluster of individuals. Punishment is not with the clan but with various organs of a government. The law reflects this continuous process of social evolution.

Other important contributors to the sociology of the law have also emphasized how the content of law is dependent on the social structure, as water takes the form of the vase. One of the founders of modern sociology[7] defined the law as a body of norms, not beliefs. The norm gives rise to the belief, and not the contrary. According to this viewpoint, primitive law was an undifferentiated system of norms, and highly irrational. Torts, a civil wrong, are not distinguished from a crime. Vengeance dominated early tribes and formal legal procedures are missing. The history of the law has gone from edicts issued by unelected occupiers of legal authority to the rationalization of the law as exemplified by Western law. The process has been legal promulgation by charismatic theocrats, the creation of legal officials, as typified by the English medieval law courts, to a systematic organization of the law profession with its lawyers and judges.

Legal history certainly has its contributions to an understanding of the nature of the law. However, particularly in the US, reconstruction of the past has given way to a realistic framework which led to embracing one of several branches of the sociological approach to the law. It is this sociological view, as subsequently developed extensively by continental social anthropologists, which has contributed the most understanding to the process of law. Our discussion begins with ideology and ends in economics.

### *Be materialistic*[8]

Marx is often associated with a general theory of social change. The Marxian view contemplates the law as a mere image of established property rights and an attempt to perpetuate the status quo. The forces of history generate opposition to the status quo and through this dialectical process society is changed. This process has been given the name of historical materialism.

However Marx also made valuable contributions to an understanding of the law. Marx's theories concerning law can be reduced to the contention that the law is a mere reflection of the economic structure of any culture, a superstructure erected on a particular mode of production. The specific mode of production which prevailed while Marx was writing and which has since become the dominant force in the global economy is capitalism. The prevailing economic forces give birth to and idealize the existing labor relations and possession of resources into principles of law. Thus the law is a consequence of ownership of property and the various constellations of social relations brought about by the productive and material forces of any society. From this viewpoint, the law is only a superstructure having its origins in the basic economical material forces which determine the relationships of individuals to one another.

Additionally, the separation of the law from its original economic source causes many people to see fetishism to the law. The law is believed to be autonomous and independent from any economic influences. It is a totem whose existence is sacred and self-sustaining. In fact, according to a Marxian analysis, the content of the law is merely a reflection of the prevailing ideology of the dominant class and has no independent existence. To a Marxist, there is no 'rule of law' if by such a shorthand description we refer to an independent body of thought applying equitable and just principles to all citizens.

The Marxian view of the law is that it is another instrument utilized by the ruling classes to enforce and maintain their ideological principles which themselves are an outcome of the material forces in which all humanity is engaged.

Furthermore, the reasoning of the law, in order to maintain an appearance of fairness, erects artificial situations. Social logic becomes subordinate to legal reasoning which itself is a mere mental artifact supported by economics. Thus the concept of property ownership extended to its extreme logic prohibits the construction of a badly-needed hospital on abandoned marsh land owned by a distant freeholder, a swamp never utilized nor even probably visited. Today, such a consequence would be avoided by expropriation, but even this concedes that ownership is the right to oppose the social welfare. When confronted with such a legal principle, a Marxian analysis would deny the legal principle any validity, being a mere idealization of the economies of ownership which in turn are but a consequence of the capitalist mode of production.

Thus through the process of intellectual reasoning erected on commercial values it is possible to segregate tangible rights from intangible rights, permitting ownership to be carved into successive estates such as landlord-tenant, licensor-licensee, franchiser-franchisee, to cite a few examples. The owners of the productive forces strive to aggrandize their profits from these assets. At any one time there are innumerable social forces at work which conceptualize their justification so that if a warlord seizes a country, all law is declared to emanate from one source, that is, the king. Should the traditions give prominence to family or kinship, the laws of inheritance are recognized so as to preserve the group assets.

In summary, for a Marxist, the law has no objective existence. It mirrors human economic existence and at times the reflection shows mostly social oppression and human degradation. Solidarity does not exist nor could it since profit and cohesion speak not the same language. The law is fettered to its origins. It has no independent existence. Worse, it is an instrument of class oppression.

Critics of historical materialism point out that multitudes have died for ideas; humans have united when economics dictated exactly the opposite. The values of human ideas may in part rest on economic realities but this basis has its limits. Marx himself saw the predicament of mankind as a spiritual one. Man was alienated from his true self through the forced sale of his labor. As contradictory as it may seem, Marx's view is essentially a humanistic vision for it presupposes that were all resources available — to each his own, one for all — there would reign a state of social harmony.

Laws would not be needed since there would be no basic structure which gave birth to a superstructure used to contain any contrary ideologies. Whether or not this is true cannot be easily verified. It is an utopian vision and until the Utopia is erected, the law, in Marx's view, is a mere social instrument, among others, to keep in check the subservient classes. As an utopia is by definition a perfect place, by logic it will never be encountered. Which no doubt explains why the predictions of Marx failed. He understood the baseness of humanity but was captivated by its imagined goodness.

*Be cultural*

From a study of the African continent and its many tribes, have come insights into the nature of the law.[9] Investigations by social anthropologists into ancestral organization enforce the opinion that a vital function of the law was, and of course still is, in resolving conflicts. Its function was to unify the society. Its application was flexible and manifested itself in various forms, ranging from actual rules to generally recognized customs.

Extracting from one social anthropologist noted for his African studies,[10] conflicts are a part of social life. Fortunately custom restrains the conflicts from destroying the wider social order. All over the world, there are societies which have no governmental institutions. Some of them have existed over long periods with internal law but little judicial organization. Nevertheless, social order and cohesion are present. Law exists. Law, then, is social order. Conflict exists at all levels of human society. Rebellion is a constant feature. One way to enforce the dictates of a law is to impregnate it with special meaning, either patrimonial, or couched in a tribal fable. Myths serve the function of imparting mystical values to customs so that conflict, when it does arise, is more readily channeled into less violent resolutions.

Another social anthropologist studying African tribes has come to a similar yet distinguishable theory.[11] The containment of conflict is important but this is only possible through a piecemeal development of law. A logical system evolves over a period of centuries. Such a development cannot reflect a consistent core of social values because history is not rational. This probably means in pre-industrial societies change was slower as there was a need to adhere to customs, even those outdated, to preserve social units. There is no evidence to suggest tribal law is different from industrial law. Law is often understood by others to distinguish between what can be enforced by a political authority, on the one hand, and the customs of local groups, implying this last category deserves mention, but not as law.

Nevertheless, in societies where there is no politically constituted authority, this distinction must fail. Without formal political cultures, social anthropologists have not encountered communities without order. There is a simple explanation.

The law addresses social relationships. The law is thus seen to be social life, rules, values, ways of life, symbols, procedures, authority, group norms. The law escapes a single, unitary definition. The absence of a highly organized judicial branch of government is not synonymous with a lack of law. The law regulates in the plurality by acting internally upon the conscience of the various social units.

### *Be not singular*

The theory of legal pluralism presents an amalgam of various explanations of the law previously considered. The concepts can be set forth in linear form as expounded by one scholar.[12] The power of the state is the bedrock of a society which promulgates the general principles of the law. The idea of what the law is, however, should not be confused with what the law ought to be. Legal reality is an inconsistent, overlapping of norms of various social groups. Legal pluralism is a state of affairs. Groups, or corporations, have their norms and these groups are effective in substantially maintaining control over its members, for example, a church, a social club, a sports association, which control is achieved through the possibility of exclusion.

Legal pluralism does not require various legal systems. Multiple norms are sufficient. Society is a structure of parallel corporations. Law deals with rules of conduct and not with rules of decision. The decision making process is a specialized aspect of legal institutions. Law is more vast. Contrary to other thinkers, the vital function of the law is to organize society, not resolve disputes. Paraphrasing our scholar, the law is a disorderly composition of social units united by obligations and duties. Social units have certain autonomy for their field of action. Finally, the law is the self-regulation of a semi-autonomous social field. Each unit wields its own power.

Moreover, when the law is perceived as the result of community parts, it is only natural that the various forms of social units, such as world institutions or multilateral organizations, understandably exert an increasingly important effect upon national laws and mores.[13] An integrated world has brought legal pluralism on a global scale. Legal cultures clash and change is wrought.[14] Nevertheless, confrontation between legal cultures requires a resolution. The disputes created by international commerce grant the dominant legal culture an opportunity to implant its jurisprudence in other nations. Thus, dispute resolution justly deserves the attention and emphasis of contemporary social anthropologists.[15] Conflict requires conceptions of legal rules to resolve social antagonisms. The law is at once a collection of verbal symbols and at the same time an exercise in power.

Another social anthropologist has addressed this elusive aspect of power.[16] The struggles for power are a constant feature of social life and of the micro-processes of society. Power is achieved through politics. To obtain power, people use strategy to achieve objectives. Thus the existing rules of law become elements which can be appropriated by groups or individuals in their quest for power. Power permeates society in all social relations. Assuming this view of society, we can see the law as a site of potential disciplinary power dependent on who has power. Groups struggle for power and access to power, the final objective presumably being to monopolize resources which are converted into assets. The 'game for gain' must be played according to the rules otherwise no social organization becomes possible.

Consequently, the contest for power must utilize current norms to avoid open, violent conflict. Law becomes a norm, a mere symbol, used as a tool in the battle for power. With this platform, we are closer to the realities of everyday life where law and its interpretations reflect struggles and contests. Change occurs when one group achieves the power to effectuate a modification of legal norms. The law is a vehicle for appropriation. It reflects ideas or symbols held as valid norms, although these icons are used for self-realization in the power arena. Law, then, has no special significance, other than as a method of manipulation.

While this approach may appear less orthodox than other classical studies, in fact, a view of society as a power engagement corresponds closely to the mundane activities of the commercial world. This takes on even further significance when it is realized that for many authors, the economic life dominates social activity and, naturally, the idea of law.

### *Be economical*

The economic system of the US has influenced many American legal writers in diverse manners which can be subsumed under the category of the 'economic' school.

One scholar[17] noted, with cynicism, that the greatest obstacle to social changes were the law courts. Far from implementing legislation designed to foster social progress, the law courts were a constant impediment. For this critic, there was a sensible reason. The answers lie in the nature of the law. Law is one of the characteristics of social organizations. It is literature, the poems and tragedies of the collective social unit deified in norms, some of which are designated as 'laws'. Phrases such as, 'All men are born free', or 'This is a country of the people, by the people and for the people', and even 'No man will be obligated to give evidence against himself' are myths enshrined in various legal norms. Law courts are therefore headed by judges who are really the high priests of the particular society. They speak a highly technical, cryptic language because they are similar in function to the sages of the ancient Greek temples: the passage of tradition from one generation to another. The ultimate purpose is to conserve the economic profit which the acolytes confiscate for themselves.

Law has no meaning apart from the organization to which it belongs. The law is essentially a power symbol. Organizations do not choose creeds. They are the creed. The Roman Catholic Church and Catholicism are but two aspects of the same social thought and structure. The myth of a democracy incorporates certain norms in its founding charter. First comes the social organization; then the theoretical formulations. Law thus develops from a combination of historical facts. The law looks backwards. The law merely restates the customs generated by history which are usually contained within an economic system.

Law, or creeds, must be a practical response to the needs of any social organization. Although creeds or myths, they are stated as universal truths. Once stated as obvious reality, any proposed new law which is seen as attacking one of the verities, will be opposed. Reform very often generates debate not about practical results but whether or not a cosmic certainty is being questioned since this will change the existing economic order. Seen in these terms, the courts tend to adhere to what is understood as being the fundamental social principles and normally will not sanction legislation or legal interpretations which tend to question basic social values, those seen as being critical to the essential beliefs of the social system.

The logic of any social system becomes more important than obvious contradictory results. Consequently, a law can give rise to diverse but undesirable conflicting conclusions simply by extension of logic. Due process for the individual must be extended to due process for the corporate entity. Since an individual's private life can not be regulated by the state, neither can the commercial activities of the private corporation be overseen. Hence, the logic of the myth is used, deliberately or not, to gloss over the underlying realities of economic power and its abuse. The law is a fable, the cherished tales which have been handed down by our progenitors in the early dawn of social history.

Similar in social stridency is another author,[18] intellectually overwhelmed by what he understood as the greed and hypocrisy of commerce. For this sociologist, the basic framework of modern civilization is the machine process and investment for profit. Law is only used to further these objectives. Within this optic, the motive of business is pecuniary gain, not to create labor for a livelihood. The aim of business is the accumulation of wealth and not to provide services. Tasks are rendered only because it is easier to gather assets in this manner, instead of resorting to violence. Business efforts are directed towards gainful ventures and not socially useful functions. In this disrespectful process, the law is an important ally.

The spiritual basis of business enterprise is the concept of ownership, formulated in laws. But ownership is only an institutional habit of thought. Ownership, through legal ideology, no longer has moral restrictions. The business economy has given birth to the concept of freedom of contract. This is the basic, commercial legal creed. Freedom of contract is sacred. *De facto* freedom — freedom in practice — is not the law's concern, only *de jure* — by law. Whether or not the consumer has actual freedom of contract before the modern conglomerate need not be examined carefully. The legal concept, myth, or fable is all important and is given precedence over social economic reality.

Law, then, is just another business tale created to reach a satisfactory commercial ending where all the participants profit with exception of the consumer or the daily worker. For most part, purchaser and laborer are the one and same person but at different times of the day. Still within an economic framework, but less cynical, are the concepts of cost efficiency, opportunity cost, transaction costs, and allocation of risk as underpinning the economic foundations of the law.[19] Here, men/women are rational in their choices. All seek to maximize individual self-realization. When faced with an alternative, men/women select what is cost efficient. This entails the use of the concept of opportunity cost.

All human activity is ordered according to the principle of selecting the optimal choice out of many. The opportunity cost lurks behind all transactions and no one will continue with a proposed commercial arrangement if the opportunity cost becomes more lucrative. Thus if my secondhand car is worth more as scrap — the opportunity cost — in face of a drastically reduced secondhand market, I will prefer to sell for scrap rather then sell the car as a working machine.

Additionally, being rational, men/women seek to minimize the cost of their activities. Thus companies are formed and preferred to individual traders because the transaction costs are less. Every purchase and sale has attendant expenses. Sensible management will always strive to rationalize and reduce transactions costs by cloistering all services under the same roof. As an example, for an enterprise to seek to obtain multiple services outside its organization becomes a hopelessly complicated legal activity. Such a task may involve hundreds of contracts which can be avoided by forming a company and hiring people to perform the services.

Furthermore, contract and corporate law reflect predetermined social norms which avoid having to negotiate each possible condition for each transaction. Phrased differently, a substantial part of commercial law and legal precedents are designed to reduce transactions costs. Finally, when faced with a social dilemma, judges gravitate towards allocating risk and responsibility where it is socially desirable. The law of trespass, which prohibits anyone from using my garage, without my permission, is founded on a simple economic principle. If the garage is necessary to the trespasser he can surely make an offer which cannot be refused. The law of trespass is merely the law of offer and demand.

The law of eminent domain exists because this prevents a few individuals profiting from the agreements of the majority, namely the last to give their consent. If a railroad company has to negotiate hundreds of contracts to obtain a needed easement, or right of way, the last to be approached can demand unreasonable prices. It is more cost efficient, and will benefit the general public, to have the price determined by a board of reasonable men who calculate the reasonable value and allow the railroad line to be built.

The family is but a simple form of household production. It is an economic unit. This being so, it is easy to see why the divorce rate is rising and the birthrate declining. For women, who do both, maintaining the home and procreating, the opportunity cost has become too high. There are too many female executive jobs to be had. Marriage is thus not very cost efficient and having children is not half as profitable as a good stock option. The law of damages for breach of contract is sound economics since the law grants to a party the right to choose which is more cost effective: perform or pay damages. Market economics infuses legal principles and sensible laws are those that honor the principles of an MBA course, namely being to reduce costs and raise your margin of profit.

## *The origin of the law*

This highly condensed presentation of the thoughts of a few scholars as to the nature of the law should be sufficient for us to reach a disagreeable conclusion. The necessary degree of concurrence as to what is the law is not easily attainable. It lies not within the reach of legal commentators to describe the law with a degree of universal concurrence for the most simple of all reasons. The nature of the law is intimately integrated with the origins of communal life and cultural affects on the human mind.

As such, there is an insurmountable obstacle to the rationalization process. It is not possible to build a science of jurisprudence on historical speculations. The origins of the law have no verifiable rootstocks, unless we are to rely on divine sources. Putting aside a religious source, any explanation for the law must be a hypothesis which explains its consistent diversity and persistent appearance. As the law is always associated with a community, an immediate candidate is the fertile imagination of humanity forged in desperation when surrounded by a screaming horde. The need foreseen is social organization which permits the realization of human instincts and desires from family to the accumulation of assets in a moderately pacific ambient.

Abundant field studies demonstrate that where there are social units, there is agreement on the essentials of community life. Otherwise, violence erupts. For whatever reasons exist as to a particular social structure, and they are as numerous as the days in a millennium, the nature of humanity is practically immutable. This nature is at once sociable but also contentious. Cooperation and aid can be quickly transformed into a predisposition towards self-help. Altruism exists yet mayhem and slaughter are frequent occurrences. History reveals the origin of the law in grand scale. Law is inescapable. It is required to maintain social cohesion. Without it, there could be no appeal to standards to which others must adhere. The idea of the law permits transferring to a collective 'we' the responsibility for the acts of an 'I' which contravene prevailing traditions.

The egoistic traits of humanity render community life a fragile association. The law had to be invented and it was, grammatically. What we therefore denominate the 'law' is a verbal icon, a grammatical fiction, a device by which authority is sought to control the irrational aspects of human nature. At any one moment in the history of a community a consensus has been reached as to the cultural values the majority of the members accept. This consensus is baptized with an icon denominated 'a law.' It does not matter for social analysis that such laws are imposed by others; or the result of unjust economic conditions; or religious canons; or derived from the state of technology. A status quo is obtained, a social equilibrium where the forces of various groups can not enforce beyond what is achieved any further expression.

An elite occupies the majority of the territory. Those without land, unable to dislodge the possessors, accept the manorial way of life. Norms are derived from this relationship and the legal icon 'lease' arises. It comes to be seen as a document with its own rules and precepts but in fact its origin is the seizure of the principal source of income, for the epoch in question, of fertile soil.

What others claim as a revolution founded on new laws is a social historical process later legitimized with new verbal icons. Behind every basic law or legal principle are those concepts which, if violated, strike at the social cohesiveness of a community. They are moral judgments which are seldom questioned. When they are, then the law may change. Consequently, the law, as distinct from its countless secondary sources, is a verbal icon, dependent on woman/mankind for its existence, as ephemeral and eternal, as human life. Marx was right. The law is an ideology built on historical social events with no inner validity or logic, looking to the past and justifying the present.

But then Durkheim was no less prescient. The law is humanity's admission of nature's dominion over us and the priority of survival. The future of the law, a law for humanity, the *ius humanitatis*, must be built on this obvious fact. For these reasons, legal globalization will follow upon the norms of the champions of the economic race. Ideology clings to economics for support. The human mind, instinctively endowed with the capacity for justification, endows successful icons with words of approval. The norm becomes the law.

## Notes

[1] The ideas formulated in this chapter owe a substantial intellectual debt to the exposition in William Twining's, *Globalisation and Legal Theory*, Northwestern University Press (2000), the many profound, philosophical viewpoints raised by him in his analysis of the law, globalization, and his summary-critique of contributions from other scholars. This acknowledgement does not in any way infer an endorsement by Prof. Twining of the contents of either this chapter or book.

[2] As of July 1, 2002, there entered into vigor the International Criminal Court (ICC) to try crimes against humanity. Unless there are laws applicable to all humanity, aptly denominated *ius humanitatis*, the ICC has no valid reason to exist.

[3] The following authors were selected for their diverse view points: Thurman Arnold, *The Folklore of Capitalism*, Blue Ribbon Books (1941), now out of print but the edition of 2000 can be purchased on internet at <www.beardbooks.com>; T. B. Bottomore & M. Rubel, eds, *Karl Marx, Selected Writings in Sociology and Social Philosophy*, Penguin Books 2nd Ed. (1963); Hugh Collins, *Marxism and Law*, Clarendon Press, Oxford (1982); E. Durkheim, *The Elementary Forms of the Religious Life*, Allen & Unwin, New York (1912); John Gledhill, *Power and Its Disguises*, Pluto Press, London, Boulder, Colorado (1994); Max Gluckman, *The Judicial Process Among the Barotse of Northern Rhodesia*, Manchester University (1955); Max Gluckman, *Custom and Conflict in Africa*, Basil Blackwell, Oxford (1963); Max Gluckman, *Politics, Law and Ritual in Tribal Society*, Basil Blackwell, 2nd Ed., Oxford (1967); John Griffiths, *What Is Legal Pluralism?*, Journal of Legal Pluralism, no. 24, pp. 1-55, (1986); Georges Gurvitch, *Sociology of Law*, Kegan Paul, Trench, Truber & Co. Ltd., London (1947); O. W. Holmes, *The Common Law*, Little, Brown, Boston (1881); K. N. Llewelyn & E. A. Hobel, *The Cheyenne Way*, University of Oklahoma Press, Norman, Oklahoma (1941); Henry Maine, *Ancient Law*, Murray, London (1861); Sally Engle Merry, *Anthropology, Law, and Transnational Processes*, Annual Review of Anthropology, 1992.21, 357-379; Sally Falk Moore, *Law As Process*, Routledge & Kegan Paul, London (1978); Richard A. Posner, *Economic Analysis of Law*, 2nd Ed., Little, Brown and Company, Boston and Toronto (1977); Roscoe Pound, *Law and Morals*, The University

of North Carolina Press, Chapel Hill, N.C. (1924); Francis Snyder, *Law and Anthropology: A Review*, EUI Working Papers Law No. 93/4, European University Institute, Florence, Italy (1993); Richard H. Tawney, *Religion and The Rise of Capitalism*, Penguin Books, London (1938 ed.); Richard H. Tawney, *The Acquisitive Society*, Harcourt, Brace and Howe, Inc. New York (1948); William Twining's, *Globalisation and Legal Theory*, Northwestern University Press (2000); Roberto Mangabeira Unger, *The Critical Legal Studies Movement*, Harvard University Press (1986); Thorstein Veblen, *The Theory of Business Enterprise*, Augustus M. Kelley, New York (1975); Gordon R. Woodman, *Customary Law in Common Law Systems*, available at <www.ids.ac.uk/ids/govern/acc/ust/pdfs/idswoodman.pdf>.

[4] Henry Maine, *Ancient Law*, Murray, London (1861).

[5] E. Durkheim, *The Elementary Forms of the Religious Life*, Allen & Unwin, New York (1912).

[6] K. N. Llewelyn & E. A. Hobel, *The Cheyenne Way*, University of Oklahoma Press, Norman, Oklahoma (1941).

[7] Max Weber, a German sociologist. All material drawing on the writings of Max Weber are based upon George Ritzer, *Sociological Theory*, 2nd. Ed., McGraw-Hill Publishing Company, New York (1988).

[8] Hugh Collins, *Marxism and Law*, Clarendon Press, Oxford (1982); T. B. Bottomore & M. Rubel, eds, *Karl Marx, Selected Writings in Sociology and Social Philosophy*, Pelican Books 2nd Ed. (1963).

[9] Max Gluckman, *Custom and Conflict in Africa*, Basil Blackwell, Oxford (1963); Max Gluckman, *Politics, Law and Ritual in Tribal Society*, Basil Blackwell, 2nd ed., Oxford (1967).

[10] Ibid.

[11] Sally Falk Moore, *Social Facts and Fabrications, 'Customary' Law on Kilimanjaro*, Cambridge University Press (1980); Sally Falk Moore, *Law As Process*, Routledge & Kegan Paul, London (1978).

[12] John Griffiths, *What Is Legal Pluralism?*, Journal of Legal Pluralism no. 24, 1-55 (1986).

[13] Sally Engle Merry, *Anthropology, Law, and Transnational Processes*, Annual Review of Anthropology, 1992.21, 357-379.

[14] Ibid.

[15] Ibid.

[16] John Gledhill, *Power and Its Disguises*, Pluto Press, London, Boulder, Colorado, (1994).

[17] Thurman Arnold, *The Folklore of Capitalism*, Blue Ribbon Books (1941), now out of print but the edition of 2000 can be purchased on internet at <www.beardbooks.com>.

[18] Thorstein Veblen, *The Theory of Business Enterprise*, 1904, Augustus M. Kelley, New York (1975).

[19] Richard A. Posner, *Economic Analysis of Law* 2nd Ed., Little, Brown and Company, Boston and Toronto (1977).

# Chapter 24

# The Profane Evangelism of Legal Globalization

*The origins of legal globalization*

In the year 2001, the US was responsible for 31 per cent of the world's production, measured at market prices.[1] The EU contributed a further 26 per cent while Japan's production was 15 per cent.[2] Contrary to popular impressions, China's economy originates less than 4 per cent of total world production.[3] With 72 per cent of world output emanating from the markets of the US, the EU, and Japan, it is hopefully not a xenophobic attitude to declare that three industrialized nations dominate world trade. Yet these simple statistics imply other consequences.

One of the most apparent is that the legal principles upon which these regions conduct their commerce are an emulative emblem for other jurisdictions. No matter that Japan is geographically part of Asia. Just as the dominant language of international commerce is English, so the assertive influence of Western law is evident in the various legal documents part and parcel of international trade spearheaded by the major industrialized nations.

These are the facts reflected in the myriad documents crossing the desks of lawyers specializing in international private commercial law. Through international investment banks, public lending institutions, private capital venture firms, mergers and acquisitions, take-over bids, global capital movements through stock exchanges, multinationals, foreign entrepreneurs, the employment of overseas investments, dominated thoroughly by Western multinationals or their Asian counterparts, is conducted through legal principles familiar to the participants. The expansion of Western capital and Western legal principles is no different in result than the extension of Christianity into African and Asian colonies centuries ago.

Nor is this statement intended to be an indirect criticism of Western legal imperialism or a signal of religious zeal. Imitation is a voluntary act. The conformity is granted in the hope of material gain. The cultural structure of the colonizer is accepted as being morally superior. The noteworthy success of the conqueror is transposed to, and associated with, the victor's laws. The invasion need not be by land, sea, or air. Global integration of commerce and media has made popular the icons, which of course includes the law, of Western thought and culture. Further contributing to the dominion of Western law over international commerce are the numerous bequests made to the globalization of Western law, of which only a modest fraction has been subject to analysis.

We have seen the effect of bits. The historic influence of public international law with its marginal recognition of individual claims is diminished and the private investment rights of the individual are being consecrated in a variety of ways. Basically this has been through requiring the nation to submit to arbitration when an investor has a legal complaint against the sovereign.

Thereafter, international arbitration, freed from municipal law principles, if not otherwise directed by the relevant legal document, seeks justice based on the *lex mercatoria*, that repository of customary international trade law. No longer anchored to the logic of municipal law which is at times chained to obsolete precedent, international arbitration can adjudicate based on the accepted commercial practices of the barons of international trade.

Moreover, regional trade agreements, such as NAFTA, have clearly usurped the province of municipal law by compelling arbitration on investment claims, even when the other party is a sovereign, before the International Center for the Settlement of Investment Disputes. Under the mandate of NAFTA, arbitration awards are based on the principles of 'international law' or 'fair and equitable treatment', which, while striving to realize justice, are far from precise.

While regional trade agreements are still in their infancy, with few constructing a firm juridical foundation, their prevalence in many parts of the world are a harbinger of the felt need to construct rules of trade not influenced by the vagaries of municipal law. The consequences for legal globalization are clear. The laws of international commerce become harmonized in a regional trade agreement and, of course, the regional trade agreement only exists to have commerce with external nations. International commerce drives forward the merchant's preference for uniformity in the rules of trade.

International commerce was the motive for the creation of the WTO. It was established upon a generalized core of principles which declares no clear legal principles but rather, similar to the *lex mercatoria*, and investment treaties, falls back upon phrases of reference such as the 'general principles of international law'. More seriously, the WTO mechanisms for enforcement of trade disputes must rely upon the offending nation voluntarily satisfying any penalties. One is reminded of the dilemma of the school boy, who faced with knowledge of an infraction by his schoolmaster, must decide between complicity or eventual reprisal. The EU has hesitated several times before attempting to enforce penalties against the US for fear of loss of trade. With international trade firmly subject to the dominion of the industrialized nations, the political process contained within the WTO inevitably compels compliance by other nations with the basic Western legal principles. Otherwise international trade will halt and the WTO will become defunct or a platform for further pamphleteering.

Complementing the WTO as a public law institution is the private club of the OECD. Committed by its statutes to promoting world commerce based on Western economic principles, the OECD is a forcible moral persuader as to the rules of conduct for transnational companies and their executives. As with any fraternity, the suggested rules of conduct for members are more powerful than any administrative code, both as to enforcement and consequences.

In parallel, various multilateral organizations such as the IMF and the World Bank are politicized by Western economic and legal principles through voting rights linked to capital contributions. The Western nations easily dominate these organizations upon which the lesser developed countries depend for economic survival. Economics without law is not a probable success story. Guided and orientated by Western legal principles, the principal public lending institutions require their sovereign borrowers to enact social and economic legislation which is a mirror image of Western economics, and of course its laws. Sovereign debtors have fewer alternatives than private mendicants, for the former may have to face street riots, while the latter can seek asylum in the many charitable refuges scattered throughout a metropolis.

Sovereign debtors and private borrowers are subject to the financial requirements imposed upon central banks by committees located far from the nation in question. From the bankers' sanatorium of Basle come edicts which no central bank would ignore, not even the US Federal Reserve Board. Disobedience to the precepts of the Bank for International Settlements and the Basle Committee on Bank Supervision concerning reserve requirements or credit standards hastens the bankruptcy of sovereigns and their citizens. A central bank cannot operate independently of an international clearing and bank system.

International alliances, mergers, and acquisitions contribute substantially to the globalization of Western law. In the year 2002, mergers and acquisitions valued at $1,198 billion dollars were consummated.[4] This is an annual and not a cumulative figure. The fact that a majority of such transactions are between the commercial enterprises of industrialized nations reinforces the globalization of Western law. The incessant transactions between Western nations impel the parties towards common, commercial international legal principles which are exported in their totality to the emerging nations.

International commercial common law and civil law precepts are borrowed and adapted from one jurisdiction to another. It is a natural consequence of transatlantic transactions. Common law lawyers are fond of affirming that equity is a distinguishing characteristic of their jurisdiction; yet the civil codes of Europe admonish parties to be bound by the principles of 'good faith'. The civil law countries of the EU have adopted many of the legal features of the common law. Franchises, consortiums, international joint ventures, and transfer of technology contracts are but a few of the juridical figures which gained prominence in common law nations but are now familiar legal concepts in the EU and Asia.

The common law preference for detailed documents and a preoccupation with minutiae, due to a fear of judicial precedents permitting avoidance, is reflected in commercial, financial, and legal due diligence procedures associated with mergers and acquisitions, lengthy commercial contracts, leases with excessive clauses, indeed, the common law penchant for legal detail and definition is one of its hallmarks. Today, an acquisition agreement drafted in Paris or Rome is no different from one assembled in New York or London.

Moving in tandem with the spectacular growth of international trade is international arbitration. The merchant's preference for international arbitration is not dampened by the fact that there is still no agreed-upon international arbitration law as to substance. Of course, arbitration procedures are fairly standardized. Nevertheless, unless the legal document establishing arbitration is quite clear as to the law to be applied, the rules invoked by arbitrators are often founded on either customary law or the alleged principles to civilized nations. With such vague generalizations, it is not possible to create a definitive core of arbitration law.

Perhaps this has a salutary effect. Arbitrators, believing themselves freed from the limits of municipal law, often accidental, historical precedents developed from economic circumstances no longer applicable, seek 'equitable' results founded on customary practices. The *lex mercatoria* looms as a viable choice even if it is still jurisprudence in its infancy as doctrinal law.

The global customs of merchants have an honorable tradition and there seems no reason not to adhere to the standards formulated. Trade associations, marine insurance policies, cargo clauses, and association model contracts are simple examples of sources of interpretation which are regulating effectively the merchants participating in the relevant trade. There appears no valid reason why the customs of such industries, the *lex mercatoria*, besides serving as a point of reference for arbitration, are not also significant contributors to the globalization of the law.

Exemplifying the best of scholastic thought and their practical applications are the multiple treaties, conventions, model laws, and uniform rules dealing with a great variety of legal topics. From wills to sales, from adoption to the taking of depositions, a variety of institutions such as the UN, UNIDROIT, or UNCITRAL are publishing texts which both homogenize the subject matter in question or leave open the possibility of recourse to general customary law, for the moment encapsulated in the expression the *lex mercatoria*.

### *The inevitability of legal globalization*

The future confirms the globalization of the law. It is a requirement for international collaboration. Unlike religion which has depended for its successful expansion upon being auxiliary to territorial conquests, the majority of legal globalization relies on material gain, but through pacific means. It is not only the pen with its ability to transcribe words which is mightier than the sword. The check, promissory note, letter of credit, share, bond, and all the other symbolic representations of wealth are also potent substitutes for the cutlass.

Swept along by international commerce and its perceived rewards, the community imagination is going global. If the law is a convenient icon for accepted values, then global symbols are needed. However, unlike the images of a singular community, global ideas require an even larger consensus. We cannot speak of the majority of the global community, but rather a mega-majority.

To obtain approval from the world community as to a set of legal principles, it is apparent that they must of necessity be broad and of unspecified application. Otherwise, there will be few adherents. This is why from the international public institutions, the world organizations, the conventions, the committees for uniform rules, the standard commercial documents, the professional associations, there emerges a typical pattern. Consensus is sought and a common front is achieved, even if by necessity built on generalities, as is the WTO. All the participants are aware that the larger the potential audience, the more pressing the need for a broad appeal based on the most uncontroversial of social norms.

After concurrence is achieved by the working groups, proposed principles are drafted. One network influences the other; ideas are filtered, shorn of novelty, and circulated. Convergence is sought before publication. Thus globalization of the law is driven by the actors associated with international commerce. Yet there is a further consequence. Commercial rationale dictates an avoidance of the local judiciary. Municipal courts reflect their inheritance. They are the guardians of the national imagination. The local court house is the warehouse of national norms. Guards are in evidence not only to ensure there is no disturbance of the peace. The cultural treasure reflected through legal principles is also jealously supervised.

The territorial laws of a nation are not sufficiently accommodative of foreign commerce. Even if they were, the distant merchants would, initially, distrust them. In this respect, international arbitration affords more opportunity for a flexible imagination than do the law courts. For this cause, arbitration is consecrated in various international legal documents. It is for this reason that international arbitration will succeed in great measure as a preference to municipal courts when issues of international commerce are at cause. International arbitration permits freedom from historical legal precedents and grants enough grammatical license so that arbitration awards, based on 'equity' are in reality confirmation of a particular trade custom.

In the name of equity, justice, the laws of civilized nations, or the universal principles of law, arbitrators are able to apply commercial commonsense to the resolution of disputes. The *lex mercatoria*, the repository of sound international commercial practice through the annals of trading, becomes now imbued with a new vigor. It gives a possible meaning to a notion in search of application, international commercial law.

International arbitration, with its territorial detachment and hands-on approach, permits the verbal globalization of the law in a way not easily attainable by the municipal courts. International arbitration is thus an accomplished ally in the globalization process. With the failure of a coherent theory as to the nature of the law a recurring theme through the centuries, it is with international arbitration that globalization will make the most strides forward. International arbitration awards are the result of commonsense doctrine which is another way of stating the King has been dethroned by the commoner. The municipal courts rely on precedent. The arbitration tribunal must seek its authority in mercantile practice.

To attribute imagination to the law's origins is not to minimize in any way its importance and function. Upon close examination, it will be discovered that all of the significant social relationships, excluding genetic affinities, rest upon contrived fictions such as husband-wife, employer-employee, landlord-tenant, creditor-debtor, trustee-ward, testator-legatee, principal-agent, guardian-ward, licensor-licensee, transferor-transferee, and assignor-assignee. Of course these examples are a fraction of the fictions the law creates.

Legal fiction reaches its sublime with its application in criminal law, that branch of the law most concerned with violence. There is a distinction in most laws between slaughter consummated in warfare and death perpetuated privately with a vengeance, normally classified as 'homicide'. Yet the result is the same: the extinguishment of life. Words cannot possibly have a constant meaning, changing as they must with the circumstances which invented them. The human being, wise and adaptable, has discovered the perfect tool for forging societies and bonds. Social conduct wrapped and packaged in legal verbiage, even if often abused, nevertheless take on an objective existence and are convincing. What they describe appears real and truthful.

One day legal globalization will be extended to criminal causes.[5] The nature of the law, originating in the urgency for social stability over violence, must accompany the historical conditions which dominate our present epoch. Not surprisingly, barter and trade may be the harbingers of a world peace.

### *Religion without ministers*

An eminent essayist and philosopher of the law[6] reminds us that globalization has many meanings and only the context can determine its particular significance. It may mean the global adaptation of cultural fads, such as fast food outlets; or, with a more serious consequence, the global dominion of a language such as English. Then again, globalization is often equated, although erroneously, with internationalization, whereby markets, services, and ideas are integrated through vast networks. From capital exchanges to international credit data banks, information is disseminated as fast as the broad band can carry it.

And of course there is globalization of issues such as climatic warming, marine pollution, or nuclear proliferation. Naturally, these are topics affecting the world population and which requires a united response. However, there is a further aspect of globalization which is significant and persistent. It is the conquest of cultural spaces by Western law but with a different context than in prior epochs.

In the sixteenth century Christian evangelists spread the gospel to the African and Asian continents. Zealous spirits were often accompanied with triumphant aggression well documented in historical and anthropological studies. Native cultures collapsed with the eradication of local religious cults. Through the missionary schools, Western culture and thought, partially absorbed, partially modified, accompanied the colonization and appropriation of native populations and their resources. The attempted dispersion and expansion of Christianity, anchored to its monotheist Judaic origins of a protective, just, yet vengeful deity, has continued unabated to the present twenty-first century. International commerce has still not severed its affinity with the Protestant ethic. The imperialism of modern neoliberalism continues to find support in morality. Yet there is strong opposition emerging.

Today, we are confronted with the rise of nationalism and the recognition of the right to cultural self-determination as an accepted and proper standard of human morality. Imperialistic territorial invasion of another nation is generally dependent on an international consensus. As a consequence, there is even being debated in academic journals the concept of extending copyright protection to 'culture'.[7] However, the final global triumph of Western religious and economic convictions has a new challenger, or perhaps it would be more accurate to say it always has existed: the law. Not the myriad legal precepts, canons, regulations, administrative codes, municipal ordinances, and country club rules, all of which naturally contribute to a more orderly world. Rather the 'law', written in letters large; the 'law' which is the expression of the basic social values of community life. 'Law' such as all people are equal if different; the prohibition of all forms of violence, whether to body or property; the protection of national culture; the consecration of national identities; access for all to the basic necessities of a dignified human condition from health to education to housing. Everyone will have their own list. But it is a secular list founded on universal human values.

Our competitor to a world subject to a divine interpretation with an economic mission is the multifaceted social engineer derived from the diverse fields of thought and experience. All the various sources of legal globalization, whether originating from multilateral organizations, or by treaties and conventions, and, of course, the promulgation of model and uniform laws, the standard forms used by associations, the imperative of integrated markets, the theory discussed and debated in academic journals and conferences, from this reduced list of activity springs forth the sensible rules of conduct for a society, deprived of obedience for reasons of religious authority but dependent on the consensus of wise and just minds.

The process of social engineering inherent in legal globalization cannot have any permanent content for what is just, what is sensible; all constitute community responses to a social and material environment which is fluid and ever-changing. In this respect, the *lex mercatoria* is sufficiently vague to permit arbitrators to adapt their awards to current commercial practices. Unlike earlier instances of scriptural dissemination, legal globalization, impelled by international commerce, owes its authority neither to clerical interpretation nor religious fiat. That Western law appears to be dominating international legal principles is but a consequence of the Western economic empire[8] which, originating in religious premises, is casting aside its birthright.

This is the irony of maturation. Finally freed from inspirational sources by the imperatives of commerce, the profanity in legal globalization should be a scholastic comfort to those interested in constructing a future, secular society. Legal globalization in the form of a global consensus on commercial norms will cast its concept of justice on property rights. But as commerce cannot be easily separated from civil claims, international commerce will prove to be the champion of the fragile dignity of humanity. A global commonwealth is not an illusory concept. Extracting the essence from the critical legal studies movement,[9] the 'power-ridden'[10] and 'manipulable materials'[11] of individuals and nations will give way to a sensible world order where economic gain will be tempered by the consensus of other powerful voices and where '... impersonal purposes, policies, and principles make sense and claim authority'.[12]

*The profane future*[13]

For future societies to be freed from their historical accidents — social obstacles imposed by class stratification resulting from conquest, inheritance, antiquated legal precepts, faulty education, racial segregation, ethnic discrimination, gender distinctions — it must be admitted frankly, without recourse to conflated language, that all law is principles and policies, or, if you prefer, social conduct wrapped in admonitions and parables. We must leave aside theological explanations as to the origins of the law. It is a question of belief and not susceptible to objective criticism. But all other descriptions are narration, the relentless unfolding of historical forces, the quest for the grail of social harmony, the emancipation of humanity founded on material progress, the social engineering by grizzled heads, the clash and conflict of social strife, no matter the theory invoked, for the results are always the same. A victor has beliefs which require administration.

Yet, if law is social conduct, it is also a received code of ethics. But morals can be changed. Norms are but a momentary belief when viewed against the stretch of history. Law can reconstruct as well as regulate. Reformulation is possible because the clever conqueror phrases its maxims in language appealing to the sentiment of ideal justice. It is proper to own property without fear of interference, even to the detriment of society, as that is an inherent natural right, or so is canted the refrain of the market economy. Still, the imposed dictate contains the seed of its modification. For there is admitted an ideal — the concept of justice — and through this mechanism a democratic society ordered and conceived upon a system of impartiality seeks through the logic of the legal mind to constantly improve and refine the abstraction of equity.

Once the cadre of forensic specialists, and in particular the judiciary, turn their intellectual prowess to the analysis of conflict and case-context, rational legal analysis demands a methodology. The process of decision becomes separated from the origin of the norms. Received legal precepts must then be subjected to a rationalizing process. It is at this juncture that a reinvention of given institutions becomes possible. What is required is institutional imagination concerning the present forms of state action, private legal norms, or public forms of representation.[14]

The adjudication of disputes and the judicial interpretation of conflict must be guided by a search for the commonsense good of the community. Judicial law-making must be tempered by the constraints of the particular social history of the group; but this should not prevent those laboring in the field of law from instilling new directions into the existing institutions.

Seeking solutions through analogies — the favorite tool of the law profession — cannot be a reason to abort the appearance of new, contemporary social norms. The life of the jurist is usually one committed to moderation, striking compromises between group interests in the hopes of uniting all around accepted social values. International commerce wrests reconciliation from its participants for that is the nature of business. The clash of interests created by mercantile activity admits institutional changes to preserve social harmony. The emergence of social groups heretofore silent requires concessions to appease and assuage the clamor for justice which is frequently access to resources.

But if we will have the clarity to understand the temporality of legal precepts; if we will accept the cultural dependency of a juridical norm; if we will concede human institutions are the result of profane norms, we will, in the words of a distinguished philosopher of the law '... make ourselves into visionaries'.[15] For, what is not sacred must conform to the commonweal and judicial precedent is no more sacred than its practitioners. As to what are the new norms which will globally emerge and further integrate the world community, there can be little doubt that the rallying point will have to serve the international commercial traders. These are the glaring facts. Western law is trawling in its wake norms which will regulate the lives of citizens everywhere who, anxious to become part of the international market place, accept the conditions this requires. For the moment, we can conclude our chronicles with the words of an eminent legal scholar:

> The internationalization of legal fields is often viewed as being more or less equivalent to Americanization. The American way of law, embedded in a particular variety of capitalism, has been exported by multinational businesses, large law firms, international organizations, development programs, cultural archetypes, and reception or imposition of US law in many other countries.[16]

Whether or not it is possible to impart humane standards into the deluge of Western commercial and legal norms emerging throughout the world requires the predictions of other investigators and the consensus of the power brokers.

## Notes

1 Martin Wolf, *Stagnation in Germany and Japan, unsustainable imbalances in the US ... will the recovery take hold?*, The Financial Times, 18 December 2002, at page 13.
2 Ibid.
3 Ibid.
4 Juliana Ratner, *The nightmare on Wall Street continues*, The Financial Times, 23 December 2002, at page 17. We are not informed as to the standard for the valuation, for example, assets or market capitalization.
5 As of July 1, 2002, there entered into existence the International Criminal Court to try crimes against humanity.
6 William Twining, Globalisation and Legal Theory, Northwestern University Press (2000).
7 Michael F. Brown, *Can Culture Be Copyrighted?*, Current Anthropology 39(2), April 1998, which contains a number of contributed articles.
8 Herb Thompson, *Culture and Economic Development: Modernisation to Globalisation*, available at <www.theoryandscience.icaap.org/content/vol1002.002/thompson>, accessed 16 January 2003.
9 Roberto Mangabeira Unger, *The Critical Legal Studies Movement*, Harvard University Press (1986).

[10] Ibid., at p. 17.
[11] Ibid.
[12] Ibid at p. 18.
[13] Many of the ideas presented in this section surged forth after reading Robert Mangabeira Unger, *What Should Legal Analysis Become*, Verso (1996), an eloquent and eclectic inquiry into the law and its methodology, legal analysis. As a unique contribution to the sociology of the law, or perhaps a philosophy of society, Robert Mangabeira Unger is an obligatory reference.
[14] Ibid, a phrase and concept developed extensively in the cited reference.
[15] Ibid, at p. 190.
[16] Francis Snyder, *Economic Globalisation And The Law In The 21st Century*, Austin Sarat, ed., *The Blackwell Companion in Law and Society*, New York and Oxford, Blackwell Publishers (2003).

# Bibliography

All references to web sites beginning with 'www' have purposefully omitted the prefix 'http://'. The major search engines automatically insert this prefix.

References to source material such as legislation, treaties, conventions, model laws, jurisprudence, or cases discussed or cited in the text have not been transposed to the bibliography nor the extensive web sites consulted and referenced in the various chapters.


Adams, John *Crisis? What crisis?*, FT Expat, February 2003, at p. 45, quotation from an "insight column: ratings agencies" signed by James Featherstone.

Adelman, Sammy and Paliwala, Abdul , *Law and Crisis in the Third World*, London, New York: Hans Zell, (1993), reviewed by Richard Bilder and Brian Z. Tamanaha, Van Vollenhoven Institute for Law and Administration in Non-Western Countries, Leiden.

Ala'i, Padideh, *A Human Rights Critique of the WTO: Some Preliminary Observations*, 33 Geo. Wash. Int'l L. Rev. 537 (2001).

Albino, Carlos, *Crime e castigo, a partir de agora*, (trans. 'Crime and punishment, as of now') Diario de Noticias, 1 July 2002, at p. 16.

Alden, Edward, *US steel tariffs illegal, rules WTO*, The Financial Times, 27 March 2003, at p. 8.

Alden, Edward, *Washington alters line on US investor protection*, The Financial Times, 2 October 2002, at p. 8.

Alden, Edward, *US proposes fines instead of sanctions in trade disputes*, The Financial Times, 25 October 2002, at p. 7.

Alden, Edward, *Transatlantic tensions set to escalate*, The Financial Times, 20-21 April 2002 at p. 4.

Alden, Edward, *Countries line up to sign US trade deals*, The Financial Times, 1 April 2002, at p. 10.

American Bar Association, *How To Negotiate an International Joint Venture*, Chicago, Il., Section of International Law and Practice (1996).

American Bar Association, *Globalization of Capital, Financial and Commercial Markets, Section of International Law and Practice,* Chicago, Il., Section of International Law and Practice (1995).

American Bar Association, *How to Conduct a Cross-Border Merger and Acquisition/Financing Due Diligence in Multiple Jurisdictions (Including Working with Foreign Counsel)* Chicago, Il., Section of International Law and Practice (1995).

American Bar Association, *How To Structure and Document Cross-Border Privately Negotiated Mergers and Acquisitions* Chicago, Il., Section of International Law and Practice (1995).

American Bar Association, *How to Draft an International Joint Venture Agreement* Chicago, Il., Section of International Law and Practice (1993).

American Bar Association, *Negotiating and Structuring International* Commercial *Transactions* Chicago, Il., Section of International Law and Practice (1991).

American Bar Association, *International Joint Ventures, A Practical Approach to Working with Foreign Investors in the US and Abroad*, Chicago, Ill: Section of International Law and Practice (1990).

Arnold, Thurman, *The Folklore of Capitalism*, originally published in 1941, now out of print but a recent edition (2000) can be purchased through the internet at <www.beardbooks.com>.

Asken, Gerald, *Arbitration and Other Means of Dispute Settlement*, pp. 287-291, at p. 287, in International Joint Ventures: A Practical Approach to Working with Foreign Investors in the U.S. and Abroad, American Bar Association, Section of International Law and Practice, (1990).

Atik, Jeffrey, *Democratizing The WTO*, 33 Geo. Wash. Int'l L. Rev. 451 (2001)

Auerbach, Alan J., *Mergers and Acquisitions*, Chicago, Il., University of Chicago Press (1988).

Braithwaite, John, and Drahos, Peter, *Business Regulation*, Cambridge University Press (2000).

Baker, Mark B., *Tightening the Toothless Vise: Codes of Conduct and the American Multinational Enterprise*, 20 Wis. Int'l L. Rev. 89 (2001).

Barbi, Celso, Filho, *Acordo de Acionistas*, Belo Horizonte, Brazil, Del Rey Editora, (1993).

Bargas, Sylvia E., *Direct Investment Positions for 1999 Country and Industry Detail*, Survey of Current Business, July 2000.

Beattie Alan, *Asia is a threat to recovery, says the IMF*, The Financial Times, 19 September 2003, at p. 1.

Beattie, Alan, *Uruguay provides test case for merits of voluntary debt exchange*, The Financial Times, 23 April 2003, at p. 3

Beattie, Alan, et al., *IMF picks its way through Latin America minefield*, The Financial Times, 2 August 2002, at p. 5.

Beattie, Alan, *IMF's plan for bankruptcy gaining favor*, The Financial Times, 18 September 2002, at p. 6.

Beattie, Alan, *Investors voice concern over bank's role*, The Financial Times, 25 April 2002, at p. 5.

Bellamy, Christopher, et al., *Common Market Law of Competition*, 4th Edition, ed. Vivien Rose, Sweet and Maxwell, London (1993).

BenDaniel, David J., et al., *International M&A, Joint Ventures and Beyond, Doing The Deal*, John Wiley & Sons, Inc., New York (1998).

Bennett, Rosemary, *Crackdown on 'vulture funds' proposed by finance minister*, The Financial Times, 6 May 2002, at p. 6.

Beynon, John, and Dunkerley, David, eds, *Globalization: The Reader*, Routledge, London (2001).

Bishop, R. Doak, and Etri, Jame E., *International Arbitration in South America*, <www.kslaw.co/library>, accessed 14 December 2001.

Blackett, Adelle, *Whither Social Clause? Human Rights, Trade Theory and Treaty Interpretation*, 31 Colum. Human Rts. L. Rev. 3 (1999).

Blake, Richard Cameron, T*he World Bank's Draft Paradigm Comprehensive Development Framework and the Micro-Paradigm of Law and Development*, 3 Yale Human Rights and Development Journal 159 (2000).

Boland, Vincent, *Congress to investigate SEC's role in policing credit ratings*, The Financial Times, 14 April 2003, at p. 21.

Bottomore, T.B. and Rubel, M., eds, *Karl Marx, Selected Writings in Sociology and Social Philosophy*, Pelican Books, 2nd Ed. (1963).

Brewer, Thomas L., *International investment dispute settlement procedures: The evolving regime for foreign direct investment*, Law and Policy in International Business, v. 26, n. 23, pp. 633-672 (Spring, 1995).

Brightbill, Timothy C., et al., *International Legal Developments in Review:2000*, 35 Int'l Law 407 (2001).

Brower II, Charles H., et al., *The Iran-United States Claim Tribunal: Its Contribution to the Law of State Responsibility*, Transnational Publishers, (1998), New York, at <www.opengroup.com>.

Brown, Michael F., *Can Culture Be Copyrighted?*, Current Anthropology 39 (2), April 1998, containing a number of contributed articles.

Bucheit, Lee C., and Gulati, G. Mitu, *Exit Consents In Sovereign Bond Exchanges*, 48 UCLA Rev. 59 (2000).

Budden, Robert, & Arnold, Martin, *Vivendi may take Cegetel stake to foil Vodafone*, The Financial Times, 18 October 20002, at p. 15.

Byttebier, et al., K., *Structuring International Co-operation Between Enterprises*, Graham and Trotman/Martin Nijhoff, London, England and Norwell, MA (1995).

Cameron, Doug, *Banks urged to hit terror funding*, The Financial Times, 18 April 2002 at p. 4.

Cantor, Richard, & Packer, Frank, *Current Issues in Economics and Finance*, Federal Reserve Bank of New York, 1 (3) (June 1995), available at <www.newyorkfed.org/rmaghome/curr_iss/ci1-3>, accessed 21 January 2003.

Canute, James, *Bahamas will reconsider reforms*, The Financial Times, 27 August 2002, at p. 4.

Carbonneau, Thomas E., ed., *Lex mercatoria and Arbitration*, Juris Publishing, Inc., Oxford and Kluwer Law International, London (rev. ed. 1998).

Casella, Alessandra, *Arbitration in International Trade*, Working Paper No. 4136, p. 1-43, National Bureau of Economic Research, Cambridge, MA (1992).

Catán, Thomas, *Argentine Legislators 'asked for bribes to stall tax law'*, The Financial Times, 30 August 2002, at p. 5.

Catán, Thomas, *Argentina urges IMF to hurry*, The Financial Times, 1-2 June 2002, at p. 4.

Chamberlin, Michael M., Executive Director, of the Emerging Markets Trade Association, *Revisting the IMF's Sovereign Bankruptcy Proposal and the Quest for More Orderly Sovereign Work-Outs*, before the Institute for International Economics, Washington, DC, April 2, 2002, available at <www.emta.org>, accessed 10 December 2002.

Coelho, Eduardo de Melo Lucas, *Direito de Voto dos Accionistas*, Rei dos Livros, Lisbon, Portugal (1987).

Cohen, Norman, and Hill, Andrew, *Governance issues lie behind Simon/Taubman battle*, The Financial Times, 14 February 2003, at p. 19.

Cohn, Marjorie, *The World Trade Organization: Elevating Property Interests Above Human Rights*, 29 Ga. J. Int'l and Comp. L. 427 (2001).

Colitt, Raymond, *Brazil plans loans to troubled companies*, The Financial Times, 13 August 2002, at p. 1.

Colitt, Raymond, et al., *Investor fears of leftwing poll win disturb fragile confidence in Brazil*, The Financial Times, 10/11 August 2002, at p. 1.

Collins, Hugh, *Marxism and Law*, Clarendon Press, Oxford (1982).

Compton, Charles T., *Changing US View Of Joint Ventures*, London, England: International Business Lawyer, 26 (3), 97-144 (1998).

Craig, W. Laurence, *Trends and Developments in the Laws and Practices of International Commercial Arbitration*, available at <www.coudert.com/practice>, accessed 26 August 2002.

Crawford, Jo-Ann, et al., *Regional Trade Agreements and the WTO*, Credit Research paper No. 00/3, Paper prepared for a meeting of the North American Economic and Finance Association in Boston, 6-9 January 2000, available at <www.dti.gov.uk/worldtrade/regional>, accessed 17 December 2001.

Croft, Jane, *Online group files S&P complaint*, The Financial Times, 27 January 2003, at p. 16.

Crystal, Paul J., *The International Finance Corporation: Encouraging the Private Sector in challenging conditions*, 165 The Courier ACP-EU, September-October 1997, pp. 45-47.

D'Ambrosio, Mary, *Ten Years of the Brady Markets*, Emerging Markets Investor, 6 (10) November 1999.

Daneshku, Scheherazade, *Development aid down to $54.4 bn*, The Financial Times, 14 May, 2002, at p. 6.

Delbruck, Jost, *Globalization of Law, Politics, and Markets — Implications for Domestic Law — A European Perspective*, 1 Ind. J. Global Stud. 9 (1993).

Dillon, Thomas J., *The World Trade Organization: A New Legal Order for World Trade*, 16 Michigan Law Review 349 (1995).

Dobson, Wendy, et al., *World Capital Markets: Challenge to the G-10*, a summary of which is available at <www.iie.com/press/worldcapitalmarkets>, accessed 8 August 2002.

Dolzer, Rudolph, & Stevens, Margrete, *Bilateral Investment Treaties*, Martinus Nuhoff, The Hague (1995).

Daniel, Dombey, et al., *The power that sits over Europe*, The Financial Times, 22 August 2002, at p. 7.

Dumberry, Patrick, *Expropriation Under NAFTA Chapter 11 Investment Dispute Settlement Mechanism: Some Comments on the Latest Case Law*, Int. A.L.R. 2001, 4(3), 96-104 (2001).

Durkheim, E., *The Elementary Forms of the Religious Life*, Allen and Unwin, New York (1912).

Duyn, Aline van, *Moody's warns of French deficit*, The Financial Times, 29 January 2003, at p. 22.

Dyer, Geoff, *Investors to increase pressure on drug groups*, FT*fm* (The Financial Times fund management supplement) 24 March 2003, at p. 1.

Earle, Julie, *US pension funds may cut links with 22 groups*, The Financial Times, 12 August 2002, at p. 16.

The Economist, survey *The Case for Globalization*, 29 September-5 October 2001, at p. 6, table 1.

Escudero, Manuel, *The world at a great crossroad*, El Pais, 10 August 2002, at p. 2.

Evans, Huw, *International Financial Architecture: Learning the Lessons of History*, Journal of International Financial Markets, 2000(3) 70-79, (2000).1

Falzoni, Anna M., Statistics on Foreign Direct Investment and Multinational Corporations: A Survey, 15 May 2000, available at
<www.cepr.org/research>, accessed at 3 October 2001.

Faundez, J., *Legal Reform in Developing and Transition Countries*, <www.worldbank.org/legal/legop/_judicial/ljr_conf_papers/Faundez3.pdf.>, accessed 29 May 2002.

Feinberg, Richard, *A vision for the Americas*, The Financial Times, 7 August 2002, at p. 11.

Fidler, David P., *A Kinder, Gentler System of Capitulations? International law, Structural Adjustment Policies and The Standards of Liberal, Globalized Civilization*, 35 Tex. Int'l L. J. 387 (2000).

Fine, Frank L., *Mergers and Joint Ventures in Europe*, 2nd Edition, Kluwer Law International, London, England (1994).

Fridson, Martin S., *Financial Statement Analysis*, 2nd Edition, University Edition, John Wiley & Sons, Inc., New York, New York (1996).

Friesen, Connie M., 'The 1998 Basle Committee Supervisory Initiatives and Their Potential Consequences of International Banking Activities', J.I.B.L. 14(2) 55-61(1999).

Garcia, Frank J., *Humanizing the Financial Architecture of Globalization: A Tribute to the Work of Cynthia Lichtenstein*, 25 B.C. Int'l and Comp. LO. Rev. 203 (2002).

General Accounting Office (US), *International Financial Crises — Efforts to Anticipate, Avoid, and Resolve Sovereign Crises*, (1997), GAO/GGD/INSIAD/-97-168, available at <www.gao.gov>, accessed 14 January 2003.

Giles, Chris, *Markets rise on Brazil's IMF deal*, The Financial Times, 9 August 2002, at p. 2.

Giovanoli, Marlo, *The Role of the Bank for International Settlements in International Monetary Cooperation and its Tasks Relating to the European Currency Unit*, 23 Int'l Law 841 (1989).

Girvan, Norman, 'International Meeting on Globalization and Development Problem', Jan 18-22, 1999, Havana, Cuba, at <www.genderandtrade>, accessed 5 January 2002.

Gledhill, John, *Power and Its Disguises*, Pluto Press, London and Boulder, Colorado (1994).

Gluckman, Max, *Politics, Law and Ritual in Tribal Society*, Basil Blackwell, 2nd Ed, Oxford (1967).

Gluckman, Max, *Custom and Conflict in Africa*, Basil Blackwell, Oxford (1963).

Gluckman, Max, *The Judicial Process Among the Barotse of Northern Rhodesia*, Manchester University (1955).

Ray Goode, *Usage and its Reception in Transnational Commercial Law*, pp. 3-36, at p. 30, in Jacobs S. Ziegel, (ed.), New Developments in International Commercial and Consumer Law, Proceedings of the 8th Biennial Conference of the International Academy of Commercial and Consumer Law, Hart Publishing, Oxford, 1998.

Griffiths, John, *What Is Legal Pluralism?*, Journal of Legal Pluralism, pp. 1-55, 24 (1986).

Gross, Daniel, *Busting up the Ratings Cartel*, 23 December 2003, available at <www. slate.msn.com/id/2075959> accessed 29 January 2003.

Gruber, Lloyd, *Rethinking the Rational Foundations of Supranational Governance: Lessons from the North American Free Trade Agreement*, Harris School Working Paper Series: 99.18, at <www.harrisschool.uchicago.edu>, accessed 24 December 2001.

Guerrera, Francesco, et al., *US warned over auditor laws*, The Financial Times, 6 March 2003, at p. 1.

Guira, Jorge M, *Mercosur As An Instrument for Development*, 3-Sum NAFTA: L. and Bus. Rev. Am 53m (1997).

Gurvitch, Georges, *Sociology of Law*, Kegan Paul, Trench, Truber and Co. Ltd., London, England (1947).

Guzman, Andrew T., *International Antitrust and the WTO: The Lesson from Intellectual Property*, UC Berkeley Law and Economics Research Paper No. 2000-20, available at <www.law.berkeley.edu>, accessed 15 December 2001.

Guzman, Andrew T., *Explaining The Popularity of Bilateral Investment Treaties: Why LDCs Sign Treaties That Hurt Them*, available at <www.jeanmonnetprogram.org/papers/97/97-12>, accessed 14 December 2001.

Hackworth, Green H., *Digest of International Law*, Sec. 228 at pp. 655-65 (1942).

Holmes, O. W., *The Common Law*, Little, Brown and Company, Boston, MA (1881).

Holtzmann, Howard M., et al., *A Guide to the UNCITRAL Model International Commercial Arbitration: Legislative History and Commentary*, Kluwer Law International, London (1989).

Ibison, David, *Fitch downgrades Japanese banks*, The Financial Times, 31 January 2003, at p. 13.

*International Encyclopedia of the Social and Behavioural Sciences*, Elsevier Science Ltd., The Netherlands (2001).

IMF, *A Sovereign Debt Restructuring Mechanism — Further Reflections And Future Work*, 14 February 2002, available at
<www.imf.org/external/NP/pdr/sdrm/2002/021402>, accessed 05 January 2003.

International Bar Association *Due Diligence, Disclosures and Warranties in the Corporate Acquisitions Practice*, Graham and Trotman, London (1988).

*Investment Treaties in the Western Hemisphere: A Compendium*, available at <www.alca-ftaa.oas.org.>, accessed 14 December 2001.

Jaffey, A. J. E., *Arbitration of international commercial contracts: the law to be applied by the arbitrators*, pp.129-151, in David L. Perrott and Istvan Pogany, eds, Current Issues in International Business Law, Avebury, Aldershot (1988).

Jayasuriya, Kanishka, *Globalization, Law and the Transformation of Sovereignty: The Emergence of Global Regulatory Convergence*, 6 Ind. J. Global Legal Stud. 425 (1999).

Jonquières, Guy de, *Foreign direct investment flows drop sharply after 2000 record*, The Financial Times, 4 July 2002, at p. 6.

Jonquières, Guy de, *WTO no better than GATT in ending EU-US trade disputes, says study*, The Financial Times, 13-14 April 2002, at p. 3.

Jonquières, Guy de, *Europe hopes to 'hit the White house where it hurts'*, The Financial Times, 26 March 2002, at p. 2.

Jonquières, Guy de, *Popular Trend is at odds with global free trade*, The Financial Times, 20 November 2001.

Jonquieres, Guy de, *Multinationals making lower profits abroad*, The Financial Times, April 27, 2000.

Katzenstein, Peter J., *A World of Regions: America, Europe, and East Asia*, available at <www.ijgls.indiana.edu>, accessed 17 December 2001.

Kazmin, Amy, *Asean and China sign deal for free trade area*, The Financial Times, 5 May 2002, at p. 6.

Kelley, J. Patrick, *The WTO and Global Governance: The Case for Contractual Treaty Regimes*, 7 SPG Widener L. Symposium. J. 109 (2001).

Kennedy, Kevin C., *The GATT-WTO System at Fifty*, 16 Wis. Int'l L. J. 421 (Summer 1998).

Khairallah, D. L., *The Developmental Role of the International Finance Corporation*, 2-Sum NAFTA: L. & Bus. Rev. Am 3 (1996).

Kissane, Mary E., *Global Gadflies: Applications and Implementations of U.S.-Style Corporate Governance Abroad*, 17 NYL Sch. J. Int'l & Comp. 621 (1997).

Korah, Valentine, *An Introductory Guide to EC Competition Law and Practice*, 5th Edition Sweet and Maxwell, London (1994).

Kregel, Jan, *The Strong Arm of the IMF*, The Sunday Boston Globe, January 18, 1998, available at <www.levy.org/whatsnew/topic/strongoped>, accessed 12 May 2002.

Krueger, Anne, *The Evolution of Emerging Market Capital Flows: Why We Need to Look at Sovereign Debt Restructuring*, available at <www.imf.org/external/np/speeches/012102>, accessed 05 January 2003.

Krueger, Anne O., *Preventing and Resolving Financial Crises: The Role of Sovereign Debt Restructuring*, International Monetary Fund, Latin American Meeting of the Econometric Society São Paolo, Brazil, July 26, 2002, <www.imf.org/external/np/speeches>, accessed 03 January 2003.

Laidhold, Michael, *Private Party Access to the WTO: Do Recent Developments in International Trade Disputes Really Give Private Organizations a Voice in the WTO?*, 12 Transnat'l Law 427 (1999).

Lamont, James, *Lesotho bribery case warning*, The Financial Times, 18 September 2002, at p. 8.

Lando, Ole, *The Lex Mercatoria in International Commercial Arbitration*, International and Comparative Law Quarterly, pp. 747-768, 34 (October 1985).

Lauterpacht, Elihu, *International Law and Private Foreign Investment*, available at <www.ijgls.indiana.edu/vol4/no2/laupgp>, accessed 14 December 2001.

Lee, Lawrence L. C., *The Basle Accords as Soft Law: Strengthening International Banking Supervision*, 39 Va. Ja. Int'l Law 1 (1998).

Lerrick, Adam, *A bankruptcy court without credit*, The Financial Times, 11 April 2003, at p. 13.

Levinson, Jerome I., *The International Financial System: A Flawed Architecture*, 23-SPG Fletcher F. World Aff. 1 (1999).

Levy-Livermore, Amnon, ed. *Handbook on the Globalization of the World Economy*, Edward Elgar, Cheltenham, UK (1998).

Lisle, Jacques de, *Lex Americana? United States Legal Assistance, American Legal Models, and Legal Change in the Post-Communist World and Beyond*, 20 U. Pa. J. Int'l Economic Law 179 (1999).

Llewelyn, K. N., and Hobel, E. A., *The Cheyenne Way*, Oklahoma Press, Norman, Oklahoma (1941).

Mackintosh, James, *GM calls on US to lobby over yen*, The Financial Times, 11 September 2003, at p. 19.

Mackintosh, James, et al., *Basle accord set to change banking landscape*, The Financial Times, 10 July 2002, at p. 8.

Maine, Henry, *Ancient Law*, Murray, London, England (1861).

Maitland, Alison, *Businesses are called to account*, The Financial Times, 28 March 2002, at p. 1.

Malinowski, Bronislaw, *Sex and Repression in Savage Society*, Meridian Books, New York (1927).

Marsh, Peter, *Multinationals more efficient*, The Financial Times, 28 March 2002, page number not recorded.

Martyn, Tim, *A Complete Guide to the Regional Trade Agreements of the Asia-Pacific*, available at <www.arts.monash.edu.au/ausapec/RTA/entirereport/PDF>, accessed 26 December 2001.

Marx, Karl, and Engels, Friedrich, *The Communist Manifesto*, London (1848).

Mataloni, Raymond J., *U.S. Multinational Companies: Operations in 1995*, available at the U.S. Department of Commerce web site, Bureau of Economic Analysis <www.bea.gov> date of access not recorded.

Jüttner, D. Johannes, and McCarthy, Justin, *Modelling a Rating Crisis*, available on <www.econ.mq.edu.au./staff/djuttner/SOVEIG.2>, accessed 2 February 2003.

McGinnis, John O., et al, *The World Trade Constitution*, 114 Harv. L. Rev. 511 (2000).

Mead, John H., *Supranational Law: How the Move towards Multilateral Solutions is Changing the Character of 'International' Law*, 42 U. Kan. L. Rev. 605 (1994).

Meltzer, Allan H., *New IMF loan will not solve Argentine crisis*, The Financial Times, 13 January 2003, at p. 11.

Meltzer, Allan H., *Back to Bailouts*, The Wall Street Journal Europe, 8 August 2002, at p. A8.

Mentschikoff, Sonia, *Commercial Arbitration*, 61 Columbia Law Review 846-849 (1961), cited by Alessandra Casella, supra.

Merry, Sally Engle, *Anthropology, Law, and Transnational Processes*, Annual Review of Anthropology, 1992.21:357-379.

Micklethwait, John, et al., The Financial Times, 27-28 May 2000, page no. not recorded.

Miller, Brett H., *Sovereign Bankruptcy: Examining the United States Bankruptcy System As A Forum For Sovereign Debtors*, 22 Law and Pol'y Int'l Bus. 107 (1991).

Moore, Sally Falk, *Certainties undone: fifty turbulent years of legal anthropology, 1949-1999*, The Journal of the Royal Anthropological Institute, 7, 95-116 (2001).

Moore, Sally Falk, *Social Facts and Fabrications 'Customary' Law on Kilimanjaro*, Cambridge University Press, Cambridge (1980).

Moore, Sally Falk, *Law As Process*, Routledge and Kegan Paul, London (1978).

Mota, Sue Ann *The World Trade Organization: An Analysis of Disputes*, 25 N.C. J. Int'l L. and Com. Reg. 75 (1999).

Munter, Päivi, *Foreign holdings of US treasuries hit record 46%*, 11 September 2003, at p. 20.

Munter, Päivi, *Fitch has bearish view of Germany*, The Financial Times, 19 February 2003, at p. 21.

Munter, Päivi, *Flight to bonds sends yields sliding to new lows*, The Financial Times, 29 January 2003, at p. 15 and the graphs presented.

Munter, Päivi, and Duyn, Aline van, *S&P warns Rome to put its finances in order*, The Financial Times, 17 January 2003, at p. 13.

Mustill, Justice, *Contemporary Problems in International Commercial Arbitration: A Reponse*, 17 Int'l Bus. Law 161, at p. 162 (1989).

Nobel, Peter, *Social Responsibility of Corporations*, 84 Cornell L. Rev. 1255 (1997).

Norton, Joseph J., *A 'New International Financial Architecture?' — Reflections on the Possible Law — Based Dimension*, 33 Int'l Law 891 (1999).

Norton, Joseph J., et al., *The Ongoing Process of International Bank Regulatory and Supervisory Convergence: A New Regulatory 'Partnership'*, 16 Ann. Rev. Banking L. 227 (1997).

Oliveira, Jose Manuel,et al., *Relacoes Internacionais e Transferencia de Tecnologia*, Almedina, Coimbra, Portugal (1993).

Oloka-Onyango & Udagama, *The Realization of Economic, Social and Cultural Rights: Globalization and its impact on the full enjoyment of human rights*, UN Doc. E/CN. 4/Sub.2/2000/13-15 June 2000 available at<www.unsystem.org>, accessed 8 February 2002.

O'Neal, F. Hodge, et al., *O'Neal's Oppression of Minority Shareholders*, West Group, Eagan, MN (1998).

Palmeter, David, *The WTO as a Legal System*, 24 Fordham Int'l L. J. 444 (2000).

Palmeter, David, et al., *The WTO Legal System: Sources of Law*, 92 American Journal of International Law 398 (1998).

Parker, Andrew, *Accounting standards move towards compatibility*, The Financial Times, 30 October 2002, at p. 6.

Parker, Andrew, et al., *OECD ponders action against tax havens*, The Financial Times, 19 April 2002 at p. 6.

Partnoy, Frank, *The Siskel and Ebert of Financial Markets?: Two Thumbs Down For The Credit Rating Agencies*, 77 Wash. U. L. Q. 619 (1999).

Paulus, Christoph G,, *Some Thoughts On An Insolvency Procedure For Countries*, 50 Am. J. Comp. L. 531 (2002).

Peel, Michael, *Squaring up to something rotten*, The Financial Times September 12 September 2002, at p. 8.

Peng, Shin-yi, *The WTO Legalistic Approach and East Asia: From the Legal Culture Perspective*, 1 Asian-Pacific Law and Policy Journal 13 (2000).

Pilling, David, *Moody's calls on BoJ to reflate economy*, The Financial Times, 15 January 2003, at p. 6.

Perrott, David L., et al., '*Current Issues in International Business Law*', chapter 8, '*Bilateral investment treaties: a comparative analysis (Pogany)*', Avebury, Aldershot (1988).

Petito, Danielle S., *Sovereignty and Gobalization: Fallacies, Truth, and Perception*, 17 N.Y.L. Sch. J. Hum. Rts. 1139 (2001).

Petrochilos, Georgios C., *Arbitration Conflict of Laws Rules and the 1980 International Sales Convention*, 52 Revue Hellenique de Droit International, 191-218 (1999).

Pollard, Duke, *The Caribbean Court of Justice(CCJ): Challenge and Response*, 3 May 1999, available at <www.caricom.org>, accessed 7 January 2002.

Posner, Richard A., *Economic Analysis of Law*, 2nd Edition, Little, Brown and Company, Boston and Toronto (1977).

Pound, Roscoe, *Law and Morals*, The University of North Carolina Press, Chapel Hill, NC (1924).

Practising Law Institute (Chair, Joseph McLaughlin), *Conducting Due Diligence*, New York (1998).

Practising Law Institute (Chair, Alfred J. Ross, Jr.), *International Joint Ventures*, New York (1998).

Pretzlik, Charles, et al., *Deal on bank reserves in sight*, The Financial Times, 11 July 2002, at p. 8.

Rashkover, Barry W., *Title 14, New York Choice of Law Rule for Contractual Disputes: Avoiding the Unreasonable Results*, 74 Cornell L. Rev. 227 (1985).

Ratner, Juliana, *The nightmare on Wall Street continues*, The Financial Times, 23 December 2002, at page 17. We are not informed as to the standard for the valuation, for example, assets or market capitalization.

Reddy, Y. V., Deputy Governor of the Bank of India, *Legal Aspects of International Financial Law*, at the International Seminar on Legal and Regulatory Aspects of Financial Stability, sponsored by the World Bank, the International Monetary Fund, The Bank for International Settlements and the Financial Stability Forum, at Basle, Switzerland, on 23 January 2002, available at <www.bis.org>, accessed 10 July 2002.

Reinhart, Carmen M., *Sovereign Credit Ratings Before and After Financial Crises*, 21 February 2001, available on <www.puaf.umd.edu/papers/reinhart>, accessed 5 February 2003.

Ridley, Matt, *Genome: The Autobiography Of A Species In 23 Chapters*, HarperCollins, New York (1999).

Ritzer, George, *Sociological Theory*, 2nd Ed., McGraw-Hill Publishing Company, New York (1988).

Roach, Stephen, *Back to borders*, The Financial Times, 28 September 2001, summary and reference available at <www.clientlink.ru/GEFdata/digests/200206607> extracting these statistics from a report by Morgan Stanley, accessed again 26 September 2003 to confirm page number of The Financial Times but none indicated. Web site contains summary of article.

Rogoff, Kenneth and Zettlemeyer, Jeromin, *Early Ideas on Sovereign Bankruptcy Reorganization: A Survey*, International Monetary Fund, WP/02/57, (March 2002).

Lina Saigoi, *Deutsche takes top slot in M&A*, The Financial Times, 3 October 2002, at p. 23.

Salzman, James, *Labor Rights, Globalization and Institutions: The Role and Influence of The Organization for Economic Cooperation and Development*, 21 Mich. J. Int'l L. 769 (2000).

Schneider, Andrea K., *Democracy and Dispute Resolution: Individual Rights in International Trade Organizations*, 19 U. Pa. J. Intl Econ. Law, 587 (1998).

Schoff, Russell B., *The International Investment Position of the United States in 1997*, available on the web site of the US Bureau of Economic Analysis at <www.bea.doc.gov/>, accessed again 26 September 2003 to confirm web site publication.

Schwarcz, Steven L., *Private Ordering of Public Markets: The Rating Agency Paradox*, U. Il. Rev. 1 (2002).

Schwarcz, Steven L., *Sovereign Debt Restructuring: A Bankruptcy Reorganization Approach*, 85 Cornell L. Rev. 956 (2000).

Sevastopulo, Demetri, *Four banks adopt IFC agreement*, The Financial Times, 07 April 2003, at p. 19.

Shapiro, Martin, *Globalization of Freedom of Contract*, pp. 269-298, footnotes pp. 361-363, in Chapter 9 of *The State and Freedom of Contract*, ed. Harry N. Scheiber, Stanford University Press (1998) at p. 270.

Shapiro, Martin, *The Globalization of the Law*, Indiana Journal of Global Studies, 1(1) (Fall 1993).

Silver, Sara, *Guatemalan 'Peace Bond' causes alarm*, The Financial Times, 08 January 2003, at p. 22.

Smith, Peter, *Banks re-examine economics of private equity*, The Financial Times, 20 March 2003, at p. 17.

Smy, Lucy, *Accounting rules find global favor*, The Financial Times, 12 February 2003, at p. 19.

Snyder, Francis, *Economic Globalisation and The Law In The 21st Century*, Austin Sarat, ed., *The Blackwell Companion in Law and Society*, Blackwell Publishers, New York and Oxford (2003).

Snyder, Francis, Law and Anthropology: A Review, EUI Working Papers Law No. 93/4, European University Institute, Florence (1993).

Stevens, Margrete, *Experience in Arbitrations under ICSID Rules Pursuant to Bilateral Investment Treaties*, International Business Lawyer, 29(8), pp. 377-380, September 2001.

Stiglitz, Joseph, *Globalization and its discontents*, at p. 21, Penguin Books (2002).

Targett, Simon, *ABP to open $250m SRI fund to other investors*, The Financial Times, FT*fm*, fund management supplement, 28 October 2002, at p. 1.

Targett, Simon, et al., *Investors to fight tax barriers*, The Financial Times, FT*fm*, fund management supplement, 22 April, at p. 1.

Tassell, Tony, *Custodians taking over the back office*, The Financial Times, Global Custody Survey, 5 July 2002, at p. 1.

Tawney, Richard Henry, *The Acquisitive Society*, Harcourt, Brace and Howe, New York (1948).

Tawney, Richard Henry, *Religion and The Rise of Capitalism*, Pelican Books, (Penguin Books Limited), London (1938 Edition).

Thome, Joseph R., *Heading South But Looking North: Globalization and Law Reform in Latin America*, 2000 Wis. L. Rev. 691 (2000).

Thompson, Herb, *Culture and Economic Development: Modernisation to Globalisation*, available at <www.theoryandscience.icaap.org/content/vol1002.002/thompson>, accessed 16 January 2003.

Thomsen, Stephen, *Investment Patterns in a Longer-Term Perspective*, Working Papers on International Investment, Number 2000/2, available on the home p. of the OECD available at <www.oecd.org>, accessed 28 April 2002.

Tomkins, Richard, *No logo can sell the true horrors of battle*, The Financial Times, 20 March 2003, at p. 15.

Townsend, Jr., Alexander, *The Global Schoolyard Bully: The Organization for Economic Co-operation and Development's Coercive Efforts to Control Tax Competition*, 25 Fordham Int'l L. J. 215 (2001).

Trachtman, Joel P., *The Domain of WTO Dispute Resolution*, 40 Harv. Int'l L. J. 333 (1999).

Tsai, Mary C., *Globalization and Conditionality: Two Sides of the Sovereignty Coin*, 31 Law and Pol'y Int'l Bus 1317 (2000).

Twining, William, *Globalisation and Legal Theory*, Northwestern University Press (2000).

UAW, *NAFTA'S hidden impact*, Solidarity, August 2002, at p. 4.

Unger, Roberto Mangabeira, *The Critical Legal Studies Movement*, Harvard University Press (1986).

United Nations Conference on Trade and Development, World Investment Report 1998 available on the web site of UNCTAD at <www.unctad.org>, accessed again 26 September 2003 to confirm web site publication.

Veblen, Thorsten, *The Nature of the Business Enterprise*, Augustus M. Kelley, New York (1975).

Vicente, Dario Moura, *Da Arbitragem Comercial Internacional* (On International Commercial Arbitration), Coimbra Editora, Coimbra, Portugal (1990).

Wadrzyk, Mark E., *Is It Appropriate for the World Bank to Promote Democratic Standards in a Borrower Country?*, 17 Wisconsin International Law Journal 555 (1999).

Walker, Gordon, *International Regulations in the Information Age: The Political Dimensions of Globalization*, Journal of International Banking Law, 10(11), 463-465 (1995).

Ward, Andrew, *Agency downgrades S Korea outlook as nuclear crisis grows*, The Financial Times, 12 February 2003, at p. 6.

Waters, Alan, *O Publico* (Portuguese daily newspaper), 21 February 2000.

Weiler, Todd, *NAFTA Article 1105 and the Free Trade Commission: Just Sour Grapes, or Something More Serious?*, International Business Lawyer, December 2001, at p. 5.

Wiener, Jarrod, *The Transnational Political Economy: A Framework for Analysis*, Uuniversity of Kent at Canterbury, available at <www.ukc.ac.uk/politics/kentpapers> with no date, although posted on internet as of August, 2,000 and accessed again 26 September 2003 to confirm web site publication.

Wellink, Nout, *The role of national central banks within the European system of central banks — the example of De Nederlandsche Bank*, 13-14 June 2002, available at <www.bis.org/review/n020620a>, accessed 11 July 2002.

Wiggins, Jenny, *US bonds face gloomier future as selling continues to increase*, The Financial Times, 8 September 2003, at p. 17.

Wiggins, Jenny, *Sovereign ratings seen as stable*, The Financial Times, 10 February 2003, at p. 19.

Williams, Francis, *WTO arms Europeans with weighty weapon*, The Financial Times, August 31-1 September 2002, at p. 2.

Williams, Francis, *M&A activity reaches record*, The Financial Times, 9 May 2000, page number not recorded.

Wine, Elizabeth, *CalPERS sticks to ethical stance*, The Financial Times, 20 February 2003, at p. 17.

Wine, Elizabeth, *Ethical Crusaders resolve to redeem the corporate sinners*, The Financial Times, 30/31 March 2002, at p. 24.

Winters, L. Alan, *Regionalism versus Multilateralism*, The World Bank, International Economics Department, International Trade Division, November 1996, available at <www.sice.oas.org/geograph/westernh/regmulea.asp>, accessed 17 December 2001.

Wolf, Martin, *The markets are too eager to discount the cost of war*, The Financial Times, 26 March 2003, at p. 15.

Wolf, Martin, *Economic Globalization, An Unfinished Revolution*, Special Report, The World:2003, The Financial Times, 23 January 2003, at p. III.

Wolf, Martin, *Stagnation in Germany and Japan, unsustainable imbalances in the US ... will the recovery take hold?*, The Financial Times, 18 December 2002, at page 13.

Wolf, Ronald Charles, *Effective International Joint Venture Management: Practical Legal Insights for Successful Organization and Implementation*, M.E. Sharpe, New York (2000).

Wolf, Ronald Charles, *A Guide to International Joint Ventures With Sample Clauses*, 2nd Edition, Kluwer Law International, London (1999).

Wolf, Ronald Charles, *A Guide to International Joint Ventures With Sample Clauses*, reprinted 1996, London (1995).

Wolf, Ronald Charles, *Corporate Acquisitions and Mergers in Portugal*, Graham & Trotman, London (1993).

# Index